TAR

MODERN IRELAND
AND REVOLUTION

MODERN IRELAND AND REVOLUTION

ERNIE O'MALLEY IN CONTEXT

EDITED BY CORMAC K.H. O'MALLEY

Introduction by Nicholas Allen
Afterword by Roy Foster

IRISH ACADEMIC PRESS

Published in 2016 by Irish Academic Press
In conjunction with Glucksman Ireland House, New York University

Irish Academic Press
10 George's Street
Newbridge
County Kildare
Ireland
www.iap.ie

ISBN: 978-1-911024-37-8 (Cloth)
ISBN: 978-1-911024-40-8 (PDF)
ISBN: 978-1-911024-46-0 (Kindle)
ISBN: 978-1-911024-47-7 (Epub)

British Library Cataloguing in Publication Data
An entry can be found on request

Library of Congress Cataloging in Publication Data
An entry can be found on request

Design by iota (www.iota-books.com)
Typeset in 12pt on 16pt Granjon with Gotham display titling
Front jacket: *Ernie O'Malley* by Brian Gallagher, print, 2010,
www.bdgart.com. Reproduced with permission of the artist.
Back jacket: *Ernie O'Malley* by Brian Maguire, acrylic on canvas,
New York, 1999. Reproduced with permission of the artist.

Printed and bound in Great Britain by TJ International Ltd.

CONTENTS

ACKNOWLEDGEMENTS   vii

PREFACE by J.J. Lee   ix

INTRODUCTION by Nicholas Allen   xi

PART I   POST-REVOLUTION PERSPECTIVES

CHAPTER ONE   On Another Man's Text: Ernie O'Malley,
                 James Joyce and Irish Modernism
                 Luke Gibbons   3

CHAPTER TWO   'Flamboyant, Gothic, Romanesque': Art and
                 Revolution in the Mind of Ernie O'Malley
                 Róisín Kennedy   17

CHAPTER THREE   From Mexico to Mayo: Ernie O'Malley, Paul
                 Strand and Photographic Modernism
                 Orla Fitzpatrick   28

CHAPTER FOUR   The Evolution of Ernie O'Malley's Memoir,
                 On Another Man's Wound
                 Cormac K.H. O'Malley   42

CHAPTER FIVE   The Importance of Being Ernie O'Malley in
                 Ken Loach's ***The Wind that Shakes the Barley***
                 Nathan Wallace   55

PART II   HISTORICAL NATIONALIST PERSPECTIVES

CHAPTER SIX   On Republican Reading: Ernie O'Malley,
Irish Intellectual
David Lloyd   79

CHAPTER SEVEN   Kindling the Singing Flame: The Destruction
of the Public Record Office (30 June 1922),
as a Historical Problem
John M. Regan   107

CHAPTER EIGHT   Witnessing the Republic: The Ernie O'Malley
Notebook Interviews and the Bureau of
Military History Compared
Eve Morrison   124

CHAPTER NINE   'The People' of ***On Another Man's Wound***
Seamus O'Malley   141

CHAPTER TEN   Literature, Violence, Revolution:
Roger Casement and Ernie O'Malley
Macy Todd   159

AFTERWORD

CHAPTER ELEVEN   Revolutionary Disillusionment
Roy Foster   185

ENDNOTES   193
BIBLIOGRAPHY FOR ERNIE O'MALLEY (1897–1957)   237
CONTRIBUTORS   243
INDEX   247

ACKNOWLEDGEMENTS

Some five years ago Joe Lee, Director of Glucksman Ireland House, suggested to me that it would be most appropriate that there be some activity or work dedicated to the various aspects of the life of my father, Ernie O'Malley, and that it be done in conjunction with Glucksman Ireland House of New York University where his manuscripts, diaries and papers on many non-nationalist matters reside. Joe ultimately insisted that any effort must result in a book being published. The Board of Advisors of Glucksman Ireland House has supported these plans all the way through, for which I am most grateful. The initial work and concept could not have come about without the oversight of Spurgeon Thompson and the assistance of Greg Londe. It is also true that nothing would have been achieved without the support of the faculty members and staff at Glucksman Ireland House, in particular Marion Casey, Miriam Nyhan, Hilary MhicSuibhne and Anne Solari.

For his assistance in the various stages of editorial revisions, I wish to acknowledge the assistance of John P. Waters and a special thanks to Victoria Harty, who helped me through the copy-editing stage while finishing up her MA at Glucksman Ireland House as well as Eli Elliot and Ellis Garey. Let me also thank Conor Graham of Irish Academic Press for starting this relationship with Glucksman Ireland House, and especially Fiona Dunne, who as Managing Editor brought this manuscript to a publishable form.

Cormac K.H. O'Malley
Visiting Scholar, New York University

PREFACE

Glucksman Ireland House at New York University is now internationally recognized for its Center for Irish and Irish-American Studies. Initiated by the vision and philanthropy of Lew and Loretta Brennan Glucksman in 1993, and sustained by dedicated members of our Board of Advisors, Glucksman Ireland House sets an ambitious teaching and research agenda for itself that is now maturing steadily. In recent years, our faculty members have been able to showcase those strengths as well as raise our visibility internationally through a series of volumes on important issues relating to Irish, Irish-American and global issues. These include *Making the Irish American: History and Heritage of the Irish in the United States* (New York University Press, 2006), edited by Marion R. Casey and myself; *The Bordeaux-Dublin Letters, 1757: Correspondence of an Irish Community Abroad* (British Academy, 2013), edited by Thomas Truxes, Louis Cullen and John Shovlin; and Nicholas M. Wolf's *An Irish-Speaking Island: State, Religion, Community and Linguistic Landscape in Ireland, 1770–1870* (University of Wisconsin Press, 2014). We look forward to two more volumes: *Ireland's Allies: America and the 1916 Easter Rising* (University College Dublin Press, 2016), edited by Miriam Nyhan Grey, and *Religious Freedom in America: Reflections on* People v Philips (1813), edited by Marion R. Casey (Fordham University Press, 2017).

But the book you have just opened is special for a further reason. It complements one of our major research initiatives, the Archives of Irish America, in New York University's Bobst Library, where the post-revolutionary and literary papers of the military leader and author Ernie O'Malley (1897–1957) are preserved. Many of the essays in this volume use his varied interests as the lens through which to see Ireland past and present. By examining the forces that led to and resulted in revolution in early-twentieth-century Ireland, particularly the nexus of modernist impulses in literary, artistic and historical endeavours that overlapped with the politics of the emerging Irish Free

State, we also gain a greater perspective on a most colourful life. We are grateful to Ernie's son, Cormac, one of our Board members, for shepherding this volume from concept to completion for Glucksman Ireland House.

J.J. Lee
Director, Glucksman Ireland House
Professor of History and Glucksman Chair of Irish Studies, New York University

INTRODUCTION

This is the first collection of essays published on Ernie O'Malley and is part of a continuing revival of interest in a writer and a radical whose art and archives offer the possibility to think again of Irish cultural history in the twentieth century. The ongoing decade of commemorations, which stops before the Civil War with which O'Malley is associated so strongly, has broadened the conversation further, with particular regard to the role of women, not only in rebellion but also in the professions, in social life and in political thought. There is a sense, however, in which the years that followed the rebellion are being recast as centenary steps of the inevitable progress to statehood. This is where this collection, and the life and work of Ernie O'Malley, prove both instructive and provocative, his role in the War of Independence and in the Civil War to follow a very public disruption of the idea that the decade of centenaries should end in 1922, where it might better have begun.

O'Malley played a leading role in these events. A young man at the outbreak of the Easter Rising his leadership of various military formations after 1918 and his commitment to an Irish republic after the negotiated settlement of the Anglo-Irish Treaty became a proxy for illegitimate extremism because of his presence at the Four Courts in Dublin when it was destroyed during the initial phase of the Civil War. With it went many of the ancient records of Irish history and so the dreadful loss of these documents has become a symbolic proxy for all those qualities that the independent state associated with a hostile republicanism. One of the more provocative essays in this collection is by John M. Regan, who suggests the story behind this disaster might be more complicated than we have come to believe in the context of documentary evidence that points to other possible reasons for the inferno. Whatever the truth of this episode, the enigma of Ernie O'Malley, and the personas projected upon him, represents a case study in the management of post-revolutionary tensions in a divided society, and a reminder of the effect these tensions can have on the foundations of scholarly study. O'Malley's own first instinct after the conflict was to flee, first to Europe and then to America, where he travelled westward until he reached the boundaries of that broad landmass. He found in the American west, as he did later in Mayo, a space to think, write and correspond his experience with that of social groups who, like him, were in exile from the centre of things. Writing offered one way back to society, as did book learning, and O'Malley spent his wandering years immersed in both.

In doing so he entered another cultural zone, which preceded the military campaign but was ambivalent about it. The literary revival was a broad based movement whose major figures represent a small fraction of the diverse interests that cultural experiment engaged with in the decades before 1922. O'Malley had less interest in the older generation that shaped the revival's first and classic phase – William Butler Yeats, George Russell and their contemporaries creating an idea of Ireland that gave partial form to the rebellion generation's ideals. But there were stark differences between the practice of rebellion and the art of nationality and once the Treaty marked a divide between those who would hold and those who would fight on, Yeats and Russell made quick compromise with the new state. This was not true of James Joyce, who created his own revolution with the publication of *Ulysses* in the same year the Civil War began. As Luke Gibbons shows, O'Malley read this book later with careful and significant attention, a fact that speaks to O'Malley's own construction of his memoir, *On Another Man's Wound*, as part biography and part modernist fiction. The genesis of this hybridity can be traced to O'Malley's lectures on modern Irish literature and history in Santa Fe at the turn of the 1930s. The substance of these talks is lost but the connection between O'Malley's writing, Joyce, and the fall of the imperial systems upon which the worlds of O'Malley and Joyce were first built is significant to an understanding of both Irish writers' comparative relevance to other times and places. This is an argument that David Lloyd follows in his consideration of the multiple ways in to understand the context of O'Malley's career beyond the narrowly republican, which is itself a concept generated by the need of the new state, as Lloyd sees it, to regulate the political advance of socially committed combatants against it. O'Malley was not in the vanguard of social change in the way that some of his contemporaries were and it might be argued that the most advanced thinking on issues like suffragism, human rights, sex and vegetarianism had peaked at the time of the Easter Rising, in part because this thinking was connected to wider patterns of social change in Edwardian Britain.

The revolution that O'Malley entered was barely worth the name in social terms, being a collapse of British political will by force of guerrilla warfare, an achievement no less the remarkable for that. It was a sporadic, intense and intimate war, the effects of which shadowed, or perhaps shaped, O'Malley for the rest of his life. There is no search for self-pity in his writing of the period, and only the occasional flicker of personal revelation with regard to the conflict's effect upon him, no matter that he constantly sought to create projects that spoke to other individuals' truth of the period. This is remarkably evident in his project to record by hand hundreds of volunteers' testimonies. Even here O'Malley has become a subject of myth, his desire to talk with combatants interpreted as his desire to create an alternative and republican archive of the conflict. Eve Morrison suggests the unlikeliness of this proposition in her insightful account of O'Malley's witness interviews and shows how closely aligned his work was to that of the official Bureau of Military History's witness statements. There is no doubt of O'Malley's dislike, whether well founded or not, of the officer in charge of the government-sponsored programme, but this cannot be said to constitute a dedicated stance against the Bureau's perspective. The major obstacle to incorporating O'Malley's research into the state archives appears rather to have been his handwriting, which is notoriously difficult to decipher. O'Malley was a creature of notebooks and a builder of archives. The pathology of this desire to capture information in reams of paper might be connected to the working out later of so much loss, emotionally and materially, in the years of disturbance. If so, the orchestration of new information was a constant refrain that did not diminish, however long O'Malley lived.

The audiences for these projects shifted according to time and context. O'Malley's interviews were an expression partly of his own sense of responsibility to record versions of the conflict that spoke to his own early adult experiences. His notebooks and diaries were more personal again and exhibit an always-restless personality, capable of sharp judgement and great in relative measure. The published works amplified O'Malley's ambition to find an audience of receptive minds in post-independence Ireland. This was no easy task and Seumas O'Malley's essay on the idea of the Irish in *On Another Man's Wound* as an undivided people is an insightful exploration of the challenges the author faced. He places these challenges in a European context that stresses again the deep transnational relationships that an encounter with Irish cultural history can generate. Macy Todd develops this argument with her reading of Ernie O'Malley and Roger Casement in context of revolutionary literature. Taking these two cultural actors as psychoanalytic case studies, Todd digs into the significance of O'Malley and Casement's responses to injustice, as they perceived it, and their consequent representation of the violence that followed their confrontations with state powers involved in the possession of contested territories.

That we have an insight into O'Malley's private mind is due in large part to the archive of his private papers. Perhaps the richest, and most individual, example of his solitary note taking was his study of the history and practice of visual art. O'Malley's notebooks are a running commentary on his reading in, and reaction to, the history of art, which was revolutionized, as his understanding of political history was in the years of Irish turbulence, by his visit to Mexico. O'Malley saw there living alternatives to the traditions of European art with which he was more familiar from his study. The modern muralists and their connection to the people they represented suggested a bond that the civil war had broken. O'Malley was invested always in the connection between representation, the public and spiritual belief. The testament for him was the republic, not the church, but he could see in his travels a living contract in art between Mexico's past and present, which had many relations, he thought, to his west of Ireland upbringing. Questions of language, indigeneity and opportunity were brought back to sharp focus when O'Malley arrived in the American southwest, his odd jobbing at building and his socializing with the artistic set around Mabel Dodge Luhan bringing him into contact with peoples made peripheral in their own land. This is the setting too for the book he began to write there, the opening scenes of *On Another Man's Wound* painted in the colours of the desert and alert to the social pressures of a coming into language. This perception impelled O'Malley to see in the visual arts a capacity for liberation that the wider culture took much longer to realize, and to which critics have only recently awoken. Nowhere is this more apparent than in O'Malley's persistent support for the oil paintings of Jack Yeats. O'Malley is the least likely of all people to have forged a friendship with an artist who has been represented as a dreamer distant from the political realities of first imperial and then independent Ireland. If it was important for a previous generation to quarantine great art from fractious politics it seems critical now to restore the connection between abstraction and commitment, a fabric O'Malley weaved into his writing and which he saw in Yeats.

The painter did not demur, the two men becoming frequent companions, a friendship O'Malley recognized in his push for Yeats to be the subject of a National Loan Exhibition in 1945. The exhibition was opened by then Taoiseach, Éamon de Valera, and the shades of civil war are in the paintings and patrons both. O'Malley did not see Yeats as an artist of historical representation. Rather, he responded to the painter's orchestration of emotion in his oils as a stateless art whose ambitions were yet to be settled, which is another way of explaining Róisín Kennedy's identification of O'Malley as a modernist. The restlessness is easy enough to equate with O'Malley's unsettled life in a body marked indelibly with the violence in which it took part. The ability to translate this disturbance into an aesthetic is one of O'Malley's abiding achievements and Kennedy's essay is instructive as a reminder of how the literary set around O'Malley, Beckett, MacGreevy and their international interlocutors in James Johnson Sweeney and John Rothenstein, created a space for experiment that is of Ireland but not in it. Kennedy makes one more telling diagnosis in her reading of O'Malley's engagement with the visual arts, which was art history's capacity to teach him how to schematize space and form. This was training, through Vasari and Ruskin, that allowed him imagine the skirmishes of revolutionary war as radical refigurations of land and seascapes long suspended in a colonial inertia. O'Malley's actions by riverbank and market town gave different shape to the national territory, as often today a car journey through country boreens will reveal a Celtic cross erected to the dead of the independence or civil wars. Over time the new state incorporated these uneven spaces back into dull conformity, the brief life of the hills beyond Mallow as a site of the transnational imagination sensible only in O'Malley's rushed escape from a British ambush, the flash of a kingfisher like a bullet beside him.

O'Malley's interest in the visual arts extended to photography, which he encountered early in his American travels with his visit to Edward Weston in California, and then later and for longer, with Paul Strand. Orla Fitzpatrick's remarkable essay charts O'Malley's engagement with and practice in photography, his experience of Strand's social documentary informing his own photography much later on in Ireland. Strand was involved in his major documentary of the Mexican people when O'Malley first met him and the two remained close friends in the decades to follow. As Fitzpatrick suggests, photography can be a collaborative practice and nowhere is this more suggestive than in O'Malley's awareness of the panel discussion 'Is Photography an Art?' The occasion was the exhibition of fifty images by the architect Noel Moffett in Dublin and the panelists included Peadar O'Donnell, the novelist and socialist republican with whom O'Malley had shared a gaol cell during the Civil War, and the painter Mainie Jellet. O'Malley had a gift for these provisional collaborations and attempted over and again to create the conditions for what is best labelled now as a bohemian social space in Ireland of the Emergency and after. His later letters especially are full of late nights and constant appointments, against which were weighed the responsibilities of his children during a failing marriage and his own worsening physical state. Fitzpatrick's attention to O'Malley's interest in photography extends to her discussion of his own project, undertaken with his wife Helen, of documenting sites of early Irish architecture, as well as sometimes striking images of the countryside and coastline, where he spent much time on his small boat.

We would know none of these many sides to Ernie O'Malley's personality were it not for one of his children, Cormac, who has spent a lifetime assembling his father's archive to share it with generations of scholars whose understanding of Ireland has been enriched by the experience. For my own part, I regard *On Another Man's Wound* as one of the great prose works of twentieth-century Ireland and a world classic on the subject of insurgency and the cultural imagination. O'Malley's account of the undoing of imperial Ireland is at once memoir, fiction and manifesto for an expanded sense of the world and its possibilities, and far from the stereotype of the dour republican in thrall to an impossible ideal. That we are able to read *On Another Man's Wound* in context of its radical suggestiveness is thanks in large part to Cormac O'Malley's work as archivist and advocate. His essay on the textual genesis of his father's major work is fascinating in itself as the account of a literary work built from the ruins of a revolutionary life. Ernie O'Malley's travels in Europe and the Americas are detailed in the collection of his later letters that were published as *Broken Landscapes* and here, as there, the influence of other languages, cultures and landscapes registers in the composition of O'Malley's Ireland. It is perhaps too much to say we would have no father without the son but our understanding of Ernie O'Malley's afterlife as a major figure in the cultural life of modern Ireland would be much diminished without Cormac's commitment, which was born itself partly of family difficulty.

This background is critical in contexts where Ernie O'Malley has become a cipher for the experiences or attitudes of many others. This is particularly true of his shadow role as an influence on the character of Damien O'Donovan in Ken Loach's Palme d'Or winning film, *The Wind that Shakes the Barley*. Nathan Wallace's essay situates this film in a historical conversation with contemporary relevance, principally the ethics of guerrilla warfare in County Cork during the War of Independence. This theatre has attracted more attention than most because of the controversial historiography that has attended it, with regard in particular to the ambush of British troops at Kilmichael by Tom Barry's West Cork Flying Column. The more concentrated the action the more difficult, it seems, to establish the facts, and Loach encouraged his scriptwriter Paul Laverty to think more of the spirit of the moment than its substance. The result is a kind of symbolic history in which the medium of cinema suggests a panorama of experience that is closer to the style of *On Another Man's Wound* than it is to the substance of O'Malley's personal history. The correspondence between art and revolution surfaces in another of Loach's films, the earlier *Land and Freedom*, which is based in Spain of the late 1930s and which suggests the ways in which events in Ireland can be understood in transnational contexts that exceed the boundaries of the old British empire. Wallace's essay traces the dialogue of *The Wind that Shakes the Barley* to a series of literary sources and suggests how the wider experiences of the period, from the women who served in Cumann na mBan to the volunteers who fought for socialism, are gestured to in the film's composition.

Roy Foster extends the horizon of these historical attachments to the literature and memoirs that populated the moment of break-up between the idea of the Irish nation and the reality of the Free State. Not that there ever was only one idea but rather a burning symbol, such as that phoenix of youthful idealism as Bulmer Hobson later described it. A rebellion, and then an insurgency, called into being by the motivating images of cultural innovation, such as those of the revival and the Gaelic movement, invited disillusion when the mechanisms of government replaced the freedom of dreams. Not that those dreams were untroubled, Desmond Ryan remembering the brutality and the death of innocents as signature conditions of the troubles. Foster associates this witness of suffering with a sensitivity absent in the memoirs of a Tom Barry or a Dan Breen, preferring to connect the scepticism of Eimar O'Duffy to the melancholy of a John McGahern. This draws the arc of twentieth-century cultural history in Ireland from one point of high culture to another, which is where O'Malley is again instructive, pitched as he was into a wider variety of life by the turbulence of his experiences. The memoirs of Barry and Breen were written for an audience fed on the wild fantasies of the Western novel and the cinema adventure, which were signatures themselves of a broader culture of imperial entertainment. Tom Barry had his first experience of military conflict in the British Army and first heard of the Easter Rising as he was part of the force that failed to raise the siege of Kut in Mesopotamia. This does not establish legitimacy for violence for one side against another but suggests the inescapable intimacy between violence and social organization in twentieth-century European culture at large, as Foster captures perfectly in his refrain of Robert Wohl's idea of the generation of 1914. Ireland's involvement in the events of the First World War becomes more than a commemorative gesture in this formula and points again to the necessity of broadening the cultural historiography's points of comparison out beyond the narrow ground of the splintering Union. It is suggestive in this regard to think of O'Malley's German publishers issuing his work in a catalogue that included the work of Gandhi; it is hard to think of two strategies more oppositional than the Irish and Indian to the end of empire but there remains much thinking to do as to why the violent and the peaceful, and all points between, were necessary for any group of people to secede from a global arrangement whose own capacity for mass violence was so catastrophically pervasive.

Ernie O'Malley's *On Another Man's Wound* is a revolutionary text because it describes the rough texture of this damaged world at the personal level. The scenes of his torture are mixed with moments of humanity from his captors, his order of the execution of captured British soldiers merged with meditations on the broken landscape around him. Writing weekly in the *Irish Homestead*, and later the *Irish Statesman*, George Russell liked to repeat the proverb that man cannot stand on tiptoes all the time. By this he meant that the period of the troubles caused a kind of emotional over-extension that the people who experienced it, men, women and children, would take long to recover from. This is another mark of that generation of 1914, the tragedy of which deepened for their dependants as they suffered at second hand from experiences that were often inarticulate. This is the brilliance, as Foster so well describes it, of McGahern's *Amongst Women*, McGahern's sympathy for O'Malley a sure sign of both their genius, the artist sensitive to divine what another might dismiss as passive suffering. This was a perspective visible to the generation after 1914 and represents a human sympathy won from such suffering as to induce melancholy in its celebration. Ernie O'Malley is the emblematic Irish figure of this European transition, congruent with Joyce, Jack Yeats and others, but solitary in his synthesis of aesthetics and experience. His archive of notes, letters, diaries and interviews is an invitation to think of Ireland as a great modern paradox, so immovable in reality and so evocative in abstraction. O'Malley, like many others, manoeuvred between these cold harbours, foundering finally on the wounds he suffered decades before.

This collection of essays offers rich suggestions of the ways in which readings of Ernie O'Malley's work can broaden our understanding of Irish literature, history and art. More than that, it establishes O'Malley as a key figure in any constellation of Irish cultural life in the troubled global history of the early twentieth century.

Nicholas Allen

PART I

POST-REVOLUTION PERSPECTIVES

CHAPTER ONE

ON ANOTHER MAN'S TEXT
ERNIE O'MALLEY, JAMES JOYCE AND IRISH MODERNISM

Luke Gibbons

> ... *[t]hrough memory [he] has made notes all his life of material*
> *which has stirred him by its emotional significance.*
> —Ernie O'Malley, on Jack B. Yeats[1]

In August 1930, the *Santa Fe New Mexican* newspaper carried a report of a series of lectures on the unlikely topic – at least for the American mid-west in that period – of Irish literature. 'General Ernest O'Malley', the report noted, gave 'a complete outline of the genesis and history of Irish poetry, from the ancient Gaelic' to the new Irish poetry:[2]

> [R]eading selected translations from the earliest poems [he showed] how these furnished, not the material, but the root soil and spiritual source and strength of the younger Irish writers – particularly that group whose lives were sacrificed in the cause of Irish freedom in 1916 – Padraic Pearse, Joseph Plunkett, Thomas McDonagh [*sic*], Francis Ledwidge [*sic*], a costly sacrifice not only for Ireland, but for poetry. Among other writers, most of them still living, whose poems Mr O'Malley read, were James Stephens, Joseph Campbell, Eva Gore-Booth, Moira O'Neill, Dora Sigerson, Austin Clark [*sic*], James Joyce and Padraic Colum.[3]

The report makes it clear that by placing the 'younger school' in the context of 1916, there is an attempt to distance Irish poetry from the first phase of the Revival led by

Yeats, Æ (George Russell), Synge and others. The engaged nature of 'the modern Irish poetic movement' is further spelled out: 'Mr O'Malley pointed out that with certain exceptions, the work of these men is not "literary"; not, that is, of the schools or universities, but of life; and he also stressed the fact that it was the Gaelic League of Ireland, started by Douglas Hyde, which really instigated the *modern* Irish poetic movement.' O'Malley's linking of 'Gaelic' to the 'modern' was not an isolated event, and it was indeed to modernism, and the distinctive literary innovations of James Joyce, that he turned his attention a few months later.

In late November, 1930, the newspaper reported on another series of lectures on Irish literature that culminated in an introduction to James Joyce, and which was delivered in climatic conditions that would not have been out of place in Joyce's story. 'The Dead': 'Last week's talks by Ernest O'Malley at the house of Mr and Mrs Raymond Otis on the subject of Irish poetry, was attended by a number of interested listeners, in spite of the blizzard.'[4] O'Malley's first lecture covered the transition from Gaelic literature to modern writing described above, but the second talk, an introduction to Joyce, proved so successful that another lecture, on *Ulysses*, was arranged for the following week:

> At the talk by Ernest O'Malley at the Raymond Otis house last Tuesday evening, so great was the interest of the audience in the subject of James Joyce that they demanded a continuation of the same subject for another evening … Mr O'Malley read many scenes from The Portrait of an Artist as a young man [*sic*], to the great delight of his listeners, and from other early work of Joyce, with a discussion of his writing based on much critical reading and a personal acquaintance with Joyce.[5]

We can assume the suggestion of 'personal acquaintance' with Joyce means first-hand experience of Joyce's daunting texts as against secondary criticism, and the final lecture 'on the great Ulysses' was delivered the following Tuesday. This received more extended treatment in the *Santa Fe New Mexican*, which noted in passing O'Malley's military background ('the general'):

> Though still reluctant to break away from what may be called professorial decorum, the general in a too-limited time covered his study of Ulysses convincingly. Certainly this was the best of his lectures. He became fluent and assuring. Beginning with an image of Joyce as a 'dark Napoleon,' Mr O'Malley began to reveal the powers of his countryman.[6]

In the course of his talk, O'Malley took issue with the over-emphasis on the Homeric parallels in the novel, preferring the *Ulysses* that 'needs move forward fulfilling its own destiny which is the tracing out with rhythmic psychological imagination the huge mind-pattern of Mr Bloom'. 'Character relationship' and the hauntings of the past drove the novel, not just literary parallels, linking 'Bloom and Mrs Bloom together to Stephen, who wandering through the timeless day haunted by the phantom of his dead mother has commiserated "Ulysses" whose ghost is sometimes twofold – both the lover and his (Bloom's) dead baby son; and finally that of Mrs Bloom to her (in the closing page) more assertive husband – these connections were all emphasized. And O'Malley read in direct quotation some of the burlesquerie, the flamboyant adjectivism, the characterology, the disssonnances [*sic*] and the guttlanguage of the stream-of-consciousness catalogue'.[7]

The detailed nature of O'Malley's talk is clear from descriptions of his adhering too closely to his script (which unfortunately has not come down to us): 'Well in a year O'Malley will probably speak extemporaneously on Joyce in a way that would now surprise him to hear. Credit, much credit is due to him for his industry and study and it is particularly gratifying to know that he has stimulated interest in the modernist literature. It is a pity more people have not been to hear him especially on Joyce who is influencing Americans.'[8] That O'Malley was not just speaking from notes but from experience, however, is indicated by his own hauntings at this time: sympathizing with Dorothy Brett earlier in the year on the death of D.H. Lawrence, he wrote that he was no stranger to ghosts himself:

> I have seen so many of my comrades die that death seems as much part of life as life itself. Yet I know there were some deaths I never recovered from. They left a strange void which has always remained, a gap, yet a communion as well for I can feel the dead, nor would I be surprised to find someday that they walked in to resume an interrupted conversation.[9]

As a result of these talks, O'Malley was able to write to Edward Weston in February, 1931: '[I] gave lectures, even on James Joyce, leaving a group behind me who were able to read Ulysses aloud!'[10] A shared interest in Joyce proved a valuable asset in other circles, such as his friendship with Gerald Sykes and Harold Clurman (of the famous Group Theatre in New York): 'We talked of Joyce and that in itself was a bond.'[11] In early 1935, O'Malley recalled these talks in a letter to Harriet Monroe, placing Joyce once again in the Irish as well as the international canon: 'In the Southwest I lectured on Gaelic and Anglo-Irish literature from our first poet to James Joyce.'[12] It was not until the post-Second World War period that O'Malley took up the study of Joyce again in earnest. In late 1947, he wrote to John V. Kelleher, a pioneer in Irish approaches to Joyce, to send on recent American books, building on the substantial number of critical studies he had already acquired.[13] By the early 1950s, he was also in correspondence with John J. Slocum, the first major bibliographer of Joyce, seeking to procure more James Joyce material, and, as late as 1953, was still studying Joyce while renewing work on his memoir of the Civil War, *The Singing Flame*.

How are we to account for this sustained engagement with the work of Joyce, and relate it to O'Malley's own formidable military reputation, and his lifelong commitment to Irish Republicanism? O'Malley's early interest in Joyce may have been stimulated by his friendship with Denis Devlin, Roger McHugh, William Fay and others in the UCD Dramatic Society, which he helped to found on his brief return to university to resume his medical studies in 1926–8.[14] His growing interest in Joyce coincided with the first systematic publication of 'Work in Progress' in *transition* magazine, edited by Eugene Jolas and Elliot Paul, and on the day of O'Malley's arrival in New York in October 1928, on a mission to raise funds for the *Irish Press* newspaper, he found his way to the newly opened Gotham Book Mart, that sold the publication.[15] The avant-garde magazine carried Stuart Gilbert's path-breaking exposition of the 'Aeolus' chapter in *Ulysses* (masterminded by Joyce himself), and other landmark essays on Joyce by Jolas, Elliot Paul, Ernst Robert Curtius, all of which feature in O'Malley's notebooks.

By 1928, Joyce's *Pomes Pennyeach* (1927) is included in lists of O'Malley's reading, and in 1929, another list included 'Anna Livia Plurabelle' (1928), 'Tales Told of Shem and Shaun' (1929), *Exiles* (1918) and *A Portrait of the Artist as a Young Man* (1916), along with Brinsley MacNamara's *In Clay and in Bronze* (1920), Liam O'Flaherty's first novel, *Thy Neighbour's Wife* (1923) and Seamus O'Sullivan's *The Rosses and Other Poems* (1918).[16] While visiting New Mexico in 1929, O'Malley recalled his futile attempts to renew his medical studies at UCD while his mind drifted elsewhere, noting ruefully in his journal:

> I heard Professor McLoughlin, old E.P. say 'Now, Mr O'M.[alley] will you please place the bone in position. What age would you say it is? Now are you quite sure?' … Oh shades of medical examination. Dear old Cecilia Street with its 'stiffs' and dissections, sitting on the College steps in the sun discussing everything from middle Irish poetry to James Joyce. Will I ever sit on the steps again with a notebook and a Materia Medica discussing everything but medicine?[17]

At a time when Joyce's status as a modernist icon was increasingly emphasized at the expense of his Irishness, O'Malley's reading of Joyce was informed by the starker, hard-edged realism of the later Revival. In his powers of concentration, fascination with maps and lists, and assiduous eye for detail, he deployed in his military activities qualities not unlike those Joyce brought to bear on *Ulysses*, and O'Malley went on to bring the same eye to his reading of Joyce's work – but with one notable difference. Not alone was nothing published but the written-up lectures have also disappeared, so that his studies of Joyce, as he said of his own vision of the Irish republic, have 'not been realized except in the mind'.[18] As in the case of Walter Benjamin's monumental *Arcades* project, which survived only in the quotations and glosses assembled for a magnum opus never completed, O'Malley's notes, devoted mainly to *Ulysses* and a wide range of critical responses to the work, are all that is left of his intensive forays into Joyce's revolution of the word.[19] The five main notebooks contain several hundred pages of notes, consisting primarily of key passages from Joyce's works; glosses and summaries; indices (of people, places, themes, etc.); and notes on his extensive reading of the already imposing body of Joycean criticism.[20] In this, they resemble Benjamin's dream of a work consisting entirely of quotations, their juxtaposition with each other bearing witness to a highly selective intelligence over and above the designs of the original authors of the passages. As Hannah Arendt writes of this aspect of Benjamin's method:

> [L]ike the later notebooks, this collection was not an accumulation of excerpts intended to facilitate the writing of the [subsequent] study but constituted the main work, with the writing as something secondary. The main work consisted in tearing fragments out of their context and arranging them afresh in such a way that they illustrated each other and were able to prove their raison d'être in a free floating state, as it were.[21]

It would be imputing too much to O'Malley's notes to consider them a self-conscious exercise along Benjamin's lines; yet in his lists, taxonomies and cross-referencing of motifs, persons, places and names in *Ulysses*, he engages precisely in the process of 'tearing fragments out of their context' and reassembling them to create new meanings. It is only when the notes are compared with the original published texts that the eclectic and even idiosyncratic nature of O'Malley's own reading becomes apparent.[22] The transcription of a passage does not, of course, mean that O'Malley agrees with it, still less that it can pass as his own voice, but if certain patterns manifest themselves across widely disparate sets of notes, it can at least be assumed that they are of interest to him. Not surprisingly, the Irish allusions and references to Irish history predominate in the home-made concordances designed to facilitate his own rereading and cross-referencing of *Ulysses*, but the extensive notes transcribed from Joycean criticism constantly set Irish aspects in the context of universal or mythic themes, rather than emphasizing one at the expense of the other.

Notes from the Underground

Two early notebooks from the period of his Santa Fe lectures testify to the background reading and concerns that informed O'Malley's talks.[23] One of the notebooks is devoted primarily to *Ulysses* and *Work in Progress*, and opens with a chapter-by-chapter outline of *Ulysses* but in a schematic manner that highlights seemingly marginal Irish political aspects alongside Homeric parallels. The scheme of 'Aeolus' is given as 'Rhetoric 111–143 News Paper Office: *Cave of the Winds*. Skin the Goat', and 'Eumaeus' as '573–622 Skin the Goat Eumaeus more of mood than of mind'.[24] That James Fitzharris ('Skin the Goat'), one of the Rosencrantzs or Guildensterns of the Parnellite period, should assume centre stage is in keeping with Joyce's own fascination with the cast-offs of history.[23]

In his notes on the opening 'Telemachus' chapter, the focus on the death of Stephen's mother and her ghoulish reappearance to him in a dream is followed by the description of the 'poor old woman', Mother Ireland or 'silk of the kine', who brings milk to the Tower, and who signals the theme of betrayal in *Ulysses*: 'names given her in old times. A wandering crone, lowly form of an immortal serving her conqueror and her gay betrayer, their common cuckquean, a messenger from the secret morning' (*U* 1.403–6). Stephen's remorse is highlighted – 'Agenbite of Inwit' (*U* 1.481) – as is his defiance of the twin sources of power in Ireland: 'I am a servant of two masters, an English and an Italian […] The imperial British state … and the holy Roman catholic and apostolic church' (*U* 1.638–44). In the notes on 'Nestor', the 'fabled by the daughters of memory' (*U* 2.7) passage is transcribed and scored at the side, ending with a passage in *Ulysses* that may well point proleptically to the destruction of Dublin in 1916: 'I hear the ruin of all space, shattered glass and toppling masonry, and time one livid final flame. What's left us then?' (*U* 2.9–10). Another quotation is underlined further down the page: 'History, S., is a nightmare from which I am trying to awake' (*U* 2.377), followed a few lines later by a comment in brackets: '(Deasy anti semite)?' In the pages on 'Proteus', the exiled Fenian in Paris 'Kevin Egan' is noted, followed by '(43 obscure)' – referring to page 43 of *Ulysses* which evokes the Clerkenwell explosion, Maud Gonne in Paris, and other tangled memories. The 'ghostwoman with ashes in her breath' (*U* 3.546–7) recurs, followed immediately by Stephen's musing, as he stands by the sea, on 'The whitemaned seahorses, champing, brightwindbridled, the steeds of Mananaan' (*U* 3.56–7).

That O'Malley's note-taking draws on his own dark night of the soul is clear, as we shall see, from the manner in which the association of the 'ghostwoman'/Mother Ireland with Mananaan MacLir, strikes a deep personal chord – that which links the O'Malley name with the mythical Irish sea god. O'Malley's early notes on his reading of *Ulysses* date from the early 1930s but when he renews his study of Joyce in Dublin in the late 1940s, the emphasis shifts to textual aids for rereading the novel (lists, gazetteers, indices) and a thorough immersion in Joycean criticism. There is a fascination with Joyce's rapid elevation in the pantheon of world literature, the emergence of a modern – and Irish – Homer or Shakespeare, recasting the universal themes addressed by myth and psychoanalysis in the idioms of Irish experience. It is for this reason that O'Malley is particularly interested in approaches that close the gap between myth and actuality, as in the noting of Stuart Gilbert's observation, in his famous essay on the 'Aeolus' chapter in *transition* magazine, that the universality of Joyce's method was achieved through 'the specific recall of a realist narrative of the past'.[24] Gilbert's emphasis is primarily on the classical or Homeric parallels but in his notes on Gilbert's essay, O'Malley was equally concerned with the byways of Irish history. He notes Gilbert's account of the comic deflation of the newspaper captions in the 'Aeolus' chapter, according to which the style passes from the 'comparatively dignified, classically allusive' mode, consistent with myth, to realist low-life 'in all its blatancy, the catchpenny slickness of the modern press'.[25]

Picking up on his earlier notes, O'Malley attends to how 'Aeolus' is a showcase for oratory and rhetorical effects, in keeping with the 'King of Winds' that blows through the original episode in Homer's *Odyssey*. Stuart Gilbert's observation that the modern press is a palace of the winds is of more than passing interest to O'Malley as he notes how the 'circulation' of newspapers guides the caprice of public opinion: 'Cities are taken by the ears.'[26] It was this 'illicit union, of aspiration and compromise, of literature and opportunism'[27] that informed O'Malley's account, in *The Singing Flame,* of how the pro-Free State journalism moulded popular opinion to accept the Treaty during the Civil War.[28] It was indeed the lack of an oppositional Republican voice that prompted de Valera to found *The Irish Press*, sending O'Malley, with Frank Aiken, on the fund-raising drive for the proposed newspaper that brought him to the United States.[29] In contrast to the ill winds of the modern press, O'Malley concentrates an another theme in 'Aeolus', that of akasic memory – the theosophical belief in the indestructibility of the records of the past (once again an ironic reflection on his own life, given his presence in the Four Courts when the archives of the Irish past were blown up during the Civil War).

It is Gilbert's discussion of a seemingly incidental passage in the 'Aeolus' chapter that catches O'Malley's eye above all else: Bloom's suggestion to use a design of two crossed keys, reminiscent of the 'House of Keys' of the Manx parliament, to illustrate the advertisement he is seeking to place for Alexander Keyes in *The Freeman's Journal*.[30] As Gilbert points out (and O'Malley notes), this links the motif 'with one of the magical themes of Ulysses, the legend of Mananaan MacLir, the founder of the Manx nation'. Stephen Dedalus's description in 'Proteus' of sea-waves as 'the steeds of Mananaan' (*U* 3.56–7) is noted, as is the connection drawn later between King Lear and the lines from Æ's play, *Deirdre* (1902): 'Flow over them with your waves and with your waters, Mananaan …' (*U* 9.190–1). Gilbert's citing of Mananaan's appearance in 'Circe' is also taken down by O'Malley: 'The bearded figure of Mananaun MacLir broods …' (*U* 15.2262), as is Gilbert's suggestion that the ancient sea god also maintains a mystical link to akasis and the God of creation:

> This linking up of the vulgar with the esoteric, as here in this sequence: Alexander Keyes' 'ad' – Keys – Isle of Man – Mananaan – AUM – Brahamata's secret Word, is characteristic of the Joycean method, and it is appropriate that several items in the series should be named in the Aeolus episode, for Mananaan MacLir … is own brother to Poseidon's son, ruler of the fog-girt isle of Aeolia.[31]

It is not surprising that this digression on Mananaan should be of more than passing interest, for the O'Malley clan were associated, through their territory around Clew Bay in County Mayo, with the great sea god in Irish legend: in Irish genealogical tradition, 'the O'Malleys are celebrated in several poems as expert seamen. They are called the Mananaans, or sea-gods, of the western ocean.'[32] O'Malley took great pride in living at Burrishoole on Clew Bay, a seat of the O'Malley clan, and O'Malley's wife, the sculptor Helen Hooker O'Malley, was so impressed with a maquette of a sculpture of Mananaan MacLir, executed by Peter Grant for the New York World's Fair of 1939, that she bought the exhibit and commissioned an enlarged version of the work.[33] It is this figure that forms the basis of the bronze monument to Ernie O'Malley, donated by his family, on the Mall in his native Castlebar.[34]

The extent to which the sea, and the related trope of the drowned body, exerts a continual fascination for O'Malley is clear from the manner in which these themes recur in his notes on Ernst R. Curtius's 'Technique and Thematic Development in Joyce'. Curtius wrote this critical commentary as a follow up to his introduction to the first German translation of *Ulysses* in 1929, and the article was translated by Eugene Jolas in *transition* 16–17 (July 1929).[35] Counting Samuel Beckett among its admirers, the article quickly established itself, along with Stuart Gilbert's writings, as a classic in the rapidly expanding field of Joycean criticism.[36] The theme of the drowned body is examined in detail by Curtius, and O'Malley transcribes the summary of Joyce's fusion of realism with symbolic/mythic allusions: 'These examples might illustrate how a motif, offered conjointly with the reality of external events and mirrored in poetic form (Milton, Shakespeare) is enlarged in the case of Stephen to a symbol of his problems of life: death, misery, sorrow, repentance.'[37] The immediate cause of Stephen's sorrow and repentance reverts to the navel cord and the maternal, prompted by his guilt over his inability to save his mother at the hour of her death: 'She is drowning. Agenbite … Agenbite of inwit. Misery! Misery!'(*U* 11.875, 879, 880). O'Malley's reading of Curtius is in a separate notebook from his earlier notes on the sea and Mananaan MacLir in 'Aeolus', but when Curtius notes Stephen's struggles with remorse, and that the 'reality of external events' is 'enlarged … to a symbol of his problems of life: death, misery, sorrow, repentance', it is difficult not to imagine O'Malley reflecting once more on the violence and suffering of his own past as he wrote the words down.

In his notes on the 'Scylla and Charybdis' chapter, these issues surface again. George Russell's (Æ) contributions to the debate in the National Library are prominent, including his pronouncement that 'The movements which work revolutions in the world are born out of the dreams and visions in a peasant's heart on the hillside … the desirable life is revealed only to the poor of heart, the life of Homer's Phaeacians' (*U* 9.103–6). The librarian Richard Best's insistence on the relationship of Hamlet to Shakespeare's personal life is emphasized, and O'Malley again underlines the moral soul-searching of Stephen, as in the repetition of notes on 'Agenbite of inwit': '<u>Agenbite of inwit. remorse of conscience</u>. Hurrying to her squalid deathlair from gay Paris on the quayside I touched his hand' (*U* 9.825–6). The attentiveness to 'Agenbite' or 'conscience' in *Ulysses* is of interest given the repeated view, promulgated first by Sean O'Faolain, that O'Malley was a man without pity or remorse.[38] This is belied by the frequency with which O'Malley reflects precisely on the emotional or moral cost of violence, as in his suggestion that in a war without the official backing of a state to absolve the individual of direct responsibility, such as in the Anglo-Irish War, conscience weighs more heavily on the individual, notwithstanding the justice of the cause: 'Action grew out of personal responsibility and individual effort rather than as an organized service of authority and a symbol which relieved the individuals of personal responsibility.'[39] Joyce's use of the term 'agenbite' diagnoses precisely this particular crisis in conscience, in which regret or remorse is felt even for actions that were right at the time, even though justice is not sufficient to appease the ghost. The operation of 'remorse' is originally connected with 'morsel', with biting and eating, and it is as if, having passed the conscious or 'mental' test of conscience, there is still a residue that passes into the body. Hence the 'gnawing' of remorse, or 'pangs' (akin to those of hunger) of conscience, somatic responses that have to do with sensitivity and humane feelings not fully resolved by acting on principle, or the 'justness' of one's conduct. These can be self-destructive but may also initiate 'reparative efforts that tend to reduce self-torment by restoring some positive self esteem',[40] through the acknowledgement of damage – not only to others but to oneself, as in the psychic injuries of trauma. The shock that passes out of the mind into the body, or that lodges in the body and does not make it to the mind at all, was classified as shell shock or, more accurately, 'neurasthenia',[41] and it is not surprising that this was diagnosed as O'Malley's medical condition, over and above the severe physical wounds that scarred his body.

Stephen's anguish in *Ulysses* over his mother's death is a clear case of conscience in crisis, as his principled refusal to grant her dying wish, that he make his peace with the Catholic church, condemns her to an agonizing death. In O'Malley's notes on 'Wandering Rocks', this is related to the theme of drowning (already noted in 'Proteus') and once more to '<u>Agenbite</u>' (underlined by O'Malley), and he notes the imperial narrative unifying the chapter: '[The Lord lieu connects them all up]'. The sound effects of 'Sirens' is noted, as is Bloom's distress as he notices Boylan entering the lounge. The entrance of the blind boy follows on the mention of the blind stripling earlier in 'Lestrygonians'; the fading of sight counterpointed by the acoustics of the ear, including the songs 'All is Lost Now' and 'The Croppy Boy'. So far from sleeping easily on another man's wound, as the old Irish proverb that informs the title of O'Malley's memoir declares, he confesses in a harrowing account of the execution of British hostages that, having been tortured and having faced death himself, 'It seemed easier to face one's own execution than to have to shoot others.'[42]

In his summary of Stuart Gilbert's essay 'An Irish *Ulysses*: "Hades" Episode', O'Malley notes Gilbert's opening comment on *Ulysses*: 'Much of the work seems a merely meticulous study of the commonplace, and its clues seem buried beneath a rubble of detail.'[43] Gilbert's discussion of the funeral/graveyard episode addresses issues of burial and rebirth, and how meaning can (re)emerge from a 'rubble of detail'. The rubble of 1916 may not have been far from O'Malley's mind as he reflected on Paddy Dignam's funeral passing by the national icons of O'Connell and Parnell ('the shades of Heracles and Agamemnon') on O'Connell Street; Gilbert's emphasis on the affinities between the ambiguous prophecy of Tiresias and Robert Emmet's 'Speech from the Dock', stipulating the birth of the nation as the condition for his own epitaph, is also duly noted by O'Malley. The downward movement or experience of descent that constitutes the 'mortuary atmosphere' of the chapter is noted, akin to the Royal Canal 'dropping down, lock by lock', but this 'downward pressure' – 'interpreting a long postponement of Ireland's freedom' in O'Malley's notes – is nevertheless counteracted by the prospect of rebirth at the end. While O'Malley had no illusions about the over-whelming defeat of the Civil War, there is no succumbing to fatalism in his work; in words that could apply to much of his life, he wrote to Paul Strand: 'This last year I went through several kinds of hell, and it was only last month I realized I was above defeat. That may sound presumptuous but it's true. I touched bottom and found that at any rate.'[44]

'Telescoped Time'

Maurice Murphy's essay, 'James Joyce and Ireland', published in the *Nation* (1929), opens with a paragraph that must have given O'Malley pause for thought: 'James Joyce has done more for Ireland than any other man of letters. It is not at all inconsistent with Irish character that he is looked on as a kind of pariah, not only of the peasantry but by many otherwise intelligent people.'[45] This could have been an image of O'Malley himself, or other Republican activists, cast as pariahs in the bitter aftermath of the Civil War. Joyce's modernism touched on another aspect of radical Republicanism as it drew closer to the daily rounds of everyday life in Dublin: the very attempt to artic-ulate popular consciousness as it is lived leads to rejection by the people whose lives are represented for the first time. O'Malley wrote of the challenge presented by the more radical images of the Revival to a complacent, popular consciousness:

> It was difficult for a people not accustomed to creative work to see themselves in print or on the stage. The sudden realization was not at first accepted, as the absence of a steadying influence of a printed creative tradition had made people glorify themselves or explain away their faults, and had made them less amenable to the writer's intuition and understanding.[46]

One of the recurrent themes in O'Malley's writing is the need to tear away the romantic illusions that provide a futile escape from harsh realities, while yet empha-sizing the equal need to challenge the conformity and passivity (Joyce's 'paralysis') that accepts such harsh realities as fate.[47] O'Malley notes Cyril Connolly's view that 'each of his [Joyce's] books reveals a growing fear of beauty; not because life is not beautiful, but because there is something exceedingly false and luxurious in the "Celtic Twilight" approach to it'.[48] For all Joyce's aloofness, it is his willingness to deal with the base metal of everyday life that constitutes his true democratic achievement for Connolly, as against the romantic images of the Revival:

> What Baudelaire and Laforgue did for Paris, or T.S. Eliot for modern London, Joyce has done for Dublin and at a time when Yeats and Synge had monopolized the Gaelic

side of the Irish, he was able to create a language of the demotic commercial speech of the Anglicized burgers of Dublin itself ... Joyce in *Ulysses* set out to revive it [literary English] by introducing the popular colloquial idiom of his own city ... [49]

It is in this sense that Joyce's 'demotic' style echoes O'Malley's own politics, particularly the Republican conviction that the restoration of the voice of the people, whether among the reading public or at the ballot box, may not initially meet with popular approval. Revolution by definition is always ahead of its time, and like the avant-garde, its justification lies in the shock of recognition, the shattering of the inertia that, in Joyce's terms, paralyses a people. This was the rationale of the Easter Rising of 1916, which had less of a mandate than the anti-Treaty position in the Civil War, and in linking revolution with the vanguard thinking of modernism, it is striking that O'Malley uses Joyce's image of 'forging' the conscience of the race to describe his own revolutionary awareness: 'We were being hammered red-hot in the furnace of the spirit and a spark was bound to fly and disclose us to each other, with a word, a look, a chance remark.'[50] O'Malley was sent down the country by IRA General Headquarters to light the spark nationwide. Though acting in the name of the nation, it was clear that many of the people he encountered as an IRA organizer were not always on his side, except in a vague way: 'I was on the outside. I felt it in many ways by a diffidence, by an extra courtesy, by a silence. Some were hostile in their minds; others in speech; often the mother would think I was leading her son astray or the father would not approve of what the boys were doing.'[51] In a description that seems once more indebted to Joyce's conception of the artist in *A Portrait*, he continues:

> I felt that I should be able to fuse with my material, the people, so that I could make better use of it, yet look at them dispassionately, as if from a distance. My approach to teaching and training the men was impersonal ... This often meant a cold quality creeping in, but few could mingle with them without gaining warmth.[52]

It is for this reason, as Richard English points out, that imagination is ineluctably bound up with political freedom in O'Malley's mind, as democracy without freedom, the cultural condition of self-determination, is empty: 'O'Malley conceived of freedom as involving both formal political and lasting cultural emancipation. National freedom and individual, intellectual freedom were interlinked.'[53] Following the classical democratic tenet which proposed that people cannot consent to their own slavery,[54] O'Malley wrote that 'it was an urge difficult to interpret; the right of a people to its own soil so long as that people would not accept domination'.[55] Remaining in the British Empire under the sovereignty of a foreign monarch was still domination in the eyes of those who opposed the Treaty. Writing from Kilmainham Gaol, following the collapse of the mass hunger strike in November 1923, O'Malley took issue with those among his own ranks who refused to face difficult truths, and who persisted in wresting victory from defeats:

> I have pointed out that our traditions are wrong and that we foster them knowingly or without thought. We are and have been slaves and so have the slave mind. The open fighting of 1920–1921 and some of the fighting of 1922–1923 has helped somewhat to eradicate slavish defects … Even though there are such outstanding deeds the mass cannot rise to them save in a certain form of enthusiasm.[56]

The appeal of the modernist turn in art towards *form* was that while rejecting passive representation, the 'slavish' reproduction of reality in politics as well as art, it acted *on* history, refusing to accept an oppressive past as given.

The point of disrupting prevailing attitudes and power relations through the jarring aesthetic devices of modernism was to break up habit and to throw off modes of domination, enabling a cowered population to reclaim their own voice and culture in the process. It is in this sense that Joyce's radicalism is closer to what Peter Burger has termed 'the historical avant garde', aligned to political as well as cultural radicalism: though initially in advance of society, the avant-garde sought to induce transformations that would eventually intervene in, and percolate through, everyday life.[57] The unexpected jolts in Joyce's use of montage migrates to the formal and stylistic shifts in O'Malley's own writing, most notably in the sudden juxtaposition of myth and realism in a key passage in his Civil War memoir, *The Singing Flame*. Hiding in a secret room at Ailesbury Road, Ballsbridge, in Dublin, O'Malley recounts how he awoke one morning in November 1922 to find the house completely surrounded by Free State troops. Resolving to shoot his way out, he describes in slow-motion cinematic detail how he dressed, gathered his gun and hand grenade, and listened in the darkness: 'I shielded a match with my hand for I did not want a light to show at the back of the house through the sepia blind' (180). At this point, the great Irish saga, the *Táin Bó Cúailnge*, flashes up in his mind, the inflated diction of the epic, recounting Ferdia's battledress on the last day of his fight, posing an ironic contrast to his own humdrum preparations: 'Outside of his brown-leathern, well-sewed kilt he put a huge goodly flagstone, the size of a millstone … On his left side he hung his curved battle sword, which would cut a hair against the stream with its keenness and sharpness. On the arch-slope of his back he hung his massive, fine buffalo shield whereon were fifty bosses …'[58] This mythic out-take continues at some length until it is brought back to earth by the stark reality of soldiers ascending the stairs and imminent capture or death: 'There was nothing very splendid about a Smith and Wesson, but I was fond of it as a good piece of mechanism, and my one grenade was not very warlike to look at.'[59] The abrupt narrative transitions raise questions about the role of myth in supplying reserves of courage, questions that surface again when, in detention at the Curragh camp, he encounters the legends that had grown around his own exploits:

> I was told stories of myself, what I had said or done in different places. I could not recognize myself for the legend. That was a difficulty. The confusion between the legendary and the real self. Time jumped a gap with us. People saw us as a myth which bore little relation to ourselves; and our real selves, where could we find them?[60]

Contesting Yeats's image of the rebel hero summoning Cúchulainn to his side, O'Malley sees myth as a poor consolation for the sundering of the Irish past: 'Ours was the country of broken tradition, a story of economic, social and political oppression, propped up by a mythological introduction innocent of archaeological or historical interpretation.'[61] The affinities between this aesthetic of disruption and the shift in consciousness that followed the Easter Rising are delineated in *On Another Man's Wound*:

> The people as a whole had not changed; but the new spirit was working slowly, half afraid, yet determined … Without guidance or direction, moving as if to clarify itself, nebulous, forming, reforming … It was as if the inarticulate attempted to express themselves in any way or by any method; later would come organization and cool-headed reason. Now was the lyrical stage.[62]

In *The Singing Flame*, this is carried over into the mindset that prevailed during the Civil War: 'There was no background into which men could imperceptibly fit. We were particles in suspension waiting for further tests of our properties. There was a recasting, a reshaping of values.'[63] Rather than masking over grim realities, it may be that the yoking together of the epic and ordinary in Joyce's work helped to retrieve everyday life itself from the banality into which it had sunk, in O'Malley's disenchanted eyes, under the new conservative Free State. Tearing away illusions, disillusionment was empowering rather than disempowering, modernist formal energies holding out for new futures that draw on unrequited pasts.

CHAPTER TWO

'FLAMBOYANT, GOTHIC, ROMANESQUE'
ART AND REVOLUTION IN THE MIND OF ERNIE O'MALLEY

Róisín Kennedy

A key incident in Ernie O'Malley's decision to become a revolutionary was a chance meeting with an art student in the streets of Dublin in Easter 1916.[1] This, given O'Malley's lifelong interest in art, cannot be coincidental. Art and revolution in Ireland were closely associated. Not only had Willie Pearse studied at the Dublin Metropolitan School of Art, but his brother had often attended the classes with him, as had Countess Markievicz and Joseph Mary Plunkett's bride, Grace Gifford. Patrick Tuohy, another former student and subsequently a teacher in the School, fought in the GPO in 1916.[2] During the War of Independence O'Malley's visits to the home of Count Plunkett can only have added to the connection of art and insurgency in his mind.[3] Eileen McGrane, in whose house he also took refuge, had a keen interest in art.[4] O'Malley's association of art with revolution was intensified in 1920 when he took cover in Lennox Robinson's flat, and spent the night hours discussing war and its effects with Thomas MacGreevy, then a burgeoning art critic, whose views on art O'Malley came to share.[5] Both came to agree that the tradition of visual art in Ireland had been shattered by colonialism and that the encouragement of modernism provided the only recourse for Irish artists.

References to art recur throughout O'Malley's correspondence and memoirs, often in the most unexpected contexts. In *The Singing Flame* he recounts, at a key moment in the Civil War, coming back to his room in the Four Courts after it has been shelled. 'I picked up some books from a shelf ... There were two bullet holes through a copy of Vasari's *Lives of the Italian Painters*. Authors had been drilled and torn out of all proportion to the number of books. "Bad luck to them anyhow," I said in the direction of a piece of artillery gone through a John Synge illustrated by Jack Yeats.'[6] He goes on to locate an undamaged volume and sits down to peruse 'old, garrulous Vasari' amid the chaos of war.[7]

As a gunman he had carried a volume of images from William Blake, Albrecht Dürer and Piero della Francesco around with him. 'I had studied them in many a strange background of mountain or bog, and my mixed portfolio of reproductions, cut to fit my pockets, had become frayed and crinkled, worn glossy surfaces stuck with rain and sweat.'[8] This passion for art, as Nicholas Allen has written, enabled O'Malley to 'imagine landscape in a deluge of images'.[9] Equally, it allowed him an escape from reality, while at the same time offering him an opportunity of exercising his ability to memorize and to schematize space and form.

Giorgio Vasari's *Lives of the Artists*, the earliest history of art, was O'Malley's first guide to the subject. Published in the sixteenth century, it was written by an ambitious and strategic artist, described by Samuel Beckett, who also relied on Vasari, as 'the even fisted pettifogger'.[10] Biased in favour of Vasari's fellow Florentines, it praises those whose work conforms to the developing criteria of academic art of which disegno – drawing and design – is paramount. When recovering from the effects of the hunger strike at the end of the Civil War, O'Malley traced the history of Italian Renaissance art in his imagination by conjuring up works of art in his mind's eye. Appropriately, given his admiration for Vasari, he tells us that 'I could reconstruct the colouring of some and the form of a few, but line I could remember best, the scientific and experimental line of the Florentines ...'[11]

O'Malley's decision to develop a sound knowledge of art began at this period while in Kilmainham Gaol. He wrote to Molly Childers confiding that, while he had developed an interest in art at UCD, he had been too lazy to read anything difficult, but that he was familiar with the prose of John Ruskin and Walter Pater, both of whom he loved.[12] While MacGreevy was dismissive of Ruskin, describing him as 'almost invariably wrong', his ideas on nature, art and society reverberate in O'Malley's later interactions with art.[13] The use of Flamboyant, Gothic and Romanesque as divisions in *On Another Man's Wound* is eminently Ruskinian in nature. In the *Seven Lamps of Architecture*, Ruskin summarizes his study as explicating the entire range of Northern architecture, from the Romanesque to the Flamboyant. Allen has described this reversed chronology of styles as drawing 'the imagination back to a source obscured by the new State's forward march'.[14] An art historical explanation might suggest a move from decadence back to the essentials of form.

Ruskin's scientific appreciation of nature as concrete fact and as an expression of divine creation is reflected in O'Malley's veneration of landscape. In addition, Ruskin's devout attitude towards art can only have reinforced the impact of Patrick Pearse's ideas on art and spirituality on O'Malley. In his letters of the 1920s he clearly sees the purpose of art criticism as 'primarily … the inculcation of a spiritual doctrine',[15] or, as he expressed it in a letter to Sighle Humphreys in 1928, 'the spiritualistic interpretation of nationalism'.[16] Years later he applied Ruskin's notion of the 'innocent eye' to the work of Jack Yeats,[17] a phenomenon which the Victorian critic explained as 'a sort of childish perception of those flat stains of colour, merely as such, without consciousness of what they signify – as a blind man would see if suddenly gifted with sight!'[18] The notion of the 'innocent eye' became a keystone of modernist criticism.

Ruskin's writings on art also provided a powerful antidote to Vasari's presentation of art as progressive. Ruskin recognized that art and architecture can decline as well as advance and he pays close attention to the impact of historical change and exchange in the development of art. In *The Stones of Venice*, the city is presented as a liminal space between East and West, an accumulation of different styles assembled through the forces of history.[19] As F.S. Connelly has written, Ruskin's method is 'rooted in disjuncture, bringing together unlike things, stressing the impurity, the hybridity of history and images …'.[20] O'Malley similarly draws attention to the imperfections and ruptures in Irish art and architecture. In an expedition to Galway and Clare in 1948, his attention is drawn to the many instances of the recycling of medieval sculpture such as the 'fine Christ in the porch of a modern church' near Kinvara which 'had been taken from an old church last year', and the incorporation of the twelfth-century chancel arch in Tuam Church of Ireland Cathedral.[21] This idea of broken traditions becomes a central preoccupation of O'Malley's understanding of Irish art, both historically and in the contemporary period. In addition to this, Ruskin's writings opened up architecture and sculpture to analysis and it was the latter that offered O'Malley a much longer and more complex artistic tradition than that of easel painting.[22]

In 1925, when O'Malley, armed with copies of Baedeker, embarked on a tour of Europe, to recover his health, he derived considerable pleasure from identifying and in some cases reattributing artworks. MacGreevy was doing exactly the same thing when he questioned the attribution of many of the works in the National Gallery of

Ireland. As in his 1921 discussion of a painting, now attributed to Botticelli's student, Filippino Lippi:

> Personally, I am content with the Botticelli ascription. It is not the artist at his most expressive, but the irregular features and the ivory complexion of the subject, and the mood suggested by the turn of his eyes, are all characteristic of Botticelli. There is also the finished painting of the queerly shaped hand, and then the little landscape in the still, sunless light of early morning which Botticelli loved.[23]

MacGreevy and O'Malley were clearly influenced by the fashionable method of connoisseurship, which relies on close observation of precise stylistic details of a painting in order to ascribe the work to a specific painter. Developed in the mid-nineteenth century by Giovanni Morelli, an Italian doctor and revolutionary, connoisseurship uses both intuition and meticulous visual comparison of specific details of an artist's oeuvre. Morelli recommended ears and hands.[24] It would have appealed to O'Malley's medical training and his experiences in espionage and surveillance.

In a letter to Kay Brady, written from Florence in 1926, O'Malley tells her, 'I performed mental gymnastics in the museum trying to find out who the pictures are by'.[25] The sort of work that attracted his attention was unusual as, for example, his admiration for Lorenzo di Credi, a relatively obscure painter whose work was frequently confused with that of the better-known Perugino and Verrocchio. O'Malley's interest in him was heightened by his association with Savonarola and perhaps also by the fact that one of his paintings was in the collection of the National Gallery in Dublin.[26] He goes on to summarize an afternoon in the Uffizi: 'Then I could have sworn to a Crivelli but it was a Vivarini; I had a stiff fight to decide between Lotto, Palma Vecchio and Veronese for one – it was a little of each but finally I decided for Palma as only the Madonna could be by Lotto. The Raphael here is not his.'[27] His quotation from Edgar Wallace's *The Murder Book of J.G. Reeder* in the same letter reveals his attraction to art history as fundamentally a type of detective work.[28]

Samuel Beckett also indulged in challenging the authority of the museum most notably in his interaction with Pietro Perugino's *Pieta*, a High Renaissance painting acquired by the National Gallery of Ireland in 1931.[29] Beckett spent hours examining the painting and concluded that, 'although it has been messed up by restorers', the dead Christ and the women in the picture were 'lovely'.[30] He told MacGreevy that 'The most mystical constituent is the ointment pot that was probably added by Raffaela. Rottenly hung in rotten light behind this thick shop window, so that a total view of it is impossible, and full of grotesque amendments. But a lovely cheery Xist full of sperm, and the woman touching his thighs and mourning his secrets.'[31]

A similar, if less irreverent, attitude to the National Gallery is evident in O'Malley's references to it. A notoriously under-visited space in the early twentieth century, O'Malley went there to think clearly and undisturbed after hearing of the Treaty.[32] Although he considered it to be 'one of the best small galleries in Europe', he criticized it in the 1940s for having no contact with the outside world, rarely holding loan exhibitions and never really being part of us.[33] It was first and foremost an institution which failed to offset the public's conservative expectations of art. For him and others it typified one of the most disappointing aspects of post-revolutionary Ireland, the lack of institutional change and the lack of imagination.

O'Malley's move to the United States in 1928 opened his eyes to the full potential of modernism. He confessed in the 1920s to knowing 'nothing of modern art'.[34] Later, rather than reading up on the subject, he advised Eithne Golden, 'It is only by seeing [modern art] that you can eventually train yourself, that is if the feeling of the quality of the pictures isn't inherent in you.'[35] This need to see art became a central preoccupation of his later involvement in art in Ireland. But its roots lie in his early fascination with connoisseurship and Ruskin's meticulous explorations of the physical structure of the artwork.

Within a year of arriving in the United States, O'Malley had become familiar with the work of a wide range of contemporary American painters and was a confirmed modernist. He wrote confidently of Mexican art, distinguishing between the murals of Diego Rivera and those of José Clemente Orozco, which he saw in Mexico City in 1931.[36] His encounters with the modernist photographers Edward Weston and Paul Strand, with whom he shared a similar solitary personality and experience, enabled O'Malley to recognize that contemporary visual art had the ability to convey complex social and historical ideas effectively. Such networks of friendship provided him with the kind of challenging discussion on art which he had often lacked in his revolutionary days. In addition, the Mexican and the American modernist art that he saw dealt with the difficulties of marginalization and regionalism that was so pertinent to the position of Irish modernism.

His time in New York in the 1930s coincided with the institutionalization of modern art in that city.[37] The friendships that he formed there exposed him to the dynamics of the art field and to the role of collectors, curators and critics in driving forward wider public engagement in art. Moving in the circles of Georgia O'Keeffe and Alfred Stieglitz, key figures in the establishment of avant-garde art in the US, O'Malley also came into contact with James Johnson Sweeney, whom he later knew as a neighbour in County Mayo.[38] Sweeney was closely involved in the Museum of

Modern Art which opened in New York in 1929, later becoming its director of painting and sculpture. O'Malley was impressed by Sweeney's 1934 book, *Plastic Redirections in Modern Painting*, which was published two years before Alfred Barr's seminal *Cubism and Abstract Art*. Like Barr's influential account, it provided a rationale for the development of avant-garde art, stressing the rejection of naturalism and the need for modern art to be a vital element in the world. In addition, its juxtaposition of the contemporary and the ancient reinforced O'Malley's experience of modernism as connecting indigenous traditions of art making with those of the present day. Its references to the role of criticism would also be useful, with Sweeney describing the only genuine constructive criticism 'as a creative act which provokes or follows up on another creative act'.[39]

In 1935, when O'Malley returned to Ireland, he found that the neglect of art begun by Cumann na Gael was being continued by Fianna Fáil.[40] In 1946, he noted that 'The government as a whole has no understanding of or feeling for creative work; nor is it inclined to consult people of vitality'.[41] While a permanent home for Hugh Lane's Dublin Municipal Gallery had been opened in Charlemont House in 1933, it was the result of lobbying by a private organization, the Friends of the National Collections of Ireland [FNCI] rather than a state-led initiative. The museum, with a room left vacant for the return of the thirty-nine Lane paintings, embodied the contemporary and ongoing sense of stasis in Irish national life. In 1946, O'Malley told Sweeney, 'I remember in all two exhibitions in the Municipal. One is not allowed to charge for admission or, I believe, to sell a catalogue of an exhibition without special legislation. There is no government grant for exhibitions.'[42] In addition, there was no acquisitions budget and the museum's art advisory committee was dominated by political appointees and conservative academic artists.

Artist-led initiatives tried to offset the potentially disastrous situation for art in Ireland. The FNCI, the most significant and influential, attempted to modernize the collection of the Municipal Gallery by giving the work of leading School of Paris artists to it.[43] O'Malley thought that the group 'had a faint hang-over air of patronage … but also they have a few good workers'.[44] He was a member in 1945 and was close friends with the 'workers' who included Evie Hone, Con Curran and MacGreevy.[45] He shared their taste for French expressionist painting, having acquired work by artists such as Jean Lurcat, Georges Rouault and Maurice Vlaminck with his wife, Helen Hooker, in Paris in the late 1930s.[46]

The height of O'Malley's involvement in Irish art coincided with the Emergency, which he recognized as a pivotal period. It encouraged 'a new attitude to the Irish scene and to the Irish landscape' and the rejection of academic realist art in favour of modernism.[47] It was epitomized in the establishment of the Irish Exhibition of Living Art in 1943. This provided an alternative forum to the Royal Hibernian Academy (RHA), and marked the ascendance of a new pro-modernist network that directed the art field in Ireland in the next generation.[48] O'Malley was a patron and friend of its leading members, Jellett, Hone, Norah McGuinness and Nano Reid. Apart from his interest in the aesthetic qualities of their work, he shared their pragmatic understanding of the dynamics of modernist art in Ireland, and the need to cultivate a sympathetic coterie of collectors and supporters who could champion their cause both at home and abroad.

The artist who made the most profound impact on O'Malley was Jack Yeats, whom he met in 1937 and with whose painting, *Death for Only One*, he 'fell clear in love' two years later (Figure 1).[49] Between 1939 and late 1945, O'Malley acquired eight paintings by the artist, astutely assembling a representative range, with a preference for his later style.[50] His name occurs in the artist's accounts along with those of Beckett, who was paying for *Regatta*, *Evening*, Con Curran and Eileen MacCarvill (née McGrane), who completed her payments for *Going to Wolfe Tone's Grave* at the same time as O'Malley started his instalments for *Evening in Spring*.[51] These were all close friends of the artist who were allowed to pay for their works over several months, even years.

Sales in Yeats's work grew considerably during the war years, largely due to the closure of London and Paris to collectors and to the consequent development of a lively art market centred on modernist Irish art. Terence De Vere White observed that 'It was a strange phenomenon this strange desire to spend money on pictures by a living Irish artist.'[52]

Victor Waddington, Yeats's chief gallerist, staged major one-man shows of his work in his newly refurbished galleries in Anne Street in Dublin. O'Malley paid close attention to these, recognizing the significance of the rising prices of Yeats's work and the possibilities it offered for the development of modernist Irish art. In his copy of a March 1945 Waddington catalogue, he listed those who admired and those who acquired works, including himself and Helen, as well as calculating the money made by Waddington and Yeats in the venture.[53]

This show was a warm up for the Jack B. Yeats National Loan Exhibition that opened in the National College of Art in June 1945 and featured 179 works spanning Yeats's long career, from his early watercolours to contemporary oils, and was attended by 20,000 visitors. Its organization required a committee of over fifty individuals including several prominent members of Fianna Fáil.[54] O'Malley was closely involved in its planning, contributing the catalogue essay as well as lending several paintings anonymously. He later asserted that not only had the exhibition 'helped many to understand aspects of good painting' but also to realize that 'until this moment there had been little of the political or economic security in Ireland needed to foster appreciation of art'. The last time this had happened had been in the eighteenth century when there was 'a monied class'.[55]

However, for O'Malley, the major achievement of the exhibition was that it made a 'large public familiar with [Yeats's] development as a painter … [and offered] for some for the first time a chance to study his work closely and to judge it, as it should be judged, in terms of paint'. He noted that 'Yeats is so poorly represented in the public galleries of the city where his most important work has been, and is being painted, that a student cannot, when it suits him, study a few consecutive good examples but must wait for an occasional exhibition.'[56] This observation highlighted the need physically to see the artist's work in order to understand it fully. Yeats resisted the reproduction of his paintings. This strategy encouraged the direct engagement of the viewer, and it was one that O'Malley understood only too well. In his catalogue essay for the Loan Exhibition, he paid close attention to the physical construction of the paintings. '[Yeats] brings a fresh experience to each canvas he paints; [...] That demands alertness of mind and an unprejudiced innocent eye [on the part of the viewer].'[57]

He took the opportunity himself of sketching several of the works in the exhibition, carefully noting use of colour and application of paint.[58] This recognition of the physicality of Yeats's work is evident in the stress that O'Malley's essay puts on elucidating the technical aspects of his practice.

> He may create homogenous surface with the brush, improvise an absorbing study in chiaroscuro, or use the priming of the canvas to aid luminosity of light and shade. At times, impatient with the brush to communicate his feelings for the richness and charm of pigment and his sheer joy of expressive power, he employs the palette knife to give swiftness and vigour to the immediacy of the emotion.[59]

Such attention to the making of the work, complimented consideration of the subject of the painting, highlighting the reciprocal relationship between the two. As David Lloyd has noted, in Yeats (as in the work of other modernist painters), the painting itself can be read as both content and form.[60] O'Malley's essay on Yeats reveals both an intimate knowledge of the artist's practice and an innate curiosity into the decisions and factors that impact on the creation of the artwork.[61] While references to the politics of modern Ireland are prominent, the account makes equal reference to environmental, climatic, historical and economic conditions (Figure 2).

While it shares many ideas with MacGreevy's *Jack B. Yeats, An Appreciation and An Interpretation* (1945), O'Malley's catalogue essay offers a more subtle interpretation. In contrast to the triumphalist tones of MacGreevy, O'Malley focused on the darker aspects of the work and particularly the later paintings. In these, Yeats's figures, according to the text, enter a subjective world in which they 'are related to the loneliness of the individual soul, the vague lack of pattern in living with its sense of inherent tragedy, brooding nostalgia, associated with time as well as variation on the freer moments as of old'. Even in the more visionary work 'all action is subordinated to thought'.[62]

Both MacGreevy and O'Malley argue that the ability of Yeats's art to refer to the experience of ordinary Irish people meant that it was fundamentally different to colonial art in the intimacy and familiarity of its themes. O'Malley later noted that: 'During this century people here, who are not reading people, have begun to see themselves on the stage and in print for the first time in their history. The seeing has caused resentment, distorted pride, acceptance or understanding. In paint also a tradition of seeing and of understanding has yet to be established as there is no national painting tradition.'[63]

If any artist was to provide this national painting it was surely artists like Yeats whose work reflected a shared experience of history but equally maintained its own distinctive and complex aesthetic. O'Malley saw something fundamentally reflective of a national mood in Yeats's work, one of uncertainty and flux rather than resolution. The essay concluded by declaring that 'the new Ireland, still fluid politically and socially has found in Jack Yeats a painter of major rank, whose vision makes us aware of inherent characteristics, psychological directives and eternal verities ... '[64]

While it was one of the functions of the critic to explain why art, such as Yeats's, was relevant and meaningful to modern Ireland, it was equally imperative to position such art within international frameworks. Privately O'Malley continued to be an important advocate of Yeats's work in this regard. He was involved with James Johnson Sweeney in a plan to hold a major Yeats exhibition in the United States.[65] In 1945, he brought John Rothenstein, Director of the Tate Gallery, to visit Yeats's studio. The following year the gallery acquired one of Yeats's major paintings of the Emergency, *The Two Travellers* (1942, Tate) a work which Rothenstein had seen in Dublin.[66]

Rothenstein's sympathetic reading reveals a keener appreciation of Yeats's work than that recorded by other British commentators of the period, perhaps reflecting the sympathetic environment in which he came to know the painting.

> The climax of the afternoon was provided by two large and elaborate pictures ... the second, two travellers in a wild Sligo landscape. This last ... is one of the most unquestionable triumphs of Jack Yeats's manifest though undisciplined genius.

No hint is given of the identities of the black, dishevelled figures or the occasion of their encounter, yet certain human values are mysteriously asserted: most positively perhaps those of human dignity and independence, of faith in Providence as opposed to carelessness and calculation, and the imaginative as distinct from the rational outlook upon life. We are certain that they live according to their values and that they consider the lilies … and that they take no thought of tomorrow.[67]

O'Malley built on the success of the Yeats exhibition and on the Rothenstein connection in developing future projects for exhibitions of Irish art in London. His vision was an outward one that recognized the increasingly international nature of the art world. In 1945–6, he undertook to interview thirty Irish artists, both to record their careers and reputations and in preparation for a planned exchange programme with the Tate.[68] This was never brought to fruition but O'Malley was credited with masterminding the major exhibition of Evie Hone's work which was held, after both their deaths, in University College Dublin in 1958 and at the Tate in 1959.[69] Like Yeats, Hone was a close friend of O'Malley's, and at her death, O'Malley described her as 'the best glass worker in Western Europe'.[70] Her extensive knowledge of French expressionist and cubist art in conjunction with her awareness of Irish medieval sculpture made her work a model for a meaningful Irish art (Figure 3).

In addition to exhibitions, O'Malley recognized the role of criticism in positioning the artwork within the wider art field, as well as being a creative process in its own right. His essay on Louis le Brocquy, for the British periodical *Horizon* in 1946, was pivotal in establishing the young artist's reputation in London.[71] It presented his Tinker paintings as an exotic and novel version of a familiar genre within European modernism and argued that this dispossessed and aloof figure was a symbol of the 'individual as opposed to organised settled society'.[72] O'Malley thus proclaimed both the universal and specific Irish contexts of the work, assessing it in ways that were accessible and meaningful to an international reader (Figure 4).

While O'Malley's fluent use of formalism reveals his familiarity with the cosmopolitan language of modernist criticism,[73] his blend of close attention to the physical characteristics of the artwork and its historical and social contexts is ultimately gleaned from Vasari and Ruskin, as well as from his close observation of art, wherever he had the opportunity to see it. His direct descendant in Irish art writing is Brian O'Doherty, who began writing on art in the 1950s. His Irish Imagination (1971) essay echoes O'Malley's blend of romanticism and pragmatism.[74] While both writers are nationalistic, their nuanced and compelling assessments of Irish art are equally indebted to meticulous consideration of the stylistic and formalist details of the artwork. O'Doherty, like O'Malley, singled out the exceptional value of Yeats's art as a blend of specific Irish experiences and challenging modernist art.[75] He too agreed that the Emergency had had a profound effect on Irish art, allowing for the development of a coterie of patrons and supporters of modernist art.

O'Malley constantly endeavoured to change public attitudes towards art in Ireland and to reconnect the threads of a broken tradition, as he saw it. But he understood that contemporary art was also an elitist activity and that his role was a collaborative one within the wider art field. In this sense he played a key role in nurturing what O'Doherty later called, 'the new audience for Irish art who discovered their souls, at the same time as the artists discovered theirs'.[76] This new audience was not the general public but a network of collectors and intellectuals who shared a strategic and practical outlook on the position of modernist art in Ireland. In art at least revolution was a gradual and often thankless process of frustrated projects and of compromise. O'Malley's contribution to it was selfless and undemonstrative. The skills of organization, observation and persuasion that he deployed in his engagement with art are the same ones that made him a successful revolutionary leader and a unique chronicler of the violent origins of the Irish state.

CHAPTER THREE

FROM MEXICO TO MAYO
ERNIE O'MALLEY, PAUL STRAND AND PHOTOGRAPHIC MODERNISM

Orla Fitzpatrick

During his travels in the United States in the late 1920s and early 1930s, the Irish revolutionary Ernie O'Malley befriended two leading modernist photographers, Edward Weston and Paul Strand. His diary entries and his correspondence with them reveal his thinking on photography and much more. He went to America at the request of Éamon de Valera to raise money for the proposed publication of *The Irish Press*; however, it was after that work was completed that he tapped into a network of modernist artists, writers and academics.[1] This exposed him to a new way of thinking and a new way of seeing, leading him to state that the 'years abroad taught me to use my eyes in a new way'.[2]

Both Weston and Strand had moved away from soft focus pictorialism to become advocates of 'straight photography'. This meant that they did not manipulate negatives nor attempt to mimic the look of paintings. Both photographers possessed considerable technical skills and they also shared the fact that time spent in Mexico provided decisive departures for their photographic careers.[3] O'Malley met Weston for the first time on 21 April 1929, at the photographer's studio in Carmel, California.[4] The following extract from O'Malley's diary outlines the type of photographs he encountered there:

> He showed me work from his studio studies of desert, rock, trees, pottery, cloud effects, female form, photographs, shells. The photos show the texture of the material. The

shells have a lustrous look on certain curves, the stones have a full[ness] of sand formation, the faces show the pores of the skin and all the lines especially on men's faces.[5]

The impact that O'Malley made upon Weston during the short time that they knew
each other is recorded in the photographer's daybooks: 'O'Malley just left for the South
– and I suppose out of my life forever: but no, not out of my life, even if we never meet
again, for our few weeks together made us real friends. We embraced and kissed at
the parting.'[6]

During this period, Weston's photographic vision was one of clarity and simplification. His close-ups reveal the formal quality of objects and he spoke of the sculptural
beauty in the natural world. The effects O'Malley witnessed in Weston's photographs
were the result of long exposures with some of the still lives taking over four hours.
Conversation on the day soon turned to Mexico, a country that was of increasing
interest to O'Malley and where Weston had lived between 1923 and 1927.

The 1920s and 1930s saw an interest in all things Mexican amongst the American
intelligentsia. Many who were disillusioned with American life sought authenticity
and inspiration in post-revolutionary Mexico.[7] O'Malley's interest in Mexican culture
was genuine and the time spent there was to have a lifelong effect upon him. His
library reveals a wealth of books and journals on Mexico, with subject matter ranging
from nineteenth-century histories to contemporary folk art.

O'Malley had access to the artistic communities of California and Taos, New
Mexico, through his friendship with the family of the Irish actor Peter Golden and
his acquaintance with the Irish mystic, poet and lecturer, Ella Young.[8] Whilst at
Taos, he came to know the community of artists and writers surrounding the former
socialite Mabel Dodge Luhan. It was during this period that O'Malley's awareness
of and empathy with the indigenous population was heightened. New Mexico was
a common gateway for many of the American artists and bohemians who ended up
in Mexico in the 1920s and 30s and in this way O'Malley's trajectory was not unusual.
O'Malley visited the country between late December 1930 and August–September of
1931 and his American travelling companions in Mexico were the painter and print-
maker Dorothy Stewart and the artist Theodora Goddard.[9]

Edward Weston provided O'Malley with an introduction to his former lover,
the revolutionary, activist and photographer, Tina Modotti; however, she had been
expelled from the country by the time of his arrival. We know that he made contact
with the editor of *Mexican Folkways*, Frances 'Paca' Toor, who lived and worked out of
the same house in Mexico City as Modotti. This artistic journal, published in Mexico
City between 1925 and 1937, included the work of contemporary artists such as José

Clemente Orozco, Edward Weston and Tina Modotti, alongside articles on folk art and folklore. It was 'the first comprehensive cross-disciplinary journal to promote rural aesthetics as part of the nation's proud heritage rather than as embarrassing evidence of backwardness'.[10] Its ethos and content chimed with O'Malley's outlook. Toor inscribed O'Malley's volume – 'Irish, No moleste-igracias, Paca, Mexico 1931'.

Wherever he travelled, O'Malley amassed postcards, clippings and visual ephemera; his Mexican journey generated a collection of photographs; the subject matter is eclectic including the Aztec pyramid of Tenayuca, baroque churches, street scenes and local customs.[11] There is also a strong emphasis on folk art and primitive sculpture. The collection includes images taken by well-known photographers including Tina Modotti and postcard images by German-born Hugo Brehme. In some ways, O'Malley's choices were quite typical of the bohemian visitor to Mexico in the 1920s and 1930s; however, they also reveal much about his ongoing development and the preoccupations that were to concern him in later years. Though at this stage he was a consumer rather than a producer of photographic images, the photographs O'Malley amassed during this period undoubtedly had an impact on the type of images he would produce upon his return to Ireland in 1935. O'Malley also met with the Russian filmmaker Sergei Eisenstein and his assistant cinematographer Édouard Tissé, who were in Mexico filming ¡Que viva México! The collection of photographs that O'Malley brought back from Mexico includes a location shot taken by Eisenstein's cameraman, Grigori Aleksandrov. The filming was beset by difficulties although it is interesting to note that one of the shorter films that came out of the project was shown in Dublin in 1940. Death Day was shown at a screening by the Irish Film Society, of which O'Malley was a member, and it was described in The Irish Times as dealing 'with curious customs, partly Christian and partly Pagan in origin, in connection with the celebration of the Day of the Dead, a feast corresponding to All Souls' Day here'.[12]

A preliminary examination of O'Malley's Mexican photographs show that he also collected images by Tina Modotti.[13] These include portraits of well-known figures such as the artist Diego Rivera and the singer Concha Michel, alongside landscapes and still lives. Another portrait by Modotti shows the Indian agriculturalist, Pandurang Khankhoje, of the Ghadar Movement, holding heads of corn. Modotti's photographs of Diego's frescoes were available through Mexican Folkways for fifty cents and perhaps this is how O'Malley obtained the image of a mural showing a naked woman with water flowing through her hands. This is the La Pureza panel of a mural by Diego Rivera at the National School of Agriculture at Chapingo near Texcoco (1925–7).[14]

O'Malley also obtained a series of photographs of folk art objects and these are annotated on their versos with the names of some well-known advocates of Mexican arts; for example, 'Carleton Beals, Apuntado 1994, Mexico D.F.' appears on the back of a photograph showing two glass figures of a crow and squirrel. This is possibly a Modotti photograph supplied to Beals to illustrate his 1929 article in a *Creative Art* special on Mexico. Beals was an American journalist and commentator who published widely on Latin America and Mexico in particular. Other names associated with these images are the silver designer Bill Spratling and the painter and caricaturist, Miguel Covarrubias, whose name appears on an image of a horned wooden devil mask from Guerrero.[15] The future director of the Metropolitan Museum, René d'Harnoncourt, is named on a photograph showing a tiger mask, also from Guerrero.

It may also be possible that some of the photographs obtained or purchased by O'Malley were those taken by Modotti for Anita Brenner's 1929 book *Idols behind Altars*.[16] The following description of her work from this period is very similar to the subject matter collected by O'Malley: 'the photographs comprised of images of carved polychrome Madonnas, colonial era ex-votos, painted calabashes, Catholic altars, Jaliscan pottery, petate-lined huts, saddlery, carved chairs, and reproductions of paintings by Francisco Goitia, Diego Rivera, Jean Charlot, and José Clemente Orozco'.[17]

His postcards include depictions of the Mexican Revolution; for example, one image is captioned *La Decena Trágica* or The Ten Tragic Days and relates to a series of events that took place during the Mexican Revolution in 1913. The image he chose shows riflemen on a rooftop aiming at a group in the far distance and had, no doubt, resonance with his own War of Independence and Civil War experiences. In contrast to the American bohemians who visited Mexico, O'Malley brought his own direct experience of post-revolutionary Ireland and the impact of violence and a civil war upon the populace. Perhaps this gave greater depth and weight to his observations of Mexican life and his subsequent comments upon Strand's photographs of the Mexican people and the country's parallels with Ireland.

During his time in Mexico, O'Malley became acquainted with the American poet Hart Crane who was in Mexico on a Guggenheim scholarship. A leading modernist, he was to share an apartment with O'Malley for a brief period in 1931; O'Malley's diaries and letters fondly mention their discussions on literature and art.[18] Whilst there is no evidence that O'Malley and Crane discussed photography, we do know that Crane was an advocate of and commentator upon photographic modernism. He accompanied his friend, the photographer Walker Evans, in his photographic wanderings around New York and chose to illustrate his poem 'The Bridge' with Evans's abstract photographs of the Brooklyn Bridge. The poem has been described as weaving 'many strands of the national experience into a tapestry of America in which the past and the present mingled' and was published in three versions in 1930.[19] O'Malley's library included an edition of the book published by Horace Liveright in New York in July 1930. This was the first occasion upon which Evans's photographs were to appear in print and reveals that O'Malley was aware of the seminal American photographer's career from its beginning.

It was with Paul Strand, rather than Weston, that O'Malley was to form a more lasting friendship. In the spring of 1932, whilst living in Taos, New Mexico, O'Malley befriended Strand, a friendship that was to remain strong for the rest of his life. Strand was to become highly influential in O'Malley's life, securing a place for him at the Yaddo Foundation (an artist retreat at Saratoga Springs, New York) and thus enabling him to complete his memoir, *On Another Man's Wound*.[20] During this period, he was also introduced, via Strand, to Alfred Stieglitz and the artist Georgia O'Keeffe.

Strand and O'Malley discussed photography and art and their correspondence reveals much of O'Malley's thinking on the medium. One of his earliest letters to Strand includes O'Malley's description of the New York sights and people whom he would like to photograph: 'I'd like to photograph the hands strap-hanging in a subway during the rush hour as seen from a platform, or boots and shoes on the Third Avenue 'El'.'[21]

The modernity of New York City was a shock to O'Malley and his desire to create imagery such as that outlined above was very much in accordance with the new photography's response to the metropolis and evidence of modernization such as mass transportation.[22] O'Malley's collection of journal and magazine articles also includes a feature on Charles Sheeler's photographs of the Ford Plant at River Rouge near Detroit.[23] Sheeler had worked with Strand on the 1921 film *Manhatta* and his series of Ford photographs embraced industrial architecture and modernity.

O'Malley was also on the lookout for the type of person that Strand would like to photograph. For example, he wrote to him in July 1934 that 'the Transient House was strange. The man in charge had been a missionary in Burma. He has a fine sensitive face. I hope you can take a photograph of him some time.'[24]

Strand's artistic and political convictions were a match for O'Malley's. Strand was sympathetic to revolutionary nationalism and travelled to Mexico between 1932 and 1934 to partake in state led efforts to create a 'new' national culture.[25]

O'Malley responded strongly to Strand's Mexican photographs. During this time Strand had developed his notion of the 'collective portrait' in which he attempted to depict a country or region through photographs of individuals, still lives and studies of architecture and religious subjects. Strand was in sympathy with the religious practice of the Mexican people, even if this contrasted with his own views and those of the anticlerical Mexican government that employed him (Figure 5). In a letter to Merriam Golden, O'Malley praised Strand's depiction of the people's interaction with vernacular church monuments and sculpture, expressing the view that Strand has captured something of the country's spirit and resilience through his photographs: 'Best of all are his studies of Mexican images of saints selected for what they tell of the people who pray through them. He has chosen random Christs and groups but the pictures tell more of the Mexican point of view than anything I know that explains a religious sense.'[26]

O'Malley saw parallels between the post-revolutionary Mexico and his own Civil War experiences and expressed these feelings to Strand. On 29 December 1934, Ernie O'Malley wrote to Strand, who was then in Mexico working on his film project for the Mexican government. This letter reveals the strength of their bond and is probably one of the most telling passages from O'Malley's correspondence: 'I wish I could see some of your stills some time. You must have learned a great deal in Mexico. I learned about betrayal, how a people is sold by spurious politicians and the futility of super names like, "revolution" and "republic".'[27] This open and explicit revelation made twelve years after the formation of a new Irish state, is a powerful indictment of the revolutionary process and points towards O'Malley's retraction from post-Civil War politics. This disillusionment led him to explore other avenues in which to forge a new reality for Ireland.

Strand published twenty of his Mexican photographs in a 1940 portfolio and this image (Figure 7) appeared halfway through the series.[28] He used vernacular architecture to contextualize the other photographs, interspersing them between the portraits and religious figures.[29] Generic vernacular buildings are elevated to a thing of beauty through Strand's skilled framing and ability to catch the Mexican light.

Strand hoped to create a 'visual social history of a nation' combining portraiture with religious sculpture and vernacular architecture such as the building depicted in Figure 6.[30] Contemporary critics condemn his naïve belief that photography could enact social change while others cite the unequal power dynamic which existed between Strand and those he photographed. He did not ask his subjects for permission to photograph them nor are any of the Mexican people captioned by name. Another criticism levelled towards his Mexican photographs was his concentration upon the rural population and his failure to depict urban poverty. According to some critics this compromises the socialist intent of his work.

O'Malley returned to Ireland in May 1935 and while the country did not boast photographers of the stature of Strand and Weston, it did, however, have a small network of individuals whose worldview stretched beyond the narrow confines of post-independence Ireland. They formed a cultural counterbalance to the prescriptive norms of the new state. This has been acknowledged recently by historians and critics. Allen, in his introduction to O'Malley's collected letters, suggests that 'culture was the presiding sphere of intellectual dissidence in the decades post-independence', and the drama, art and literature produced by Dublin's bohemian set during this period counters the notion of Ireland as insular and unquestioning of the new state's orthodoxies.

Upon his return, O'Malley kept up with international avant-garde art, photography and literature through the little magazine *transition*: an international quarterly of creative experiment. This publication, which was founded in Paris in 1927, not only showcased modernist writers but also the work of those at the forefront of photographic innovation such as Man Ray, Moholy Nagy, Karl Blossfeldt and Eli Lotar. The autumn 1936 issue of the journal included a series of stills from Paul Strand's Mexican film *Redes* (*The Wave*) and this issue is included in Ernie O'Malley's library.[31]

O'Malley corresponded with his friend, James Johnson Sweeney (1900–86), one of the magazine's editors, the Irish-American art collector and curator. During his time at the Museum of Modern Art (MoMA), Sweeney showed leading modernist artists such as Paul Klee and Alexander Calder; however, he also curated large-scale exhibitions of African, Mexican and Pre-Columbian Art. A contemporary reviewer noted that the museum's programme and publications offered 'a basis for a thorough introduction to modern art and those fields of the past from which it has drawn inspiration'.[32] Modernism's interest in the 'primitive' and how it reimagined indigenous and ancient cultures is a theme which recurs in O'Malley's collection of art books, journal articles and postcards.

O'Malley's library includes several MoMA exhibition catalogues published during Sweeney's tenure, for example, *African Negro Art* (1935), for which he commissioned the photographer Walker Evans to take 477 images.[33] O'Malley also owned the museum's later publications, procured after his return to Ireland, which demonstrate his ongoing interest in the arts of Mexico and Latin America; for example, *Twenty Centuries of Mexican Art* (1940) and *The Latin American Collection of MoMA* (1943).

It appears that O'Malley's taste in photography rested with romantic modernists such as Strand rather than with avant-garde practitioners like Man Ray and Moholy Nagy, who also featured in *transition* but whose experimental techniques could be construed as 'art for art's sake'. This preference is also evident in his role as a collector of and commentator upon Irish art. He felt that radical technique alone was not enough and that an engaging work must also have a meaningful content. Mary Cosgrove notes that 'although valuing technical innovation, he expected it to be used in the service of a national art that would establish the truth-value of a painting when placed against social and historical conditions', going on to state that he 'would have agreed with Jellett who saw her work as tradition reinterpreted according to the spirit of the age'.[34] It would appear that similar aims and values can be found in his photographic project which aimed to reinterpret medieval Irish sculpture through the modern medium of the photographic image and book.

The vibrancy of Dublin's cultural life, in the midst of the Second World War, is demonstrated by an event which took place in late 1941. A photographic exhibition of fifty images by the modernist Irish architect Noel Moffett occurred at Sean Dorman's Picture Hire Club at Molesworth Street, Dublin. Moffett's photographs included not only Mayo and Donegal landscapes but also abstract studies of sand, cloud formations, nudes and groups which reference the Ballet Jooss.[35] His subject matter was not dissimilar to that of Strand and Weston. Indeed his image of a Donegal cottage has much in common with Strand's depictions of Mexican dwellings (Figure 8).

A debate took place to coincide with the exhibition on the topic 'Is Photography an Art?' The panel included the artist Mainie Jellett and the socialist Republican writer Peadar O'Donnell. No record of the debate's content exists; however, notes cited in Jellett's biography state that although interested in photography she felt 'a photo is a fragment and a work of art is a whole'.[36] Perhaps it was left to the other members of the panel to defend photography as an art form.

The interconnected nature of the Dublin art and cultural scene is evidenced by the fact that O'Malley knew at least two of the panel members: he had shared a prison cell with O'Donnell and was to act as the literary editor for his journal, *The Bell*. He knew Jellett personally and purchased several of her works. I do not know whether or not O'Malley attended this exhibition, but given its content and Dublin's close-knit arts scene it is likely that he was aware of it. We do know that O'Malley and Moffet's paths were to cross later on in the decade.

In 1947, Moffett commissioned O'Malley to write the introduction to a special Irish issue of the English journal *Architectural Design* for which he was the guest editor. It marked the conference of the Royal Institute of Architects which was taking place for the first time since the Second World War. Dublin was chosen as the location and the journal content reflected contemporary Irish architectural practice and traditional or vernacular Irish buildings and design. O'Malley's introduction paints a broad picture of Irish culture and society and also refers to vernacular housing, the rural nature of the country and its oral tradition.[37]

O'Malley also selected the art works reproduced on page 175 of the journal, namely, *The Two Travellers* by Jack B. Yeats and *In Fear of Cain* by Louis le Brocquy.[38] These were two of O'Malley's favourite artists, about whom he wrote and whose work he collected. The captions which accompany these images echo O'Malley's earlier criticism. For example, that which appears alongside the le Brocquy watercolour bears a similarity to O'Malley's 1946 *Horizon* article on the artist.[39] The caption reads as follows:

> Louis Le Brocquy, now aged thirty, had no formal art training, nor had he been interested in painting for more than ten years. Yet now he is one of Ireland's leading artists, with for inspiration, the Connemara landscape and the tinkers – primitive, fey wanderers of the countryside, tinsmiths and horse jobbers by trade, but to Le Brocquy symbols of the individual as opposed to the collective.[40]

O'Malley's piece was published alongside Moffett's photograph of a 'developed' cottage in Donegal. This is not just another generic Irish cottage. Like O'Malley's approach to photographing medieval sculpture, Moffett researched his subject matter thoroughly and this image of an extended house type references the work of Estyn Evans, the Ulster folklorist. Moffett explained how new rooms were added and the materials used, stating that the 'developed Irish house is never more than one room width, for it was considered unlucky to widen a house'.[41]

Upon his return to Ireland, O'Malley and his American wife, Helen Hooker, set about photographing the medieval Irish sculpture which was dotted throughout the country, a countryside familiar to O'Malley from his revolutionary days. This project can be viewed as a natural outcome of their shared interest in art and sculpture (Figure 9).

Helen Hooker's interest in photography pre-dated her meeting with Ernie O'Malley and her vast output reflected her previous travels and her art works. In addition to architecture and sculpture, which she photographed with her husband, she also recorded rural life in the West of Ireland, such as portraits of the people of Clare Island in Clew Bay, County Mayo. This body of work, when combined with the sculpture and architectural elements, in some way replicated Strand's attempts at a complete portrait of a nation.

Photography is often a collaborative endeavour and authorship is not always easily assigned. O'Malley's photographic project was not undertaken alone. In addition to his wife Helen Hooker, whose photographic expertise was above his, he was sometimes accompanied by his brother Kevin, or the Limerick County Librarian, Robert Herbert. Diaries and letters reveal that O'Malley's role was somewhat akin to that of an art director: selecting and researching locations which would yield a wealth of sculpture and architecture. On one occasion, when his camera broke, he instructed Bob Herbert to take photographs for him.

O'Malley described the project as follows:

> I had intended to work on sculpture from the 12th to the 17th century. It was unknown even to scholars and archaeologists: a good deal of it was not even recorded. I slowly built up knowledge, visited remote graveyards by myself or with Helen to study detail and position of figures for architecture. This study continued from 1937 for a number of years.[42]

On his excursions he recorded fascinating sculptures such as a panel featuring apostles on the side of an upright rectangular tomb in Ennis, County Clare, and the details of a chancel arch depicting belt wrestlers from Kilteel Church, County Kildare, dating from the twelfth century.

It does not appear that the O'Malleys printed their own photographs and Ernie's diaries do not reveal any references to setting up or working in a darkroom.[43] Instead they sent their negatives to the Dublin firm of Thomas H. Mason, 5 & 6 Dame Street, for development and printing.[44] Thomas Mason was a well-known antiquarian and photographer whose publications on the islands of Ireland and other subjects were well received. He would have been known to Ernie O'Malley through his member-ship of the Royal Society of Antiquaries of Ireland.[45] Helen and Ernie preferred matt prints and notes in her handwriting contain detailed instructions as to how to crop and print certain images. A letter from Ernie from early 1940 refers to a photographic project upon which Helen was engaged; however, it doesn't outline whether it relates to a publication or an exhibition: 'I hope the photos are doing well and that you have made a complete selection of them. Can I give you any assistance? It is just as well to get them printed while you can personally supervise them.'[46] It does, however, provide further evidence of the serious manner in which both Helen and Ernie approached their photographic endeavours and their careful attention to detail.

In preparation for these photographic forays, O'Malley immersed himself in long periods of research at both the National Library of Ireland and the National Museum of Ireland. He was given access to the collections at the museum through a friend, Michael Heaney (Mícheál Ó hÉeanaigh), who was an Assistant Keeper in the Irish Antiquities Division during the 1930s.[47] Pat Wallace, in an article tracing the influ-ence of the Director Adolf Mahr, states that Heaney's political leanings hampered his career: 'Heaney was more political and in his letters to Mahr showed his anti-Cos-grave/pro de Valera views with which he may not have been as ingratiating as he hoped. His Irish salutations might have hurt Mahr by making him feel inadequate about his inability to use the first official language.'[48] This is an interesting insight into the Ireland which O'Malley returned to. It points to the sometimes political nature of promotion within the civil service and to an atmosphere tinged with post-Civil War animosities.

O'Malley's approach to medieval sculpture differed to that favoured by the museum's archaeologists and antiquarians, who photographed purely for research purposes. He railed against what he saw as the 'museum outlook, with its emphasis on catalogues and dates, [which] supersedes sensitive understanding'.[49] For archaeologists, photography was a tool, providing visual evidence which enabled them to compare, contrast and sort objects into typologies. O'Malley often filled the frame with sculptural details which were overlooked or contextualized by other photographers. He considered the medieval sculpture as art while at the same time aiming to create beautiful artistic photographs. He articulated his position in his review of the art historian Françoise Henry's seminal work, *Irish Art in the Early Christian Period*. He had an aesthetic approach and, like her, he did not emphasize typologies.[50] He recommended her treatment of Irish art, and though he thought that some of the photographs in her 1940 work were poor, he praised those in her later works.[51]

He also provided Henry with his photograph of the North Cross, Ahenny, County Tipperary, reproduced as Plate 38 of her 1940 book.[52] There is evidence of their collaboration on several other occasions, either through the Royal Society of Antiquaries of Ireland where they were both members, or through their shared interest in the antiquities and archaeology of County Mayo. Henry spent a period of time excavating at Iniskean, off Blacksod Bay, in 1938.[53] On other occasions he advised her on lecture content and appears to have been a sounding board for her career concerns.[54]

Interestingly, O'Malley does not appear to have written for any of the many archaeological, antiquarian or local history journals which were published throughout the country. He did gather many off-prints from these publications and his diaries mention the possibility of providing photographs for the journal edited by Bob Herbert, but he preferred to channel his scholarship into the visual recording of medieval sculpture, with a planned photographic book as the outcome of his endeavours. Perhaps he felt that a book would expose a wider public to the beauty and importance of this sculpture, thereby removing it from the rarefied field of antiquarianism.

O'Malley also recommended the approach and photographs used by the Harvard medieval historian Arthur Kingsley Porter in his 1931 work, *The Crosses and Culture of Ireland*.[55] Porter and his wife Lucy, who took many of the photographs, had moved to Ireland in the 1930s and purchased Glenveagh Castle, County Donegal, before his mysterious disappearance (presumed drowning) in 1938.[56] Many of the theories contained in his book have now been debunked; however, the photogravure plates in the first edition of this work appealed to O'Malley; he singled out Kingsley Porter's approach to Irish archaeology and medieval sculpture from the viewpoint of aesthetics.[57] His aesthetic rather than archaeological approach chimed with O'Malley's, who viewed these sculptures as a living vibrant part of the Irish landscape. They reflected the country's essential nature in the same way that Strand's Christs reflected the spirit of Mexico.

O'Malley delighted in travelling the country and being immersed in the Irish landscape was part of the attraction of the project. Of course, the Irish climate threw up problems for the photographer. He writes of difficulties presented by cloudy skies and rain and, in a letter to James Johnson Sweeney sent in 1939, he states that 'some time I hope to finish a book on Irish sculpture, if the sun would show itself more frequently here it would make the work easier'.[58] There is evidence that he chose to light some of the subjects artificially, such as a late-sixteenth-century cross-slab from the St Nicholas Collegiate Church, Galway (Figure 10). His was not a casual snapshot approach; diary entries record the optimum time of day in which to capture a monument.[59] A letter from the 1940s tells of how he waited for hours for just the right light to illuminate a tomb:

> Later up along the edge of the Burren mountains up the pass to Corcomroe in its valley of limestone. There we photographed, waited for light to swing on the figures and capitals and drank. The drink was good as was the sun. We slept, on limestone, waking to watch the light come on to the noblest figure in Irish personal sculpture: O'Brien buried there 1276 I think.[60]

O'Malley and his wife were not the first to photograph these medieval sculptures and indeed the nineteenth-century amateur antiquarians, such as the Tenisons in Roscommon and the Dillons of Clonbrock, were quick to employ the new technology of photography to record Irish sculpture. Much has been written on the manner in which such Victorian and earlier antiquarian studies were to feed into national identity. However, O'Malley's use of them in a new state was to offer a different vision.

Even as late as 1953, O'Malley's remarks on publishing in Ireland are an indicator of the market for photographic books. In a letter to Paul Strand, acknowledging receipt of Strand's publication [*La France de Profil*, Lausanne: Guilde du livre, 1952], he mentions again the possibility of Strand photographing in Ireland. However, O'Malley outlines his misgivings in relation to the market for books of this calibre and Irish publishers' capacity to handle such an undertaking:

> I liked your photographs very much, and I admire the carefulness with which you selected your people and your places. It would be fine if you could do an Irish book, and I would be very glad to help. There is, however, no Irish publisher who would produce a book at the cost of your book, £2.10.0, but then the proposition has not been placed before them. There are a few publishers here, but they are not big publishers. When I return to Ireland I can see some of them about the book. [61]

The photogravure printing process favoured by Strand and most serious photographers was unavailable in Ireland. However, this may not have been that large a problem, as Strand arranged to have all his books printed in East Germany.[62] Strand decided to photograph the Scottish Island of Dura instead. The resulting book, *Tir a'Mhurain / Outer Hebrides*, was published in 1962.[63] It is considered a classic although some critics have accused it of pastoral nostalgia. Like Strand's other regional studies, it contextual-izes portraiture within elements of the landscape and architecture and 'renders people an integral part of the natural world, emphasising how they are shaped, nurtured, buffeted by nature and in thrall to it'.[64]

The possibility of Strand exhibiting in Dublin was mooted by Helen in a letter to the MoMA curator, James Johnson Sweeney, in 1946. In it, she mentions that the avant-garde Ballet Jooss were performing in Dublin, and she also refers to a recent international photographic exhibition. Both demonstrate that there was an appetite in Ireland for photography and non-mainstream artistic endeavours:

> Ernie comes down from Mayo to-night, for the Jooss Ballet, who are in Dublin for three weeks … Jooss was extremely interested in Paul Strand's prints as he is unfa-miliar with work of his and experience in the reproduction process of his photograph album which was specially printed. I have also wondered if it were possible for an exhibition of Paul Strand's work to be sent to Ireland as there is keen interest in photography, and nothing of the quality of Paul's work was sent in the International Photographic Exhibition held early this year, but the exhibition was a great profit to the public in allowing them methods of progressing in other countries.[65]

Unfortunately, as with the proposed collaborative book project, an exhibition of Strand's work failed to materialize in Ireland.

Although it is unlikely that an Irish publisher would have done justice to the project, personal circumstances prevented the publication of the photographs of medi-eval sculpture in book format. The small market for high-quality books meant that few purely photographic publications were produced in Ireland until many decades after the Second World War. This failure does not lessen the importance of the project which attempted to reinterpret Ireland's rich sculptural tradition according to the spirit of the age. Commenting upon Ireland in an article on the arts in Mexico, O'Malley clearly articulates how he felt: 'Sculpture is a definite and important heritage which should be a source of true pride to our imagination and to our eyes, and a challenge to creative inspiration.'[66]

CHAPTER FOUR

THE EVOLUTION OF ERNIE O'MALLEY'S MEMOIR, *ON ANOTHER MAN'S WOUND*

Cormac K.H. O'Malley

Ernie O'Malley used his diaries to prepare himself to write his first published work, *On Another Man's Wound*, and to develop a writing manner that incorporated the essential elements of a good novel or compelling memoir, namely, detailed description of landscape, character analysis, dialogue and action.[1] His challenge was to tell the story of the struggle of the Irish people for their freedom over time, as well as his role in that fight in the early twentieth century, and yet, not to allow his recitation to become a history book.

Preparation for Writing

O'Malley probably did not know how or what he wanted to write when he started what became *On Another Man's Wound*. He eventually found that his own story echoed the fighting struggle of so many others before him, many of whom had been recalled in folktales and songs.

In the first instance, O'Malley was extremely well read, as he had been a voracious reader from an early age. He read broadly in his secondary school and during his days at University College Dublin when he should have been studying medicine. While in military confinement for over twenty months, after his arrest by the Free State Army in late 1922, he had plenty of time to read, as the books and magazines he requested were allowed to be sent to him in prison regularly. Indeed, he had a small library in his prison cell during the Civil War era.[2]

By the end of his internment, O'Malley had read a broad spectrum of the classics and expressed an abiding love for Shakespeare, Chaucer and Dante but had also covered Milton, Spenser and the standard English nineteenth-century writers – Pope, Blake, Wordsworth, Shelley, Keats, Coleridge, Morris, Browning, Stevenson, Tennyson, Masefield, de la Mare, Conrad, Dickens, Lamb and Scott, as well as Cervantes, Papini, Tagore, Turgenev, Tolstoy and Chekhov, among others. On the American side, his favourites were Melville (*Moby Dick*), Whitman, Twain and Hawthorne. His fields of interest included art, art history, drama, fiction, folklore, history, poetry and travel. His reading of Irish literature appears quite limited at the time but Colum, Gregory, Shaw, Stephens and Yeats are mentioned though no doubt there were many others. During his European travels in the mid-1920s, he read mostly contemporary literature, drama and fiction, and later while in America he kept himself abreast of the developing modern literary trends including Joyce, Pound and Eliot, and even younger writers like Hemingway. He had also read broadly in modern poetry including Hart Crane, whom he would later meet in Mexico.

Erskine Childers' encouragement of O'Malley to write in early 1921 was, no doubt, significant. O'Malley had written, at Childers' request, the story of his own harrowing capture, torture and escape from Kilmainham Gaol with its many tribulations.[3] In his memoir, O'Malley recalls Childers saying to him: 'That's good. It will be of use … You can write.'[4] Those words from a published author, a senior Irish Republican Army publicist and someone whom he trusted and regarded highly, must have been encouraging. His other writings up to that point had been terse and perfunctory military dispatches which did not need embellishments, though one can see in his personal letters from prison that he had the capacity to write reflectively and philosophically.[5]

Perhaps it was Childers who also told O'Malley to practise his writing by writing regularly, writing about anything, writing letters, diaries or even just notes. O'Malley was a keen observer and a prodigious note-taker. He wrote detailed observations of anything he thought relevant to his military campaign, be it the strength of the Royal Irish Constabulary in the local barracks, the timing of their patrols, the conditions of the roads, the number of men in a local IRA company, their knowledge of arms, and such matters. Twice when he was captured – in Kilkenny in 1920 and again in Dublin in 1922 – his extensive and detailed notes regarding names and positions of his own local IRA men placed them and himself in perilous difficulties.[6]

From the start of O'Malley's post-military European travels, undertaken in 1925 and 1926 to help recover his health, he kept a diary faithfully. His entries were in a narrative form recording where he was and what he was doing; they were not reflective as to his feelings or perceptions. He wrote daily while in France and Spain, especially about life in Barcelona and climbing the Pyrenees. In his Italian diaries, he recorded his visits to art galleries, the paintings and art objects he saw as well as gardens, castles and churches. He kept lists of books and plays he was reading and continued this habit when he returned to his medical studies in Dublin in the autumn of 1926. The lists of plays illustrate how much he had read in established and modern drama, and thus it is not surprising to find him as a founding member and first director of the University College Dublin Dramatic Society in 1926–7, along with the poet Denis Devlin.[7]

O'Malley started his *Irish Press* fundraising activities in the United States in October 1928; on his first day he started to keep a daily diary to record his reactions to the new sights, sounds and personalities of American society, including what he saw of Irish America. He wrote in New York and Boston and continued in California in the spring of 1929. When he travelled from Pasadena, California to Taos, New Mexico, he even wrote in the car as he bounced across the desert, complaining of the bullets rattling against his bones. Three months of his diaries in New Mexico in late 1929–30 and three months of his diaries in Mexico in 1931 have survived.[8]

Examination of Diaries

O'Malley's first known non-military diaries were written during his European travels, and they include his diaries of Spain and France, his ninety-seven-page manuscript on climbing the Pyrenees, and his walks through Italy – all in 1925 and 1926.[9] Although rich in descriptions of what he was doing and seeing, there is practically no dialogue and only limited description of characters and landscape. These diaries include his daily spending, his search for good books and stamps (he was a philatelist), recitation of facts about the history of the village, church, town or museum he visited, but they do not offer much reflection by, or on, himself.[10]

In his next diaries, those written in America, there is more personal detail on what he was doing, whom he was meeting and his own reactions to New York, Boston, Carmel and San Francisco. It is with the diaries written in New Mexico and Mexico in 1929–31 that O'Malley developed a different, more literary style. In some of these notebooks he wrote his daily diary in the front but included notes and research details or ideas for his memoir on the pages starting from the back cover. The latter included his notes on his Irish history research for the 1914–24 period, as well as comments on books he was reading. Some of his other notebooks are devoted entirely to his notes on military, political and social research, but it would seem that when he was travelling he used a single notebook, and when he was in residence he used more than one notebook as the subject matter required.

What does one learn from examining O'Malley's New Mexican and Mexican diaries in terms of his writing development? His description of landscape became more colourful and his style more lyrical, with painting-like detail. He focused on characters he met, added dialogue and included folklore references by describing at great length the folk festivals of Native Americans. He included occasional references to some Irish folklore.

In his landscape depiction, O'Malley placed himself stage centre with observations as to what he sees to the left and to the right, close by and on the horizon, as if writing for a movie script, and then describes the immediate scene whether it be mountains, desert, trees, river gorges, mesas, the road itself or other aspects of the topography. By way of example: 'The road was an earth track leaching over wooden plank bridge, wild plants grew on either side, also a red berry, raspberry from which they made jam … Below … with steep sloping sides was a valley well watered, extending down for a mile or more lying against the mountain side where in the distance shaped in to form a narrow neck with the opposite bank' or 'The light climbs up the [mountain] slowly. The snow becomes mauve … and wine … Often in Taos I saw the snow, wine red.'[11]

O'Malley also started to embellish details about the people he met, sometimes with short, incisive descriptions of their physical, mental and emotional characteristics. In his IRA days, when organizing down the country, he was used to making quick judgements about a person, whether he could trust that person with his life shortly after their first meeting; perhaps this speedy, self-defensive decision-making process required him to pay attention to the many details of character and physical characteristics at his first encounter. In his New Mexican diaries he brought this skill to bear on character descriptions. For example: 'Mary Tucker. She wore a white silk blouse, a bright brown velvet skirt. She looked better with her hat. A quiet faced girl, with large brown eyes, long black lashes … Her finger nails were well cared for, her fingers long and slender. Quiet, no very obvious traits of sex. We talked Indians.'[12]

Of Ella Young, the Irish mystic whom he sought out as a mentor, he wrote, 'She looks youthful, her eyes are always young,' and '… a blue scarf on her head, a white leather skin around her and colouring appeared in between'.[13]

Also, in 1929, O'Malley started to make his diaries more vivacious by including streams of dialogue for the first time. For example, when his friend was talking to an unresponsive Native American, he noted:

'Is the church open?'
'No, 'm.'
'When is service held on Sunday?'
'Yes, 'm.'
'Does the priest from Laguna visit here?'
'Yes, 'm.'

Then he commented, 'I felt that "Yes, 'm" would be an answer to all her questions.'[14]

O'Malley captured some of the tension between Mabel Dodge Luhan and her husband, Toni Lujan, in dialogue rather than in descriptive form:

'The habit of eating the plant came from Mexico.'
'No,' said Toni. 'It just happened.'
'But they do it in Mexico,' said Mabel.
'Well it did not come; it happened.'[15]

O'Malley sometimes used his dairy as a way to record the substance of a conversation and only included some of the subjects discussed rather like an encapsulation or summary. At the end of his first week in Taos, as he conversed with the illusive Ella Young, he listed topics covered as well as those not covered. For Ella, he noted: 'we talked of Ireland, at least I did as she bade me. She is anxious to have the old traditional singing taken on records and feels sure that Monsignor Rodgers [sic] would be willing to put up the money. I promised to compile and get others to compile information … She asked me if I felt [the] American country as I did the Irish country … Had I ever felt the same about European countries … Had I ever seen fairies.'[16]

Again, of a dinner conversation with Ella, Mabel Dodge Luhan, Dorothy Brett and others, he recorded, 'We talked of things: what experiences had I, the sense of fear, of being strayed, of the disappearance of time … the Pyrennean [sic], the long hound on the Kilrush road, of the Donegal noises near the bridge of Gweedore, the Newcastlewest story of the man who could not find his way and was then drowned.'[17] 'We adjourned to the red room where I was placed beside Mable L[uhan] by Ella and told to talk so we talked of America, of the Indians, Carmel, she knew Jeffers, but did not like his wife … San Francisco, the MacDowell colony … I told her of Una Jeffers and her friendship for me when I spoke of Moore.'[18]

O'Malley's diaries were also peppered with his reflections on Ireland, his family, his friends, and his IRA organizing days. Sometimes he wrote of his own inner debates, the ones we all have with ourselves but which we do not usually reduce to writing. A good example is his Examination of Conscience written six days after his first experimentation with this type of dialogue.

'What the hell are you doing near Indian country? Why aren't you working? … What good are you to yourself or anyone else out here?'

'None.'

'Then examine your conscience.

You did not report back to your office?'

'No.'

'You risk arrest?'

'Yes'

'You are liable to be refused entry to this country again?'

'Yes'

'You have not brought along your Physiology so that you could study …?'

'No'

'You have spent what money you have …'

'True, O King.'

'I thought you were going to do a Library course in Paris … ?'

'Yes'

'Your "Yes" is becoming monotonous, my friend. It is not humility. It is a habit of disarmament. Then why are you here?'

'It brings ease and peace, the heights of the desert, and what does it matter if one has little money if one can be independent. To be content is the main thing.'

'Could you not have remained at home in your own country? I have often heard you say that immigration was a curse, one should endeavor to remain?'

'Yes, but I could not get work. My name was enough to damn me.'

'I think you are a fool.'

'Foolishness is relative. I might think you were one. Anyway I call my soul my own!'[19]

These dialogues become more frequent in his diaries. Their intensity and rationale vary greatly. Their frequency suggests that he was practising the form rather than merely attempting to record or convey something of particularly great merit or intensity. This practice flowers in *On Another Man's Wound*, which includes extensive stretches of dialogue, sometimes with short, staccato-like exchanges – covering up to several pages – to draw out and heighten the dramatic effect of a tense scene. O'Malley used this technique in the retelling of the initial rough interrogation he received when captured in 1920 in Kilkenny, the more extensive and harsher cross-examination and torture in Dublin Castle as well as his refusal to drink to the health of the king of

England at the Christmas dinner in the Dublin Castle British Army officers' mess.[20]

O'Malley was interested in folklore from an early age and was well read in that field. While trying to organize an IRA company on the Aran Islands in early 1919, he regaled the local fisherman with his tales of 'Till Eulenspiegel, some of Hakuylt's sea tales, Bricriú's Feast and the Story of Burnt Njal. Eulenspiegel and Bricriú were favorites; they rocked with delight and I had to repeat them often.'[21] He mentioned some of his favourite works from his youth: 'Hackulyt [sic] and Morte d'Arthur, we knew best of our books.'[22] The Voyages, with seamen's directness, simplicity and detailed objectivity, were as real as Robinson Crusoe.[23] 'There were two books on Ireland: Kings and Vikings, which we knew by heart, and Donegal Fairy Tales of Seamus MacManus.'[24] As O'Malley travelled around Ireland as an IRA organizer, he heard local folk stories and variations of well-known folktales. In Clare he recalled hearing stories from two men of Rafferty or Donnchadh Ruadh MacNamara, of which he only knew the English translations, but he noted that 'here the seventeenth and eighteenth centuries lived again, for these two men could tell story after story of their poets' pranks, drinkings and songs and describe them as if they lived in the same parish'.[25]

O'Malley's first line of his memoir referred to such oral folk culture. 'Our nurse, Nannie, told my eldest brother and me stories and legends.'[26] He went on to mention Nannie's tales of 'the mighty Fionn and his great strength, the epic of Cúchulainn, the boy hero, the Hound of Ulster … Ferdia of Connacht'.[27] Indeed, throughout his memoir he referred to folktales such as Conchubar who broke his word, Balor's advice and Balor of the Evil Eye in Clare, Ildana, Lugh of the Long Arms, and many others. He also included portions of thirty-six ballads and songs which he explained 'express what the people thought and amplify, in so far as they are concerned, the situations described'.[28]

It is thus not surprising that O'Malley's New Mexican and Mexican diaries included his research into local practices, customs and legends to help explain the folk dances that he witnessed and the stories that he heard there. In Coolidge, New Mexico he met Berton Staples who ran a small Navajo trading post and was most knowledgeable in the Navajo ways. O'Malley wrote that Staples was

> a well-built man with a weak voice … He showed me his museum. Well arranged, glass cases on the walls with shards of pottery, many maps. Maps are the most intelligent form of concentrated information. The development of pottery from basket bowls in one case; the modern method of making pottery in another case. A linguistic map on the wall … Staples discussed fluidity in the origins of Indian tribes. He gave me a list of Navajo words … The words are sent by the tongue to the back of the mouth and then spat out in some instances.[29]

And he continued on with details of a Zuni dance:

> I saw the Shalako, six of them outside the village, surrounded by Indians. One Indian waved the spectators away. They were mainly whites, The Shakalos, the representatives of the gods, were supposed to enter at sunset. They crossed the river on a specially prepared path, bridged in two places by planks … At the West was an altar hanging from the roof, in the centre was a small altar. A line of meal lead in a curve from the door to the foot of the altar … On the North wall with their backs to it were the gods, opposite them were men seated with heads slightly bent …[30]

Impact of O'Malley's Diaries on His Memoir Writing

O'Malley undertook research in libraries wherever he visited – in newspapers and books in New York, Chicago, San Francisco and Santa Fe – to find out about the general background to the War of Independence and Civil War, statistics about arrests, murders, attacks, dates, military manpower and executions. He wrote this research up in his notebooks too, sometimes in the back of the most current diary notebook he happened to have with him; at other times he used a separate notebook. He designated some notebooks with 'L' for literature, 'I' for Irish, and 'F' for folklore. He also jotted down his own recollections of his movements during the period, and other subjects to be included in the narrative. For example: 'rest of command makes patrols, cycle and walk, steel bridges, conscription of labour, Coughlan and column, on being afraid, sense of relief when a raid did not materialize, the Order in Council, youth of prisoners, the Glass House, Price, Des Murphy and Lemass, TD when in goal, refusal to pay taxes'.[31]

Next O'Malley started to weave the elements of facts and recollections into a framework at once chronological as well as architectural. He ultimately named the three sections of his memoir – Flamboyant, Gothic and Romanesque – the reverse of their actual chronological development. O'Malley explained in his Introduction that he wanted to 'show my own progression in development. Each of the divisions of the book deals with a certain phase of events and with my changing relation to them.'[32] My own interpretation of these headings is that the Flamboyant section is the cultural background of Ireland; nothing concrete, partially mythical, the folklore, the country ways, and the West. The Gothic section is where some limited brigade organizational structure is in place, where a commitment to a desired political and military objective is made by the men, and where training is started. The Romanesque section sets out the details of what is done to make a success on the ground of the ongoing revolution;

training results in action with concrete results. The last section is also the story of how he operated by himself, of his capture, torture, escape and succeeding command positions – the mature, solid soldier.

O'Malley worked on two parallel fronts at once in his diaries. On the one hand he researched and annotated the factual framework for the entire period in his diary notebooks; on the other hand he developed a style to relate his own daily life. Eventually he started to write and revise the narrative. He took four elements – landscape, character, dialogue, folklore – and used them to transform the recent chronological history into a more personal narrative, one that resonated with the legends and history of Ireland as well as the long struggle of its people. His early notebooks show him working on the most basic elements of his own life – where he was, when, and what he was doing. Then he embellished these factual narratives and added in the elements of character, enriching the people he describes, expanding the description of the landscape to provide a better sense of place, inserting dialogue to make the story more dramatic, and including folklore and songs to remind the reader of the cultural background. Not all of these elements were present in his first drafts.

Textual Development

O'Malley's process was to examine his notebooks and diaries, write up a section in longhand on single sheets of paper, revise it several times page by page by writing another longhand draft, and when he was satisfied, send the draft off to someone in New York who would type up the manuscript for him.[33] Then he would do the same thing with the typed version – edit and rewrite. To maintain a logical order of the pages he kept the same page number, but if the corrections required an additional page he inserted a letter after the page number, such as 299A, 299B, so that the overall page sequence remained the same.[34]

Regarding the iconic title to his memoir, O'Malley mentioned in one of his New Mexican notebooks – not his daily diary – the Ulster expression, 'It is easy to lie on another man's wound' and yet the ultimate version he used was, 'It is easy to sleep on another man's wound', with the actual title of the memoir being a shortened version, On Another Man's Wound.[35] There are different ways to interpret the words 'lie' versus 'sleep'. For example, to 'lie' could suggest a prevarication or boast by the person not wounded, namely the telling of great deeds not actually done. It could mean to lie down – but not to sleep – while someone else fights on. To 'sleep' could suggest that the person not wounded can rest securely and even sleep soundly because someone else is fighting or was wounded during a successful engagement. For me the sleep implies a higher level of sarcasm.

An author's initial sentence is always critical. O'Malley's original opening sentence was:

> How to reconstruct a spiritual state of mind. How to explain or interpret a feeling that seems to be indefinable. Our nurse told my brother and myself stories and legends, the King of Ireland's son, his adventures and exploits, faery tales of the 'good people', the story of Fionn, the heavy handed tales of the fairies. She described the fight at the ford.[36]

In his final version O'Malley's opening is far more compelling: 'Our nurse, Nannie, told my eldest brother and me stories and legends. Her stories began "Once upon a time and a very good time it was," and ended with "They put on the kettle and made tay, and if they weren't happy that you may."'[37] These two sentences grab the reader's attention and prepare one to hear a story rather than an intellectual discourse explaining an 'indefinable feeling'. Most people would recognize the 'once upon a time' line as a storytelling mode and by reading it would be ready to settle in to hear a bedtime story which by definition is not a history.

O'Malley edited dramatically the typed draft of his twenty-four-page first chapter. He cut nine pages out or modified them significantly. In his second chapter, ten of the eighteen pages were cut out or modified though he also added some new text. The drafts in his archive reflect the other edits he makes in other chapters in a similar manner.

In the course of this editing process, O'Malley eliminated passages with colourful dialogue, no doubt, because they did not enhance the narrative of the principal nationalist story. One such passage was his memory of going to confession.

> 'How long since your last confession?'
> 'Three weeks.'
> 'Well. What?'
> 'I had distractions during my prayers.'
> 'How often? Did you try to drive them away?'
> 'I tried to drive them away, but they came back … I was disobedient to my parents. I forgot to say my prayers.'
> 'You know you must not forget that, my child. God does not forget to think of you.'[38]

O'Malley was quite conscious of trying to get the proper narrative tone for his memoir. He wanted the story to be readily comprehensible by anyone who was not familiar with Irish history and legend. He was telling a story of a struggle 'between an empire and an unarmed people'. An important editorial technique he used was to read his manuscript aloud to friends to solicit their comments.[39] While he was at the Yaddo Foundation in September 1932, he allowed some friends, such as George Milburn, Betty Todd and Mary Heaton Vorse, and no doubt others, to read his draft chapters; they later helped him to place his manuscript with their friends at publishing firms.[40] No doubt, this process also allowed him to hear how the words sounded and to observe their impact on the various listeners. Though he sent sections of his manuscript off to friends for their comments, there are no written reactions with specific feedback on the manuscript.[41]

One of O'Malley's most beautiful lyrical descriptions of the Irish countryside, covering the change in vegetation, weather, cloud formation and living conditions was developed with considerable research over some time.[42] He first wrote down on separate pages, month by month, all the factual information he needed such as the types of vegetation, flowers, animals, birds, insects, weather, farming activities, and then later he wove all the facts together into a seamless lyrical description of the four seasons in rural Ireland.

Publication History

During O'Malley's stay in the United States he received at least seven letters of rejection for his memoir from various publishers.[43] The first bad news came to him from a New York publisher, Harcourt Brace, shortly after he had arrived in Taos and was addressed to him care of Mabel Dodge Luhan.[44] His book could not have been completed by that time in 1929 and so the rejection might have been based on the publisher not seeing his entire manuscript. This coincidence of timing suggests that Luhan had given him an introduction to the publisher or perhaps even an endorsement. In any case rejection letters followed over the next five years. When O'Malley attended Yaddo Foundation in August–September 1932, he was still working on his manuscript; and he referred to working on it thereafter as well, but presumably he felt it was complete by late 1934 or early 1935.

The scope of O'Malley's manuscript when completed covered both the War of Independence up to the Truce in July 1921 and from the Truce through the end of the Civil War. In his mind the Civil War continued the struggle for independence, to avoid any Free State Government Oath of Allegiance to a 'foreign king', and for a country composed of thirty-two counties not just twenty-six. The manuscript was not divided into two volumes until O'Malley's return to Dublin in June 1935, when Peadar O'Donnell advised him to do so. It was not the length that concerned O'Donnell but the greater potential for libel action in connection with the Civil War half, as it was then only thirteen years after the outbreak of that conflict.[45] In fact, O'Malley was sued for libel even on the first half, and he lost that action in 1937.

O'Donnell had a friend, Feirn French, who was the Dublin-based reader for Rich & Cowan, a distinguished London publishing house. Apparently French was captivated by O'Malley's manuscript, which he read overnight and immediately asked if he could arrange for its publication. A Rich & Cowan contract was prepared in the autumn of 1935.[46] The next twelve months must have been agony for O'Malley as he saw his manuscript go through what for other authors is the normal publication cycle, with enquiring editorial comments from the publisher; in this case they insisted on deleting a six-page segment about the rough interrogation of O'Malley by British Army intelligence officers in Dublin Castle.[47] He must have felt then the way he did in 1952 when Dan Nolan tried to edit his work and O'Malley promptly withdrew his IRA Raids manuscript.[48] However, in 1935, perhaps with the exigencies of a recent return to Ireland, his newly married life, the expected birth of a child, the continuation of his medical studies, and the potential to start his literary career, he was less intransigent.

In 1936, O'Malley allowed the section of the book covering the attack on the British Army's Mallow Barracks to be published in *Ireland Today*, edited by Jim O'Donovan.[49] Then Éamon de Valera's *Irish Press* proceeded to publish the entire book in a daily series over several months, and finally the book itself was published both in London and Dublin and received great reviews.[50] Rich & Cowan in 1951 replied to O'Malley and said that given the recent state of the market they could not reprint 'your excellent book'.[51]

In 1937, Houghton Mifflin of Boston published an American edition under the title *Army Without Banners*, again to great acclaim.[52] *The New York Times* heralded it as 'a stirring and beautiful account of a deeply felt experience'.[53] The American edition included the six pages of the Dublin Castle interrogation scene.[54] It may surprise some that the memoir was also published in Germany as *Rebellen in Irland* in late 1937, by Alfred Metzner, a Berlin publisher of liberal authors including Mahatma Gandhi. In fact, Éamon de Valera, who was president of the League of Nations at the time, had recommended the book to Wolfgang Metzner, who had been sent to Geneva to see if he could pick up any leads for new books on one of his first assignments when starting to work for his father's small publishing firm. His father decided to republish the book in 1942 and again in 1943 to support the liberal anti-National Socialist German Worker's Party's cause under the pretext of it being an anti-British book.

After O'Malley's death in 1957, efforts were made by his executor, Patrick Malley, to republish the memoir. Four Square Books Ltd of London brought out editions in

1961, 1967 and in the early 1970s. I also tried to get some Irish publishers interested, but they deferred, probably due to the increase of violence at the time in Northern Ireland.[55] Finally, Dan Nolan of Anvil Press in Tralee agreed, and in 1978 he published an edited second half, covering the 1921 Truce through to July 1924, called *The Singing Flame*, and then followed with a new edition of the original memoir in 1979. Mercier Press took over the publication of the Anvil Press titles in 2009.

Conclusion

By studying Ernie O'Malley's diaries, one can see the evolution of his writing from a personal narrative to a more complex, literary and involved text, with some extraordinarily beautiful, poetic, lyrical passages that marked the book definitely, as he said in his introduction, 'not as history'.[56] The final published memoir included his descriptions of landscape, both rural and urban, his development of characters with his pithy comments, his folklore elements of traditions and myths, and his dialogue used to heighten the dramatic effect of a particular moment. It took more than four decades from the completion of the original manuscript for *On Another Man's Wound* to be published with the second half as *The Singing Flame*. We can see now that this was a period during which Ireland itself evolved in its understanding of the struggle for its independence.

CHAPTER FIVE

THE IMPORTANCE OF BEING ERNIE O'MALLEY IN KEN LOACH'S *THE WIND THAT SHAKES THE BARLEY*

Nathan Wallace

It has often been observed that *The Wind that Shakes the Barley*, Ken Loach's Palme d'Or-winning 2006 film about the Irish War of Independence and Civil War, draws heavily from Ernie O'Malley's memoirs of that period, *On Another Man's Wound* (1936) and *The Singing Flame* (1978). This is not, however, a biopic. Loach has identified O'Malley as a paradigmatic figure of his time, whose 'life says so much about the struggle and reveals so much about the tragedy of the Civil War'.[1] He has also said that a line from the introduction to *On Another Man's Wound* –'my attitude towards the fight is that of a sheltered individual drawn from the secure seclusion of Irish life to the responsibility of action' – 'absolutely sums up the character' of the film's protagonist Damien O'Donovan (played by Cillian Murphy).[2] It would not be accurate however, to say that the film was based very closely on O'Malley's life.[3] Damien has some of O'Malley's characteristics, and these enhance the audience's sympathy for the film's Republican perspective on the Civil War. Like O'Malley, Damien is a well-edu-cated, multi-faceted, intellectual guerrilla fighter. Looking at the era through eyes like these, the film can present an alternative to the stereotypical image of the hard-line

Republican: he is neither an ideological fanatic nor a naïve romantic supporter of a doomed cause. Loach's scriptwriter, Paul Laverty, used various aspects of O'Malley's character not simply to make a sympathetic Republican protagonist, but also to address characterizations of the Cork IRA in the literary and historical writings of Frank O'Connor and Peter Hart.

While it would indeed be a mistake to over-identify the fictional Damien with the actual O'Malley, there are nevertheless several important parallels between the stories. Similarities include the following: both were medical students who became guerrilla fighters during the War for Independence. Both were taken prisoner by the Black and Tans during that war. While in British custody, both underwent torture. Both subsequently escaped the British with the help of sympathetic guards, and both executed hostages between the time of their escape and the announcement of a truce in July 1921. Both joined the anti-Treaty (Republican) forces in the Irish Civil War, and both were taken prisoner by Free State troops. While this is a compelling set of parallels, the differences between these stories are nonetheless substantial. Most important of these are the facts that O'Malley and Damien come from different places in Ireland; they have different ranks in the IRA; they have different relationships with siblings; they have different romantic attachments; they have different ideological reasons for participating in the revolution; they have different experiences of being captured in both wars; they execute different prisoners for different reasons; and as prisoners of war one is executed and the other is not. O'Malley did not have Damien's commitment to Socialism, while Damien does not have O'Malley's knowledge of literature, drama and visual arts.[4]

O'Malley inspires many aspects of the character, but Loach's protagonist is primarily a fiction. In 2007, Loach told David Archibald that he and Laverty 'wanted fictional characters' in the film 'because they can embody the conflict rather than follow what the actual characters would have done in real life'.[5] In his notes to the published screenplay, Laverty also stressed their 'key decision to have fictional characters, rather than real historical characters', because this would let them 'explore a range of voices that, we hope, are true to the times without being bogged down by the biographic and geographic detail'.[6] Laverty made people up, but each invention was carefully calculated, as he put it, 'to examine broader ideas that were in the air at the time. It was a challenge to create a range of characters who could reflect that rich complex mix of the times, but try to make them real, three-dimensional personalities.'[7] Usually the characters' emotional realities come through their personal relationships to Damien, and we encounter multiple perspectives coming from within the Republican movement. In this regard, it helps that Damien is an attentive listener who readily engages in political debate. For instance, Laverty invents Sinéad (played by Orla Fitzgerald), whose story provides a glimpse of Republican women's experiences at that time, from participation in Cumann na mBan and running the court of law in the shadow-government, to caring for families in crisis, and even suffering abuse at the hands of British soldiers.[8] Laverty also introduces a train-conductor turned IRA Volunteer, Dan (played by Liam Cunningham), in order to demonstrate the relationship between Republicanism and the Labour movement.[9] And finally, Laverty includes a fictional brother Teddy (Padraic Delaney), so that he could present the Civil War as a family tragedy.

Coming up with a fictional group of people offered the screenwriter the opportunity to draw freely on a range of materials, including what Laverty called 'the extensive and contested literature', and

> (contradictory accounts), personal letters, the songs, [and] poetry ... of the times. I spoke to the sons of men who were actually in the Flying Column in West Cork. Looking at their photographs and reading their accounts – sometimes in their own words, sometimes in academic studies – gave me a feel for it, and gave me the confidence to try and build an imaginary Flying Column.[10]

There was a very personal aspect to the script as well: Laverty drew on the personalities of family members and friends he knew as a child on his uncle Pat's farm in West Limerick, and he was inspired by the stories of older family members (such as his grandfather) who provided support to the IRA.

Among other sources, Laverty's script draws heavily from *Guerilla Days in Ireland*, the war memoir of Tom Barry, who led the legendary West Cork Flying Column and later fought on the Republican side of the Civil War. In addition to O'Malley and Barry, Laverty also drew on the stories of two other Corkmen: Tom and Sean Hales. Like the fictional O'Donovan brothers of *Wind*, these real-life brothers fought together for the IRA during the War for Independence but took different sides in the Civil War. Although he initially rejected the Treaty, Sean was persuaded by Collins personally to support it; he became a member of the Dáil and was assassinated on its steps in 1922 in retribution for the Free State's executions of Republican prisoners. During the Anglo-Irish War, Tom had been captured and tortured by the British but he would not betray Michael Collins's whereabouts – even after they ripped out his fingernails. This happens to Teddy in *Wind*, but even so Laverty told Archibald, 'For the actual torture scene I tried to imagine the horror of what happened to Hales and many others. I was informed by those incidents. But the fictional character, Teddy, was not Hales.'[11] It was with bitter historical irony that just a few years later Tom would lead the Flying Column that ambushed and assassinated Collins at Béal na mBláth.[12] Sean was the senior Free State officer in the area, and was not far away from Béal na mBláth on the day when Tom led the ambush party. Collins died in the arms of one of his closest associates, Emmet Dalton, who later resigned his generalship in the Free State army in protest against the execution of Republican prisoners. While Laverty did not fit these particular reversals of fortune into his script, he did construct the plot around the similarly tragic irony of having Teddy order Damien's execution in the very prison where both endured torture rather than turn over information.

As mentioned above, Laverty was intrigued by the fact that historical accounts were 'contradictory', and the literary tradition was 'contested'. He drew on elements from O'Malley's memoirs to deal with a current historical debate and also with a longer-term literary debate. First, he used O'Malley to address the Revisionist debate over the IRA's execution of informers, and furthermore he used O'Malley's example to contest Frank O'Connor's idea that the Irish Civil War could be understood on an aesthetic level as a conflict between realism and romanticism.

When Laverty was conducting the research for writing his screenplay about the Republican movement in revolutionary-era Cork, it would have been impossible not to be aware of the furore that had arisen among Irish historians over Peter Hart's 1998 monograph, *The IRA and Its Enemies: Violence and Community in Cork, 1916–1923*. This would have been a major source for his knowledge of Tom and Sean Hales, and also for his awareness that there were contradictory accounts of the Kilmichael ambush. Hart's book was so controversial because it formidably challenged what had been, largely thanks to Barry's memoir, the best-known image of the IRA's heroic exploits in the Anglo-Irish War. *Wind* deals significantly with two subjects that were deeply contested in the debate over Hart's books, the first of which was Kilmichael. Hart had charged that the West Cork Brigade were excessively brutal during the ambush operation because Barry had ordered his men to kill Auxiliaries who had already surrendered.[13] *Wind* has an ambush scene that is largely based on Barry's account, although this scene is not identified with it by name. 'At the end of the day,' Loach said to Archibald,

> the detail about that particular ambush doesn't really matter. If we were doing the story of Tom Barry, we would have every anorak under the sun saying this was done on such and such a day, and so on. You could be so easily crucified on historical detail … [which] becomes a burden and stops us becoming true to the spirit of the times.[14]

Loach evades crucifixion a little too easily here, because the screenplay clearly follows the account in *Guerilla Days*; the Column commander Rory gives a speech right after the ambush that echoes Barry's own rationale for the heightened 'savagery' that the Black and Tans have obliged them to adopt. Calling this scene a fiction sidesteps the issue of having to choose between Hart and Barry in an immediate way, but these writers' differences in characterizing the ethos of the IRA in those days speaks directly to 'the spirit of the times'. Whether they named the battleground or not, negative criticism of that scene would be a matter of ideology rather than pedantry, and Laverty acknowledges this dimension of the conversation by adding that '[w]e reveal our politics, values, and way of seeing the world in a very deep sense by choice of premise, character, and point of view. It's like a historian who reveals himself by what he selects or doesn't, and how he interprets it.'[15] Accordingly, the two most hostile reviews of the film in Ireland came from the Revisionist historians Roy Foster and Stephen Howe (who are not 'anoraks'). These critics differed on the aesthetic value of the film, but both faulted its historicism for privileging the romantic nationalist Barry's perspective over that of Revisionist historian, Hart.[16]

The most pressing historiographic question to impact Laverty's script had not so much to do with Kilmichael as it had to do with the theme of executions by the IRA. In *Guerilla Days*, Barry offered a pragmatic justification for the Republican policy of executing informers. These killings, Barry wrote, led to 'an extraordinary drop in our casualty list. The enemy, deprived of the guidance of their civilian agents, were now raiding blindly, and … were more careful about murdering IRA prisoners.'[17] The concern over Republican prisoners' torture and execution is voiced again and again in the film, from the first arms raid to the tragic finale. In order to win the war, the IRA had stepped up its espionage programme. In *The IRA and Its Enemies*, however, Hart took direct aim at Barry's pragmatic account. 'The war on informers,' he wrote,

> must be seen as part of the tit-for-tat dynamics of violence, driven by fear and the desire for revenge. It was not, however, merely (or even mainly), a matter of espionage, of spies and spy-hunters. It was a civil war within and between communities, with the battle lines drawn by a whole range of social bonds and boundaries … beneath its official rhetoric of courts martial and convictions, the IRA were tapping a deep vein of communal prejudice and gossip: about grabbers, black Protestants and Masonic conspiracies, dirty tinkers and corner boys, fly-boys and fast women, the Jews at No. 4 and the disorderly house at No. 30.[18]

With a purposefully inflammatory choice of words, which he later retracted, Hart even went so far as to say that the IRA ran what amounted to a campaign of 'ethnic cleansing'.[19]

The political rhetoric of this analogy offended many, but it must be admitted that so many Protestants did actually flee Cork at that time, that Barry saw a need in *Guerilla Days* to address claims that the IRA were engaging in sectarian intimidation. 'The British Imperialists down the ages,' he wrote,

> owe in the main, their successful conquests of many peoples to the technique of 'Divide and Conquer.' They have consistently urged class against class, district against district, creed against creed, and in the resultant chaos of warring sects and factions, they established themselves and maintained their rule of exploitation. So in 1920 and 1921, they fanned the flame of religious intolerance between Catholics and Protestants … This was in keeping with the general British propaganda to make the Protestants of Ireland believe that they and their faith would be victimised and destroyed under a Republican Government of Ireland.[20]

According to Barry, that is, the IRA was a national (rather than sectarian) organization with an effective counter-espionage operation; Protestants who did not inform on the IRA had nothing to fear from them, and any who actually feared them were unfortunate dupes to the British imperial propaganda machine. Although this particular argument does not make it overtly into the film, we can tell from interviews that Loach was inclined to accept this explanation of Protestant fears because he was himself primarily interested in the way British imperial strategies (such as 'Divide and Conquer') had wreaked havoc on the countries it colonized.[21]

In his review of the film, Foster alleged that Loach had been duped by Irish Republican romanticism, but rather than being a gullible romantic he simply seems to have been more interested in the analysis of imperial policy than in the ethics of anti-colonial resistance. Whatever the historical reality might have been, Laverty's Republicans are an earnest rather than a cynical group, motivated by principles rather than immature romanticism or social prejudice. Indeed, the only character in the film to voice religious prejudice is the Protestant informer.[22] Moreover, the fact that one of the two captives Damien executes is a fellow-Catholic, contradicts the notion that the IRA were primarily interested in killing Protestants.[23]

In response to these and other charges, that the Cork IRA were secretly motivated by resentments and prejudices, Laverty drew on various confidence-inspiring aspects of O'Malley's character to shape the film's protagonist. Most importantly, he expanded greatly on the idea that O'Malley had once been a medical student. In the autumn of 1915, the eighteen-year-old O'Malley began to study medicine at University College Dublin on a scholarship. He had not been at it for very long before the Easter Rising took place, however, and after this he went on to become a revolutionary instead of a doctor. O'Malley resumed his training ten years later, but his interest in medicine gave way to his interest in drama and he failed his second-year exam before leaving Dublin for America with Frank Aiken in 1928. This medical training was also an important point of character reference for Cillian Murphy, who wrote in his cast notes that

> The fact that Damien is a doctor who finds himself having to kill people is dramatically very powerful – but there are actual historical instances of it. Ernie O'Malley, who wrote about his experiences as a volunteer, was a doctor. I feel that the only way Damien could handle this situation is to have a goal, and then numb himself to it.[24]

The idea of a doctor undertaking the kinds of military operations that O'Malley undertook proved extremely useful from a dramatic point of view, and it would be particularly so in the scene of Chris's execution.

Expanding on this medical training also helped move the plot along with greater economy than that which we find in O'Malley's memoirs. The story of O'Malley's conversion is told in Chapter 3 of *On Another Man's Wound*. When O'Malley becomes aware that the Easter Rising is happening, it is not apparent which side he will take in the battle. At first he accepts an offer given by students at Trinity to hold up with them inside the locked college gates and fight off the rebels. He tells them he will be right back, but does not return. He speaks with Nationalist friends, one of whom dissuades him from taking up arms against fellow Irishmen, but he remains undecided about what actions to take: 'I walked around in a detached manner. I had no feeling for or against, save irritation at those fellows for doing the unexpected, seizing the Post Office and those other buildings.'[25] He ultimately comes to a decision after bravely walking up O'Connell Street to the Parnell Monument one night and talking to members of the Citizens' Army – who are singing songs about 1798 and plotting (unsuccessfully) to blow up Nelson's Pillar. O'Malley returns to his parents' home, and by the next morning he has made his decision. O'Malley's conversion story is dramatic and even cinematic, but it lacks the economy and visceral immediacy of the train station scene in Laverty's tightly plotted screenplay. In *Wind*, Damien's moment of conversion happens at a local train station in County Cork. He has graduated from the medical school at UCC, and has won the opportunity to complete his training at a world-class hospital in London. He is on his way to emigrate and become a doctor, therefore, when he witnesses British officers beating a train conductor (Dan, played by Liam Cunningham) for refusing to carry troops because this is the Transport Workers' Union policy. Although Dan isn't yet a member of the Flying Column either, his heroic example convinces Damien to stay in Cork and take his oath as an IRA volunteer.

Although nothing resembling this moment-of-truth conversion actually happens in *On Another Man's Wound*, the scene reflects Loach's sense of Damien as both a 'realist' and also 'a sheltered individual' before joining the IRA.

Wind is not the only film about this period to draw inspiration from O'Malley's having been a medical student, although it is the only one to invoke it for an anti-Treaty perspective. That is, we also find it in director Michael Anderson's *Shake Hands with the Devil* (1959). The protagonist of this film is an Irish-American, Kerry O'Shea (played by Don Murray), who joins the IRA rather than completing his medical studies at Trinity College Dublin. Unlike Damien (or O'Malley), however, Kerry remains loyal to the Michael Collins character ('the General', played by Michael Redgrave) in the Civil War. The wildly implausible villain of the film, played by James Cagney, is both the leader of the anti-Treaty IRA and a professor of medicine at Trinity College. Whereas *Wind* uses the idea of an IRA medical student as protagonist to humanize the Republican side of the Civil War, *Shake Hands* had used the same device to make the anti-Treaty position seem psychopathic.[26]

In his memoirs, O'Malley's self-portrait as a man of culture far outweighs his self-image as a medical man. In the chapters of *The Singing Flame* devoted to the Four Courts, for instance, O'Malley does not talk about dressing his fellow soldiers' wounds (which is what Damien would have been doing), but he does take a quiet moment to inspect his travelling collection of literature and art history – which has been damaged by Free State gunfire.[27] Near the end of the siege, moreover, while sitting under the dome contemplating the forthcoming surrender, O'Malley recites sonnets 25 and 90 from memory to his senior officer, Rory O'Connor.[28] Denis Flannery notes that O'Malley, having chosen Sonnet 90 to fulfil O'Connor's request for a 'hopeful' poem, leaves out the final couplet: 'And other strains of woe, which now seem woe, / Compared with loss of thee, will not seem so.'[29] Flannery argues that, had he spoken it, O'Malley would have risked making an overt declaration of love to his senior officer. Rather than seeing this as a failure of nerve, however, Flannery interprets it as a negative statement, appropriate to Shakespeare's own exploration of queer subjectivity. This omission amounts, therefore, to a 'rejection of maturity, first by making military erasure part of the scene of love and then by O'Malley's erasure of a declaration of static love, albeit one carried out in the interests of maintaining the restraint that guarantees in this queer scenario, love's survival'.[30] We should also remember, however, that O'Malley omits the couplet when O'Connor interjects a comment that the previous lines ('so shall I taste / At first the very worst of fortune's might') do not sound very encouraging about what might happen to them as soon as they lay down arms and walk out of the building. They were waiting to learn whether or not the Free State forces (led by Emmet Dalton) would accept their terms of surrender. Once they were in Free State custody, O'Malley did slip away from the guards but O'Connor stayed behind and would later be executed by Free State forces in retribution for the assassination of Sean Hales.

Intricately playing off the way these two real-life revolutionaries connect over poetic recitation in a time of defeat, however, in *Wind* Damien and Dan (meeting again in prison) bond over memorized literature while the former awaits almost certain execution. Damien has just written his goodbye letters, and he becomes interested in a fragment of Blake's 'Garden of Love', which he finds scratched into the cell wall. Dan is also imprisoned there, and he, knowing the rest of the poem by heart, completes it: 'And Priests in black gowns, were walking their rounds, / And binding with briars, my joys & desires.'[31] This is probably coincidental, but it is worth noting further parallels that in *Wind* the final lines are supplied through dialogue rather than omitted, and, in both 'The Garden of Love' and Sonnet 90, the final two lines refer to unregulated sexuality and forbidden love. The two do not try to interpret Blake, however, but rather move on to bond over a shared memorization of James Connolly's Dublin Lockout speech. Like O'Malley, Damien appreciates English poetry but like Loach he gets more from Blake's radical critique of oppressive political and religious authority than from Shakespeare's meditations on unrequited, forbidden love. Again echoing this section of *On Another Man's Wound*, when Damien finds himself once again in prison at the end of *Wind*, he willingly goes to his death rather than turn over information on a Republican leader named Rory (played by Myles Horgan).

Damien's story explains why a well-educated and self-aware young intellectual such as Ernie O'Malley might join the IRA, even though the fight seemed unlikely to succeed. This does not make him so much a representative figure, as an exemplary one. Moreover, Damien provides an ethical justification for the Republican policy of executing informers, against Hart's argument that this was really just an indiscriminate policy of ethnic cleansing. If Damien does brutal things, this is only because (as Barry had insisted) the British created a situation necessitating a brutal response. However, Laverty went beyond simply providing us with the representative kind of volunteer Barry assured us he commanded. Rather, in Damien, we find an exemplary figure who goes the utmost distance of living and dying by the principles Barry says his men generally followed. He takes full responsibility for carrying out the execution, and part of that responsibility implies that he will give up his own life in order to observe the principle for which he ordered his friend's death. In short, we know that

Damien kills informers out of principle (rather than personal interests or community prejudices), because he takes that principle seriously enough to sacrifice himself for it. Of course, coming up with a fictional character who lives and dies by that principle proves nothing about the IRA's war on informers in West Cork. It does, however, reflect very clearly the fact that Free State and anti-Treaty leaders of that time played the alternating roles of martyr and executioner out of principle, and they proved this again and again by overseeing the deaths of close comrades.

While Laverty was interested in the historians' debate, he was also intrigued by the 'contested' literary tradition, and his intervention into this literary contest gave him even more occasion to make deliberate use of O'Malley's memoirs. This is not a contest over what happened when – or even why. Rather, this is an argument over what James Chandler has called 'the politics of style' in representations of the period. Laverty's screenplay rigorously contests the idea that Republicanism is an ideology of naïve romanticism, and in doing this he pushes back against the image of the Flying Column that had been popularized by Frank O'Connor's short story, 'Guests of the Nation'.[32]

The debate over realism and romanticism in Ireland stretches back to the nineteenth century, and these terms have been key to the critical comparisons between *Wind* and Neil Jordan's *Michael Collins* (1996). Eleftheria Rania Kosmidou, for instance, reads both of these films as interventions into the Revisionist debate in Irish historiography.[33] Among Irish historians, Revisionism implies a rejection of myths and romanticism in Irish history, with the understanding that those myths promote conflict rather than peaceful coexistence on the island. Revisionists have also tended to accept and even defend Irish Partition, however, and critics of this school have therefore seen it as an academic version of Unionist propaganda.[34] One might therefore expect these two films, taking opposing sides of the Civil War, to lend themselves quite readily to the terms of the Revisionist debate. The films do not at all fall in line that way, however, and Kosmidou acknowledges this when she argues that *Michael Collins* tips its hat to both the Revisionists and the anti-Revisionists because it is both mythic and realist by turns. A nostalgic film, it 'presents history in terms of a heroic past', and thereby 'contributes to the anti-Revisionist, Nationalist discourse which justifies past Republican action. At the same time, its nostalgia is also reflective (and by implication Revisionist) in its support of compromise solutions to conflict situations and the critical depiction of de Valera.'[35] She persuasively identifies the even-handedness of Jordan's intervention, which by turns romanticizes and distances itself from Irish Republican violence: Collins was in the right when he waged an idealistic war against the British Empire, but he was also right when he fought for the compromise Treaty against his former Republican comrades.

James Chandler, who has also written about the comparison between Loach's and Jordan's takes on the Irish Civil War, has gone so far as to read Loach's style in the film as a critical intervention, deliberately countering Jordan's over-reliance on 'Hollywood' conventions.[36] This contrast is very real, but Loach's style developed prior to the appearance of *Michael Collins*; Chandler's comparison with Jordan highlights the brilliance of how Loach and collaborators operate as realist filmmakers, but that approach reflects his career-long development as a British socialist director rather than an ad hoc defence of the anti-Treaty position. Loach, one of the world's great realist directors, is an heir to the Italian Neorealist tradition of Roberto Rossellini, Vittorio De Sica and Gillo Pontecorvo, and in *Wind* he approaches his subject with a realist perspective that is not bound by the protocols of any previous Irish debate about ideology and style.[37] As is the case with his Italian predecessors, Loach's highly sophisticated practice can be deceptively simple. In *Wind*, as in many other films, he opposes top-down perspective on history and society on multiple levels. As a socialist realist, Loach is uncannily resourceful and so what we find in this film, therefore, is Laverty's screenplay focusing the depth of Loach's realist vision on an old Irish debate. This collaboration effectively blows the traditional debate over realism and romanticism in the Irish Civil War wide open.

It is worth asking at this point, however, whether Collins himself wanted to be remembered in anything resembling the terms of realism and romanticism. There is no likelier source by which to answer these questions than the pamphlet collection of his speeches and writings, *The Path to Freedom*, issued shortly after Collins's assassination at Béal na mBláth in County Cork, in August 1922. The first of the samples included in this volume was entitled 'Notes by General Michael Collins', which must have been written within weeks if not days of his death. Formulated during the heat of Civil War, these notes constitute a sustained criticism of Éamon de Valera's anti-Treaty position. The essence of his argument here is that the Irregulars' war was 'not against an enemy [i.e. the British state] but against their own nation. Blind to facts, and false to ideals, they are making war on the Irish people.'[38] In defying the results of the 1922 election, in which the majority of Irish citizens voted to ratify the Anglo-Irish Treaty, and rejecting Collins's understanding that the British would reoccupy the country with irresistible force if the new Irish government could not unify the people in holding to that Treaty, Collins insisted that 'we have to face realities'.[39] If he figured the Republicans' idealism as a betrayal of the actual Irish people, he recommended a form of realism that would be in service to an ideal Irish Republic:

> We must be true to facts if we would achieve anything in this life. We must be true
> to our ideal, if would achieve anything worthy. The Ireland to which we are true,

to which we are devoted and faithful, is the ideal Ireland, which means there is always something more to strive for. The true devotion lies not in melodramatic defiance or self-sacrificing for something falsely said to exist, or for mere words or formalities, which are empty, and which might be but the house newly swept and garnished to which seven works devils entered in. It is the steady, earnest effort in face of actual possibilities towards the solid achievement of our hopes and visions, the laying of stone upon stone of a building which is actual and in accordance with the ideal pattern.[40]

Here Collins straddles the line between the real and the ideal, but he clearly delineates the contrast between a solid, stone-like quality of the actual, and the empty abstraction of the Irregular commitment to 'melodrama'. Given the force of his emphases on the primacy of the actual in reaching the ideal, we might trace the ideological formulation of realism as a post- Republican aesthetic register, to Collins himself.

After the Civil War, however, a number of former anti-Treaty writers (including Sean O'Faolain, Liam O'Flaherty, Frank O'Connor, Peadar O'Donnell and Ernie O'Malley) emerged to shape mid-century Irish intellectual culture. Some took up Collins's argument and, curiously enough, turned it against themselves. These were all literary realists, and with the exceptions of O'Donnell and O'Malley they saw their realism as a way to distance themselves from their early political romanticism. In some cases, these writers figured their turns to realism as a turn to a mode of artistic, personal and political maturity. Perhaps the most influential of these post-Republican realists was O'Connor. He was best known internationally as a short story writer, but he was also a literary critic and a biographer. His most famous short story was 'Guests of the Nation', in which the protagonist, Bonaparte, is an IRA volunteer whose perspective changes utterly when he takes part in the execution of two British soldiers (Belcher and Hawkins), whom he has paradoxically befriended while holding them prisoner. He does not realize until late in the game that these men are actually hostages; it turns out that the British army has executed some IRA prisoners, and so now Bonaparte's party, led by the cold-blooded Donovan, must execute Belcher and Hawkins. Once the soldiers have been killed, the narrator describes feeling 'very small and lonely. And anything that ever happened [to] me after I never felt the same about again.'[41] Key elements of this story have been repeated in various ways in subsequent films about Irish Republicanism, from such movies as *Shake Hands with the Devil* and Neil Jordan's *The Crying Game* (1992).[42]

Much of the story's authenticity and ambiguity comes from O'Connor's conflicted thoughts about having been in the IRA. At first we might think that the author identifies solely with the naïve Bonaparte, who only shoots Belcher after Donovan has shot

Hawkins in the head. O'Connor was only a *nom de plume*; however, when we remember that the author's real name was Michael O'Donovan it becomes clear that he must have identified, at least subliminally, with the unsympathetic villain as well. Laverty's script catches this trick and plays with it in the names of its Republican characters. First, he gives O'Connor's real last name to Teddy and Damien. Secondly, the first execution in the film comes when a similarly named young man, Micheail Ó Duigneain (played by Laurence Barry) refuses to identify himself in any language but Irish. In another instance, when the IRA come to kidnap Sir John Hamilton, he significantly refers to the leader as 'Mr O'Donovan', after having made a joke that the notorious Teddy O'Donovan, to whom he pretends not to have realized he was speaking, must be 'short and thick'. By playing with O'Connor's names in this way, Laverty was pointing to the very source of the post-Republican realist tradition.

In his 1963 book *The Lonely Voice: A Study of the Short Story*, O'Connor explained his model of the short story as a quiet moment in which a protagonist's perspective on life is changed unalterably. 'If one wanted an alternative description of what the short story means,' he explains, 'one could hardly find better than that single half-sentence, "and from that day forth, everything was as it were changed and appeared in a different light to him." If one wanted an alternative title for this work, one might choose "I Am Your Brother".'[43] True to this model, the tragic conclusion of 'Guests of the Nation' affirms the principle of human brotherhood, a principle apparently denied by the IRA, and so it is clear that Bonaparte's future will include a growing disenchantment with Irish Republicanism. The story implicitly produces an ideology of the aesthetic whereby narrative realism stands in for the Irish subject's process of disaffection from Republicanism.

O'Connor further articulated this linkage in his biography of Michael Collins, *The Big Fellow*, published shortly before his own death in 1966. In his own life, O'Connor had taken the anti-Treaty side in the Irish Civil War, but in his preface he identified his much-later writing of Collins's biography as 'a labour of love' and 'an act of reparation' after 'the fever of the Civil War died down'.[44] That is, when the author matured into a post-Republican realist, he came to recognize Collins's principled leadership of the Free State as the political corollary of his own mature literary principles. Both spoke to the Irish future, and paved the way for modernity in Ireland: 'It is as a realist Collins will be remembered, and as a realist he should be an inspiration to the new Ireland. From the Civil War and the despair that followed it sprang a new honesty in Irish life and thought. The old sentimentalism against which Collins almost unconsciously strove has suffered.'[45]

At the end of that book, O'Connor's recounting of Collins's death scene echoes the conclusion to 'Guests of the Nation'. O'Connor describes the killing in short, declarative sentences followed by longer, lyrical observations of the countryside at dusk:

> The glen was quiet again, only the wind stirred in the bushes. Over all a wild and lovely county night fell; the men came in from the fields, gathered at the crossroads for a smoke, sat about the fire where soon they would say the rosary; clearer in the darkness sounded the wheels of the little country cart thumping over the ledge of stone, a cart such as Collins had seen and thrilled at in the Shepherd's Bush Road. But he would hear it no longer. The countryside he had seen in dreams, the people he had loved, the tradition which had been his inspiration – they had risen in the falling light and struck him dead.[46]

This reads like a classic short-story ending, and it encapsulates the author's explicit formulation of the Irish Civil War as a fight to the death between realism and romanticism. This description of the Cork countryside as murderous also implies a rebuke of O'Connor's mentor Daniel Corkery, who encouraged O'Connor to join the Irregulars, and whose attempts at literary realism, according to O'Connor, were compromised by romanticism. In *An Only Child*, O'Connor voices this disappointment in a story from Corkery's *A Munster Twilight* (1917), 'The Ploughing of Leaca-na-Naomh', in which a man dies while ploughing sanctified ground. O'Connor calls this 'a typical bit of symbolism that seems to sum up a deep personal conflict. It describes the suicidal destruction of the creative faculty as an act of revolt against the worldliness of everyday life.'[47]

We might also diagnose O'Connor's theory of realism as a literary version of Stockholm Syndrome. According to O'Connor's memoir of the Irish Revolution, *An Only Child*, the author underwent his decisive transition to post-Republican realism in a Free State prison. It 'came as a relief' and even 'a real blessing', he wrote, when 'I was captured effortlessly one Spring morning by Free State soldiers.'[48] Beyond this understandable feeling of relief that captivity had removed him from some dangers, however, O'Connor also came to identify with his captors precisely through observation of their brutality. In a key recollection he recalls encountering a young Republican who had been beaten nearly to death by the gaolers: the victim had been reduced to 'a bundle a rags … trying to raise itself from the floor', whose face and hands now looked and felt like 'a lump of dough'.[49] The young man, Pat Henley, would be executed a few days after this, and O'Connor describes this experience in very similar terms to those used in 'Guests of the Nation' and *The Lonely Voice*. 'That scene haunted me for years,' he wrote,

> mainly because I was beginning to think that this was all our romanticism came to … the battered face of that boy was something that wasn't in any book, and even ten years

later, when I was sitting reading in my flat in Dublin, the door would suddenly open and he would walk in and the book would fall from my hands. Certainly, that night changed something forever in me.[50]

As he settled into prison life, he came to discern 'some relationship between Irish nationalism and the Romantic movement'.[51] The political implications of this connection were dramatically realized one night when he spoke out about his fellow prisoners for singing a new ballad romanticizing Henley's death. He was the only person to voice this criticism, just as he was the only one to stand up for another Republican prisoner, Frank Murphy, who went on hunger strike to protest the Republican leadership's policies within the prison (rather than those of the official authorities).

Here we can find one of the greater points of divergence between O'Connor and O'Malley. O'Connor was the only internee to vote against the hunger strike by all Republican prisoners during the post-Ceasefire 'Prison War', whereas O'Malley was arguably the most famous Republican prisoner to engage in it (despite ill health and the fact that he did not entirely agree with the idea). O'Malley's resolution on this point, in fact, would be taken as an inspiration by the Provisional IRA hunger strikers at Long Kesh in the 1980s. At any rate, O'Connor's dissident position on this occasion inspired his later theory of short fiction, which centred on 'outlawed figures wandering about the fringes of society, superimposed sometimes on symbolic figures whom they caricature and echo – Christ, Socrates, Moses', and who thereby imbued the form with 'an intense awareness of human loneliness'.[52] Ironically, O'Malley's experience after the Civil War would seem to match O'Connor's description of this lonely, visionary figure. Nonetheless, this association of Irish realism with revolutionary disenchantment constituted the abiding theme of O'Connor's literary career, and it is largely thanks to his popularity that this association enjoyed a more or less unquestioned hegemony in the Irish Republic until the appearance of the Field Day Theatre Company in 1980.

The Wind that Shakes the Barley revisits the question of Republicanism and realism in its own execution scenes, although various characters express competing claims to realism in other scenes as well. One key scene takes place in a Republican court near the end of the War for Independence, and in it our main characters conduct a debate over how the new authorities should deal with a local property owner who has been exploiting the poor but who has also been purchasing weapons for the IRA. Damien's brother Teddy, who leads the Flying Column, is motivated by the 'real' need for weapons, while Damien and Dan argue for the no less vital need for the Republican courts to have legitimacy. Who is the realist in this situation? Another IRA leader,

Rory, says their true goal is to get rid of the British, calling for 'a little clarity, in the name of God!' in reply to which the socialist volunteer Dan makes a direct appeal to the realism of class struggle:

> Turn out your pockets, lads. Come on, how much money have you got in your pocket? … Have you a blade of grass to your name? … Right, you're paupers, just like me. Now you want to take a look up and down this country and see the amount of volunteers that are involved in land seizures and cattle drives. Do you want to know why that's happening, do you? The IRA are backing the landlords and crushing people like you and me. You sat down and had dinner with the IRA last night – These boys are backing the local bigwig and selling out a mother who hasn't got a penny in her pocket, just like yours!

It is clear that Loach sympathizes with Dan's claim to realism more than with that of the IRA leadership. We do not find this socialist perspective in O'Malley's writings, but the bare outline of his story lends the opportunity for Loach's film to voice that social-realist perspective with real drama and eloquence. It also forecasts the real criticism of the Irish Free State that would emerge later in the film.

The debate over realism intensifies in a later scene where Damien and Sinéad walk out of a Church in response to the Priest's anti-Republican sermon. Damien shouts: 'Once again, with honourable exception, the Church sides with the rich!' Teddy follows him out of the church and tries to win him back over to his side. Damien provides a number of concrete examples of why he won't turn back, demanding that Teddy recall the occasion when

> … our own father … fired Pat McCarthy because he was sick, and we couldn't even look his son in the face because of the shame of it? … Look, Teddy, there's one in four people out of work in this country, right? I have seen children and … families starving. Do we expect them to head off to New York and London like before? Is that what we fought for? … Look, it's too late, Teddy! You're not gonna convince me!

> TEDDY: You've always been a dreamer, Damien.

> DAMIEN: I am not a dreamer. I'm a realist, Teddy … You can't see it, boy. You really can't see it. John Bull has his hand down your pants and his fist round your bollocks, and you can't see it … This treaty makes you a servant of the British Empire. You have wrapped yourself in the fucking Union Jack. The butcher's apron, boy.[53]

Damien's speech may turn from concrete realist images to rhetorical ones by the end, but his denunciation of the Free State's anti-democratic alliance with Church, Property and Empire is unquestionably the superior form of realism by Loach's lights. This was also precisely the way Murphy understood the character he was playing: 'very much a realist'. Furthermore, this exchange also highlights the way Teddy's attribution of Damien's resistance to some dreamy romanticism merely serves as a hollow self-justification of his own flawed position. It was precisely this hegemonic idea that Laverty's screenplay sought most thoroughly to contest.

The crucial first execution scene of Loach's film, wherein Damien puts to death his former comrade Chris Reilly (played by John Crean) alongside the Anglo-Irish landlord Sir John Hamilton (played by Roger Allam), is the turning point in Damien's story. In his review of *Wind*, Foster wrote that this scene 'suggests … [a] passage from O'Malley's book, or Frank O'Connor's "Guests of the Nation", but without the tragic ambiguity beneath the surface'.[54] We have already discussed this scene in 'Guests', but in the section from *On Another Man's Wound* to which Foster refers, O'Malley recalls the execution of three British officers he ordered in Tipperary not long before the Anglo-Irish ceasefire in 1921. Although the rationale for these executions differ in various ways, the resemblance between the execution scenes in Loach and O'Malley gives them a shared contrast with O'Connor's conclusion.

For instance, O'Connor's Bonaparte has a low rank and therefore lacks the authority either to deliver or to refuse the order for execution. In *On Another Man's Wound*, the decision fell to O'Malley, and in *Wind* the decision falls to Damien – both of whom insist on going ahead with it despite appeals for leniency from others. In 'Guests', the killings are a reprisal for the execution of four Republican prisoners in Cork. O'Malley, on the other hand, was responding to the British army's general policy of executing Republicans. In all cases, the prisoners are treated with dignity. For example, O'Malley recalls saying that he would release the prisoners in case of a firefight: '"If we are surrounded," I said to the one whose face I liked best, "I'll let you go. I'm not going to shoot you like dogs."'[55] He furthermore defends them from the derision of his subordinates and, late that night, O'Malley considers his connection with the prisoners: 'I was putting myself in the place of the men inside.'[56] Before he actually does have them shot, O'Malley gives his prisoners the opportunity to turn over letters, and forward their possessions to friends and loved ones. He records their last words, and then

> The volley crashed sharply. The three fell to the ground; their arms twitched. The quartermaster put his revolver to each of their foreheads in turn and fired. The bodies lay still on the green grass. We stood to attention. Then slowly we went up the hill across country, making for the centre. None of us spoke until we had crossed a good many fields where wind had snaked the rye grass.[57]

These lines also read like the conclusion to a short story, and they conclude the penultimate section of the book. Given their blunt description of violence followed by a poetic evocation of the landscape, this even sounds like the end to O'Connor's 'Guests'. For O'Connor, scenes like this were only exercises in Republican madness and futility, whereas O'Malley seems to point out the policy was effective because it takes place only a few days before the Truce of 11 July.

O'Connor does not accuse the IRA of ethnic cleansing the way Hart does, but in 'Guests' and other places he does suggest that the policy is brutal and short-sighted. Even Barry was not sanguine about what this policy had wrought in the Republican psyche, and he writes:

> We were now hard, cold and ruthless as our enemy had been since hostilities began. The British were met with their own weapons. They had gone down in the mire to destroy us and our nation, and down after them we had to go to stop them. The step was not an easy one, for one's mind was darkened and one's outlook made bleak by the decisions which had to be taken.[58]

This idea of necessary brutality is echoed by the character of Rory in Loach's *Wind* – right after the controversial ambush scene – and Liam Neeson makes similar remarks in Jordan's script for *Michael Collins*. The darkness, bleakness and ruthlessness to which Barry refers here suggests a slide towards the mire of realism rather than an ascent into dreamy clouds of romanticism. Nonetheless, when Stephen Howe criticizes *Wind* for its insufficient scepticism towards Barry, he ascribes the IRA's brutality not to their realism but to their 'romantic, culturalist, separatist, and sometimes necrophiliac brand of nationalism'.[59] He faults the film not just for its historical departure from what Hart says about the IRA's real motivations, but also because it reverses the aesthetic categories by which Irish history and politics have so often been understood by the intellectual critics of Irish nationalism.

In sharp contrast with these fictional examples, O'Malley's description of the execution of three British officers is able to provide the reader with the who, the how, the where and the when of a real event – in which he not only took part but for which he was fully responsible. O'Malley knew what he was doing, and the experience did not lead him to any O'Connorite movement to a post-Republican version of realism. Here is perhaps the most significant point by which Loach's treatment of the scene follows O'Malley rather than O'Connor: the execution fails to signal any movement for our protagonist away from his Republicanism.

Loach's film is like O'Malley's memoir in that the main character knows what he is doing, and after doing it he does not lose faith in the cause. In *Wind*, Loach establishes

Damien's shocking awareness of what the execution means, by stressing that he, like O'Malley, is a medical student. Murphy's lines illustrate this beautifully when he says: 'I studied anatomy for five years, Dan and now I'm going to shoot this man in the head … I've known Chris Reilly since he was a child … I sure hope this Ireland we're fighting for is worth it.'[60] These lines show not just that Damien, as a student of medicine, understands what the bullet will do to the men's bodies, but he is also thinking about the uncertain ends towards which these killings are directed.[61] Right after Damien has shot the men, we see him in a long shot, stumble away from the camera, about to disappear down a hill, barely able to withstand the shock of what he had to do. We know he will be haunted by this event for a long time, and indeed he later tells Sinéad that this has made him numb. Despite this numbness, even when he realizes by the end of the film that the ideal Republic is not coming soon, he does not repent of the choices he made while trying to bring it about. The experience of doing these things made Damien more of a realist than he had been before, but taking responsibility for their consequences also makes him more of a radical. This is the turning point of the script because, as we later learn, this action makes his own execution inevitable. As O'Malley said of the event in *On Another Man's Wound*: 'My turn might come too, and soon.'[62]

In each of these texts, the meaning of the execution scene is largely determined by its position within the plot. It appears near the end of *On Another Man's Wound* because in actual fact these executions did take place near the end of the war. In 'Guests', however, the placement of this scene at the end signals that a lifetime will be spent contemplating the wrongness of what has just happened. In Neil Jordan's *The Crying Game*, what had been O'Connor's lonely turning-point-as-conclusion, becomes instead the inciting action for a three-act feature. In *Wind*, however, the scene appears halfway through the film and this gives it a completely different meaning from what we find in these other two examples. It radicalizes the protagonist and makes his self-sacrifice understandable.

Turning to the end of the third act, which is set during the Civil War, *Wind*'s climactic scene features tragic irony recalling the history of Tom and Sean Hales: Teddy is in charge of Free State forces, who kill Dan and capture Damien in a botched weapons raid. It falls to Teddy, therefore, to interrogate Damien in the same gaol where they had been tortured after Chris informed on them. Teddy literally begs Damien to save his own life by turning informer, but Damien sits patiently at the table and does not look up until his brother has finished his appeal. When Damien does look up, there is a shocking intensity in his eyes. He leans in and speaks the devastating lines: 'You listen to me. I shot … Chris Reilly … in the heart. I did that. You know why? I'm not going to sell out.'[63] Here we see that the first execution scene has made the final one inevitable because Damien cannot betray the cause for which he has killed Chris, to whom his last words had been 'I'll protect you.' That had been an unexpected choice of words, and it was more memorable than 'God protect you' which appears in Laverty's screenplay. The change is meaningful, however, because by putting himself in the place of God, Damien takes an almost unimaginable responsibility for his actions. The alteration also gestures towards another change of words in the scene between Teddy and Damien in the prison. In the screenplay, Damien is surprised by the death sentence and says 'Christ', whereas in the film he says nothing because he already seems to know what is going to happen. Again, cutting a reference to religion means that the protagonist has an even greater acknowledgement of his own responsibilities. Death by firing squad may not come as a relief, but there is at least some sense that he is finally delivering, in some strange way, the 'protection' he earlier promised.

O'Malley never faced this precise situation, but Damien's self-sacrifice also brings to mind another comment about the execution at the end of *On Another Man's Wound*: 'It seemed easier to face one's own execution than to have to shoot others.'[64] By the same token, Teddy would clearly also have preferred his own death to the duty of ordering his brother's. The stark choice between martial law and family loyalty also recalls the ethical conflict Hegel identified in Sophocles' *Antigone*; Teddy may be playing the role of a tyrant, but like Creon he is neither pleasing himself nor pursuing any ulterior motives. According to Laverty, both he and Loach 'were really keen to ensure that Teddy was not seen as a fall guy. We really wanted him to be a man of principle who really believed that the Treaty was the best possibility, that it was, as Michael Collins argued, "The freedom to achieve freedom."'[65] Teddy is more devastated by Damien's death than Damien had been devastated by Chris's, and his subsequent actions are accordingly more reckless. He delivers Damien's message to Sinéad by motorcycle personally, and without an escort. These risks practically invite a reprisal shooting, and insofar as these characters' relationship echoes that of Sean and Tom Hales, or even Michael Collins himself, we should not assume that Teddy will survive the war either.

In conclusion, *The Wind that Shakes the Barley*'s contribution to the cinema of Irish Revolution is best understood when recognized as a dynamic collaboration between two great artists at the peak of their creativity: Ken Loach and Paul Laverty. As a director, Loach is primarily interested in harnessing an inventive realist film style to raise consciousness about Britain's imperial history. While Laverty shares this concern, his highly literate script intervenes, with great sophistication, into the historiographic and creative legacy of the Irish War for Independence and Civil War. Loach's style proves that realism can be much more than simply a post-Republican mode of representing Irish history. Ernie O'Malley is essential to the film partly because some of his character traits lend the protagonist credibility, but also because his life and writings have so often demonstrated that very same thing. Of the distinguished list of anti-Treaty IRA members who went on to become realist writers after the Civil War, O'Malley was one of the few not to attribute his Republicanism to artistic immaturity and political naïveté. O'Malley's memoirs are realistic and unsentimental, and they do not equate the Irish Free State's acquiescence to the demands of the Anglo-Irish Treaty with realism as such. Laverty's script takes us back through the history of writing about the period, and asks how realism may still be used to explore Ireland's revolutionary history. O'Malley is an essential influence on the script because his memoirs, like Loach's film style, have suggested many rich ways to answer to those questions.

PART II

HISTORICAL NATIONALIST PERSPECTIVES

CHAPTER SIX

ON REPUBLICAN READING
ERNIE O'MALLEY, IRISH INTELLECTUAL

David Lloyd

'… *the whole might be useful, in extract, to any of our literary people who feel inclined to devote attention and proper interpretation of a much unstudied period of our history, which has simply been glossed over by the words: murderers, fanatics, gunmen, wild foolish boys, idlers, looters, impractical idealists.*'
—Ernie O'Malley to Molly Childers

'*This was no academic seminar consumed with the search for truth. Physical force would decide. It was a reality check for the Irish delegates – as for any account of Irish history with the British gun left out.*'
—J.J. Lee

Over the last decade, the gradual publication of the papers and other previously unpublished manuscripts of Ernie O'Malley has performed a signal service to the scholarly and public reassessment of the significance and traditions of modern Irish Republicanism. It is the kind of endeavour that promises to disentangle the ideological tendencies and the practices of Republican activists from the skein of myth in which historical Revisionism has wound them and to allow a more complicated image to emerge of the spectrum of political positions that Republicanism has embraced. It also helps us to locate the Irish experience of decolonization in relation to subsequent such movements internationally and to highlight both its anomalies and its normality. The first of these volumes, *'No Surrender Here!' The Civil War Papers of Ernie O'Malley, 1922–1924*, has already proven to be an indispensable book for anyone concerned with the history of decolonization in Ireland. It is also a very odd book.

It is not a body of political writings like Gramsci's *Prison Notebooks*, nor a statement of a utopian political vision. What it offers instead is an intimate and detailed picture of the unfolding of a struggle, of the interaction of principle, improvisation and pragmatism that informs it, and, above all, a sense of the complexity of that interaction that belies the historian's tendency to view the revolutionary as zealot, anti-modern fanatic, or brutal idealist. It is, indeed, to riff on Ranajit Guha's famous essay, an instance of the 'prose of insurgency': a body of writings produced for the most part in the heat of the moment, lacking by circumstance an overall perspective on the dispersed and fragmentary armed resistance of the Republicans to the Free State and the Treaty that they regarded as a continuation of the war against British domination.[1]

The book's third section, the letters from prison, also furnishes some sense of the broad intellectual curiosity and culture that would come to characterize O'Malley's post-independence trajectory, his absorbing interest in literature and art, and the auto-didacticism that drives his never-institutionalized erudition just as it drove his military intelligence. There is no particular reason to believe that O'Malley was alone among Republicans in these characteristics. Indeed it is among the peculiarities of a Republicanism that historians generally seek to characterize as narrow, superstitious and backward-looking, that it included in its ranks and among its sympathizers many of the most advanced feminists and most radical socialists in the nationalist movement, together with most of the important artists and intellectuals of the post-independence decades: O'Malley himself, Francis Stuart, Frank O'Connor, Liam O'Flaherty, Peadar O'Donnell, Thomas MacGreevy – the list goes on and might extend to include both of O'Malley's eventual friends, Jack B. Yeats and Samuel Beckett. The paradox is that while the historical record emphasizes the refusal of the Republicans to compromise with the Treaty and the Free State it dragged into being, characterizing them as fanatical idealists, it remains the case that it was to be the Free State that became the organ of a narrow and intolerant nationalism, subservient to the most repressive forms of Catholic morality and to cultural provincialism. The Republican tradition, to the contrary, with the often admirable capacity for critical reflection on its own legacy that O'Malley himself everywhere exhibits, gave rise to some of the most vigorous currents of cultural criticism and cosmopolitanism in the first decades of Irish independence.

It is perhaps this paradox that gives rise to some of the oddness of the collection. Ernie O'Malley was a crucial actor in both the Anglo-Irish and the Civil Wars and, as Richard English emphasizes throughout his insidiously ambivalent biography, *Ernie O'Malley: IRA Intellectual*, an indispensable example for understanding both the Irish nationalist struggle and the intellectual and cultural perspectives of Irish Republicanism.[2] Deeply and widely read, an art critic and historian, a traveller and a farmer, he was perhaps the most articulate and conventionally 'cultured' of the Republicans who survived the Irish Revolution; a fine if not tremendously innovative writer whose memoirs of the conflict, *On Another Man's Wound* and *The Singing Flame*, continue to retain compelling literary interest, writings, moreover, stand as vital documents for understanding the processes and vicissitudes, and the violence, of decolonization – a theoretical term markedly absent from the historians' vocabulary, but which is as appropriate to describe Ireland's independence struggle as it is to characterize the global anti-colonial movements that Ireland's experience foreshadowed. This conjunction of the cultured intellectual with the man who unrepentantly took up arms in a nationalist struggle clearly sticks in the craw of the contemporary academic historian even as it fascinated the writers and artists O'Malley would meet in his US sojourn in the late 1920s and early 1930s. It is a strange and remarkable thing that the editor of O'Malley's Civil War papers, Anne Dolan, would commence her introductory essay on the papers by citing no less a rancorous and inveterate anti-Republican than journalist Kevin Myers, who accuses O'Malley of being '[t]he literary model for the killer-as-writer' who 'oozed the cant of the artist-killer, flaunting the exquisite sensitivity of the terrorist unflinchingly attending to a regrettable historical necessity: poor creative me'. The self-advertising excess of such invective, which with grand moral self-delusion rehearses the evident but comforting fallacy that culture and violence are normatively antithetical, lacks the restraint of Sean O'Faolain's terser judgement of *On Another Man's Wound*, that it was 'a book without pity', with which Dolan opens her essay.[3] But in their conjunction these quotations nicely present the well-worn stereotype of the pitiless gunman and sentimental terrorist, old turfs around whose carefully banked embers Revisionism has for a long time warmed its hands, fostering its cozy belief in its own moral and intellectual superiority over the 'simplified version of history' which, they claim, justifies 'contemporary brutalities in relation to Northern Ireland'. As English, typical in this respect, sententiously, and rather comfortably, continues: '[s]uch validating certainties offer some comfort and are frequently used to sanction political violence; historians tend instead to offer complexities which subvert both the comfort and the sanction'.[4] Dolan understands the project of *'No Surrender Here!'* in quite similar terms (indeed, her introduction and prefatory notes for each section are consistently indebted to English's biography). That project is to retrieve from both popularly circulated myth and from the 'character' produced by O'Malley's writings themselves, a more complicated picture of the man. 'The point of this book, one could argue, is to escape his memoirs. This book is Ernie O'Malley's Civil War in his own words, Ernie O'Malley's Civil War in its own time. There is no artistry, little hindsight, there are perhaps a few more complications.'[5]

Complications there are, indeed, and the papers as a whole belie any simple image of the pitiless terrorist gunman. Taken alongside the memoirs, and set in critical but informative relation to them, they reveal both continuities and ruptures between the Anglo-Irish War and the Civil War that have equally much to say about the complexities of a decolonizing struggle, its monumental difficulties and its political momentum. In a far more finely grained way than the theoretical writings of, for example, Frantz Fanon or Amilcar Cabral, and with a considerable degree of tactical realism, O'Malley recounts the almost insuperable tasks of mobilizing a population long accustomed to being ruled by superior force, with only the most sporadic memories of insurrection, without continuous traditions of military organization (though many who fought between 1919 and 1923 had received some training in the British Army), and often sceptical as to the possibilities of overthrowing British rule when not openly hostile to the very idea. O'Malley's writings of all kinds are eloquent about the exhaustingly demanding task of organizing the IRA out of the dispersed, ill-trained and inexperienced groups of Irish Volunteers around the country, as well as the challenge of improvising guerrilla strategies, practices, flying columns, literally and figuratively 'on the run'. The officers with whom he worked were rarely promising material for guerrilla struggle, lacking in discipline and experience as they were in weapons, uncomprehending of the need for careful planning, detailed mapping, constant training, and often half-hearted in their commitment to the struggle in ways that were dangerous to those they were elected to command. The essence of guerrilla warfare is, as Tom Barry once put it in a phrase echoed later (if not borrowed from him) by both Mao Zedong and Che Guevara, 'discipline, speed, silence and mobility'.[6] None of these were easy to achieve or instil in volunteers accustomed to the rhythms of agrarian labour or traditions of easy-going conviviality. O'Malley is everywhere clear both about the enormous obstacles that the cultural formations of a long-colonized people present to mobilization and organization and about the degree of earnestness, moral and political as well as military, that the decision to engage in armed struggle demanded. Nothing in O'Malley's writings suggests the casual adventurer, the pathological killer, the fanatical terrorist. He was, however, at a remarkably young age what in a state-sanctioned military force would be called, with some admiration, a professional.[7] But he sought always to be a professional against the grain of most of those he worked with and in circumstances, human and military, that made the sustained organizational structures that shape the professional soldier impossible to achieve.

It is this commitment and its frequent frustration that counterpoints, in surprisingly moving ways, the passages of lyrical description of the Irish countryside or the accounts of raids and ambushes for which *On Another Man's Wound* is probably more commonly remembered. In both the encounter with a rural Ireland largely unknown to him before and in the slow and frustrating process of getting to know the people with whom and among whom he worked, O'Malley, indeed, anticipates the dilemmas of the decolonizing intellectual militant whom Fanon so memorably describes in *The Wretched of the Earth* as the inevitable product of a colonial formation.[8] And O'Malley is by no means oblivious to the contradictions his position entails any more than he and other Republicans were to the deconstructive *mise-en-abyme* that faces *any* political organization that is obliged to forge the very people in whose name it clams to speak, a dilemma exacerbated by the mentalities of the colonized:

> I was on the outside. I felt it in many ways by a diffidence, by an extra courtesy, by a silence. Some were hostile in their minds; others in speech; often the mother would think I was leading her son astray or the father would not approve of what the boys were doing. We of the Volunteers were talked of at first: 'Musha, God help them, but they haven't a stim of sinse.' Yet there was a tradition of armed resistence [sic], dimly felt; it would flare up when we carried out some small successful raid or made a capture. Around the fire it would be discussed; it would heighten the imagination of those who were hostile. In their minds a simple thing became heroic and epical. Perhaps the sense of glory in the people was stirred, and the legend that had been created about myself, whom they did not know, helped them to accept me as part of it.
>
> I felt that I should be able to fuse with my material, so that I could make better use of it; yet look at them dispassionately, as if from a distance. My approach to teaching and training of the men was impersonal; they would have to learn to do without me, to depend on themselves and to avoid too much trust in what they considered leadership. This often meant a cold quality creeping in, but few could mingle with them without gaining warmth.[9]

To read O'Malley on the process of forging and waging guerrilla war, on the obstacles and the hindrances, on the groping and cumulative lessons of experience and often fatal error, is far from the reading of an adventure story by John Buchan, to whom Dolan in passing compares O'Malley. His writing is far too attuned to the costs and losses, the peculiar mix of instrumentality and human warmth, violence and compassion, that compose both the terrain of guerrilla war and the underlying conditions of colonial culture from which it seeks emancipation.

With hindsight it is easy to cast the Republican struggle as the misguided product of inflexible principle and idealism and, worse, as the enactment of a fundamentally anti-democratic and religious adherence to a cause bound to failure, callously taking with it the lives of many former comrades and Irish non-combatants. This is the politics of blood sacrifice that has become the commonplace of analyses of a later generation of Republicans since Richard Kearney's myth-making essay of the 1970s, 'Myth and Terror'.[10] It is a motif that Dolan uncritically repeats in her assessment of O'Malley and of the Republicans in general – 'the obstinate man who seemed so desperate to fight', 'a man who always seemed to know that he had failed', a soldier with a 'contempt for electoral politics … that he shared with many of his republican peers'.[11] But to a reading less predetermined by the conventional myths about Republicanism, the memoranda reveal a genuinely complicated picture. They are, of course, documents composed by soldiers already committed to a cause and a campaign, written to record the day-to-day activities of an underground organization, and accordingly lacking any general discussion of political principles or utopian hopes.[12] What they provide, through the tantalizing picture they offer of one small segment of a war fought from locality to locality, is a sense of the process of the struggle and, more importantly, insight into what at least some of the Republican commanders thought they might achieve. Aware that they have no control of the apparatuses of the state or of the media for propaganda, O'Malley remains for some time convinced that through proactive military engagement with the Free State forces, public opinion might be swung to the anti-Treaty side. His often expressed desire for 'a return to the field, a return to active command in the west' seems less the Buchan-ish man of action's intoxication with action for its own sake, than part and parcel of his conviction that only by taking the fight to the Free State could the propaganda as well as the military victory be won.[13] It is a strategic more than a psychological or quasi-religious conviction, and one he came to in the light of the gradual development of the IRA's popular support during the Anglo-Irish War in which O'Malley had just played so active a role.

But the need to portray O'Malley as the callous, fanatical diehard slants the editor's reading of the documents assembled here throughout, and often in interestingly symptomatic ways. There is the peculiarly insensitive response to O'Malley's apparent indifference to his younger brother's death as compared to his sorrow at the death of a fellow prisoner, Jimmy Mooney: 'There was little sadness at his brother Charles's death … He had more in common with a fellow prisoner than with a brother he no longer really knew.'[14] Dolan here omits the crucial evidence that O'Malley's writings supply. He writes with considerable cultural as well as personal insight in a long – and invaluable – autobiographical letter from prison to Molly Childers, Erskine Childers' widow, about his middle-class Irish family and its inability to foster loving relations: 'There was very little love in the family. I can honestly say that I never loved my parents, but I respected them.'[15] Home life, he explains, 'was none too congenial as its ties were never strong enough'.[16] The sense of lack of affect is hardly unique to the O'Malley (or Malley) family in the Ireland of the time or for many generations since, and it would be more valuable to consider how the intersection of Victorian values and colonial culture may have impacted the 'structures of feeling' in Ireland at the time of the revolution than resort to normative family values that imply that there is something essentially inhumane in O'Malley's lack of grief for a brother whom he had hardly seen during long years on the run. Jimmy Mooney, to the contrary, was not merely 'a fellow prisoner', but a young man who acted as O'Malley's orderly and effective nurse in prison and with whom O'Malley shared music and probably reading.[17] Indeed, the portrayal of O'Malley as a man with little affective relation to others and limited capacity for friendship, an assumption that Dolan shares with Richard English, is belied in a passage of the letter to Childers that is appalling in its matter-of-fact roll call of dead friends, lost not only in the Irish wars but also in the British military – fifteen in all, including his older and closest brother Frank, who died in the British Army in East Africa. It is scarcely an index of his lack of feeling that O'Malley should remark: 'now I am often afraid to make friendships'.[18] Indeed, a later letter from O'Malley to Dorothy Brett, written while he was living in Taos, New Mexico, on the occasion of her friend D.H. Lawrence's death, is both sensitive and moving in itself and further evidence of O'Malley's own meditations on the question of loss and grief that the Irish wars so clearly forced him to confront:

> I have seen so many of my comrades die that death seems as much part of life as life itself. Yet I know there were some deaths that I never recovered from. They left a strange void which has always remained a gap, yet a communion as well for I can feel the dead, nor would I be surprised to find someday that they walked in to resume an interrupted conversation. I found it easier to get over the losses in my own family than I did those of my friends. Somehow a family makes some kind of barrier and the members of it often live in little compartments of their own. Their very intimacy in adolescence seems to prevent a fusion when growth has been reached.[19]

Yet this shadow of unfeelingness constantly haunts the reception of O'Malley in what one can only term counter-insurgency historicism. The convention that a commitment to revolutionary principles goes hand-in-hand with callousness and indifference to ordinary human affects has a long genealogy, finding its classic expression in Edmund Burke's *Reflections on the Revolution in France* and its invocation of the notoriously callous Marie-Antoinette as the repository of humane traditions and right feeling. Not surprisingly, then, it is around O'Malley's relation to the women to whom he writes from prison that the ascription to him of a certain emotional indifference unfolds. Dolan suggests that 'the letters by Ernie O'Malley's mother are particularly telling. Notably changing her name from Malley to O'Malley for her later correspondence, she presents a very different perspective of civil war than that of her son ... By the time of Ernie O'Malley's capture in November 1922, Marion Malley had lost two sons – Frank in East Africa and Charles, aged seventeen, in the Dublin fighting in July 1922. Two more boys were imprisoned and Ernie was reportedly dying with multiple bullet wounds.'[20] This – her 'great heartbreak and worry' – writes Dolan, 'was a mother's understanding of war'.[21] To O'Malley's mother, as opposed to Molly Childers and Sighle Humphreys, 'who sang from the same republican hymnal', 'there was nothing more than "those wretched awful Irish affairs", that had in whatever form taken the lives of two of her sons and imprisoned three more'.[22]

The stereotype, quite evidently posed against the Pearsean virago-mother who is willing to sacrifice her sons for the nation, presents Marion Malley as the vessel of feeling, as the grieving, desperate mother, at the same time depriving her of agency or intelligence, political engagement or analysis. We are supposed to receive the response to the Anglo-Irish and Civil Wars as 'those wretched Irish affairs' (which can scarcely include Frank's death in British wars to hold on to their other colonial possessions in East Africa) as the index of true maternal feeling, free of ideology or myth. If the stereotype of the sacrificial Mother Ireland has its genealogy in Yeats's Cathleen ni Houlihan and Pearse's poems, this counter-stereotype has an equally distinguished genealogy in O'Casey's melodramas, novels like O'Flaherty's *The Informer*, or films like *Some Mother's Son*. It requires, of course, the consistent denial of women's agency in the Republican struggle, even as it seeks to imply the illiberal masculinism, even misogyny and anti-feminism of the Republican struggle – indeed, of anti-colonial struggles in general. Republican women activists and supporters are reduced to automatons, singing from 'the republican hymnal'. And Marion O'Malley (to use the name she herself adopted) has to be effectively censored by selection to produce this image of her. One statement, unsigned but apparently in her handwriting, also on O'Malley's medical condition, presents a quite different sense of her than that 'she thought only of her child in danger and pain'.[23] In it, she records her conversations with the doctor treating O'Malley in prison, Henry Barniville: 'I spoke that day about the shooting of

[Erskine] Childers. His remark was – you need not fear – the four men were robbers and Childers was a spy. Well, I spoke up and said I am ashamed of you and his reply was you and I won't agree. I said not on your politics anyhow.'[24] She continues with an entirely political judgement of Barniville: 'In my opinion (and a good many Dublin people know it) Dr Barniville acted a real blackleg and did the Free State dirty work well by treating his patient so badly – and he will yet suffer for his lack of attention to that poor wounded boy.'[25] It is hard to square such political statements with the image of Marion O'Malley as the apolitical grieving mother. The tone and contents of this document, that was apparently not written for official consumption, is quite different from those Dolan relies on, written to Free State Minister for External Affairs, Desmond Fitzgerald, and begging for official intervention on Ernie's behalf. Like so many of the documents in this collection, her letters need to be read in their contexts and can be seen clearly to be acutely attuned to them. Ironically, though, the attempt to pose Ernie's callousness against his mother's 'natural' grief ends up, as so often in Revisionist interpretative selection, to be itself quite misogynist.

Comparable simplification takes place in the effort to portray O'Malley's class position in relation to the Republican movement as a whole. Sometimes it is simply silly, as in Dolan's caricature of one of O'Malley's Civil War safe houses, that of the Humphreys family on Ailesbury Road, during a two-month period that ended in his bloody capture, a period that she describes as being 'like civil war the Jeeves and Wooster way'.[26] As O'Malley explained in *The Singing Flame*, the location was chosen for its very unlikeliness: it was in a 'sedate, leisurely, respectable and imperial' neighbourhood and the house itself 'was so frankly Republican that I thought it would not be suspect'.[27] It would have been difficult, given the necessity of his location in the capital, for him to have hidden out 'in the barns of the simple farmers', and given the house-to-house searches then in progress throughout Dublin, the choice seems a quite logical bluff.[28] The point of such caricatures is, of course, to dispel the myth 'of a united band of comrades fighting for Irish freedom'.[29] But the myth is itself yet another historical myth. No one who studies nationalist movements anywhere is unaware of the peculiarities produced by the fact that what they seek to achieve is what the Indian historian Bipan Chandra has termed the 'vertical integration' of class-stratified colonial societies, rather than the 'horizontal comradeship' by which Benedict Anderson characterizes the dream of the nation.[30] It is the process that Fanon explores in depth in his essays on the role of the intellectual in decolonizing movements, where the acculturated and generally middle-class nationalist intellectual has to overcome a range of prejudices, tastes and distastes, and ideological assumptions in order even to begin to comprehend 'the occult spaces where the people dwell' as he puts it.[31] In his memoirs, O'Malley – in rather less poetical and perhaps more self-ironizing and dispassionate terms – explores with some honesty his difficulties in entering into the mores, diet and poverty of rural Ireland while staying among small farming families (whom he never describes as 'simple' nor holds, as Dolan claims, in contempt). When O'Malley admits in his autobiographical letter to Childers that he 'was hated thoroughly', it is clear in the context Dolan withholds that he was hated not for his class but for his rigorous discipline and expectations.[32] Indeed, the resentment that O'Malley suffers and any contempt that he shows rarely concerns the ordinary volunteers but mostly involves the largely middle-class officers who failed to carry through orders and instructions and consequently endangered the men under their command. As he reflected from prison to Liam Lynch, in a letter that probably refers to an article on him in *An Phoblacht*, 'Most of all I would have liked to talk about the rank and file where I found much solace when broken hearted with the officers.'[33]

One could enumerate at tedious length numerous other such distortions-by-selection that riddle the prefatory material of each section of the book. They share a single tendency, one they have in common with English's biography, which is to present, under the rubric of historical complexity, a simplified portrait of O'Malley as intransigent Republican, as out of touch with the plain people of Ireland, as a romantic committed to violent struggle for its own sake. The portrait is one that it is difficult to sustain in the face of voluminous evidence, much of it presented in the invaluable two volumes of his papers now available to us, that furnishes material for a genuinely more complex picture of Republican militancy and of the contradictions they worked with in a war of decolonization. Such a portrait would, of course, require a much broader context for comparison than most academic Irish historians are willing or able to engage, and a much richer and more critical theoretical framework for doing so. Within such a context, the contradictions O'Malley both confronts and articulates, the difficulties of engaging in a war of decolonization in a country whose population still has, in language he draws from a long tradition of Irish nationalist analysis while anticipating later thinkers like Cabral and Fanon, 'the slave mind', even the reasons for the relative brevity of the post-Treaty civil war, would be both illuminated and illuminating.[34] Certainly none of these aspects of the period could be so crassly reduced to the psychological peculiarities of individual participants. We might, indeed, learn to read O'Malley's and others' memoirs as often self-critical theoretical reflections rather than as tissues of '[e]mbellishment, artistry, hindsight, lies'.[35] For example, O'Malley comments in *On Another Man's Wound*, to give just one example, that '[a]reas of the country had a habit of going to sleep. They would wake up after a century or more and step into a gap. This unexpected quality was there in what I knew to be a bad area. It might awaken of itself: the times and situation might start the spark.'[36] Such remarks are richly suggestive as to the peculiar rhythms and temporalities of popular resistance to colonialism. Similarly, there has been little work in Irish historiography to compare with that of, for instance, Reynaldo C. Ileto, on the Philippines, that could illuminate imaginatively what 'spirituality' (understood by both Dolan and English in unhelpfully restrictive terms as Catholicism and romantic nationalism) might actually represent in terms of the ways in which anti-colonial popular movements lay hold of and transform for radical purposes the available religious rhetorics.[37] Governed by the kind of division between the spiritual and the material that Partha Chatterjee has explored as an essential – and deeply gender-coded – aspect of nationalism, and that recurs as an essential aspect of the division of spheres in the liberal state, they are unable to read as fundamentally political a terminology expressed as spiritual. Consequently, they can only read the use of a language of spirituality by imprisoned Republicans as a recursion to the institutional Catholicism that would come to dominate the Free State and to which, on the contrary, such usage may be deeply opposed.[38] The intellectual damage suffered by Irish historiography by its leading exponents' casual and usually sparsely informed dismissals of postcolonial theory, not to mention their apparent lack of awareness of the long and voluminous histories of decolonization globally, is nowhere more evident than in the limited and ideologically driven scholarship on the Republican movement and on the Irish Revolution.

This is hardly surprising, since what underlies the dismissal out of hand of colonial contexts for the understanding of Irish history is itself a contest over legitimacy and sovereignty, with all the consistently deferred questions about the normativity of violence or coercion that shadow such debates. Thus Richard English's biography of O'Malley postures about objectivity and complexity and performs a pseudo-ethical fastidiousness about O'Malley's participation in an 'elitist' militarist movement that 'acted in the name of the people while disavowing much that the people actually believed'.[39] Yet the assertion turns out to be little more than a covert legitimation of the establishment of Northern Ireland – that 'Protestant state for a Protestant people' – against the will of the majority of what was then the political unit of Ireland. The traces of the repressed are very close to the surface here. What is always at stake in delegitimizing Republicanism is the legitimation of a state forged out of the refusal, backed by the very real threat of force by both an armed minority and the colonial power, to accept what was the will of the electoral majority. That that state had to survive by the virtually perpetual exercise of a state of exception in the form of the Special Powers Act, in order to coerce the large minority incorporated into the state, is what brings to the fore over and over again the problem of sovereignty and the roots of *both* post-independence states in violence. To a historiography a little more theoretically informed, and less driven to hide behind the conventional humanist truisms of academic historicism, this insight would provoke a little less anxiety and make of Ireland a remarkably interesting case study through which recent debates on violence and sovereignty that derive from the contemporaneous work of Weimar political theorist Carl Schmitt and of critical theorist Walter Benjamin could be comparatively addressed.[40]

But to do so would mean relinquishing a cherished belief in the merely curative intervention of state-sanctioned violence as in the innocence of civil society and the status quo that defends it. It would demand addressing the violence of the colonial state itself, rather than understanding the police work of the state to be directed at a primordial violence that emanates from the colonized. It would mean confronting the fact that non-violent civil disobedience movements in Ireland, from the Repeal Association to the Northern Ireland Civil Rights Association (NICRA), have been understood and confronted by the British state, just as in other colonial contexts, as if they were violent insurrections and therefore subject to coercion. This is so precisely because, as Benjamin understood, such movements question the legitimacy of the state, challenging its very existence.[41] It would mean understanding that the context for the Irish Revolution and for its violent unfolding lies in the consistent reliance of the British state itself on the use of force. It is another of the peculiar oddities of *'No Surrender Here!'* that, despite its possibly even unwitting ideological agenda, it should be introduced by a remarkably forthright essay by the eminent historian J.J. Lee that argues precisely this. Lee commences his essay on the background to the Irish Revolution by pointing out the simple fact that 'The British were by this stage [1898] normally stationing between 25,000 and 30,000 troops in Ireland, and maintaining about 10,000 police, the Royal Irish Constabulary, as an armed force, in contrast to the unarmed police of Britain.'[42] (This presence of an *armed* police force is among the many things that make colonial Ireland resemble colonial India or West Africa more than Britain itself.) The constitutionalist Nationalist party 'simply assumed this as a fundamental reality'.[43] The fact that that assumption was determining has, however, often been occluded by historians and it is testimony to the efficacy of British self-representation as a 'civil' power that this occlusion has been so consistent. As Lee points out:

> The gun was already there, as the fundamental fact of political power, the bedrock on which British domination was based. That it can be conjured out of existence is

either wishful thinking or testimony to the hallucinogenic impact of British mind games. The power of domination derives even more from capturing the minds than the bodies of the dominated – whether in terms of nationality, race, ethnicity, religion, class, gender, age or any other marker of identity. Part of the genius of British domination skills in Ireland was to so skillfully disguise the elementary fact that British gun-power determined the framework within which Irish politics operated. The suffocating skill of British control techniques had ensured that for many, British guns in Ireland were somehow purged of any association with violence. Conquest was not violence. It was only resistance to conquest that was violence.[44]

If, as O'Malley well saw, this context made the Irish resort to arms 'an exercise in basic political education ... stripping away the beguiling but self-deluding facade of "constitutionalism", behind which the British gun was disguised', the force of British and Unionist guns no less determined the partition of Ireland against the will of the majority of the population.[45] Richard English is typical of Revisionist historians and journalists who are accustomed to accuse the Republicans of having sought to exclude 'large numbers of Irish people' from the Irish nation[46] in an undemocratic resort to force, but, as Lee points out, '[t]he line of the border stood as irrefutable evidence that far from achieving nothing, [Unionist] command of violence was crucial in determining the outcome of the conflict over partition'.[47] Along with other Republicans, O'Malley 'grasped the terrible simplicity that so many others chose to ignore, the elemental truth that the gun was the basis for British control over Ireland. Getting the British gun out of Irish life was a prerequisite for the creation of a sovereign Irish state.[48] What Republicans understood themselves to be resisting was, in effect, the acceptance by their counterparts of state terrorism, encapsulated in Lloyd George's infamous threat of 'immediate and terrible war'.[49] But fundamentally at issue, if veiled by its expression through the symbolic form of the oath of allegiance, was the question of sovereignty; sovereignty is not merely a question of 'symbolic supremacy', of 'honour' or 'status', as Lee suggests.[50] 'Sovereign is he', as Carl Schmitt put it, 'who decides on the exception'.[51] Sovereignty is at once the decision over the power of lawmaking itself and over the life and death of the subjects of the state. Or, as Benjamin was to put it in an essay Schmitt much admired, 'Lawmaking is powermaking, assumption of power, and to that extent an immediate manifestation of violence.'[52] That is, the state's sovereignty, its authority or *Gewalt*, rests on its monopoly of violence. For Republicanism, the limited sovereignty offered by the Treaty was a contradiction in terms, leaving the monopoly of violence in the hands of the colonial power. Ironically perhaps, the terrible miscalculation of *force majeure* that led O'Malley and others to believe that resistance to the Free State could be a further 'exercise in basic political education', and bring the coerced majority to their side, may have concluded by establishing, with British assistance, the monopoly of violence effectively in the hands of that very Free State. For, as Kevin O'Higgins well knew in ordering the execution of Republican prisoners in reprisal for ambushes, 'in the exercise of violence over life and death, more than in any other legal act, the law reaffirms itself'.[53] The fratricidal violence of the Civil War was as terrible as it was precisely because it was at every level about the state's non-negotiable monopoly of violence. But it would be the merest 'wishful thinking' to believe that the surrender of the Republicans removed the shadow of violence from the state, any more than the establishment of Northern Ireland could avoid casting forward the perpetual question of its legitimacy.

It is of course the ruse of the state to persuade its population that what it represents is a normative state of peace and non-coercion to which violence is the irruptive exception. Essential to that ruse is the division of social spheres. While the state retains the right of resort to force to preserve the law and to protect the citizen, civil society is assumed to operate normally without coercion. Yet at the heart of civil society, and at the core of what the law is established to preserve, is the principle of private property, a principle in its essence predicated upon violence. Historicism, whose means and end are the civil society that sanctions its supposed academic disinterest, offers to legitimate the established state by proposing a critique of violence that always stops short of the critique of state violence. Masquerading as an ethical humanism, pretending to a judicious complexity its caricatures and predictability belie, it maintains a posture of moral purity and empirical scruple against the terrible certainties of the idealist while residing comfortably in the sanctuary of the violence of the state. The challenge that a figure like O'Malley presents to such comfortable assurance lies less in the violence in which he engaged than in the principle of non-violence that he aspired to make possible, one embodied in the Republican aspiration for a society predicated on non-domination.[54] While the liberal democratic state has shown itself remarkably accommodating to coercion and domination, whether by transnational corporations or the security apparatus, European political elites or military alliances, the alternative to violence as means and foundation of the political order may yet be found, not in the pieties of Revisionist moralizing, but from the perspective of a radical non-violence. Only from such a perspective could the means to which O'Malley resorted, for ends that were ultimately their antithesis, finally be adjudicated. O'Malley's post-Civil War life and work embody those ends: he connects the legacies of Irish Republicanism to international modernism, integrating an aesthetic commitment to the local with a cosmopolitan interconnection and a philosophy of non-domination with the safeguarding of cultural difference.

*

Jack B. Yeats's haunting painting, *The Funeral of Harry Boland* (1922), is unusual in his oeuvre. Its uncharacteristic quality is not due to its explicitly political theme, commemorating the funeral of the anti-Treaty Republican who was murdered by Free State forces while seeking to escape arrest, for it belongs among a number of such paintings, sympathetic to Irish nationalism and to the Republican struggle, that Yeats produced throughout his life.[55] It is, rather, unusual for its formal qualities. Yeats's paintings are generally composed around a strong triangle converging at a vanishing point away from the picture plane, occasionally with such triangles overlapping one another. *The Funeral of Harry Boland*, however, is marked by a line of vertical forms – mourners, gravestones, trees – that virtually bisects the painting horizontally, and these elements are united by the lower portion of a round tower that amplifies the vertical thrust of the painting and dominates the centre. Separated from it by the line of mourners, and balancing it, as the visual centre of the painting, is the wreath-covered grave of Boland, which forms a visually peculiar horizontal void among the standing mourners. It succeeds in emphasizing the isolation of the figure generally identified as Kevin O'Higgins, Free State Minister of Justice, from the other mourners, and also interrupts what might otherwise have been the left side of a dark triangle running from the black-clad mourners centre left through a small group of similarly dark figures on the far side of the grave and then culminating in the tree-shadowed upright of an obelisk or monument to the right of the round tower. At this point, that dark line might have met the corresponding line running from O'Higgins through another group of dark mourners, completing the visual triangle that should unify the composition. It is as if the absence of Boland in death prevents the completion of his commemoration, making of memorial a rupture and leaving a void at the heart of the work. That void, indeed, in a kind of visual pun, is re-echoed through the hollow forms of the wreaths laid on the grave and borne by the mourners who face the viewer.

The presence of the Free State's first Minister of Justice, who presided over the executions, carried out as reprisals for Republican actions during the Civil War, and who was therefore responsible for the elimination of many of the movement's foremost leaders and intellectuals, may suggest that this void constitutes a challenge to the very legitimacy of the state that his insistence on the prerogative of legally sanctioned violence was designed to establish. The moment of commemoration fails to represent the consolidation of the new state, laying to rest the conflicts out of which it was forged, but shelters instead an absence at its core. As Nicholas Allen has argued in his recent *Modernism, Ireland and Civil War*, the persistent failure of the republic to be realized remains as a kind of absent centre in Irish culture, even as the surviving figures who had stood most clearly for it either withdrew much of their commitment or felt themselves marginalized in the culturally conservative Free State.[56] Yet, politically and institutionally marginalized as they may have been, or may have felt themselves to be, Republican intellectuals and artists maintained a constant critique of the state which, far from being the atavistic and backward-looking caricature of recent Revisionist writings, was often associated with the most aesthetically advanced and culturally progressive work of post-independence Ireland and with the ongoing project of decolonization. Yeats, the leading and probably the most experimentally restless of twentieth-century Irish painters, may be one prime instance of this tendency, such that Samuel Beckett, in his review of MacGreevy's book, foregrounded Yeats's commonalities with the great European painters even as he balked at MacGreevy's specifically spiritual and expressive version of nationalism.[57]

Certainly Ernie O'Malley, friend to all three of the above, may be considered among an extensive group of internationalist, socially and culturally critical Republicans who contributed to the shaping of an experimental, cosmopolitan, and decolonizing culture at the margins of official Irish culture. In the wake of the Civil War, after a somewhat frustrating tour of the United States seeking to raise funds for de Valera's *Irish Press* (a paper O'Malley hoped, perhaps over-optimistically, would further an independent, decolonized public opinion Ireland), he spent several years in New Mexico, Mexico, and around New York and New England, where he befriended numerous artists and writers in the bohemian subcultures of Taos, Yaddo and the Group Theatre workshop. Among those he encountered, some of whom would become lifelong friends, were photographers Paul Strand and Edmund Weston, Hart Crane, Clifford Odets, Lee Strasberg, and Georgia O'Keefe. In Ireland, after his return, his friends included Liam O'Flaherty, Denis Devlin, the painters Evie Hone, Nano Reid, Mainie Jellett, and Louis le Brocquy, in addition to MacGreevy, Yeats and Beckett. His letters and notebooks furnish the record of his generally ethically and aesthetically demanding responsiveness to a remarkable range of artists and art forms, from Mexican art to Asian music, from old Irish sculpture to contemporary theatre; a responsiveness that, on account of the format of these mostly private remarks, is singularly woven together with his judgements on individuals and on politics and society, as well as with the often desolating daily history of a crumbling marriage and with the efforts of a committed father to maintain his relationship to his children. They also reveal an intense engagement with art and artists that is part of what O'Malley himself understood as part of his own 'spiritual self-culture'.

The link O'Malley makes between spiritual culture and decolonization – or its truncation – is never fully theorized but is a constant of his writings from the time of his imprisonment, when he had cause to reflect on the failure of the Republican project of a total decolonization of Ireland. That project, which involved both political sovereignty and the liberation of Irish cultural attitudes from their continuing subservience to English values as to British domination, was the ideal for which Republicans fought and for which partition and the oath to the crown were vital obstacles in distinct registers. O'Malley's own adherence to a left-wing interpretation of this struggle, which clearly embraced a spectrum of ideological positions, is everywhere evident. It is evident in his description at several points of the Irish Revolution as being one 'between exploiters and exploited'; in his consistent anti-fascism and support for Republican Spain; in his respect for indigenous peoples in New Mexico and Mexico; in his association in the United States with left-wing cultural movements like the Group Theatre; and in his sympathy with the down-and-out, unemployed and striking men during the Depression that he experienced firsthand on his American sojourn.[58] However, the scepticism that he shows at every juncture towards what he regards as the 'clichés' and 'isms' of political organizations challenges the reader to assemble some consistent sense of O'Malley's post-independence politics.[59]

It is in the context of his imprisonment that O'Malley begins to reflect in a sustained way on the failure of Republicanism and in this context that he begins to place his emphasis on what he recurrently terms the 'spiritual' aspect of the struggle. That this has little to do with spirituality in the New Age sense, and equally little to do with organized religion, is quite clear. His concern is with the failure to move beyond immediate, pragmatic political or military goals and to engage with the question of nationality, by which he seems to mean precisely the problem of decolonization understood as the realization of cultural difference. If the problem of colonization, as so many theorists of decolonization have argued, is the assimilation of the cultural norms and mores of the colonizer, together with an implicit assumption of their superiority, then the process of decolonization necessarily involves a cultural – or spiritual – declaration of independence and its actualization. For O'Malley, the Treaty represented not only a succumbing to British state terror – to Lloyd George's threat of 'immediate and terrible war' – but additionally the consequence of a failure to develop a decolonized sense of national culture. Writing to Sheila [Sighle] Humphreys, a fellow Republican prisoner, in the wake of the failed hunger strike of 1923, O'Malley sketches a critique of the superficial national sentiment ('enthusiasm') that the Republican struggle engendered and an assessment of the need for a more thorough decolonization:

Previously I have pointed out that our traditions are wrong and that we foster them knowingly or without thought. We are and have been slaves and so have the slave mind. The open fighting of 1920–1921 and some of the fighting of 1922–1923 has helped somewhat to eradicate slavish defects, but at heart we are still slaves and have slaves' meannesses and lack of moral qualities. It is inevitable. All enslaved nations have ever been the same …

I'm afraid it will take a big length of time to make up for the personal loss of the [19]16 group. [Patrick] Pearse and his group set out to minister to the spiritual side of the nation. They were replaced by [Michael] Collins and [Richard] Mulcahy neither of whom, from what I could see of them during the 1918–21 fighting, were spiritual; they had genius for work though. For years these men directed and in the end, attempted to direct a guerilla war – a most demoralising form of the most demoralising kind of war. If at the same time they had directed effort to keep the national soul up to the proper pitch of spirituality and not of enthusiasm all would have been well.[60]

We await, even yet, an objective and internationally comparative assessment of Pearse's understanding of Irish decolonization, but it is clear from the bulk of O'Malley's writings that he stands, not for the spirit of blood sacrifice and fanatical spiritual nationalism that he has come to represent, but rather for a Republicanism vested in the popular ownership of land and resources and a decolonization predicated on undoing the 'slave mind' inculcated by British education and media. This is what O'Malley describes as 'the right of a people to its own soil so long as that people would not accept domination.'[61] Despite over a century of nationalist organization and propaganda, the resistance to domination, as O'Malley seems to see it in his reflections, was forged in the struggle rather than pre-existing it as a fully theorized body of principle or analysis. Even at the late stage of Republican discussions of their failure in the Curragh internment camp, 'all they seemed to have in common was that they resisted economic, social and clerical pressure together'.[62] Yet that very triad of qualities belies the notion that the decolonizing process could ever be either solely military or solely 'spiritual'; the problem was rather that the different aspects of that process were out of kilter: 'Driving force was there, but no vision or attempt at economic solution. There was an economic root to the fight, though many on our side would not better their position by a result in our favour. Freedom comes religious, political, economic. We were at the political stage. We had not the faculty for thinking things through sufficiently.'[63]

O'Malley proceeds to quote George Russell (Æ), himself a half-hearted proponent of nationalism, who speculated that the Irish fought for freedom 'because they feel in themselves a genius which had not yet been manifested in a civilization, as Greek, Roman and Egyptian in the past have externalized their genius in a society with a culture, arts, and sciences peculiar to themselves. Ireland, through Sinn Fein, is fighting for freedom to manifest the Irish genius'.[64] In invoking Æ in this fashion, O'Malley links his interpretation of the 'spiritual' dimension to the Revivalists' earlier efforts to forward a concept of Irish culture that was defined against what they considered the limitations of English industrial society and its monopoly on what could constitute progress or modernity.

It is, of course, all too easy at this juncture to critique such notions of genius and spirit as a legacy of romanticism that would inevitably culminate in fascism or blood-and-soil nationalism. Yet it is not a language peculiar to Irish, or even to major European state-nationalisms, but one that Irish nationalists hold in common with, for example, W.E.B. Du Bois in *The Souls of Black Folks* or Indian nationalists like Sri Aurobindo Ghose.[65] It is, indeed, their common legacy from the German romanticism of J.G. Herder and Wilhelm von Humboldt and, while it could furnish the ground for a deeply reactionary cultural politics, it could also, as the instances of Æ and Du Bois suggest, subtend the claim to the rights of small nations or oppressed peoples and assert the specific contributions of diverse cultures. If it can lead to Heidegger, it can lead no less to the cultural anthropology of a Boas or the linguistics of Sapir and Whorf; it can lead no less to the language of decolonization that refuses to admit that the only conceivable course is that of assimilation to the dominant power.[66] In the latter case, there is no contradiction between a deep investment in the cultural or aesthetic specificity of a particular people or region and a comprehensive cosmopolitanism, one grounded not in the idea of advanced civilizations but in a radical equivalence of diverse cultural modes. It anticipates what we might now think of as a kind of cultural ecologics that insists on the necessity of cultural and of biological diversity. O'Malley's career, both his travels and his reading and writings, make clear that, in the wake of Republican defeat, it is his overall project to further his own self-education as a means to a certain kind of exemplary cultural decolonization in an Irish context.

It is surely as a result of discussions in the gaols that O'Malley determines that his future work on behalf of the Republican movement would be neither military (of which he was probably no longer physically capable) nor practically political (work for which he had little inclination or aptitude), but cultural. Writing to Mabel Fitzgerald from Kilmainham in December 1923, he claims that, being physically unfit, he wishes 'to place at my country's service what training I can by reading, and think[ing]'.[67] This determination follows an exhaustingly long list of books that he has read while in gaol or intends to read and queries of other things with which he should be acquainted. The list is characteristic of many of his letters, both in his post-Civil War imprisonment and throughout the rest of his life. O'Malley was a relentless autodidact and constantly sought advice from an extraordinary range of acquaintances as to reading that he should undertake in literature or art history or music that he should hear. Given what was available to him before he had mastered languages other than English, and the limiting circumstance that he depended on books lent by friends, the lists he enumerates tend to be dominated by English Literature, from Shakespeare to Shaw, Galsworthy and Wells, even as he follows an extensive curriculum in the Anglo-Irish literature that he had started to read after 1916. In recent times, O'Malley's love of English literature has come to betoken the possibility of reconciliation, as if culture were the site of a rapprochement without decolonization, a detente that bridges domination with understanding. Declan Kiberd concludes Irish Classics with the following fable regarding Patrick Mayhew, then British Secretary of State for Northern Ireland:

> One day as this [peace] process was beginning to take shape, Mayhew read the prison letters of Ernie O'Malley, an IRA veteran of the War of Independence. He found in them to his amazement an unambiguous celebration of the masterpieces of English literature. This confirmed – even if Mayhew might not have so phrased it himself – those postcolonial theories which held that nationalism was doomed to frustration by the myth of its own singularity: only by contact with the art of other peoples could anything approaching a national culture be born. O'Malley clearly revered English literature as deeply as many of the great Anglo-Irish writers had admired Gaelic culture. What struck Patrick Mayhew most was an account of how the wounded IRA man, as he lay waiting for first aid during a long gun battle, took comfort from his pocket edition of the sonnets of Shakespeare. On the basis of that strange epiphany he concluded – rightly as it turned out – that a meaningful peace process between ancient enemies might yet be possible. Irish, or British, or both.[68]

It is a fable that appeals to – and records – a certain cultural narcissism, to be sure, and it is accordingly hopelessly partial. It is not simply that the conclusion implied, the continued partition of Ireland, is one that O'Malley could scarcely have regarded as the grounds for a 'meaningful peace process', but also that it drastically simplifies both O'Malley's attitude to English culture and the place of English literature in the larger scheme of his reading and thought. Throughout his life he took rather more seriously than this anecdote implies the need for nationalist culture to have 'contact with the art of other peoples'. What is perhaps most striking in O'Malley's efforts to reach beyond the 'prison-house' of English in the gaols and moreover in his process of self-education throughout his life, is the urgency of his need for perspectives that exceeded those that English education imposed on Irish colonial culture. It could be said, indeed, that he opposed those influences even as they persisted through Irish school and university curricula long after independence.[69] With a certain self-satisfaction, perhaps, the eye of a Mayhew, or of biographer Richard English, arrests itself at the litany of English literature to which O'Malley has access and in which he systematically immerses himself. A self-serving parablepsis occludes his equal interest in French, Russian and American writing, his insistence on teaching himself Greek, Latin and Spanish, even while in gaol, and, in particular, his lifelong reaching over the dismal wedge of England to the richer intellectual and artistic culture of the continent and beyond. 'France, Spain, New Mexico, Mexico, Italy, are my second countries', he writes to an American friend in 1955.[70]

What is at once fascinating and instructive in following the evidence of O'Malley's reading, as in following his interest in art history, is less its anglo-centrism than its breadth and its resolute modernity. Accustomed as we are to the insistence that Republicanism is and has always been a backward-looking and anti-cosmopolitan movement, insular and repressive, it is a peculiar thing to find O'Malley as a young man engaged in guerrilla warfare reading Blake and Villon 'on the grassy edge of the road' or discovering Tagore, Dostoyevski and Melville while in gaol.[71] Though Tagore and Dostoyevski (like Turgenev, Chekov and Tolstoy whom he also reads) may represent instances of alternative modernity of immense value for a Republican intellectual in a culture whose achievements were all too often evaluated in relation to English canons. Melville, and in particular *Moby Dick*, remained a touchstone throughout his life. He read *Moby Dick* aloud and passed it around in both Kilmainham and the Curragh, and a late letter in *Broken Landscapes* depicts him reading it, accompanied by much laughter, to his young children. *Moby Dick* perhaps represents the Republican allegory *par excellence*, with its heterotopic vision of a community of differences, its various struggles for both co-operation and against dominance, with its ambiguous pursuit of an ambiguous object. Certainly O'Malley interprets it thus in *The Singing Flame*:

> Moby Dick was a favourite. I had copies of it sent in to me for the men. I had re-read it many times, now I knew some of it by heart. Was not the white whale the whale of empire which devoured us, or was it the idea of freedom, which would make *brus* of us until we could improve the harpoon of a social system that would bring it alongside.[72]

Not accidentally, O'Malley's circulation of this complex work is at one with his faith in the possibility of 'spiritual' work in the gaols, confirming his belief that '[t]he feeling of the men was instinctively for what was good in subject matter'.[73] His own self-pedagogy, and his apparent indifference to institutional academic sanction throughout his life, might be seen as an unspoken commitment to that principle.

Shakespeare, of course, appears, but not always with either the solemnity or the pre-eminence Kiberd's anecdote would seem to accord him. Typical is an interlude in

O'Malley's account of the siege of the Republican-occupied Four Courts by Free State troops in *The Singing Flame*:

> My leather portmanteau had been cut and torn, my clothes and books damaged. I picked up some of my books from a shelf. Baudelaire, two al fresco prints, Tintoretto and Piero della Francesca, a portfolio of drawings. There were two bullet holes through a copy of Vasari's Lives of the Italian painters. Authors had been drilled and torn out of all proportion to the number of books. 'Bad luck to them, anyhow,' I said in the direction of a piece of artillery gone through a Synge illustrated by Jack Yeats. 'They mustn't like books or anything to do with books.' ... Cuchulainn had suffered most of all ... I turned over another undamaged volume of Vasari, and sitting on my bed read his remarks on Andrea del Sarto ... A volume of Montaigne had escaped shell and bullet. He would have been a good man to have here with us; he could have joined our philosophic discussions under the dome. I put him in my pocket where he lay beside a thin copy of Shakespeare's Sonnets which I had been reading last night. Beneath a red plush chair I found my bright yellow boots, untouched; a terrible colour to wear.[74]

Much like the Bible and Shakespeare on the desert island, The Sonnets in a military tunic pocket is a cliché of military reminiscence from the First World War to the Malvinas (Falklands). O'Malley gently ironizes it here, pairing the Sonnets with a tasteless pair of boots. Synge and Yeats, and of course Cúchulainn, one might expect in a Republican's canon, but the accompaniment of Baudelaire, Vasari, Montaigne comes as a considerable surprise on first reading this passage. Is this Republican reading? The sceptic and the biographer of the Renaissance, the epitomes of an inaugural moment of modernity and of the questioning rather than dogmatic possibilities of European catholic culture, appear alongside the dark angel of urban modernity even as another modern city is being reduced to rubble, not by Haussmannization but by government shelling.

The episode, like O'Malley's engagement in the next decade with American modernists, reminds us that Republicanism is not, as Kiberd characterizes nationalism, 'another in the long line of attempts to cope with modernity', but itself an agent and an effect of modernity.[75] But what O'Malley's intellectual career suggests is that what he finds at stake here is not the modernization of Ireland, understood in accord with capitalist modernization internationally, but an alternative modernity that seeks to assert its difference from that path. Despite O'Malley's highly prized self-discipline, he remained an autodidact and his intellectual formation was haphazard and interrupted and often conditioned by the contingencies of his encounters and by the resources available to him in rural Mayo where he settled after the mid-1930s. Nonetheless, reading through his assembled papers and published writings, one can discern the outlines of a consistently held set of principles that conjoin his interest in the art of Western Europe with both his enduring concern for Irish art and his interests in culture further afield. Within these contexts, he grasps both Ireland's 'incongruity' and its affiliations. The Anglo-Irish War was 'a clash between two mentalities, two trends in direction, and two philosophies of life'; differences that were never seen by O'Malley in essentialist terms, but – as they also were viewed by James Connolly – as specific characteristics determined by Ireland's anomalous history.[76] As O'Malley was to put it in an article for *Architectural Digest*:

> Ireland is a country difficult to assess, for the ordinary measuring stick may not give the best results …
>
> Her people carry into the modern world some qualities which belong to another age and which may appear incongruous. Either by accident or design the Irish have avoided some incidents in world history which have helped to shape the European scene: Roman occupation, the Renaissance, the Industrial Revolution and in recent times, the last world war and conscription. The lack of a sense of centralized authority might have come from the Romans; instead it came very much later in time, through the British [*sic*]. Explicit participation in the Renaissance can be dimly sensed in a study of poetry in Irish, but aspects of the medieval mind can be more easily seen in every day use …
>
> We speak English but, with mouths shaped from long centuries of a native language, our pronunciation and lack of stress is different. English with us has also a different intuitional and psychological value as it represents a completely different consciousness and tradition.[77]

Part of the European Catholic cultural and philosophical world, Ireland is also anomalous in it. But its anomaly is not understood simply as backwardness in relation to some norm of modernity, but as a set of alternative resources the Irish 'carry into the modern world'. For O'Malley and other Republican intellectuals, these resources are not hindrances to be overcome in order to modernize, but potentialities to be unfolded in their own terms.

It is perhaps for this reason that O'Malley's encounters with Indians in New Mexico, with whom he worked in 1930 while employed in rebuilding Dorothy Brett's cabin near Taos, and with the indigenous and mestizo peoples of Mexico, remained so important to him. Initially he understands colonial relations in Mexico by analogy with Ireland. 'This is of course an Indian country though it has been ruled by whites and maztitos [*sic*];' he remarks, 'it's the problem of mixing Gaelic and Anglo-Irish and solving the problems of both …'[78] He accordingly retains his impatience with the white tourist or anthropologist in New Mexico 'who goes out there to escape humanity or to become interested in ceremonies, dance or legend of the Indians and who does not care a damn for the actual spoliation of the Indians or Mexicans there'.[79] His later essay for *The Bell* on 'The Background of the Arts in Mexico' maintains a similar perspective and insists on the same connections. 'Mexico', it opens, 'is of interest to Ireland because for over three centuries it has been subject to foreign domination and for close on a century and a half it has been struggling to integrate itself.[80] The essay ends with a more extended reflection on the similarity between the position of the Irish and the Mexican Indian:

> The burden bearer, the Indian, in passive despair and apathy threw [*sic*] all conscious-ness of contact with his oppressors although in remote regions he could preserve his enduring bodily strength and his way of life. His culture had been destroyed and despised, monuments of his race had been heaped over with earth or split by forest growth and the Indian was not even vaguely aware of the contribution of his race to world history.
>
> In some such manner the Irish of the 18th century have been isolated from and unaware of their achievements in the past. They had withdrawn from the conscious life of their conquerors as if they were living in another dimension. The plastic arts were not even a dim memory. Literature was a survival of the tongue, history was kept alive by folklore memory alone. Criticism in the creative sense had neither material to work on nor educated people to work with.[81]

O'Malley continues to make some unexpected remarks that distinguish the situation of Mexican from that of Irish art:

> Mexican pre-conquest art has an advantage over Irish material in that the former has little history associated with the objects unearthed or already in position. This lack of history can help when objects are looked at for their own sake and as an end in them-selves. They have then less to do with factual information or with literary association, but demand more attention from the eye and a more sympathetic perception of form and design.[82]

In Ireland, on the contrary, 'history is used as a compensation for a vanished past for which there has been no critical understanding as a result of the lack of continuity in the tradition of scholarship'.[83] Such remarks may seem odd, coming as they do from one who devoted his life to the study of Irish and Western European art history and who has just demonstrated considerable mastery of Mexican art and history. Yet it is, on consid-eration, of a piece with the praise he gives to the French archaeologist Francoise Henry for her rich 'aesthetic approach'.[84] He opposes this approach to the 'museum outlook', which, 'with its emphasis on catalogues and dates, superseded sensitive feeling'.[85] What is striking in his assessment here, however, is that what he promotes is not a pure and abstract aesthetic apprehension of the object, but a vivid juxtaposition of the contemporary and the 'primitive': 'Now that contemporary art has paid more attention to feeling, to basic rhythm and design, it has helped our age to understand and appraise primitive art work.' Not that early Irish art was primitive in any negative sense. On the contrary, it evidences a cosmopolitan 'native aptitude for seizing on an idea and altering its character' – Irish art is characterized by its capacity for 'meeting waves of foreign influences, absorbing them or possibly rejecting them, for centuries, though never scorning them'.[86] The aesthetic sense that O'Malley espouses, then, becomes a capacity for grasping the distinctive in Irish (or Mexican) art precisely by the juxtaposition of what is contemporary with what is past, what is foreign with what is local, through comparison and differentiation alike. It is, in effect, a refusal of what Walter Benjamin termed historicism, that insistence on the continuity of history or tradition through 'empty homogeneous time',[87] a refusal that is perhaps crucial to a culture whose experience of history has been that of rupture rather than continuity and for whom the artefacts of often jarringly disparate traditions are often violently pressed into alignment.

Something of this appears in O'Malley's description of the energy and clash of Mexican Baroque, with its confluence of Spanish and Indian elements: 'Line was broken at every possible angle to form recessions, and facades became as richly exuberant as interiors whilst Indian craftsmen elaborated their designs in a maze of carved or sculptured detail.'[88] On the other hand, the achievement of modernist artists like Diego Rivera, David Siqueiros and, especially, Jose Clemente Orozco, whose frescoes O'Malley preferred, was to have brought the Indian into representation, absorbing the 'high purpose' of folk art that had survived colonization and was 'invariably aesthetically satisfying'. Part of that achievement is to have 'drawn on the sculptured faces of his countrymen', faces that 'were unlike the academic Greco-Roman European tradition'.[89] In the Irish context, in his various writings on Jack B. Yeats and Louis le Brocquy, in particular, it is on the effects of landscape and light that his attention falls as much as on both artists' interest in the portrayal of Irish popular culture. Landscape becomes almost an allegory for the clashes of colonial culture, throwing up 'improbable colour combinations', 'subtle, unrelated colour which is not easily seen as pattern, but develops in strange orchestration'. The consequent 'strong dramatic sense' demands a rupture with academic convention[90] just as it fails to furnish '[t]he sense of formal composition and defined pattern met with in French landscape and elsewhere'.[91]

But in both Yeats and le Brocquy, O'Malley also discerns a tendency towards the representation of the outsider – the circus clown, the tramp, the rogue, the prisoner[92]

– that is the human correlative to the unconventionality, in painterly terms, of Irish landscape. They are also indices of the survival of a Republican mentality, as they were for MacGreevy, in his book on Yeats, and of a persistent resistance to domination. Le Brocquy's paintings of 'tinkers' of this period draw O'Malley's attention for this reason:

> Their aloofness, intractability, and fierce independence interested le Brocquy. They are, he could see, outside of the closely organized life of the parish unit, looked on with mistrust and suspicion, but generally treated with the tolerance given in the country to groups outside of its parish life. They become the symbol of the individual as opposed to organized, settled society, and to the growing power-control of the State; a symbol, also, of the distressed and dispossessed people of Europe wandering, unlike the tinkers, without hope of changing their condition by individual effort. For the creative worker they could represent the artist who deals in the unexpected and the unrecognized, and who suffuses with meaning familiar things against the inanition of their too facile and unmeaning acceptance.[93]

The enfolding here of the aesthetic and the political judgement lodged in the particular work of a given artist is typical of O'Malley's reflections on art. So also is the movement from the local condition and observation to the recognition of a wider historical situation to which Ireland has a distinct relation. At the very moment that his acquaintance Samuel Beckett is writing back to Ireland from Normandy, promising 'a vision and sense of a time-honoured conception of humanity in ruins, and perhaps even an inkling of the terms in which our condition is to be thought again', O'Malley is writing out from Ireland with a parallel vision of the legacies of dispossession and displacement that bring the Irish experience of the past into conjunction with Europe's devastated present.[94] Indeed, both in art and culture, O'Malley grasps Irish neutrality and the Emergency less as confining Ireland to a stultifying isolation than as an opportunity to fall back on itself and discover independent and distinctive resources. His perceptions, unelaborated but none the less intense, draw the traditions of Irish Republicanism into alignment with the philosophical critique of the nation state and of governmental modernity that has stemmed from Hannah Arendt's concern with the post-war displaced peoples in *The Origins of Totalitarianism*, to the work of Giorgio Agamben on the fate of the Roma and other minorities in the contemporary period.[95] It also foreshadows a later Republican solidarity with the Palestinians, displaced from their own historical lands by a Zionist settler state.

But what is crucial to O'Malley's arriving at such networks of relation and solidarity is precisely the imbrication of the aesthetic and the political. If, as Philip Pettit has argued, the European Republican political tradition, of which the Irish forms part, has emphasized not the liberal concept of freedom in the form of non-interference, but the understanding of freedom as non-domination, there follows from that principle the primacy of cultural – or 'spiritual' – independence.[96] Just as for the individual, culture also requires freedom from domination in order to realize its own potential as a distinctive ecology of human historical experience. The demand is as much aesthetic as it is political or social: every culture takes its formation from specific historical and geographic factors that have shaped it and the function of political freedom is to allow for the unfolding of the aesthetic possibilities, in the broadest sense, that a culture implies. It is for this reason that the logic of Republicanism has tended to be anti-capitalist: O'Malley's discomfort with the homogenizing tendencies of urban American society as he saw them, is not untypical. But it is also why Republicanism has tended to remain illegible to Marxism, insistent as Western Marxist analysis has tended to be on industrialization and modernization as pre-conditions for revolutionary struggle. The Irish Republican tradition, which grew out of the conditions of primitive accumulation in eighteenth- and nineteenth-century Ireland and was articulated through the Fenians, Connolly and the left Republicans, among them O'Malley, always affirmed other possibilities than the destructive passage through industrialization and modernization for the radical transformation of the colonial order. What O'Malley discovered among the Irish people as a guerrilla fighter, the latent persistence of recalcitrance to colonial domination that could flare up into open resistance according to its own peculiar rhythm or tempo, he sought to articulate in his writing and thinking as a post-revolutionary intellectual in the form of a lifelong meditation on the specificity of Irish cultural possibilities and on their disjunctive relation to other cultures, most notably those of Catholic Europe and of Mexico. If the patterns of his thought are at times hard to decipher, it is not only because of the disparate and fugitive nature of most of the writings collected here, but largely on account of the fact that, in no way an institutionalized or formally trained intellectual, O'Malley inhabited the Republican tradition more than he reflected upon it.[97] In many ways, he embodied its principles, with the unfortunate consequence that all too often, in the wake of the defeat of Republicanism in the Civil War, his own individual disdain for subservience stands in for any larger reflection on the *collective* conditions for furthering decolonization. Yet the political and aesthetic principles he did embody in his own individual way were by no means unique to O'Malley, nor are they unique to the Irish context. One finds resonances everywhere, not only with Connolly or Fintan Lalor, for example, but with Hugh MacDiarmid in Scotland or David Jones in Wales, in their appeal to specifically

Celtic cultural formations, and, more remotely, with the writings of anti-colonial intellectuals like Amilcar Cabral or Ngugi Wa Thiong'o. Precisely at a moment when a restructuring of the global order promises a more violent imposition of domination under the cover of modernization and liberal democracy, and in which the forces that defy the renewed injustices of accumulation are mostly dispersed and localized, the resources of such traditions of culturally differentiated and ecologically distinct resistance still have much to teach us.

CHAPTER SEVEN

KINDLING THE SINGING FLAME
THE DESTRUCTION OF THE PUBLIC RECORD OFFICE (30 JUNE 1922), AS A HISTORICAL PROBLEM[1]

John M. Regan

The destruction of the Public Record Office by fire and explosion on 30 June 1922 marks both the opening salvo in the Irish Civil War and a cultural atrocity unique in modern Irish history.[2] The Public Record Office, housing Ireland's national archive, and its Registry building, formed part of the building complex comprising Dublin's Four Courts of Justice. Containing documents dating to as early as the twelfth century, much of the archive was destroyed or irrevocably damaged in the conflagration.[3] This chapter addresses the different ways historians have interpreted this tragic event, alongside the role the destruction of the Public Record Office plays in the contemporary public memory. What has been in question since 1922, is on whose shoulders responsibility for the destruction lies, and the extent to which blame can be apportioned to one or other party in the Civil War. This article revisits the primary sources used by historians to examine how they have interpreted evidence and events before reaching their conclusions.

Answering somewhat mundane questions about causation and evidence, however, raises challenging issues about the relationship between the professional historian and society at large. These issues concern the tensions between what may be called 'public histories' and 'historical research'. Public histories are identified here as histories produced for mass and, therefore, often easy consumption, in textbooks, newspaper articles, television and radio documentaries, dramas, websites, and the like.[4] This approach to telling the past can be distinguished from historical research mostly published in scholarly monographs and academic journals after being subjected to peer review by other scholars. Historical research advocates a rigorous empirical approach, and is written primarily with more expert audiences in mind. Historical research produces, for the wider public at least, less digestible renderings of the past. This is partly because the conclusions historical research arrive at tend to be tentative, usually ambiguous (not to say messy), and are open to forms of challenge and reinterpretation that historians call 'historical process'.

Public histories are seldom completely divorced from historical research. These days, most professional historians, whatever approach they adopt to the past, straddle both activities in their career and are encouraged to do so. Nevertheless, where the aims of public history and pure research sometimes conflict, tensions emerge. Notably, friction occurs where in comparison to historical research, public histories become oversimplified and even distorted, sometimes horribly so. Where it occurs, reductionism of this kind may alter the historical record so much as to make it wholly inaccurate, on occasion even unintelligible to the research historian. In the slide towards error, where the story departs so far from the source evidence that the interpretation no longer has any historical truthfulness, we observe public histories becoming utterly ahistorical.

On the morning of Wednesday, 28 June 1922, the anti-Treaty IRA garrison inside Dublin's Four Courts of Justice was given an ultimatum to evacuate the buildings by the pro-Treaty Free State army.[5] The Four Courts' garrison was opposed to the December 1921 Anglo-Irish Treaty; some among its members were the most hard-line of IRA Volunteers.[6] Ostensibly, they opposed the Treaty because they believed it disestablished the Irish republic proclaimed at Easter 1916, and after 1919 constituted in Sinn Féin's Dáil Éireann assembly. Led by Michael Collins and Arthur Griffith, the pro-Treatyites countered that the Treaty and the Irish Free State it would eventually establish, had received, alongside their government, a democratic mandate in Southern Ireland in the June 1922 general election. In addition, during June, the British government insisted that the Four Courts garrison's defiance of the Treaty settlement had to be brought to an immediate end.[7] Under combined pressure to establish its authority and the threat of British military re-intervention, the Free State forces issued an ultimatum to the Four Courts' garrison to surrender. Shortly after four in the morning on 28 June 1922, after this ultimatum was ignored, the Free State army began its bombardment with field guns hastily borrowed from the British.[8] More than any action during the previous six months, the attack on the Four Courts propelled the pro- and anti-Treaty forces toward all-out civil war.

Fire and two massive explosions (the second detonating after the IRA garrison had surrendered), levelled the Four Courts on 30 June, making the Public Record Office and its Registry among the first casualties of a war lasting until May 1923. Ever since, responsibility for the destruction has been a source of disagreement among historians.[9] That it was historical documents that were destroyed, the bricks and mortar of historical research, has sometimes infused this debate with professional indignation and the occasional emotional outpouring.

Published in 1978, in his memoir of the Civil War, *The Singing Flame*, anti-Treaty IRA leader Ernie O'Malley wrote about the final hours of the Four Courts' siege on Friday, 30 June 1922:

> As we stood near the gate there was a loud shattering explosion … The munitions block [the Public Record Office] and a portion of Headquarters block went up in flames and smoke … The yard was littered with chunks of masonry and smouldering records; pieces of white paper were gyrating in the upper air like seagulls. The explosion seemed to give an extra push to roaring orange flames which formed patterns across the sky. Fire was fascinating to watch; it had a spell like running water. Flame sang and conducted its own orchestra simultaneously. It can't be long now, I thought, until the real noise comes.[10]

For many anti-Treaty Republicans, the Four Courts' siege was remembered as a heroic defence of their republic against the combined forces of British imperialism and the Irish Free State. O'Malley's lyricism turned the destruction of Ireland's documentary heritage into a maudlin elegy for the revolutionaries' republic. When his memoir was first published, its dust jacket sported the striking image of an enormous smoke plume bellowing from the devastated Four Courts.[11] In the Republican narrative, the Treatyites' attack on the Four Courts signalled the betrayal of the struggle for the republic. Well into the 1970s, annually, Fianna Fáil Presidents, Taoisigh, and senior government ministers attended mass in Dublin Castle and wreath laying ceremonies at Glasnevin Cemetery commemorating the attack on the Four Courts and the later killing of the garrison's leaders in a reprisal.[12] In 1978, for many Republicans, the smoke plume remained emblematic of the inferno metaphorically consuming the republic below, O'Malley's eponymous 'singing flame'. In this view, the republic born in the flames of Easter week 1916, could be seen as being reduced to ashes in late June 1922, from where no doubt it would be seen to rise again. In this story, the contents of the Public Record Office are incidental, if not irrelevant.

More recently, that same image of the smoke plume has become closely associated with a determined act of cultural vandalism: the intentional destruction of Ireland's national archive. Rehearsing pro-Treaty narratives from 1922, it is sometimes said that in an act of egregious defiance against the Free State, at the end of the Four Courts' siege the surrendering IRA purposely destroyed the Public Record Office. Most often responsibility for this outrage is directed toward anti-Treatyite IRA leaders like Rory O'Connor or Oscar Traynor or, indeed, O'Malley. In recent years, this blame game has become integral to interpretations advanced by some professional historians, and likely their attribution of culpability has informed the public's memory of events in 1922. Moreover, the Public Record Office's destruction by so-called 'republican vandals' has become important to a revised foundation myth, which describes the birth of a democratic Irish state in opposition to a tyrannical IRA.[13]

Using the example of the Public Record Office's destruction, this chapter condenses a broader critique advanced since 2007 by the present author.[14] At its core this critique explores the relationship between the Irish historical profession and its publics. It considers how some historians attempt to influence the public toward adopting a revised, some say 'improved', memory of the past, one said to be better suited to society's needs in the present. This chapter also addresses the distorting pressures this approach places on the use of historical evidence in academic writing. The association of Republicanism with cultural vandalism in 1922, has of course wider historiographical contexts. In some recent historical writing other negative values, among them sectarianism supposedly leading to 'ethnic cleansing', sexual violence, and the persecution of vulnerable minorities, is exclusively associated with, or used to explain, anti-state Republicanism in the Civil War period.[15] A problem with some of these associations, as we shall see, is that they have been advanced by professional historians, unburdened by the weight of verifiable evidence.[16]

The argument advanced here is organized around three discussions. The first of these explains why some historians see in the past doctrinaire certainties, where others recognize only ambiguity and contradiction. Using the destruction of the Public Record Office as a case study, the chapter examines how some historians have arrived at doctrinaire, sometimes ahistorical, conclusions from contradictory evidence, from unverifiable evidence, or indeed from no evidence. Latterly, the chapter reflects on some of the implications of what is described as 'ahistorical public history' for the historical profession and its public alike.

Once the infelicities of public histories are recognized, a complex and perhaps irresolvable question forces itself. Is society best served by striving for an accurate historical record or, alternatively, by a more inventive account of the past, supposedly tailored to society's needs in the present? This chapter cannot attempt a definitive answer to any of this. Rather it is concerned to discuss the implications of ahistorical public histories for the communication of ideas and understanding concerning the past.

*

The past, or at least the past interpreted using a rigorous empirical method, is an uncertain place. Some historians wish to replace this uncertainty with more doctrinaire interpretations. On occasion, in their quest for more reassuring certitudes, doctrinaire historians provide us with the consolations found in binary interpretations of the past. That is to say, 'black and white' histories populated by recognisable 'goodies' and 'baddies'. Inevitably these accounts force gross reductions. Eliminating inherent complexities, binary histories brutally revise the past to produce easily digestible stories. Said to suit to our needs in the present, sometimes these stories carry messages, often in the form of morality tales. These stories contribute to what are said to be 'useable' histories. Reviewing the present author's recent book *Myth and the Irish State* (2013) in *The Irish Times*, Professor Diarmuid Ferriter references an example of useable history relevant to this discussion. Ferriter observed, 'that ... reordering the revolutionary generation as pro-State democrats or anti-State dictators was common, as numerous scholars felt it vital to define the IRA in 1922 as anti-democratic in order to undermine the Provisional IRA during the Troubles'.[17] What Ferriter describes is commonly known as the 'democrats and dictators' interpretation of the Civil War.[18] Precisely how consciously biased writing on the Irish Civil War (or any aspect of Ireland's history), could be 'vital' to undermine the Provisional IRA goes unexplained by Ferriter or by anybody else. A problem with this approach, as Ferriter concedes, is that despite endorsement by 'numerous scholars', the interpretation is also utterly ahistorical. Explaining why this might be acceptable to some, the work of Bernard Lewis is instructive. Lewis, an English-born historian of the Middle East, has since 1974 been professor at the Institute for Advanced Study at Princeton in the United States. Notable among Lewis's impressive corpus of writing is his brilliantly lucid 1975 collection of lectures, *History: Remembered, Recovered, Invented*.[19] It is Lewis's lectures on the 'invention of history' that is of most interest here.

Following Lewis's example, we can identify some species of usable history as being what he labels 'invented history'. In these interpretations, the usability of the history is dependent on degrees of fabrication, both great and small. Rejecting any strict empirical interpretation of the evidence, invented history offers possibilities for a purposefully more fictional rendering of the past. And where the invention is deemed to have a beneficial influence on public consciousness, Lewis calls this approach 'the improvement of memory'.[20]

The improvement of memory approach is closely identified by Lewis with authoritarian regimes, notably the former Soviet Union. There, a historical profession long existed, directed by the state to endorse the state. Historians who balked at this Soviet arrangement were customarily denounced. Commonly diagnosed as a form of mental illness, the condition of historical dissent sometimes led to incarceration by the authorities in asylums for corrective psychotherapy. Famously, the best exposition of the interdependency between invented history and authoritarianism is provided by George Orwell in his novel, *Nineteen Eighty-Four*. In Orwell's dystopian state of 'Oceania', we witness the all-seeing dictatorship of 'Big Brother' and the 'Party' propagating the slogan: 'Who controls the past controls the future: who controls the present controls the past'.[21] Applied to political realities (not the least in the former Soviet Union and its successors), the Party's statement is most likely delusional, but it is, nevertheless, a delusion embraced by dictatorships the world over.

For authoritarian states, as Lewis explains it, the invention of history is a relatively straightforward choice between carrots and sticks; or state-sponsored patronage and salt mines, metaphorical and real. Lewis's innovation in 1975 was to advance a model for the invention of history in non-authoritarian societies, employing various methodologies and strategies, including patronage and, as he admits, 'force'.[22] Directed at the state of Israel, Lewis's short 1975 book offers instruction on how to reconstruct a society's collective memory by embellishing certain helpful stories, part fact, part myth, when creating an 'improved' past. In 1986, Lewis's invented history impinged upon the Irish academy's consciousness when it was advanced by an up-and-coming historian, Ronan Fanning, as a possible approach to the writing of modern Irish history.[23] Anticipating Ferriter, Fanning appeared to endorse Lewis's invented history as a means of undermining the controlling narratives of Irish revolutionary Republicanism, notably the strain espoused by the Provisional IRA.

Writing invented history, Lewis tells us, the search for evidence is always pre-directed towards information endorsing some or other 'improving' narrative. Our enemies in the present have always been bad democrats, for example, or, alternatively, our friends in the present share our glorious past. It is the pre-direction towards source evidence that differentiates invented history from scholarly empirical historical research: the latter properly resisting any temptation to seek evidence to bolster foregone conclusions. Inevitably, invented history involves ransacking archives for supporting evidence. And, with equal inevitability, invented history demands ignoring or marginalizing evidence that spoils the helpful stories that will populate the improved memory. By carefully selecting and arranging helpful historical information, gifted historians can conjure up from the archival morass almost any story that they wish. But where no suitable sources are available, the improvement of memory approach may demand the fabrication of evidence.[24] This is a tricky procedure, but one not altogether unknown to some Irish historians. Embellishing the narrative is of course the oldest of tricks, as old as storytelling itself. In various guises, the improvement of memory approach is employed by historians, professionals, amateurs, propagandists and publicists; everywhere, and in every generation. As an approach, the improvement of memory technique works best where audiences are comforted by stories that they know to be true, or at least nearly true. In this manner, the past becomes the condescending mirror of the present.

Invented history is never about attempting to understand the past on its own terms, and this differentiates it from a quality intrinsic to historical research. Recognizing all the available evidence, the results of historical research remain unpredictable, ever shifting. Sometimes, unhelpfully, historical research may endorse the 'wrong' story at the 'wrong' time: our enemies were not always bad democrats or, conversely, our new friends were not always friends at all. This unpredictability greatly complicates the past. Conversely, because it is written to order, an attribute of invented history is its inherent predictability – inventive historians find in the sources what they look for or what they are told to look for by those who wield power. It is for this reason, that authoritarian and similar regimes take solace in the certainties invented history provides. Invented history's primary function is therefore to control the past for some vested interest, be it a government or a political party or the 'establishment' going by some or other appellation. These observations go some way towards identifying the often times oblique connection existing between power-holders in society and the desire to own the past as a political commodity.

As in Israel–Palestine, Lewis's example, where history informs identity politics (or indeed in Britain–Ireland, the example advanced here), those who hold power take an interest in history and memory, towards their better management. Following hard on the heels of historical invention and dressed in the tattered robes of the academy, the improvement of memory approach is really nothing more exotic than history as propaganda. In wartime, when anxieties about identities are exacerbated (and may even become matters of life and death), history as propaganda is in high demand. In 1975,

Lewis gave careful instruction on how to dress up propaganda as historical research in democracies, where sending dissidents to mental asylums or salt mines is seldom a realistic option. Because we cannot be sure what kind of history historians' practise, it is always useful to attempt to differentiate historical research from invented history and its derivatives. The best procedure available to us to distinguish what methodologies historians employ is to compare their considered interpretations, alongside their original source evidence. This kind of scrutiny can be instructive, but it is a time consuming and costly affair.[25]

To be clear, what is not argued here is that any particular approach to the past intrinsically is 'right' or 'wrong'. Instead it is argued that the approaches discussed, principally invented history and empirical historical research, while seldom totally divorced one from another, nevertheless are different, and can be demonstrated to be different. Empirical historical research is grounded in verifiable and credible evidence, whereas invented history cannot be. Within recognisable legal and ethical bounds, historians should of course be free to propagate any kind of history they wish, be it empirical or invented or fictional or pure fantasy. Mine, therefore, is a permissive argument for freedom of expression. The corollary of this argument is, however, that historians should feel themselves free to engage other historians' work openly, and without fear of sanction or denunciation. But it must not be forgotten that the modern approach to the improvement of memory originates in authoritarian societies, where such freedoms are at a discount, if indeed they are not denied altogether. And it is well to be reminded the prescription of academic freedom in authoritarian societies exists to keep those who hold power in power.

An intractable problem in the improvement of memory approach is that its inventions rest on misinterpretations or unreliable evidence or on no evidence whatsoever. Consequently, the invention is always vulnerable to being exposed as ahistorical nonsense. For the reasoning student of history, any such exposure dissipates the power to influence that the original invention might have had. Consequently, invented history must rely on unscholarly procedures to defend itself against adverse criticism. In the Soviet system, in almost every sphere threats from within the state exerted their pernicious influence over the manufacture of knowledge. In the Irish example, denunciation of critics as 'cranks', 'conspiracy theorists', and, sometimes, apologists for predatory paedophiles or Republican terrorism or Nazi atrocities, may suffice to inhibit unorthodoxy.[26] Inside most academies, in most circumstances, fears about unemployment and non-preferment may encourage self-censorship among scholars and lead towards uncritical conformity. If in authoritarian states or in liberal (and not so liberal) democracies invented history is to achieve success, its advocates will be tempted to resort to illiberal practices to silence critics or risk failure.[27] At the end of this chapter we will briefly revisit these ethical issues. In the next section we return to a concrete example of the supposed 'improvement' of our memories, the destruction of the Public Record Office at the end of June 1922.

*

Published in 1996, in a collection of essays marking the bicentenary of the Four Courts buildings, the Honourable Mr Justice Ronan Keane (later Chief Justice of Ireland) wrote, 'belief persisted for many years that Rory O'Connor, in a Samson-like gesture, had deliberately set fire to the Four Courts or exploded a mine before the garrison surrendered'. Justice Keane concluded: 'There is no evidence to support that thesis.'[28] Soon afterwards, contrary interpretations were advanced by political scientist Tom Garvin, and historians David Fitzpatrick and Michael Laffan.

Also writing in 1996, in his book *1922: The Birth of Irish Democracy*, Garvin rightly noted: 'Rory O'Connor ... had been appraised by officials of the immense cultural value of the Public Record Office'.[29] Garvin then went on to say of O'Connor that he: 'deliberately mined the buildings and timed the mines to go off two hours after the surrender, which they duly did ... and the contents of the Public Record Office ... were distributed in tiny fragments all over the city. The enormous cultural loss to the Irish nation perpetrated by these putative patriots, actual vandals, has been irreversible. The Civil War then began in earnest.'[30]

The destruction of the Public Record Office frames Garvin's thesis of a civil war supposedly fought between the new democratic Irish state and the forces of anarchy following in the train of anti-state Republicanism. To support this thesis, Garvin identifies evidence in his footnotes apparently overlooked by Justice Keane, alongside several other historians.[31] As his evidence, Garvin cites a handwritten volume of inter-view notes dating from the 1940s or 1950s, which Ernie O'Malley had taken down from IRA veterans.[32] After painstakingly reading O'Malley's notebook, nothing has been found to support Garvin's interpretation of the anti-Treaty IRA setting mines to explode inside the Four Courts following their surrender. Additionally, Garvin cites two files in the papers of former Free State Attorney General, Hugh Kennedy.[33] In these files, alone, one contemporary document from 1922 entitled 'Destruction of the Four Courts' does indeed endorse Garvin's interpretation.[34] The value of the docu-ment as evidence, helping to explain what happened in 1922, is undermined somewhat, because it was circulated by the Free State army after 4 July 1922, and is thus a propaganda leaflet. Where in 1996, he said there is 'no evidence', Justice Keane was mistaken. However, it is correct to say that the propaganda document is not 'credible evidence', where it is relied on in a reconstruction of contested events. The solution Garvin demonstrates to the problem of there being no credible evidence is to draw on unreliable evidence. This procedure, though, is obscured in a disarmingly short citation referencing many hundreds of pages of handwritten notes, letters, official documents, and other papers. The silent substitution of war propaganda for want of more credible evidence, provides an example of embellishment intrinsic to Lewis's invented history.

In 1997, David Fitzpatrick wrote that Oscar Traynor, the officer commanding the anti-Treatyite IRA in Dublin at the end of June 1922, 'demonstrated his regard for procedural niceties when ... blowing up the Four Courts in 1922, together with their archival contents'.[35] Fitzpatrick offers no citation or reference to support his statement about Traynor's supposed actions. A possible reason for this oversight is that no credible evidence is to hand.[36]

In 1998, Michael Laffan wrote of the Public Record Office: 'Some republicans stored petrol and paraffin in the Four Courts, determined to burn or blow up the buildings rather than obey any orders to hand them over.' Laffan continues:

> In an act of vandalism pre-eminent amongst so many other comparable atrocities, the Public Record Office ... was turned into a munitions factory and was mined by its defenders; as a result it was destroyed in an explosion when the building caught fire. Independent Ireland's opportunities for understanding the country's past were impoverished as fragments of irreplaceable documents floated over the city.[37]

Laffan's account is more ambiguous than either Garvin's or Fitzpatrick's. The act of vandalism identified by Laffan is the turning of the Public Record Office into a munitions factory and laying mines inside it. The reader is therefore left in no doubt where, ultimately, blame lies – with the IRA garrison. No consideration is given by Laffan to the cause of the fire. Nevertheless, Laffan is correct to assert that some IRA volunteers said they would destroy the Four Courts rather than surrender to the Free State. Laffan cites no evidence to confirm this threat (endorsed and recorded by O'Malley), was ever acted upon.[38]

In his memoir, O'Malley explicitly says that the IRA ordered the destruction of the Public Record Office on the evening of Thursday, 29 June.[39] However, that order was rescinded when it was discovered that having entered the Public Record Office through a breach blasted by their artillery, Free State troops already occupied the building. Overnight explosive materials and munitions found inside the Public

Record Office and Registry were removed by Free State engineers to garages at nearby Smithfield and stored in inspection pits.[40] According to a Free State source, no IRA mines or explosives were present in the Public Record Office and Registry when it was destroyed the next day.[41]

On the morning of Friday, 30 June, the Free State soldiers launched their assault on the rest of the Four Courts from the vantage the Public Record Office offered[42] (see Figure 11). At about 11 am, accounts agree, a ferocious fire erupted. Ultimately, it was fire that destroyed the Four Courts, igniting as it spread to mines, chemicals, commandeered vehicles, petrol, and as much as two tons of commercial explosives. The first of the two massive explosions (described by O'Malley above) happened shortly after mid-day. A second larger detonation happened at twelve minutes past five in the evening shortly after the garrison vacated the Four Courts following their surrender.[43] The fire determined the siege's outcome by making the garrisons' position hopeless, and ultimately prompting Traynor's order for the garrison to surrender.[44]

Precisely how the fire started remains of no small interest. In *The Singing Flame*, O'Malley offers no explanation for the fire's origins, though in his later interviews with veterans O'Malley investigated its source.[45] Alongside IRA sabotage, although the idea of the garrison burning themselves out seems illogical, possible explanations for the fire include the impacts from high explosive shells or the accidental ignition of explosives or chemicals. Simon Donnelly, a garrison officer and eyewitness, claimed that 'about 11 a.m. incendiary bombs thrown [by Free State soldiers] into the GHQ block in which there was the chemical shop took fire, owing to the inflammable substances in the building the fire made great headway'.[46] Donnelly's account may, however, be another piece of wartime propaganda.

In his memoir, one of the Free State officers leading the assault on the Four Courts, Padraig O'Connor, recollected being supplied with rifle grenades in the Public Record Office and Registry.[47] These rifle grenades might be construed to be the 'incendiaries' Donnelly identifies in his account: the word 'thrown', though, suggests something else, perhaps petrol bombs. For his part, Padraig O'Connor denied responsibility for starting the fire, claiming it was already underway before he began his assault mid-morning on Friday, 30 June.[48]

A week later on 5 July, to drive the anti-Treatyite IRA from their strongholds, the Free State army burned large parts of Dublin's city centre. The tactic of fire-bombing followed the British cabinet's decision the previous day not to supply the Free State army with poison gas.[49] Instead, IRA incendiary bombs recovered from the garages at Smithfield were used by Free State army officers to burn much of Upper Sackville

Street (later O'Connell Street), including the Hammam and Gresham Hotels.[50] The order to fire Upper Sackville Street was given by general J.J. 'Ginger' O'Connell, but it was most likely sanctioned in advance by Michael Collins.[51]

None of these events excludes the possibility that the IRA garrison deliberately set fire to the Four Courts or planted mines to go off after their surrender. Nevertheless, to avoid assaulting buildings in the city centre, Free State soldiers resorted to incendiary bombs and this tactic may have been anticipated during the Four Courts' siege. Despite photographic evidence of the Free State's soldiers using incendiaries on anti-Treaty strongholds, curiously few historians reference this tactic.[52] As in the Four Courts, fire proved decisive when ending the anti-Treatyite IRA's occupation in the city centre. With Upper Sackville Street in flames, the battle for Dublin ended in a Free State victory on the evening of 5 July.

Following the surrender of the Four Court's on 30 June, Thomas Johnson, the leader of the Irish parliamentary Labour party, visited those of the garrison imprisoned in Mountjoy Gaol. Johnson became convinced that the garrison had not timed any mines to explode after their surrender, and he told the Treatyite government: 'justice demands that this denial ... should be made public'.[53] Unsurprisingly, the Treatyite government replied in the negative to Johnson, adding it had evidence contradicting the prisoners' self-serving account.[54] The government did not disclose its evidence to Johnson.

Supporting the Treatyite government's claim, that the garrison had indeed set mines to explode after the surrender, to date the only evidence to come to light is to be found in a government file documenting the Four Courts' salvage. It is a pencil note, unsigned and undated, written on a torn slip of brown paper and reads: 'Sergeant Major Doyle 1st Batt. 1st Dublin Guards heard the click of a mine from the cellar when calling for [the garrison's] surrender.'[55] Less than conclusive, this document helps explain why it is that those who say the IRA garrison booby-trapped the Four Courts look to war propaganda for their evidence.

Understandably, what is presented in this chapter is both contradictory and inconclusive, and this argues that the destruction of the Public Record Office remains a more ambiguous event than some historians would have it. Writing in 2011, Liz Gillis, author of *The Fall of Dublin: 28 June to 5 July 1922*, wrote: 'If the answer to the question of what actually caused the explosions [in the Four Courts] is to be answered definitively, further investigation is needed.'[56] As for establishing that the IRA garrison was responsible for the fire, Gillis echoes Justice Keane's earlier conclusion where she writes 'no proof has been found'.[57]

Nevertheless, the interpretation that anti-state Republicans destroyed the Public Record Office proves useful when reshaping a particular memory of the Irish state's birth. In the revised memory, where they are blamed for destroying Ireland's national archive, anti-state Republicans are forever tied, inexorably, to an act of unforgivable barbarism. This is just another attempt to 'reorder' the past and retell it as a morality tale. For any accepting the argument that in 1922 the anti-Treatyite IRA 'prefigured what was to happen in fascist Italy and Nazi Germany during the 1920s and 1930s', the destruction of the national archive finds powerful resonances in later fascist public book burnings.[58] In the popular imagination it is almost axiomatic that, as Matthew Fishburn has put it, 'book burners are fascists, and fascists are book burners'.[59] Anticipating Fishburn by almost two hundred years, German poet and playwright, Heinrich Heine, made a terrifying equivalence: 'Where one burns books, one soon will burn people.'[60]

The idea that in Ireland Republicanism is essentially a manifestation of fascism gained momentum among some intellectuals and historians after 1970.[61] If the idea of 'green fascism' had purchase, partly it was because militarist Republicanism had long been associated with authoritarianism. More importantly, equating Republicanism with fascism also formed part of the contemporary propaganda war against the Provisional IRA. Conor Cruise O'Brien gave expression to a shared perception of equivalence in his familiar rallying call: 'those who want to oppose fascism in Ireland will start opposing it where it is really to be found: at the heart of the Republican Movement'.[62] The association, in 1922, of anti-state Republicanism with sectarianism, ethnic cleansing, the persecution of minorities, sexual and other crime, no more than with the destruction of the Public Record Office, form part of the attempt to find equivalences with continental fascism. However, these associations cannot be historical where the interpretations are unsupported by credible evidence. Yet, such ahistorical constructions now form part of a sophisticated propaganda informing the collective memory of the Irish Civil War.

All this is only to remind ourselves that burning a book, a library, or an archive, holds particular and powerful meanings for contemporary audiences. On this reading, the smoke plume rising high above the Four Courts signals a secular act of sacrilege, alongside the division of the revolutionaries into anti-fascists and fascists. Unsurprisingly, this binary reduction is just another rehearsal of the old 'democrats and dictators' story advanced by 'numerous scholars'.

*

Broadcast in June 2010, *The Limits of Liberty* was a three-part documentary series commissioned by the Irish state broadcaster RTÉ, and substantially funded by the Broadcasting Authority of Ireland (BAI).[63] Co-written by historian Diarmaid Ferriter and writer Nuala O'Connor, the series offered a purportedly left of centre critique of political power in independent Ireland. Once again, the destruction of the Public Record Office framed the origin story of the Irish state. To contextualize fully the documentary's treatment of these events, it is necessary to reproduce two extended extracts from the programme.

Delivering to camera, Diarmaid Ferriter says: 'In April 1922 the anti-Treaty IRA took possession of the Four Courts Building, which included the Public Record Office.' He continues:

> Two months later the army of the pro-treaty Government began a military bombard-ment of the Four Courts in order to force the republicans out. This marked the opening phase of the Irish civil war. Two days after that bombardment began a huge explosion ripped through the Public Record Office destroying most of the contents. Some of the charred fragments of the documents were blown as far as the Bailey Lighthouse nine miles away. At the time of the IRA's occupation of the Four Courts its commander Rory O'Connor was interviewed by the *Irish Independent*, 'Every care will be taken to preserve all documents,' he said. But the IRA had packed the Public Record Office with gelignite and munitions in the midst of a priceless repository of Irish history. Some seven hundred years of documents went up in smoke including census returns, Land Registry deeds, baptismal certs, marriage certs. During the occupation they barricaded the windows with the 1821 County Antrim census returns. The cultural vandalism involved in their destruction was not deemed significant by those inside. They were consumed with the internal power struggle of the Irish republican move-ment. Rory O'Connor was visited by two scholars and republicans, Eoin Mac Neill and Seamus O'Ceallaigh, they implored him to keep the records safe, but their pleas fell on deaf ears.[64]

In the interest of balance and accuracy, it might be fairly said that the cultural vandalism involved in the destruction was not deemed significant by those inside or outside the Four Courts. Earlier in the proceedings, the British army contemplated an aerial bombardment of the Four Courts, should they have to intervene.[65] Meanwhile, Free State gunners lobbed hundreds of shells into the Four Courts, and on the second day of their bombardment, they targeted the Public Record Office in order to make a breach. During three days of siege, this was the only violence purposefully directed at the Public Record Office. All of this is only to notice that the Four Courts' garrison did not have sole responsibility for the destruction of the national archive. It is also true, that in the conflict all sides subordinated any desire to conserve the national archive to the achievement of strategic military objectives. In time of war, such are the lamentable priorities of soldiers. That in his treatment Ferriter loses sight of any of this, identifies his as a partisan treatment.

Immediately following Ferriter's presentation to camera, the documentary enlists the testimony of archaeologist, Dr Niamh Whitfield. A problem with Ferriter's interpretation of events remains the absence of credible evidence apportioning blame exclusively to the IRA garrison. Superficially, Whitfield's testimony addresses this problem. While apparently restoring a degree of balance to the programme's interpretation, she recounts a story told about her grandfather, the physician Dr Seamus O'Ceallaigh, who in 1922, Whitfield tells us, was an opponent of the Treaty. 'Well now as I have been told this as a child,' Whitfield begins, 'and I cannot remember who told me but it is something I feel I have always known.' She continues:

> Our story is that the Irregulars were holed up in the Four Courts for three months, at the end of the three months it became apparent that they would have to surrender. Initially [Rory] O'Connor, who was an engineer, his plan was to tunnel out under the Liffey and get his men out that way but that turned out not to be feasible. So he wanted to go out with a bang rather than a whimper and he planned a gesture of defiance, and that was the destruction of the Public Records Office. And my grandfather [Seamus O'Ceallaigh] got wind of this plan, as did Eoin Mac Neill, they were both northern Catholics, they were both on the side of the [anti-Treaty] Irregulars, but they were both historians, and they both appreciated the value of the records in the Public Records Office. They were horrified, they went together out to the Four Courts under fire, I believe, and they pleaded with [Rory] O'Connor not to blow up the Public Records Office. And their argument was that it was completely mistaken to believe that these were records which were solely concerned with the English. That these were actually records of the Irish people, so, if they blew them up what they would be doing would be destroying part of the history of their own people. They went away and a few days later my grandfather was in the street on a beautiful sunny day and he heard a huge explosion and he was so horrified he burst into tears. And that was the only time he wept in public. So his reaction [to the destruction] was absolute horror and I think he was completely right: it was an extremely vandalistic and stupid thing to do.

Dr Whitfield's testimony rehearses the story of Rory O'Connor's 'Samson-like act of defiance'. She also recounts another story circulating in 1922, that of two respectable professional men pleading with Rory O'Connor to save the Public Record Office.[66]

It may be that Dr Seamus O'Ceallaigh, as Whitfield says, did approach Rory O'Connor during the bombardment. Endorsed by Ferriter, there is, however, no evidence corroborating the statement that Eoin Mac Neill remonstrated with Rory O'Connor during the siege. And contrary to Whitfield's testimony, Eoin Mac Neill was not an 'Irregular' opponent of the Treaty. Instead, Mac Neill was not alone a supporter of the Treaty, but also a prominent member of the Treatyite government. That, unnoticed and unrecorded, a government minister entered the Four Courts during the bombardment to plead with Rory O'Connor seems highly unlikely.

In the absence of credible evidence, the documentary-makers employ hearsay oral testimony to retell the story of the IRA garrison's vandalism. Rehearsing a usable story, this testimony introduces inaccuracies into the programme's account of events, if not elements of fantasy. This is not to dismiss Dr Whitfield's testimony, which is of intrinsic value to any study of the relationship between narrative, memory and history in the Irish Civil War. However, her testimony is less useful where it is employed in an 'expository history', attempting to show how and why events happened. Employed in an expository mode, the use of Whitfield's testimony provides an example of dire methodological confusion, because she is a witness to her family's story about the destruction of the Public Record Office, not the event itself.[67] Nevertheless, Whitfield's testimony is indispensable to the documentary-makers, because it lends credence to the blame game being played out in the programme. In these ways, the 'Limits of Liberty' provides an example of the ahistorical public history identified at the beginning of this article.[68]

*

While we can never definitively establish what motivates historians to produce their histories, it is, nevertheless, fair to speculate that the association by some historians of the anti-Treaty IRA with cultural vandalism is related to the exclusive association of the same IRA, as Ferriter identifies, with anti-democratic values. Indeed, sometimes these and similar interpretations have been advanced in parallel by the same authors. Yet it is true, a television documentary broadcast in 2010, realistically cannot be said to have been directed at undermining the long defunct Provisional IRA. Describing the origins of the state, the *Limits of Liberty* subscribed to a foundation myth endorsed by Garvin, Fitzpatrick, Laffan and treatyite propaganda dating to the Civil War. What makes that myth attractive to so many historians is the still current polemical responses to the Northern Ireland crisis. These sometimes reconceived the democratic Irish state as being in perpetual opposition to fascistic Republicanism.

The destruction of the Public Record Office offers concrete examples of the demands 'reordering the past' places on historical evidence. This is because historical experience, complex, ragged-edged, and frustratingly elusive resists being forced into pre-formed boxes. Nevertheless, pouring the past into binary moulds is what some historians attempt to do. In 2001, J.J. Lee has reflected that in recent decades much historical scholarship 'reverted to being a variety of war propaganda'. Continuing, Lee said that it is 'one of the sadder features of the intellectual history of the past generation that the standards of use of evidence set in the first generation of the *Irish Historical Studies* school lapsed so lamentably'.[69] What some historians have achieved when writing and broadcasting is the seamless integration of civil war propaganda into the historical record. Lending their professorial authority to this error, unavoidably, they influence the public's memory. Historians have every right to revise the past as they wish, or indeed to invent it anew in more satisfactory forms. Invented history necessarily is not wrong in any moral sense (as long as it involves *no deception*), and, like other forms of expression, ordinarily, it should not be censored. Instead, invented history must be loudly applauded, if only to draw attention to its form and function, not to mention its occasional creative ingenuity.

Introducing error into historical knowledge, unconsciously or consciously, debases historical understanding of the past and our memories. Where the error services crude propaganda, that debasement finds its completion. This observation reminds us that historical information, no more than the news information conveyed to us by journalists, has a particular value where it informs our decision-making in the present. It is for this reason that those who seek to control memory and historical understanding have always resorted to various forms of coercion. Some will deem this unavoidable and often necessary. What matters in the end is the value society as a whole places on both its memory and its historical understanding, and by what manner and means this value is defended or indeed allowed to lapse for the want of effort.

CHAPTER EIGHT

WITNESSING THE REPUBLIC
THE ERNIE O'MALLEY NOTEBOOK INTERVIEWS AND THE BUREAU OF MILITARY HISTORY COMPARED

Eve Morrison

> As regards question of neurasthenia: his conduct would strike the average individual as strange. He wanders and has been wandering for some years past over the United States and Mexico, going from one job to another, seldom staying in one place long. He appears indifferent as regards making any provision for the future and although he works and studies he appears to have an antipathy to making any mater[ial] use of his knowledge.[1]

So wrote Frank Murray, a New York City doctor assessing the extent of Ernie O'Malley's disablement due to 'neurasthenia' (post-traumatic stress disorder) and several other ailments. The medical examination was in aid of his application to the Irish government for a disability pension. O'Malley was considering returning home, but had not decided: 'America seems such a good country when I think of Ireland and Ireland such a pleasant place when I think of America that it is hard to resolve my doubts.'[2] Over his revolutionary career, the former OC of the Irish Republican Army's [IRA] 2nd Southern Division during the War of Independence (1919–21) and Director of Organisation and Assistant Chief of Staff of the anti-Treaty forces in the Civil War (1922–3) had been arrested three times, wounded on six separate occasions, imprisoned in several different gaols or internment camps (escaping twice), and spent over forty days on hunger strike.[3] A decade later, he was living in the United States, eking out a living as a housepainter and in receipt of transient relief.[4] One publisher after another had rejected the manuscript of *On Another Man's Wound*, now acknowledged as arguably the finest memoir of Ireland's independence struggle.[5]

Word of O'Malley's ill health had crossed the Atlantic, prompting an indignant letter in August 1934 to Frank Aiken, then Fianna Fáil's Minister for Defence, from the brother of a man in New York who was helping O'Malley get back on his feet: 'he was worn out and hungry until he wrote to my brother ... It remains for our Govt. at home to do something to help him ... I would like to inform you this matter is for yourself and the President and the head Members of your Government.'[6] The letter obviously struck a chord. O'Malley's disability pension claim was ranked as 'very urgent', and Aiken personally invited him to apply for a second pension, this one for military service.[7] The success of both claims transformed O'Malley's prospects: 'I have been given a pension of £120 a year,' he wrote to Paul Strand in December 1934, 'I am due to receive it in a month or more and can apply for another pension for services from 1916–1924 which should bring me in about £300 a year. That means I can go back to Ireland.'[8]

In the decades after independence, the Irish state passed a host of disability and service pension acts for former combatants who fought on both sides in the Easter Rising, War of Independence and Civil War. The majority of claims were made for military service and awarded under the two Military Service Pension (MSP) acts. A Cumann na nGaedhael government brought in the first act in 1924, in an effort to dispel unrest among pro-Treaty forces in the wake of demobilization and the army mutiny.[9] It was limited to pro-Treaty Civil War veterans with pre-Truce (1916–21) service in one of the main separatist military organizations: the Irish Volunteers/IRA, Irish Citizen Army, Fianna Éireann or Hibernian Rifles. In late 1934, Fianna Fáil passed a second pensions act allowing applications from anti-Treaty Civil War veterans with pre-Truce service, neutral Easter Rising and War of Independence veterans whose service ended at the Truce, and for the first time from Cumann na mBan (the women's auxiliary force). Administering the 1934 legislation proved to be an equally contentious, torturous business. The Department of Defence was swamped by over 50,000 applications by the end of 1935. Only a minority of veterans were awarded pensions, and the work of the adjudicating Referee and his panel of advisors was painfully slow.[10] By 1957, less than 20 per cent of the 82,000 applicants were successful, but O'Malley numbered among the highest ranks of this already exclusive grouping.[11]

He was one of just thirty-nine individuals to qualify for the top grade of Lieutenant General under the 1934 MSP Act.

Securing a regular income allowed O'Malley to lead a remarkably productive and energetic post-revolutionary life in Ireland, despite continuing to suffer from neurasthenia, 'general nervousness', insomnia, an impaired memory and the long-term effects of several gunshot wounds.[12] He married and started a family, pursued a writing career after failing his university medical exams, promoted the arts, and embarked on extensive research into the independence struggle and Civil War through interviewing his former comrades in arms. Around 450 of those interviews survive, transcribed and rewritten into over one hundred notebooks now held in three separate repositories, the majority in University College Dublin Archives (UCDA).[13]

O'Malley was something of an oral history pioneer though he did not use this terminology. In the 1940s he interviewed a number of artists for the Irish Exhibition of Living Art including Evie Hone, Jack Hanlon, Louis le Brocquy, Norah McGuinness and Nano Reid, and went folklore-collecting around Clew Bay, County Mayo.[14] He described his combatant interviews as 'folklore' as well.[15] Conducted, it seems, primarily as private research for his still unpublished Civil War memoir and other pieces of writing, the interviews also helped him manage mental and emotional trauma. His 1916–23 experiences clearly haunted him for the rest of his life: 'When I was too disturbed I thought it better to collect the information, because in Ireland the men will tell me the truth about themselves. I take notes at speed as fast as they can talk, but again that had to be re-written into notebooks. It is a long piece of work.'[16]

Direct evidence as to exactly when he started interviewing former combatants, and what he intended to do with the material, is limited to scattered references in his diaries and personal correspondence (particularly to his friends Paul Strand and John Kelleher), and a few interview schedules and lists of interviewees jotted into his notebooks. Consistent dates for the interviews exist from September 1950 onwards, but he seems to have started in the late 1930s. By 1945, O'Malley's efforts had coalesced into a planned project. He consulted Florence 'Florrie' O'Donoghue, a Cork IRA veteran, who had just drawn up his own proposal to collect statements and documents about the 'Tan war'.[17] O'Malley's interviewing gradually expanded in chronological and regional scope. Most were collected between 1948 and 1952. O'Malley's health was precarious, and the idea of leaving his interviews for others to use might only have come into focus as he became ever more aware that his life would not be a long one. He had transcribed most of the early interviews by September 1950. The onerous task of rewriting the rest seems only to have been resumed in earnest a few months before March 1953, when he

Figure 1. Jack B. Yeats, Death for Only One, *1937, oil on canvas, 61 x 91.5 cm, Private Collection, Estate of Jack B. Yeats, DACS London / IVARO Dublin, 2016.*

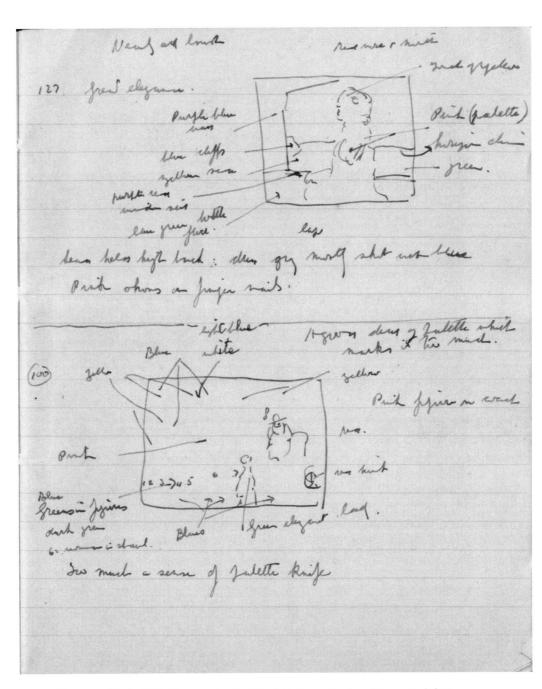

Figure 2. Ernie O'Malley, notebook of Jack B. Yeats National Loan Exhibition, 1945, Ernie O'Malley Papers, AIA060, New York University Library.

Figure 3. Evie Hone, Deposition, *1940, gouache and watercolour on paper, 29.7 x 56.4 cm, IACI O'Malley Collection, University of Limerick.*

Figure 4. Louis le Brocquy, View from Burrishoole Lodge, County Mayo, *1946, watercolour on paper, Private Collection, © Estate of Louis le Brocquy.*

Figure 5. Paul Strand, Cristo with Thorns, *Huexotla, 1933. Source: Krippner, James,* Paul Strand in Mexico, *New York: Aperture Foundation, 2010.*

Figure 6. Paul Strand, Plaza, State of Puebla, *1933. Source: Krippner, James,*
Paul Strand in Mexico, *New York: Aperture Foundation, 2010.*

*Figure 7. Paul Strand,
photographer;* Woman and Boy,
*Tenancingo de Degollago, 1933.
Source: Krippner, James,* Paul
Strand in Mexico, *New York:
Aperture Foundation, 2010.*

Figure 8. Noel Moffett, Donegal Cottage, *c.1941, photographic print 204 mm x 135 mm.
The Irish Architectural Archive courtesy of Patrick Moffett with thanks to Shane O'Toole.*

Figure 9. Ernie O'Malley, Two Apostles, *Ennis Friary, County Clare, c.1939,* © Estate of Ernie O'Malley.

Figure 10. Ernie O'Malley, Detail of Cross Slab, St. Nicholas' Collegiate Church, Galway, County Galway, c.1939, © Estate of Ernie O'Malley.

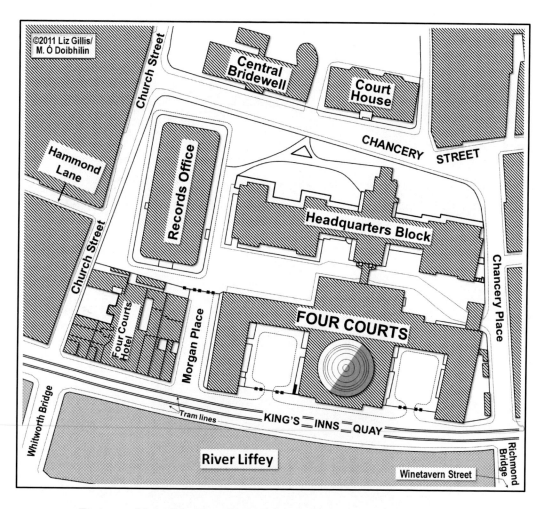

Figure 11. Map of the Four Courts Area, Dublin, in 1922, prepared by and courtesy of Micheál Ó Doibhilin and Liz Gillis, © 2011.

Figure 12. Eugene Delacroix, Liberty Leading the People, *1830, Museé du Louvre, Paris, ART 147488.*

Figure 13. Jacques-Louis David, The Death of Marat, *1793, © Royal Museums of Fine Arts of Belgium, Brussels / photo: J. Geleyns – Ro scan.*

suffered a serious heart attack, from which he never fully recovered. By November of that year, he was working every day 'to put them into better shape for reading so that they could be of use in case anything happens to me'.[18]

Grittier than his own self-consciously literary memoirs and far more graphic than virtually any other collection of veterans' testimony currently available, apart from the Father Louis O'Kane interviews discussed further on, O'Malley's interviews are peppered with language associated in witness statements almost exclusively with British soldiers and spies. At their best, they capture a ribald, bawdy irreverence:

> There was a clerk of the chapel then who used to look after stuff for us. Barlow's in Shragh used to give it to him, and the clerk would 'go over to St Joseph's statue': and the directions for finding it were: 'put your hand up his hole and you'll find a revolver. Then go over to the Blessed Virgin's hole and you'll find four hundred rounds of 45 ammunition.' Poor Pake Dalton was a big, huge man. One day when the men were resting Lynch came in 'Lads come out quick' and the column men all ran out. 'Look over the ditch' said Lynch 'he's after making his shit it's like the Treaty Stone of Limerick and there are steps leading up to it.[19]

Whether O'Malley would have published all the material he gathered without toning it down is a matter of conjecture. O'Malley's combatant interviews were just one of many attempts by separatist nationalist veterans, both independently and officially, to document their war. From very early on, and particularly after Fianna Fáil came to power in 1932, various government representatives and departments pushed for projects to collect first-hand accounts from veterans to be undertaken.[20] In January 1947, after several years of negotiations and proposals from various quarters, the Bureau of Military History – the first employment of the MSP records as an aid to historical research – commenced its work. It was understood to be (and to a significant extent was) a means of complementing and expanding on the pension records, which became the single most important methodological and administrative control utilized by the project. Administering the pension legislation had engendered a massive, thirty-two county re-investigation into the organization and conduct of the 1916–23 separatist nationalist military organizations. Defence amassed thousands of files relating both to individual claimants and organizations, creating the most significant repository of available material relating to the independence struggle in Ireland. In 1943, the department agreed in principle to allow its vast revolutionary archive to be consulted for historical purpose.[21] As Defence held the records, the army was a natural choice to administer the scheme, and the confidential status of the pension files made it almost inevitable that the project would remain 'in house'.[22] Bureau members John McCoy and Seamus Robinson had both served on the MSP Board of Assessors and the pension referee's Advisory Committee. One of their main tasks was to compile lists of potential interviewees, and to advise investigators on subjects and periods where MSP material was lacking or incomplete.[23]

The Bureau was in operation for a decade, accumulating 1,773 oral testimonies, known as 'witness statements', 334 collections of contemporary documents, and twelve voice recordings, as well as newspaper cuttings and photographs.[24] These, along with O'Malley's interviews, rank among the most fully realized of a host of historical schemes instigated, managed and/or conducted by veterans after 1923. In all, over 2,000 former combatants gave a first person account to either O'Malley or the Bureau, concerning some aspect of their involvement in Ireland's independence struggle from 1913 to 1923. The often scant descriptions of IRA actions in newspapers, British records and IRA brigade and battalion reports can now be fleshed out with hundreds of accounts of ambushes, engagements, arms raids, assassinations, intelligence gathering, prison life, hunger strikes, the separatist movement's wider organization and supporting networks during the Easter Rising, War of Independence and Civil War. There is more information available about Ireland's revolutionary decade than ever before, and it has never been easier to access. The witness statements (available since March 2003) and the first releases of the vast MSP archives are freely accessible online.[25] The O'Malley interviews are in the process of being transcribed and published in Mercier Press's *The Men Will Talk to Me* series.

The popular and scholarly perceptions of each collection, however, could hardly be more different. O'Malley's privately conducted interviews have achieved iconic status, despite (or perhaps because of), the fact that his notoriously difficult hand-writing tends to defeat all but the most diligent. O'Malley's interviews are often posited as a deliberate and more authentic rival to the witness statements. In the highly competitive atmosphere surrounding its initiation and running, the Bureau – and particularly Michael McDunphy, its director – was subject to a stream of public attacks and private criticisms by Robert Dudley Edwards, the UCD historian, and Florrie O'Donoghue. Both men were members of the Bureau's Advisory Committee of historians and archivists who had hoped to play a more direct role in the Bureau's administration.[26] The Bureau is often characterized as a 'Free State' project that – by reputation – intentionally eschewed controversy and the still divisive Civil War, and is commonly associated with unprofessionalism and state censorship. The reality is more complicated.

There is, in fact, a surprising amount of common ground between the O'Malley project and the Bureau in terms of provenance, political outlook, personnel, interviewees and methodology. They are more distinctive in style and subject matter, though not to the extent that is often suggested. The Bureau's approximately 2,000 administrative records confirm that the project's methodology and decision-making were generally much better than studies drawing mainly on the private papers of Edwards and O'Donoghue suggest.[27] The two initiatives, operating concurrently for several years, are each a good source for the other. O'Malley refused to give a witness statement on the grounds that everything he had to say was in *On Another Man's Wound*, but he was obviously interested in the Bureau's work. There is little evidence of hostility on either side. The Bureau was aware that O'Malley was collecting material about the Civil War, and in 1951 helped him identify and locate Leitrim Brigade officers.[28] He likewise promised to let the Bureau make copies of any 'Tan War' documents in his possession. O'Malley transcribed at least fifteen witness statements into his interview books, and stayed in regular contact with individual Bureau staff, interviewing five of them.[29] Both of O'Malley's interviews with Florrie O'Donoghue discuss the material collected by the Bureau, including a copy of the notorious 'K' Company, Auxiliary diary, long reputed (inaccurately as it turns out) to have listed the names of local Protestants shot as spies in West Cork in April 1922.[30]

This reasonably congenial reality has been obscured by a lack of concrete information about the provenance of O'Malley's interviews, and the considerable misconceptions that persist to this day about the Bureau. One of the most widespread and puzzling mischaracterizations of the latter is that it was a 'Free State' project. In reality, the Bureau project was supported by, and to significant extent reflects the values of, the Republican middle ground that coalesced in Fianna Fáil after 1926. The Bureau was initiated by a Fianna Fáil government. Éamon de Valera played an instrumental role in its creation. Several key Bureau staff were his long time close associates and party stalwarts. He and Michael McDunphy (de Valera's personal choice for the position of director) had been discussing the project since the early 1930s.[31] McDunphy, a pro-Treaty senior civil servant and barrister, had worked in successive administrations since the foundation of the state. Acting assistant secretary to the Executive Council and private secretary to its President in the 1930s (under a Fianna Fáil administration), he also played an important role in formulating the government's early archival policies and was a member of the committee established by de Valera in May 1934 to draft what would eventually become the 1937 Constitution.[32] John McCoy and Seamus Robinson were also closely associated with Fianna Fáil. Paddy Brennan, the Bureau's affable secretary, had attended Fianna Fáil's founding meeting on Good Friday 1926. His brother Seán was both a Bureau investigator and de Valera's aide-de-camp.[33]

The Bureau was promoted at the time as a symbol of Republican reconciliation: a forum in which former Civil War adversaries could unite in common purpose to leave a record of the independence struggle that would act as a corrective to the 'British' version of events. Great care was taken in selecting Bureau staff and members of the Advisory Committee to ensure that all shades of political opinion were represented. Likewise, O'Malley showed little inclination to involve himself actively in politics on his return to Ireland. He remained on good terms with both Fianna Fáil anti-Treatyites who had reconciled themselves with the state and Republican irredentists who remained implacably opposed to it. Support for this kind of post-Civil War reconciliation was not universal. Both O'Malley and the Bureau were advised by prominent veterans about potential candidates for interview,[34] but hardliners on either side of the Treaty split were generally unwilling to co-operate with the Bureau. Despite considerable efforts made to secure witness statements from them, prominent pro-Treatyites Gearóid O'Sullivan, Diarmuid O'Hegarty, Joseph Vize and Richard Mulcahy, and Republican militants Pax Whelan, Moss Twomey, Peadar O'Donnell, Elizabeth Grennan and Tom Maguire, all refused. It was a sign of the times, however, that the Bureau sent out investigators to Twomey and Maguire, and that O'Donnell and Whelan helped Bureau investigators contact potential witnesses on the ground.[35]

Republicans who remained in Sinn Féin and the IRA after the 1926 split, often described Fianna Fáil as the 'new Free Staters'.[36] The Bureau's 'Free State' tag is almost certainly this irredentist slur taken out of context. There is little concrete evidence to suggest that significant numbers of anti-Treatyites refused to co-operate with the Bureau on political grounds, although this claim remains a feature of the negative historical gossip associated with the project. O'Malley was undoubtedly more successful than the Bureau in securing interviews with radicals such as Twomey, O'Donnell and Maguire (as well as Fianna Fáil luminaries such as Frank Aiken and P.J. Ruttledge) but the majority of interviewees in both collections were anti-Treaty. Ill feeling towards the Bureau, where it existed, was more often driven by current circumstances and issues such as the harsh treatment of the contemporary IRA by Fianna Fáil or controversies relating to the administration of the pensions legislation. Even where Civil War intransigence did inform attitudes, there was almost always more to it than that. Richard Mulcahy and Piaras Béaslaí, for instance, were clearly irritated at not being invited to take up a position in the Bureau.[37]

It is often hard to explain attitudes towards the project in terms of the (much over used) generalization 'Civil War bitterness'. One of the Bureau's most overarching difficulties was procrastination, even among willing witnesses, and knowing what side individuals took in 1922 was no help at all in determining who would come through in the end. Among East Limerick veterans, Major General Liam Hayes (pro-Treaty) was always extremely enthusiastic about the Bureau and promised to give statements to several investigators over the years. He never did. Cornelius Kearney (anti-Treaty) flatly refused to give a statement in 1952: 'you can hope for no reminiscences from me', he wrote, 'I look on the events of the period referred to as a very silly and stupid adventure. I remember those times with a feeling of aversion and self-disgust which increases as the years go by.'[38] By 1954 he had changed his mind, though he remained a 'difficult witness' to the end. The investigator taking his statement noted that he was the only person he was aware of who had voluntarily given up his military service pension 'because he considered that he had not earned it'.[39]

Gaining the interviewees' trust was among the most important factors influencing success for both projects. Neither O'Malley nor the Bureau was always successful. Bureau witnesses sometimes refused to discuss incidents or issues, or would tell investigators things informally which they would then decline to include in their statements.[40] O'Malley's notes suggest that he was quite a good interviewer, but he still encountered individuals whose reticence could not be overcome, such as Jack Harty, a former flying column member and Captain of B Company, 2nd Battalion, Tipperary I Brigade. O'Malley inserted this frustrated comment into his interview notes: 'Evidently they did a number of things which Harty wouldn't talk about so I am none the wiser as to how the columns behaved.'[41]

Both the Bureau and O'Malley collections cover the revolutionary period with a similar operational and distinctly Southern focus on, for the most part, a single organization – the Irish Volunteers / IRA, though smaller numbers of Irish Citizen Army, Hibernian Rifles, Cumann na mBan and Fianna Éireann veterans were also interviewed. Bureau and O'Malley interviews concentrate primarily on the experience of officers rather than the rank and file, and on how, when and why military actions were organized and conducted, as well as the combatants' prison experiences. The Bureau interviewed many more northern veterans and female Republicans than O'Malley, and also has much better coverage of the Easter Rising. About 350 individuals who gave Bureau testimonies about their experiences up to and including their involvement in the 1916 Rising did not discuss later events, even where they were involved in them. O'Malley's interviews tend to cover fewer topics in greater detail and are less regionally inclusive than the Bureau's but contain far more wide-ranging coverage of the Civil War.

The majority of witness statements span the entire period, from the founding of the Irish Volunteers in November 1913 to the Anglo-Irish Truce on 11 July 1921, and do not discuss the Civil War. The decision to exclude the Civil War period from the Bureau's official chronological terms of reference was pragmatic rather than ideological, taken in hopes of convincing wary pro-Treatyites to co-operate.[42] The cut-off point (July 1921) soon began to be ignored by Bureau investigators, and in October 1951 it was quietly jettisoned.[43] In all, over 250 Bureau testimonies contain some discussion of the Truce and post-Truce periods. Although the Bureau's Civil War content will never rival O'Malley's, a few statements deal entirely or at length with the later period, and several of the Bureau's document collections also contain Civil War material.

Ernie O'Malley's notebook interviews and the Bureau of Military History witness statements are the two most important currently available collections of personal testimony from the generation of Irish revolutionaries who fought against British rule. Apart from a few pre-written, re-transcribed memoirs, the vast majority are conversations rendered as solid blocks of written testimony. Discrepancies in the amount of available evidence relating to the provenance and conduct of the O'Malley interviews make extensive methodological comparisons between the two collections difficult, but they are essentially the same kind of source. Methodologically, neither is as straightforward to use as the recorded question and answer sessions of modern oral history interviews, primarily because their structure, by excluding the questions asked, masks the role of the interviewer. Consulting a pension board interview transcript in a 1934 MSP file provokes an instant awareness of the extent to which the general context of the interview, the questions asked and the status of the person asking, drives the answers given. The recorded interviews with Northern IRA veterans conducted by Father Louis O'Kane in the 1960s, held in the Cardinal Tomás Ó Fiaich Library in Armagh, demonstrate how much of the tone and rhythm of an interview is lost in even the best transcription.[44]

Nonetheless, O'Malley interviews and Bureau statements are oral history of a kind, and display the chronological fluidity and fusion of facts and representation that are the distinguishing hallmarks of oral testimony. Taking full advantage of these testimonies involves assessing both the wider context and provenance of their production as well as their specific characteristics as texts. Oral sources are, as Guy Beiner notes, 'social products, and text cannot be meaningfully separated from context'.[45] Interviewees were recounting events that formed part of a public, collective history. Their narratives document both individual experience and social memory, reflecting the distinctive *mentalités* and practices which developed among former combatants after 1923. The more acquainted the reader is with this wider 'context of remembering', the richer they become.[46] The tendency of historians to characterize the two projects as being in conscious opposition has obscured far more important contexts for both: the military service pensions acts, the writing and lobbying for rights and pensions that developed among separatist veterans after 1923, the general culture of remembrance and the post-Emergency reconciliation between former Civil War adversaries promoted by Irish governments after 1945.

The state's decision to provide some measure of practical compensation through pensions to those individuals who had fought for independence, shaped and informed both the O'Malley and Bureau projects indelibly. It is unlikely the Bureau could have operated on the scale that it did without access to the MSP records, and the financial security provided by O'Malley's pension played an equally important role in facili-tating his interviewing. That said, the process was very controversial, and the Bureau in particular had to contend with the disillusion that set in among thousands of failed pension applicants. The most common reason given for declining to give a witness statement was dissatisfaction over the outcome of a pension claim. Several individuals who did speak to the Bureau used their witness statements as a platform to vent their frustration or make a case in relation to their claims.[47] Fianna Fáil ministers, such as Seán MacEntee, were only too aware of the potential for storms over the MSPs to alienate their support base:

> we should not lose sight of the fact that very likely the vast majority of these disap-pointed applicants were very active political workers for Sinn Féin, and, we may assume, subsequently for Fianna Fáil. If we turn them down flatly now, they may be so completely estranged that they will become an effective element in the several left wing organisations which are hostile, not only to the Government, but to the State.[48]

There is no evidence that failed applicants were radicalized as a result, but resentment was widespread.

*

Scores of Old IRA and other separatist veterans' associations were formed in the decades after independence.[49] Through the pensions process, Defence established contacts with networks of veterans' organizations in every county in Ireland (including Northern Ireland), the United States and Britain. They became the main advocates for separatist veterans in post-revolutionary Ireland. The associations worked closely with Defence to secure pensions for their members, lobbied the government and local businesses for preferential treatment in employment and land distribution, organized annual commemorative events, and fund-raised for monuments. In the early 1930s, Moss

Twomey, then IRA Chief of Staff, feared that the veterans' associations would be used by the government to undermine the IRA. He deemed them 'freakish combinations of Republicans-Free Staters' and advised members to steer clear of them, although irredentist hostility seems to have gradually ebbed as the decade wore on.[50]

The veterans' organizations initiated in the wake of the 1934 MSP Act wielded considerable power. In order to build up a repository of corroboratory evidence relating to the activities of separatist military organizations (the exceptional amount of paperwork generated by the IRA was still very sparse compared to the records kept by regular forces),[51] Defence asked Old IRA, Cumann na mBan, Irish Citizen Army and Fianna Éireann veterans throughout the country to set up advisory committees 'irrespective of the political and other differences which divided them'. From 1935 until c.1945, these bodies compiled nominal rolls of members and activity reports for validating individual applications and nominated former officers to act as verifiers for pension applicants from their area.[52] These organizations often played a decisive role in determining who would receive a pension. As one pension Referee noted: 'it should be made clear that perhaps this is the only Act in this country, and perhaps in any other country, where the actual certifying authority is vested in persons or bodies not on the State Pay Roll'.[53]

By the time the Bureau and O'Malley began interviewing, former combatants had developed a distinctive 'separatist veterans' culture' of traditions and practices relating to remembrance, sociability, commemoration, self-protection and promotion. Each project negotiated, reflected and in some respects deviated from the common practices and dominant sensibilities of that culture. The idea that veterans were the most, indeed the only, suitable candidates to deal with the period ran very deep and across political divides. O'Malley's conviction that the men would 'tell me the truth' was likely a general reference to his veteran status. Likewise, almost all of the Bureau's initiators, advisors, administrators, and all but one of the Bureau's field workers, were veterans, mostly IRA, from a range of political backgrounds. John McCoy and Seamus Robinson were both anti-Treaty. Florrie O'Donoghue had been neutral in the Civil War. Colonel Dan Bryan was pro-Treaty.

Commissioning, composing, collecting or facilitating popular accounts of the independence struggle – generally drawing on first-hand accounts from the men and women who had taken part in events – were important expressions of separatist veterans' culture. Veterans' committees were sometimes able to exert a significant measure of influence over how they were represented. In 1947, for instance, Dan Nolan, editor of the Kerryman newspaper, submitted a draft of *Kerry's Fighting Story* to a local brigade committee for correction and approval.[54] Well-established conventions for constructing accounts of the revolutionary period had evolved. The idea that participant narratives were the most reliable kind of evidence co-existed with competing and conflicting attitudes about how best to deal with inconsistencies in remembered fact. Personal testimony was frequently communally reviewed by groups of veterans to verify accuracy, and accounts were often devised collectively. This was the method employed by many of the Old IRA Brigade committees in compiling records for pension purposes, and the 1916 Garrison committees when collecting accounts for a proposed 'Historical Record of the 1916 Rising and Events'.[55] The Old Irish Citizen Army Comrades Association also collected and reviewed personal testimonies for R.M. Fox to use in *The History of the Irish Citizen Army* (which they commissioned).[56]

The traditions of communal compilation and review were to a certain extent rooted in anxiety at the lack of consensus among veterans. The former combatants and activists, interviewers and interviewees, populating the O'Malley interviews and Bureau witness statements were simultaneously documenters of and subjective participants in a dialogue between veterans and the public sphere. They were active agents of memory, interacting with a larger 'community of memory' of which they were part. They regularly framed their recollections of the events in which they had been involved as commentary on published memoirs or well-known accounts of those events by other participants. These discourses can be traced through published accounts, witness statements, Bureau administrative records, MSP applications and O'Malley interviews. In November 1949, a man stormed into the Bureau offices on Westland Row with a copy of Robert Holland's witness statement, which named this man's family as forming part of a 'mob' who attacked Irish Volunteer prisoners being marched to Richmond Barracks after the Rising. Insisting that the accusations were untrue, the man described them as 'part of a political vendetta that was being carried on against members of the Fianna Fáil organization by Holland and his friends who were members of Clan na Póblachta'.[57]

There were long-lasting allegiances and friendships, many notorious rows and less-well-known ones. By the 1940s they resembled layers of an onion. Enmities and alliances, often predating the Treaty split, were cemented by the Civil War and then further fuelled by events which post-dated the revolutionary era. Accusations and rumours followed some individuals for the rest of their lives. All sorts of animosities and disagreements had to be managed. Practically every published account was publicly or privately contested by some veterans and approved by others. *On Another Man's Wound* was no exception. O'Malley's memoir certainly deserves the description of 'one of the great works of twentieth century Irish prose';[58] but, in common with other participant testimonies, it was a forum in which the author paid tribute to some, caricatured others, took venomous swipes at those he really did not like or (worst of all), failed to mention someone's contribution. Maureen McGavock took O'Malley to task in her witness statement for not acknowledging the assistance rendered to him by Josephine Clarke.[59] Several Kilkenny veterans were enraged by his account of his arrest in that county in December 1920.[60] O'Malley was successfully sued by Joseph O'Doherty in 1937 for alleging that he had refused to participate in a Donegal arms raid.[61] In *Guerilla Days in Ireland*, Tom Barry portrayed O'Malley as a pretentious know-all sent by GHQ: 'His language during his exposition of the document and his constant use of long military words and phrases left no doubt in the minds of his listeners that he had read a military book of some sort'.[62] Responses to Barry's own memoir were as mixed as those to O'Malley's.[63]

*

Accusations of cowardice levelled by O'Malley and others at John V. Joyce, in charge of army officers working as Bureau investigators from June 1948, are another case in point. O'Malley, on good terms with several Bureau staff, clearly despised Joyce. Joyce fought for the Free State during the Civil War, but it was undoubtedly his post-revolutionary career that made him a hate figure among Republicans. He and two other Bureau appointees had served on the Military Tribunal set up by the Cosgrave government in 1931, and later the Special Criminal Court established under the 1939 Offences against the State Act passing death sentences on Republicans.[64] A former medical student and 1916 veteran of the South Dublin Union, as captain of C Company 4th battalion, Joyce had cancelled a planned operation at the Standard Hotel, one of several attacks aimed at British intelligence and courts-martial officers by the Dublin Brigade on 'Bloody Sunday', 21 November 1920. Colonel Dan Bryan, a member of C Company, who had taken part in the action, said the decision to call it off was taken by Joyce only after consultation with other officers, because the job was considered 'too big'.[65] O'Malley pilloried but did not name Joyce in a passage from *On Another Man's Wound*, in which he described meeting him the night before, 'An excited captain from the university whispered to me in the dressing room: "My God, it's awful, a GHQ job, damned awful"... He laughed with a nervous whinny as he pressed back his hair ...'[66]

Joyce came up again in O'Malley's interviews with Bloody Sunday veterans. Andy Cooney (IRA Chief of Staff in 1925) and Joe Byrne, a former member of Joyce's company who agreed with O'Malley that Joyce was a coward, were scathing.[67] O'Malley, bracketed his own comments within the interview: 'It was lucky that others thought that Joyce was a coward, otherwise he would have taken an action against me for what I'd said about him in my book.'[68] O'Malley's and Cooney's assessments seem to be based on conversations with Joyce before the action, not direct experience. There is enough contradictory detail in MSP files and witness statements from other anti-Treaty men who had actually taken part in the abortive Standard Hotel attack to suggest that much of what O'Malley implied should be treated with caution. Joe Byrne's pension application, for instance, contains a glowing reference from Joyce, and Byrne told the pension board someone else had demobilized his company on Bloody Sunday.[69] Patrick Mullen, interviewed by the Bureau but not by O'Malley, says Joyce was in charge, but that the job was cancelled because the two British targets had left the hotel.[70] Thomas J. Doyle, in both his O'Malley and MSP interviews, also said that the attack was called off because the officers had been replaced by others: 'We were in a very bad position, but it would be a bad thing to shoot the wrong fellows.'[71] The MSP testimony of Patrick Lamb, however, claimed that one of the two officers was still there. Oscar Traynor, former OC of the Dublin Brigade, was critical of Joyce in general but unconvinced by Lamb's testimony: 'I could not really say, several of them [the intended targets] were absent … but that would be typical of Lamb, he would say he was on the premises maybe when he did not know whether he was or not.'[72]

Joyce did not give a witness statement about Bloody Sunday, and his pension claim under the 1924 Act did not require the same level of detail as the 1934 procedures.[73] He does not seem to have made any effort to contradict O'Malley and, as he successfully sued a British newspaper in 1958 for referring to him as the 'Hanger Joyce' (in reference to his former role as military court judge), he was not averse to taking libel action as such.[74] If what Doyle says is true, then O'Malley's accusation of cowardice seems overly harsh. If Joyce's silence is interpreted as assent, as O'Malley supposed, then we have our answer, but who knows?

Either way, the distinctive 'off the record' quality of O'Malley's Bloody Sunday interviews make them among the most significant in the collection. Both the pensions board and the Bureau had difficulty in establishing who had taken part in Bloody Sunday because several of the men involved simply would not discuss it.[75] Yet more than one veteran who did little more than confirm his involvement to the pension board spoke quite candidly to O'Malley.[76] The dispute over the Standard Hotel action was far from being the only acrimonious controversy to generate a miasma of claims and counterclaims for which there is very little other evidence to go on apart from what one warring side says about the other. Despite O'Malley's occasionally withering asides in his notebooks, both he and the Bureau generally chose to document rather than try and resolve such disputes.

Neither the O'Malley nor Bureau projects replicated the traditions of communal compilation and review established by other schemes. There is no evidence to suggest that O'Malley's privately collected interviews were reviewed or corrected by his interviewees. Undoubtedly the most important methodological decision taken by Michael McDunphy was to revise the Bureau's earliest procedural guidelines drafted by Florrie O'Donoghue. O'Donoghue had recommended that all statements be reviewed by groups of veterans and that Bureau investigators should correct perceived mistakes in the witnesses' evidence in order to avoid recording 'faulty and misleading' evidence.[77] McDunphy's procedures, issued in May 1948, by contrast, directed that no attempt be made to make a witness's story more plausible or to adjust it in any way.[78] Only the witness could review or correct his or her own statement. If they could not account for 'apparent contradictions' in his evidence, McDunphy wrote, the 'matter should be left there and the story recorded exactly as it was told'; and if that story conflicted with others in the Bureau 'it is not for the investigator to decide which is right. That is a matter for the historian'.[79] McDunphy's decision to prioritize the subjective truth of individual experience – recording it 'exactly as it was told' – rather than attempting to mould memories into conformity with other accounts – was prescient, and foreshadowed contemporary oral history practice. In the context of the time, it was a brave step, and not always accepted. Bureau investigators were occasionally involved in tussles with cantankerous local committees or individuals over the issue of editorial control, and were deliberately obstructed in some areas. Tom Barry, former commander of West Cork's famous flying column, argued that witness statements should be pre-vetted by a veterans' committee. Some of the Dublin, Cork City and Limerick veterans' associations insisted on submitting only pre-examined or group statements.[80]

Witness statements are more formal and formulaic than O'Malley interviews. They are rarely as blunt in their depictions of political violence, war and bodily functions but are still, in their own way, just as sophisticated. Variously dragooned into the service of insular, 'anti-Revisionist' (whatever that means) polemic or rejected as inherently less trustworthy than other records, witness statements deserve more subtle and intuitive models for interpreting and comparing them than is often employed: 'Ambushography' (Peter Hart); a 'ubiquity of serious factual errors and self-justifying distortion' (David Fitzpatrick).[81] That the Bureau and O'Malley collections are often still dismissed on such grounds is more reflective of the narrowly positivist predisposition in much scholarship relating to the revolutionary period than an accurate assessment of the material. There is a tendency to characterize veterans as mouthpieces for nationalist myths (to be either supported or derided). Anne Dolan's decontextualized narrative analysis of the Bureau and O'Malley Bloody Sunday testimony is original and powerful in its exposition, but assumes rather than proves that the explicitness of the men's descriptions of violence provides insight into their emotional psychology (with a lack of gruesome detail read as moral failure or dishonesty).[82]

There is much more involved in consulting witness statements (and O'Malley interviews) than the straight extraction of factual detail. Memories are complex constructions, inherently dynamic and unstable rather than linear or chronological. Retellings over the years are shaped by the passing of time, as the significance of the events change. Josephine Clarke, in her witness statement, recalled an incident during the Civil War when Liam Tobin, a Free State officer, secured her release from custody so that she could continue her search for the anti-Treaty column in which her husband served:

> We were brought to the Aerodrome in Tallaght which was filled with Free State troops and while we were waiting there who should come in but Liam Tobin all decorated with stars and stripes. He and I knew each other in Kilkenny and played together as children - he was Billy Tobin then. He got an awful drop when he saw me and said, 'For God's sake, Josie, what are you doing here?' 'You see I am a prisoner' said I. He took me aside and asked me where was Liam [her husband]. I told him he was with the Column around Rathfarnham. He said, 'You had better get in touch with him. I'll have you sent in the first car that leaves here, and tell him I have orders to get all those fellows, dead or alive.' I'll remember that to Billy's credit as long as I live.[83]

The revolutionary generation's dialectical, transitional memories are as reflective of the period in which they were collected as the years being discussed, and formed as much by the Ireland they fought to overthrow as the one they helped create. A whole range of circumstances, associations and events from Clarke's life are invoked to explain the significance of her meeting with Tobin. In her self-reflective nod to her and Tobin's shared history and former identities, the present intrudes into the past, and the past is employed to explain the present and a world that no longer existed: 'he was Billy Tobin then'. Her narrative shifts from the Civil War to late-nineteenth-century Ireland with its anglicized names and the Irish Parliamentary Party, then back to the Civil War, fought between people who had known each other all their lives. Clarke ends by calling attention to the elderly lady that she was in 1952, remembering all this.

As oral historians have demonstrated (time and time again), distinctions between 'reliable' written evidence and 'unreliable' oral evidence tend to dissolve under scrutiny.[84]

It is not that oral testimonies do not sometimes contain factual errors, distortions, omissions – they do – but so do written sources. How 'true' any source is depends a great deal on what you want to know. A lie or a silence can reveal a great deal of truth. British and Irish government records from the revolutionary period, for instance, are full of them. Surviving primary sources are an essential starting point when using oral testimony, but historical documents of all kinds, even the most traditional, are limited, partial, and almost always contain a mix of accurate and inaccurate information. A far more important distinction is that a retrospective personal account – be it a published memoir, MSP testimony, witness statement or O'Malley interview – is a different kind of source than a contemporary record. Its historical value is rooted in its subjectivity.

As the German philosopher and essayist Walter Benjamin once observed, while actual events are 'confined to one sphere of experience, a remembered event is infinite, because it is only a key to everything that happened before and after it'.[85]

CHAPTER NINE

'THE PEOPLE' OF
ON ANOTHER MAN'S WOUND

Seamus O'Malley

A long concern of Irish historiography and political theorizing has been the inadequacy of continental models of political parties to explain the Irish situation, either in terms of its many revolutionary moments, or its subsequent establishment of two political parties that make little clear ideological distinction. Nationalism is generally held to be the altering agent, but in fact there is another formulating element in Irish politics that has clear correspondence with other nations, and that is the politics of populism. Irish politics, especially before Independence, closely adheres to models of populism like those formulated by the Argentinean theorist Ernesto Laclau. For Laclau, via his work *On Populist Reason* (2005), 'the people' as a discourse is produced when a series of local demands are unanswered by an established power, and the groups making these claims begin to form discursive links.[1] Unlike the traditional Marxist model of a working class organizing into labour unions, or a neo-liberal model of isolated citizens utilizing parliamentary politics and a free market, populism mobilizes large and loosely defined groups, and especially contingent allegiances of groups, often led by a charismatic leader who comes to embody the aspirations of 'the people'. O'Connell and de Valera meet many of Laclau's definitions of the charismatic leader.

Hearing the phrase 'the people' usually spells trouble: societies functioning without a great degree of strife do not produce 'the people', and only when there is 'the drawing of an antagonistic frontier' between clamouring groups and the entrenched system do the necessary conditions for populism exist.² Laclau argues that the language and images of the grieving groups eventually unify 'into a stable system of signification'.³ How stable can vary tremendously, however, and in the case of Irish history, the long nineteenth century witnesses a total transformation of the term. The early 'Patriot' politicians were generally referring only to their own class when using the phrase, and as John Fitzgibbon acutely (if uncharitably) remarked in 1789, 'when we speak of the people of Ireland, it is a melancholy truth that we do not speak of the great body of the people'.⁴ Later in the nineteenth century, Young Ireland and the Land League embraced the term in vaguely national and class terms, respectively. By the end of the century 'the people' meant anyone except the Anglo-Irish, and thus the phrase slowly morphed, from 1789 to 1889, into its own antonym. The discourses of the Irish Renaissance and agitations for independence inherit this late usage of 'the people', as compellingly evidenced in Ernie O'Malley's *On Another Man's Wound* (1936).⁵

At populist moments, one group within a larger, loose alliance of groups becomes the rallying point for the entire discourse of 'the people'. Laclau terms this 'privileging', as when 'a certain identity is picked up from the whole field of differences, and made to embody this totalizing function'.⁶ In works of the Irish Renaissance, like those by Lady Gregory, and later in O'Malley's memoir, the rural, peasant Irish of the West become the privileged identity that 'embodies' the entire set of grievances launched by Dublin workers, Sinn Féin intellectuals, Irish exiles, nationalist aristocrats like Gregory or radicalized students like O'Malley. At stake in this process of privileging is the question of legitimacy. For the United Irishmen, Enlightenment ideals embodied in the more forward-thinking of the Anglo-Irish caste legitimize Irish independence, whereas Lady Gregory's use of 'the people' to speak broadly of her peasant neighbours, or O'Malley's portraits of the homes in which he found shelter, indicates that during the revolution a different social grouping will be called upon to legitimate Irish nationalism.

This process of privileging poses 'the horizon of the social, the limit of what is representable within it'.⁷ If the phrase 'a people' is merely descriptive, 'the people' carries power and moral authority while simultaneously establishing boundaries and exclusions. 'A people' can be one amongst many worldwide; 'the people' implies an inevitability to its power, but also casts a negative judgement on any individual not 'of the people'. Laclau writes that the discourse of 'the people' 'is something less than the totality of the members of the community: it is a practical component which nevertheless aspires to be conceived as the only legitimate totality'.⁸ The rural peasants of

Ireland are the part that not just stands for, but legitimizes, the whole; 'a partiality which wants to function as the totality of the community'.[9]

Laclau is not blind to the limits of populism as a privileged mode of political organization, as the links that are formed to produce the people will only ever be contingent and temporary.[10] Thus when we investigate historical formulations of the people, their inevitable disintegration is usually clear to hindsight. The phrase's history is most evident in painting of the French revolutions. Eugène Delacroix's *Liberty Leading the People* (1830) may be the visual masterpiece of this discourse, but it also stages the complex strategies involved in deciding how to represent the people (Figure 12). In the figures that dominate the left and bottom of the painting, Delacroix opts for a representative mode, both in terms of their non-abstractness – they are not allegorical like the bare-breasted Liberty, nor symbolic like the tricolour flag of the Republic – but also in the sense of representing various strata of the Parisian population, who are selected to embody 'the people' as a legitimating force. The foregrounded figure with a sabre from the far left has the visual signifiers of a printer, one of the most radicalized of Parisian trades. Next to him is the representative figure of the lower bourgeoisie, dishevelled but still in possession of top hat and vest. Other lower-class workers appear less prominently but still distinctly.

The work is a powerful record of 1830, and yet glaringly visible are the social fractures that will lead, not to a government of the people or by the people, but rather to an Orleanist monarchy with close ties to large capitalism. (While the aristocracy had never been the people, the big bourgeoisie could be for a few years after 1789.) With every subsequent revolution, the bourgeoisie had a harder time identifying as the people, and by 1870 their severance from revolutionary activity was complete. Delacroix's armed petit bourgeois would be the last we would see on this side of the barricades.[11]

Class thus disrupts the unifying power of the phrase, but French painting also demonstrates how, as T.J. Clark writes in *Farewell to an Idea: Episodes from a History of Modernism* (1999), 'The question of the People is a question about representation.'[12] For Clark, since the usage of 'the people' is always oppositional, employed against the aristocracy, or the powerful and wealthy, 'the categories themselves had better be kept free from empirical detail, lest the actual distinctions and tensions that existed within the people's ranks take on political form'.[13] This is precisely the case of Delacroix's painting, whose representative empiricism makes it the ideal expression of 1830 but completely incompatible with 1848 or 1870.

A more fascinating mode of handling the concept of the people is the strategies of avoidance or redirection that we see in Lacques-Louis David's *The Death of Marat*

(1793, Figure 13). Clark writes that, in the revolutionary period, 'never before had the powers-that-be in a state been obliged to improvise a sign language whose very effectiveness depended on its seeming to the People a language they had made up, and that therefore represented their interests'.[14] In David's painting, Marat – *L'Ami du Peuple* – does not represent the people per se. He is their friend and spokesperson, and for David offers a convenient means to elide any empirical depiction of the people. Clark writes that Marat's death took many representational forms throughout 1793, all part of the struggle to depict the signs of revolutionary ideals:

> The category 'People' had to have something be its sign. Among the signifying possibilities on offer in 1793, 'Marat' seemed one of the best. At least in him the category was personified. That might mean that the welter of claims, identifications, and resentments wrapped up in the word could at least be concentrated into a single figure – and therefore shaped and contained. It would take some doing.[15]

The result is David's secularized idol that became the blueprint for the public display of the corpses of Lenin and Eva Perón, some of the stranger emblems of the politics of populist modernity.

But just as Delacroix's painting lays bare the contradictions within revolutionary discourse, David's provides the signifiers of a contested social process, and Clark argues that 'this is what makes it inaugural of modernism'.[16] For Clark, modernism is the cultural transmission of the contingency of modernity, as 'painting [is] being forced to include the accident and tendentiousness of politics in its picture of the world'.[17] While David is trying to be a good Jacobin, 'the picture enacts the contingency of claims to truth and falsehood at the moment it was made. This is its modernism, so to speak.'[18] The painting questions the very values of nation, liberty, and the people that it offers. The modern world then begins on or about Year Two, since with Marat, 'contingency rules. Contingency enters the process of picturing. It invades it. There is no other substance out of which paintings can now be made – no givens, no matters, and subject-matters, no forms, no usable pasts. Or none that a possible public could be taken to agree on anymore.'[19] The constant forming and breaking of social links that Laclau theorizes is, for Clark, part of a wider symptom of modernity. What is fascinating about the concept of the people, then, is that it is born at the same time that its representational existence becomes impossible. While Laclau is generally defending the possibilities of populism, he does point to what he calls the 'emptiness' of its formulations, since as the discourse of the people grows hegemonically, 'it becomes intensionally poorer, for it has to dispossess itself of particularistic contents in order to embrace social demands which are quite heterogeneous. That is: a popular identity functions as a tendentially empty signifier.'[20] The resulting vagueness is anathema to artistic production, which is why David's particular strategies in Marat maintain their hold.

David, of course, is not Picasso, not eagerly seeking out the possibilities of contingency and its implications for painterly representation. The political and representational doubts of Marat are 'foisted on it by the very urgency of its effort to guarantee truth, to show it inhering in the world', Clark writes.[21] The painting resists contingency even as it embodies it, in keeping with what Clark terms the modernist 'rearguard action against the truths it has stumbled on'.[22] And this was not just true of early modernist works: we might say that Yeats, especially the mature Yeats of 1916–23, was launching the most sustained and impressive rearguard action against modernity in works like 'A Second Coming' and 'A Prayer for my Daughter'. 'Easter 1916' is relevant here as well: Clark writes that, while *Marat* is hardly the first political painting, it might be the first 'to leave the accident and tendentiousness of politics in the form it makes – not to transmute it', a process that could explain the belated tone of Yeats's reaction to the Easter Rising.[23] What that poem recognizes is the already aesthetic nature of the Rising. Thus the event may be mediated but not 'transmuted'.

It is this acknowledgement of contingency, whether willingly or not, that animates the style and discourse of O'Malley's *On Another Man's Wound*. What emerges in that memoir – written just before de Valera's Constitution – is a series of attempts to depict the people, and a struggle on behalf of the people. The voices of the people are even included, in a sense, in the popular ballads that often close the chapters. But the text also enacts the contingency of the people as a social or political construction, as the memoir's unflinching and austere honesty cannot help but ingest the fractured and stratified nature of Irish social classes and the mechanics of Irish populism. Like David, O'Malley is a good Republican who cannot help but include the contingent. Also like David, and unlike Picasso or Joyce, O'Malley does not revel in modernist self-doubt, and to conclude Clark's reading of *Marat*, we could theorize various modernisms that emerge from French painting. Clark turns to the top, supposedly empty, half of David's work to theorize a kind of modernism that would become hegemonic in the twentieth century: 'the endless, meaningless objectivity produced by paint not quite finding its object, symbolic or otherwise, and therefore making do with its own procedures', that is most visible in Abstract Expressionism.[24] Clark also links this to the discourse of the people, as the emptiness that David encounters trying to include the notion of the people sends him to technique as pure technique. I do not believe that we encounter such an attitude in *On Another Man's Wound*, which might explain why it does not fit easily into the canons of modernism, Irish or otherwise. But, in O'Malley, 'contingency rules', not only in its political acknowledgements but in its very style and aesthetic strategies.

French revolutionary painting is especially apt because of the shared vocabulary of Irish and French Republicanism. Despite the obvious differences of historical context, both movements, in all their broad range, struggled with the depiction of res publica.[25] Michael Hopkinson writes of the 'strong Robespierrist tendency' in Irish Republicanism that especially emerged during the Civil War.[26] Clark, describing the politics of Marat, could equally be commenting on the IRA, and especially O'Malley: 'A terrible determination to forge or preserve those weapons that (in his opinion) the revolution might need combines with a wish to speak for the despised and rejected.'[27] For both Marat and O'Malley, a substitution of armed revolutionaries for the people is necessary for the political victory of the people. As Richard English argues in his biography, *Ernie O'Malley: IRA Intellectual* (1999), 'according to O'Malley, one should lead the people rather than follow their expressed preferences' and the movement was 'as much about creating the conditions for Revolution as about responding to them'.[28] At one point in his memoir, O'Malley recounts how he wrote to Frank Gallagher of the *Irish Bulletin*: 'It's time for you to acknowledge the IRA at last … Previously we had been referred to as a suffering people who in desperation were attacking their oppressors.'[29] Paradoxically, the very professionalism of the Irish Republican Army, which by definition means the separation of the army from the people, is what legitimates both the IRA and the Irish Republic. Paradoxical, and yet commonplace around the world: nations of all kinds have professional armies – but only nations. Early in the war, O'Malley argues, 'we had thought in terms of a general, simultaneous rebellion throughout the country; now Headquarters endeavoured to teach us to train, arm and equip and to carry out minor operations for the seizure of arms'.[30] A 'general' uprising might directly express the will of 'the people', especially in nineteenth-century terms, but newer strategies envisioned a fighting force made up of, but separate from, the people. The existence of the IRA was thus necessary to allow the Republic to come to birth, and in both O'Malley's military organizing and later life-writing, he is performing on behalf of the people, but always acknowledges that he is not of them.

French painting is apt in O'Malley's case due to his deep interest in the visual arts, during his youth as a sometimes-student of art, when he would pass long hours contemplating Italian painting, and especially the post-war years when he was immersed in modernist networks in New Mexico, New York and Dublin. O'Malley's interest in modernist art from Jack Yeats to native Mexican art was linked to his theorizing regarding representations of the people. O'Malley's role in Irish visual culture is only now coming to the proper attention of Irish criticism, but the vexed issue of political representation was never absent from debates on Irish art of the period.

The phrase 'the people' is deployed over thirty times in *On Another Man's Wound* (over twice the amount that appeared in *The Singing Flame* – appropriate given the later text's recurrent anxiety over the unpopularity of the Republican side during the Civil War). In most cases, O'Malley's compact prose becomes vague when discussing the people, as in these typical examples:

> The effort at repression continued. Boys were arrested for marching in groups, for singing 'The Soldier's Song', for carrying the tricolour; concerts were prohibited, newspapers heavily censored. Baton charges broke up meetings, freedom of speech was denied, bayonets began to glitter and threaten. The people met the new measures passively; but militarism, without excessive physical repression, evoked the same memories and produced the same results as it had once done when it could shoot and hang, burn and confiscate, transport to the West Indies or employ the boiling pitch-cap.[31]

> The life of the people was hard enough, but money or comfort were not standards that interrupted their contentment; above all they were alive and personal. The struggle with the soil rarely ground them down.[32]

The language in these passages is overly broad, never displaying the concreteness, both physical and emotional, of his stronger moments. These 'people' passages pass on recycled ideas, depicting a general state of affairs that only serves dutifully to give readers a larger context for the progression of the war. Such moments violate his stated desire in the Introduction: 'I have endeavoured to explain action as I then saw it and, as far as was possible, to avoid all retrospective realisation of the implications of events. As the survey is seen through my eyes I had to show my own progression in development.'[33] O'Malley generally succeeds in his ambitions, which make these vague lapses all the more conspicuous.[34]

Of course, the vague use of the phrase was widespread in nationalist discourse. But what is so fascinating about *On Another Man's Wound* is not just that O'Malley usually avoids such an empty tone; it is that he intuits the nature of the difficulties of representing the people and, like David, looks for aesthetic solutions to an ideological problem. O'Malley perceives the inadequacy of the phrase, and I suspect it is his immersion in visual art, both European and Mexican, that provides him with the awareness of the issue and an aesthetic designed to redress the challenge.

On Another Man's Wound is so full of sharp observations of social particulars that, as in Delacroix, the empirical aspect of O'Malley's recordings cannot fail to lay bare the heterogeneous nature of 'the movement'. Note how in the following passage on class stratification 'the people' is absent as a phrase:

> Our fight was a beginning not an end we knew, but in what direction would it go? We could not say. In the country the small farmers and labourers were our main support, and in cities the workers, with a middle-class sprinkling; towns we could not count on. The countryman, sympathetic enough where a land revolution was concerned, was hostile to the revolution of organised labour; the farm labourer could understand the city workman, and was organised in labour unions with him. The movement as a whole was hostile to labour claims even though labour had helped to prevent conscription, had not contested the last election and was now refusing to carry armed troops.[35]

While general, O'Malley's summary here is never reductive or abstract, and presents an intellectually honest account of economic gradation during the revolution and the challenges it posed to nationalist organization. 'The people' as a phrase could not survive in such a passage that resists nationalist shorthand.[36] Much later O'Malley writes, 'Our comradeship in a desperate cause was reducing our disparities and was uniting us in a bond, yet class distinctions would jut out, and our merging in what we were glad to call "the people" was a figment.'[37] Contingency rules as O'Malley questions the very discourse of the people that he elsewhere employs.

While questioning 'the people' as a representational concept, O'Malley is also depicting the fractures that threaten the unity of the nationalist efforts: 'We fought boys from Belvedere and Protestants from Mountjoy School or MS; they were Swaddlers and Proddy-dogs; we were papishes, RCs pronounced quickly, and O'Connell's Sausages from the "OCS" on our caps; their "MS" meant Monkey Slops … In the towns tuppence-ha'penny looked down on tuppence, and throughout the country the grades in social difference were as numerous as the layers of an onion.'[38] These social fractures, however, could be accommodated within the nationalist movement generally. They are hurdles, but not insurmountable ones (and are a feature of any nationalist moment). The 'we' above is simply the young O'Malley and his friends. Once the 'we' become the IRA, heterogeneity functions differently:

> We, like all city companies, were mixed: professions, unskilled labour, students, government clerks, skilled labour, businessmen and out of-works; mostly young men, some boys. University students were scattered among the city companies where they learned to meet and know that fine type, the Dublin working man. Through him and others they were brought into touch with the slums and with living conditions; they found the Cause had united men of different classes, outlooks, creeds.[39]

O'Malley, throughout both memoirs, shows little interest in politics as traditionally conceived, and is comfortable with the IRA representing nationalism at large. What he never does is assume they represent the people, and thus in the passage above, the 'mix' of groups within the movement is not on par with a fractured discourse of the people. To highlight heterogeneity within the IRA is acknowledging a challenge to organization; to point out the mixed nature of the people is to undermine the stability of the discourse itself.

Economic class is the most prominent point of fracture within 'the people', and in the passage above the phrase does not appear but in its stead we get 'the Dublin working man', another vague generality, although with more regional and class particularity than 'the people'. (Although O'Malley's most memorable passages are describing the countryside, much of his writing takes place in cities, although often behind bars cut off from urban life.) Is the Dublin proletariat part of the people? The question cannot, of course, be empirically asked or answered, and yet its presence in O'Malley's text distinguishes it from so many other Irish works during de Valera's ascendancy (especially de Valera's constitution itself).

The differences of class or religion that O'Malley records could be accommodated within a nationalist framework, and again Irish nationalism is not unique in confronting these divisions. It is the geographical divisions that were more troubling to Sinn Féin and the IRA, and O'Malley pays particular attention to how location operates in the Irish consciousness:

> Jerry Kieley left for Tipperary. The Corkmen would not give him a rifle. He felt he deserved one after Mallow, but rifles were rifles; they belonged to the brigade in which they were captured and Jerry, angry with me because I would not insist on his claim, went off in disgust. It was hard to keep men outside their own counties; in the column some men made excuses to get home on leave. Mountainy men were the worst; their girls or the mountains made them unsettled when far away.[40]

These regional feuds bedevil O'Malley throughout his career as a military organizer, but more crucially destabilize the notion of Ireland as its own geographical entity. O'Malley's line regarding the 'mountainy men' make them appear a separate race altogether: how could they possibly share interests with an Arthur Griffith or the young medical student from Dublin turned IRA organizer? In O'Malley's memoir, local attachments threaten Irish nationalism to a much greater degree than religion or class. While imprisoned by the British in Kilmainham Gaol,

> It was easy to begin an acquaintance when I could talk of a county that I had liked. The men carried their home places in their minds; it was pleasant to take them out of

themselves by building up the skeleton of what they had known well; their memories would supply details, and people the new country of their minds. When you knew a man's district well and could talk about its personal geography, you became, for a time, closer than a blood relation.[41]

What does this local, county attachment do to Ireland as an 'imagined community'? While the men 'carry their home places in their minds', 'home' is not Ireland but Kerry or Cork or Donegal. Is there room for Ireland in their imagination? O'Malley is often dubious, and the 'new country' of their minds is not a future Irish nation but the local regions of their pasts. (Although elsewhere he writes that 'in gaol, boys learned to carry on a gaol war; they mixed with men from other provinces and widened their national horizon'.)[42] Note too the use of 'people' as a verb, meaning 'to populate': while nationalism generally is attempting to people their minds with a modern notion of Ireland, 'the people' themselves seem resistant and retain local attachments.[43]

Questions about the people also involve voice. Can the people speak? The people are not necessarily subaltern, although the subaltern is often one of the groups included in the discursive networks of populism. But if Laclau is correct, then the people defining themselves is a logical impossibility, given their non-existence as an essential category: they only exist after they are named.[44] The people are always spoken for, either by a David or a Delacroix: Laclau writes that the people who get called 'the people' 'can never fully control which demands they embody and represent'.[45] Marat was a Friend of the People, not one of them. When Lady Gregory writes that 'I hear the people say now and then …', we can never verify if what she hears is what they say.[46]

O'Malley is yet another spokesperson, in the literal sense, and while Gregory is equally honest about her difference from the people, O'Malley's aesthetic is more aggressive in positioning himself apart from them as objects of representation. He never pretends to be of the people, or even their friend, and in fact goes to great efforts to highlight his difference from them, not to establish his superiority but to call into question his right to speak on behalf of people very unlike himself: '"A stranger" I was spoken of in their houses. It would be easy for information to be brought to the police, but though the people talked much amongst themselves, as if making up for lost time when they met, yet there were walls between them and the outside world';[47] and 'I found the country strange. Life had been very sheltered at home. We had been well clothed and cared for; neatness had always been insisted on. I did not understand the people.'[48] Throughout the memoir, either he is a stranger to the people, or they are strange to him. This should come as no surprise given what he has already established about the divisions of class and region: O'Malley remains throughout, a

Dublin medical student, if lapsed. As a military organizer he has to generate strategies to surpass these barriers, but as a writer his challenge is aesthetic: how to represent what he 'did not understand'? O'Malley's austere honesty precludes any easy identification. As Nicholas Allen has remarked in *Modernism, Ireland and the Civil War* (2009), 'O'Malley reveals a proximity between representation and deployment that suggests the imaginative negotiation of a landscape at once aesthetic and military.'[49] We see this operating in several passages regarding O'Malley's struggles with local divisions (in both senses of that term):

> The clan spirit as such, deeper than the isolation and accent of individual counties, had to be overcome or switched to rivalry in organisation and action with those across the border. Distrust and jealousy had to be fought by fostering their own development in command; the dead weight of tradition grinding us between millstones had to be diverted to a new outlook and in a new hold on the present.[50]

While ostensibly describing military organization, we could also, as Allen suggests, read this as a meditation on the challenges of nationalism generally, and the need for a new kind of writing that could maintain the 'new hold' on modern Ireland. O'Malley's interest in modern art and literature, especially James Joyce,[51] is of course relevant here, but in other passages O'Malley expresses a desire, again ostensibly military, that Allen encourages us to read as aesthetic: 'I felt that I should be able to fuse with my material, the people, so that I could make better use of it, yet look at them dispassionately, as if from a distance.'[52] This desire to 'fuse' is precisely the insolvable problem, but equally a source of creative animation, for *On Another Man's Wound*. The entire work reads like an effort at drawing closer to an object that the text acknowledges will never be grasped:

> At home gatherings I sometimes felt the people withdraw their already partly granted family intimacy; the eddy that had taken me in would fling me out again. I would be like a hole in the wall then. That was all right, I thought later. They had their own dignity and aloofness; there was a seemingly unconscious boundary beyond which I could not get.[53]

The people remain elusive from representation, but by establishing the representational borders of 'the people', O'Malley can suggest, in the Hegelian sense of the finite approaching the infinite, what is beyond his immediate powers of observation.

O'Malley's strategies involved techniques we associate with modernism, and, as Richard English demonstrates, O'Malley's immersion in New Mexico during the composition of his memoir informs so much of his thought from that period: 'Mexican reflections both echoed and reinforced his view of Ireland.'[54] O'Malley was particularly impressed with the Mexican muralists like José Clemente Orozco and Diego Rivera, modern artists employing folk techniques. Mary Cosgrove notes the inspiration these artists provided O'Malley: they 'drew upon their [Mexican] folk tradition to inspire national cohesion. The Mexican government's mural project, like O'Malley's own writings and artistic projects, aimed to restore nationhood and national consciousness after the country's civil war.'[55] In 1947, for a BBC broadcast entitled 'Traditions of Mexican Art', O'Malley looked back on his 1930s immersion in Mexican art: 'Here, then, was a folk tradition which was enriched in memory as I wandered through Mexico. It had strength, interest, and vitality. In colour, form and design it was invariably aesthetically satisfying.'[56] This aesthetic pull was, of course, invested with an awareness of the postcoloniality of both Ireland and Mexico: in an article for *The Bell* from the same year, he writes, 'Mexico is of interest to Ireland because for over three centuries it has been subject to foreign domination and for close on a century and a half has been struggling to integrate itself.'[57]

Naturally, then, Mexican and New Mexican art informs much of the final shape of *On Another Man's Wound*, especially the depictions of landscape. However, another strand of O'Malley's writings from that period expressed his difficulties in communicating with what he usually termed 'the countrymen' of New Mexico. Thus the staging of his difference from 'the people' re-emerges. In 1930, he wrote in his notebook that 'Their customs are difficult to know as an Indian hates to be asked questions.'[58] In the poem titled 'Time of Day: Cordova' (1930), note the distance between the speaker and the New Mexican countryman:

> 'What time is it,' I asked,
> Juanito shrugged a shoulder
> As if to say 'Why seek.'
> He smiled a Quien sabe look:
> There was a yesterday,
> You see today,
> For sure there'll be a morrow.
> 'Is it near twelve o'clock?'
> His brown eyes scan the sun.
> 'It is not yet the midday.'
> He knows only the dawn,
> The half-way house of noon,
> Indefinite evening,
> Sunset and sleepy night.[59]

Here the narrator tries in vain to initiate some sort of interaction with Juanito, but, literally, cannot even get the time of day out of him. While this demonstrates O'Malley's anxieties regarding his ability to communicate with the countrymen of New Mexico, it also lays bare the aesthetic difficulties of representing the people's voice. 'Quien sabe' ('who knows') might well answer the question as to what Juanito is thinking, as he remains outside the scope of O'Malley's honestly limited perspective.[60] An almost identical passage occurs in prose in *On Another Man's Wound*, further evidence of the connections between Mexico, New Mexico and Ireland: 'Time did not matter to a countryman who judged time by the sun or his stomach. Dawn, breakfast, noon, dinner, afternoon tea.'[61]

Ultimately, what O'Malley learns from Mexico and New Mexico is not the ways of the Mexican natives, but rather how educated, middle-class artists struggle with incorporating native traditions into their own work. He was close with other artists not of 'the people': Hart Crane, Georgia O'Keefe, Paul Strand. Even Orozco, O'Malley's favourite Mexican artist, was the son of an urban businessman. These are Fanon's intellectuals, both alienated from the people, but also essential for allowing the people a political voice, if problematically inflected with issues of class and power.

One aesthetic strategy that adapts folk material to depict the people is the inclusion of popular ballads that relate to the Irish wars. (Ballads were of course central in Irish culture, but in O'Malley's papers from his New Mexico era are some ballads in Spanish that he most likely requested someone transcribe for him.[62] Thus his exposure to Mexican and New Mexican culture partly prompted the inclusion of the ballads.) Do the ballads allow the people to speak? Their function in *On Another Man's Wound* is akin to a Greek chorus (and again, they are conspicuously not included in *The Singing Flame*.[63] That text never saw completion in O'Malley's lifetime, which accounts for their absence, but such a gap also dramatizes the lack of popular support in some regions that plagued O'Malley and the Republicans throughout the Civil War). Ultimately, however, the ballads only play a marginal role, and while O'Malley wore many hats throughout his lifetime, ethnographer was never one of them. He does not share much of the sensibility of Lady Gregory or the young Yeats. It is the other Yeats brother that O'Malley is emulating.

In the 1940s, O'Malley became one of Jack Yeats's biggest supporters, purchasing his paintings and also providing critical appraisal through a series of prominent articles. The end of the Second World War began an intense period of critical output for O'Malley, and Yeats, who became a close friend, was one of his central subjects. What O'Malley saw in Yeats, via his critical writings from the 1940s, makes explicit some of the notions of landscape from *On Another Man's Wound*, and it is in his lyrical depictions of Ireland's sparsely habited regions that O'Malley advances his most creative formulation of 'the people'. Both O'Malley and Yeats were drawn to Irish landscapes, and some of the most moving passages in *On Another Man's Wound* are the attentive sketches of nature. His landscapes, however, are more complex than mere lyrical evocation, and his writings on contemporary art can help illuminate some of his strategies.

What O'Malley admires in Yeats is precisely what he was aiming for in his memoir. In an introduction to the catalogue for the Jack B. Yeats National Loan Exhibition in the summer of 1945, O'Malley praises Yeats's attention to the visual details of landscape, and insists that the empirical ability to render visual impressions could not account for such a talent; instead, some knowledge of the land and its people were necessary for greatness:

> This subtlety and its opposite, and strongly dramatic sense, must be the despair of academic painters whose minds have been trained to accept the conventional impression, but whose eye may fail to record the sudden unexpected impact. Memory must play its part, for painting hours are episodic, broken by rain or rebellious wind. The sense of man is present in enclosures of light-filigreed stone walls which map land hunger, or in unobtrusive cottages, dwarfed by mountain and hill to an almost tragic insignificance.[64]

The 'academic' ability to reproduce faithfully the visual can never capture the 'unexpected impact' that a social memory allows, and any visual consideration of the land must include 'the sense of man as well'. It is ultimately the relationship between landscape and humanity that draws O'Malley's attention in Yeats's work, and I would argue that such an attraction stems from the similar concerns he encountered in the production of his memoirs when he was first struggling with the challenges of the people and their representation. As Allen writes, O'Malley's 'obsession with landscape can be easily equated with a romantic nationalism, except that his descriptive attention was drawn reiteratively to landscape's ephemeral human geography. Just as O'Malley carried a notebook everywhere to take down scraps of folklore, he thought of the country through which he moved as aesthetic, not essential.'[65] The people endow the landscape with its value.

O'Malley goes on to write in the catalogue introduction that 'artists whose energy is turned to observation see the relationship of people to each other, to events and to their environments'.[66] Even pure landscapes should reflect human relations. O'Malley's description of Yeats's human figures could equally be applied to his own writings: 'His figures now enter a subjective world in which they are related to the loneliness of the individual soul, the vague lack of pattern in living with its sense of inherent tragedy, brooding nostalgia, associated with time as well as variations on the freer moments as of old.'[67] We can see such a dynamic in moments like this one from *On Another Man's Wound*:

> The officers were slack. They talked but none were willing to come with me when they had to. I could feel the rugged wild nature of the land, the craggy, cliff-bound or shelving coast with its jutting headlands and small bays; but for the most part it was a blur, undetached from the bleakness of my mind and the bumpings of my body on the penance of a bicycle.[68]

Yeats's Romanticism that we can detect in a work like *Two Travelers* (1942) animates O'Malley's use of landscape in this passage as he charts his own gloomy thoughts.

O'Malley's other significant essay on Yeats also sheds light on his own literary practices. In a 1946 book review in *The Bell* of Thomas MacGreevy's *Appreciation and Interpretation of Jack B. Yeats*, titled 'A Painter of His People', O'Malley argued that Yeats did not need access to a tradition of painting the people (he references Daumier and Constable).[69] Instead, Yeats had the ability to go, unmediated, to the people: 'to one reared as Yeats was reared, in the West, with his access to people whom he later painted, there would be no need for an emphasis on direction from another painter who was interested in the relation of people to land'.[70] As an art historical claim, this is spurious, but it can help us appreciate moments like this from his memoir: 'towards Arigna, the land was rugged with small stretches of wood. Plantations were scarce enough; the war had made the unfortunate country barer than ever; soon it would rival Iceland. Near Lough Meelagh there were ferns and dense growth, green sedge blades flowering brown and purple and a damp leafy smell of humus.'[71] Land for O'Malley always has a past and a future, and embedded amongst the lovingly particular depictions of the smells of the region are its history, and humanity's impact on the landscape. Often history is not far from his portraits of land: 'I preferred the Rosses and the north where I founded companies and felt at home. It was a pleasure to see a clump of trees; but if they were in any quantity it meant good land which had been planted by English or Scottish settlers.'[72] Note how for O'Malley the landscape is not a place of simple celebration of past nationalist victories, nor is it only a reminder of imperial violations. History animates the land in ways beyond popular ideology.[73]

Ultimately for O'Malley, to paint the landscape is to paint the people. This means being attuned, not just to how humans have altered the landscape, but how the landscape shapes humanity:

> Each county was different; the very map boundaries in many places seemed to make a distinction. The land seemed to determine the nature of the people often enough; whether pasture, grazing, tillage; good or bad; nearness to the sea; whether remote

from towns and cities; hilly, mountainous or undulating. Sometimes I came to a town-land where there was a company of twenty or thirty men and boys. Tall, well set-up or lanky, eager, lithe, willing to learn and anxious to take risks. Six miles away across the barony the people were cowed; the men had no initiative. They were irresolute. The captain of the company sometimes made the difference, sometimes the men themselves, but in parts it was the nature of the land and the long struggle against odds that had told.[74]

The fact that the land shapes the people presents a problem for the very conceptual-ization of 'the people of Ireland' as a master category: the people are scattered and diverse, as heterogeneous as Irish topography. For O'Malley, however, it is not the final product that offers a site of unification – that is, the people's diversity is not a barrier to their formulation, as it is the very process of the struggle with nature, regardless of the diverse results, that defines who the people are. This is an idea that we see not only in his writing on Yeats, but also the painter Louis le Brocquy: 'Man and his work merge slowly and unobtrusively with the land. Houses sink into or join with a slope or foreground; men fuse with the walls they sit on, or lean against. Sometimes people and landscape are one, and take on a consciousness of organized growth; a painter cannot separate them as independent in meaning.'[75] Nor, it seems, can a writer. Note how O'Malley depicts the people in relation to the land in his memoir:

> Again I visited the companies from Ardara, where homespun is made to enrich retailers far away, to the Rosses, the Irish-speaking district. Bare, boulder-strewn land backed by purplish heather and misty mountains. The people lived close to the soil, pushing back the soft bog and making it give food; a barren, troubled existence. Yet this country grips their body and soul; it haunts the imagination in its cruelty, strength and beauty, and the bleak coast with its wild angry sea, changing skies, crashed rocks, as if old gods had sported with pieces of granite mountain, can be recalled when sleek fat land is forgotten.[76]

Note the absence of verbs in the second sentence; the agency imparted to 'the people' by the verbs 'lived' and 'pushing back' in the third sentence; but then the dominance of nature in the fourth sentence with the verbs 'grips' and 'haunts'. The people exist in a dialectical relationship to the land, both shaping and being shaped. And this is not a Romantic harmony: the land is not always an ally (and is often portrayed as more of the antagonist than the British). What is so crucial for O'Malley's formulation of the people is how his focus on their relationship to the land avoids the problem of empir-ical embodiment that troubles Delacroix's painting. For O'Malley, 'the people' may be a process as much as a collection of individuals or groups.

The problem of the agency of representation remains, however. Jack Yeats, like Orozco or O'Malley himself, could never be taken as one of the people, despite his gifts for depicting them on canvas. O'Malley addresses this in his *Bell* review: 'Into this effect of light, which even when seen is difficult to believe, the painter builds and relates his humanities, based on his understanding of the Anglo-Irish as well as of the people, to fit into the imaginative and seeming extravagance of colour values.'[77] Here we see O'Malley's notion that even non-human aspects of a painting like an 'effect of light' have to be related to the social, but what is also made quite clear is the utter distinction between the Anglo-Irish and the people.

His consideration of the Anglo-Irish and their role recurs in his essay 'Renaissance', which appeared in French in the journal *La France Libre* in 1946. In that piece O'Malley surveys several decades of Irish history and reports on the complex state of affairs during and just after the Emergency. Of interest to an analysis of the people is his brief aside on the Anglo-Irish:

> The English in Ireland were known as the Anglo-Irish only when their allegiance was given to England and when their interests and mentality were hostile to Ireland. When they contributed in any way towards freedom, they were immediately accepted and regarded with affection. Some of them have laid the basis for the understanding of political freedom, yet in all movements of revolt it has been the people themselves who supplied the motive power.[78]

Less important than O'Malley's estimation of the contributions of the Anglo-Irish are his very clear distinction between them and 'the people'. The Anglo-Irish may be Irish, and could have legitimate nationalist credentials, but could never be mistaken for the people themselves. While this might appear exclusionary, we have seen how O'Malley always presented himself as equally distanced from the people, despite his efforts of fusion. O'Malley certainly saw room in Ireland for people other than the people: educated intellectuals like himself, the Anglo-Irish, and maybe even the Ulster Protestants could fit easily into his imagined Republic, but none of these groups could ever lay claim to being the people.

We might contrast O'Malley's statement with W.B. Yeats's famous senate speech on divorce from 1925. Yeats was alarmed at the idea that 'the Catholic conscience alone must dominate the public life of Ireland',[79] and wrote: 'We against whom you have done this thing, are no petty people. We are one of the great stocks of Europe. We are the people of Burke; we are the people of Grattan; we are the people of Swift, the people of Emmet, the people of Parnell.'[80] As much as Irish criticism has debated the difficulty of defining the Anglo-Irish – they are a hybrid class, 'our side – which is no side' as Hugo puts it in *The Last September*[81] – in fact Yeats bequeaths a perfectly functional definition of the Anglo-Irish, because of the qualifications he is allowed to bring to the phrase 'the people'. The 'of' that follows the phrase five times is crucial, and we might read Burke, Grattan, Swift, Emmet and Parnell as the 'empirical details' that T.J. Clark saw as so threatening to French Revolutionary discourse on the people, but that bolster, rather than disturb Yeats's attempt at establishing an Anglo-Irish genealogy.[82] It is the people of Ireland – not always synonymous with 'the Irish people' – that are much harder to define or represent, although defining the people has certainly been the spur, since 1789, to works of creativity like David, Delacroix and O'Malley.

Comparing O'Malley with the mature Yeats allows us to see two contrasting intellectual attitudes towards the people. O'Malley desires to 'fuse' with them, while Yeats in his divorce speech might also be concluding his divorce from the people that began with the *Playboy* riots in 1907. Neither intellectual was of the people, but in the post-war period Yeats draws his creativity from a widening gulf, O'Malley from his efforts to bridge it.

CHAPTER TEN

LITERATURE, VIOLENCE, REVOLUTION
ROGER CASEMENT AND ERNIE O'MALLEY

Macy Todd

> *But this is not the old sea*
> *Nor this the old seashore*
> *What gave that roar of mockery,*
> *That roar in the sea's roar?*
> — W.B. Yeats

Tucked away in an unpaginated section at the beginning of one of Ernie O'Malley's notebooks is transcribed a portion of a speech W.B. Yeats gave to the Irish senate. Written presumably while O'Malley was in the midst of interviewing former soldiers who he asked to talk about their experiences fighting for Irish independence, Yeats's words provide a somewhat startling frame for the war stories that come after it. The speech is a suggestion that the government fund translations of Irish language stories, from which O'Malley copied out the following: 'The greatest portion of my own writings have been founded upon the old lit of I –. I have had to read it in translation *but it has been the chief illumination of my imagination all my life.*'[1]

These words suggest a dissonant relation between the Ireland that was promised by the spirit of revolutionary zeal that led O'Malley to fight and the Ireland that came into existence. Much of what he recorded in the notebooks included a deep sense of regret over how much was lost in the fighting and how little it seemed was gained. Yet there is an additional point of resonance in this transcription, a parallelism between the poet and the freedom fighter that coalesces in the section O'Malley chose to highlight: 'the chief illumination of my imagination'. Both Yeats and O'Malley knew well the struggle of making public the work of a private imagination. Whether it is the process of bringing a nation into being, or a process of bringing a work of art to the public, there is a necessary ethical component added to a fantasy when it will inevitably become an object of value on the social scene. Both men struggled to produce objects worthy of this distinction.

A material analysis of revolution, violence, and literature provides the space wherein relations between these terms can be examined without making those same relations into transcendental truths. Such an analysis is key precisely because these concepts stand as pillars of liberal ideology, in large part because of the work of mystification. For example, Alain Badiou, refers to the task of materially analysing literature and revolution as 'searching for a language for the unnameable', and striving 'to name the latter without naming it … instruct[ing] its vague existence without specifying anything whatsoever within it'.[2] Rather, in the case of modern Ireland, it is possible to highlight the emergence of a collective act of violent resistance that bore a constant and avowed relation to literature. Of those responsible for planning and executing the Easter Uprising, often given credit for instigating the Irish Revolution, Patrick Pearse, Thomas MacDonagh, Joseph Mary Plunkett and Roger Casement were all published poets. Note, for example, MacDonagh's posthumously published introduction to his essay collection, where he explicitly frames Irish literature as 'a movement that is important to English literature, because it is in part a revolt from it'.[3] There can be no doubt that this 'movement' isolated in Irish literature is intended not only to reform English letters, but to disrupt them and produce new meaning in the wake of violent opposition.[4] Three months after publishing a call-to-arms for Irish authors, MacDonagh would be executed for the time he spent firing at British soldiers in the streets of Dublin.

The tone of MacDonagh's text recalls Franz Fanon's explanation of a 'third stage' of colonial writing, in which the colony has both assimilated imperial artistic practices and traversed a stage of drawing those practices into question. Finally, convinced that there is a need to produce an art that would produce the potential for a collectivism unheard of in the colonial scene, the author is capable of revolutionary acts.[5] Fanon asserts reality not as a limit to the imaginative activities of the author, but as the site of revolution, reinvention and possibility. Ireland, at the end of the nineteenth century, had produced many 'colonized intellectuals', to use Fanon's phrase, who believed and practised not only the gestures of a literary revolution, but also a revolution that can be read through its literature.

Reading a revolution as though it was literature means also taking seriously the revolutionary potential of literature. The guiding premise behind this form of analysis is that there is an equivalence between the violence produced in wars of liberation and the violence of true artistic sublimation. It is my hope that this violence will be taken seriously as violence, and not mistaken for an aggression only readable as such through metaphor. There can be no dissimulating on this point because the stakes are so high – namely, what precisely literature can offer to any critique of ideology, to any potential understanding of justice. The Republic of Ireland, born from early-twentieth-century violence, must therefore be read concomitantly – even if it is, as Declan Kiberd claims, a political structure 'ready to build if not the land of saints and scholars then at least an island of silos and silicon'.[6] Even before the moment Kiberd uses to identify this industrial enthusiasm – the 1966 celebration of the fiftieth anniversary of the Easter uprising – Ireland's path from revolution to republic, was fraught with anxiety. This is obvious from the fact that, in the immediate wake of the revolution, Ireland experienced a civil war. If one is to claim that literature contributes or is formally related to revolution, literature must also be involved in the outcomes of those revolutions, no matter how disparate they seem. Ernie O'Malley attempted to find resolution to the violence of early-twentieth-century Ireland in artistic practice, writing both literary memoir and art criticism in the wake of the revolution. Having been transformed by the Irish government in a matter of years from national folk hero to war criminal, O'Malley recalls openly questioning the Irish rebellion's cause while looking at the faces of his fellow prisoners in a war camp. His comments speak to the difficult task of reading the signs of revolutionary action once they have been written: '[w]hat had they fought for, I often thought, as I watched the men in my hut. They were from country, city, and small town, and, on the surface, all they seemed to have in common was that they resisted economic, social, and clerical pressure together. It was an urge difficult to interpret.'[7]

Interpreting this urge entails an examination of the interrelation of revolution, literature and violence in the years surrounding the Irish fight for independence. In particular, the revolutionary decisions made by Sir Roger Casement and O'Malley demonstrate that if there is a relation between these concepts, it is not as complimentary as a first glance might suggest. Indeed their mutual interrelation reveals the blemishes of each: revolution loses its potential for total change, literature is unsustainable as a stage for moral uplift, and violence lacks the symmetry of perfect opposition between enemies. Casement, a dedicated employee of the British empire who firmly believes in the principle of British honour and righteousness, having his resolve in the justice of his task ground away by harrowing accounts of systematic torture and murder. No longer able to imagine the British empire as a check to this species of cruelty, he commits treasonous acts in an attempt to aid and co-ordinate the Irish fight for independence. Furthermore, O'Malley's memoir *On Another Man's Wound* renders a literary revolution through its material effects in a literary mode. For this reason, the moment of revolutionary decision can be explored in both genres – armed resistance and literature.[8] These two figures and their acts attest to the possibility of a reading of revolution, literature and violence that grants them access to a potential rewriting of reality without recourse to transcendental abstraction.

Roger Casement and the Dead End of Reason

There is no such place as Putumayo
—Roger Casement

At the tail end of what is referred to as the period of real growth within the Celtic Tiger, Irish Taoiseach Bertie Ahern made an impassioned call for a vigorous investigation into a specific critical question regarding the life of Roger Casement. Speaking at the annual Fianna Fáil Arbour Hill commemoration, Ahern stated forcefully, 'The issue is not one of interpretation but of fact. The truth ought to be possible to determine, using modern forensic and analytical techniques.'[9] The hard sciences, with their unimpeachable ability to investigate an object, are trusted to put to rest any question of moral ambiguity. In view of the graves of many Easter 1916 rebels who, like Casement, were killed by the government for their revolutionary acts, objective thought is privileged as the mode of intervention in ethical questions.

Two features of Casement's life make this episode particularly chilling. One regarding the specifics of the actual question involved: Ahern is suggesting that forensic science can definitively answer whether or not the notorious 'black diaries' were actually written by Casement, or if they were forgeries intended to smear his name during his trial for treason in 1916. The content of the diaries includes descriptions of the genitals of indigenous boys Casement encountered in the Putumayo region, and the diaries generally suggest Casement was homosexual. The critical debate over the authenticity of the diaries will not form a major portion of this chapter, yet it is crucial to note that – in the twentieth and twenty-first centuries – this debate marks the intersection of desire and scientific interrogation. The question of what provided the impetus for what Peter Costello calls an 'extraordinary' energy hinges on whether or not Casement's altruistic exposition of slavery within the rubber trade was tinged with libido.[10]

That the government would take up this line of inquiry is especially noteworthy because Casement's concern in the Putumayo was with the relation between government, science and desire. Any reader of Casement's diaries from the time (either the official diaries or the black diaries) will be immediately struck by the copious charts and graphs that have been glued into the pages, as well as the mass of text dedicated to the weight of rubber, the measurements of the natives, the varying costs for supplies at different trade posts along the river, and the debt accrued by employees of the company. Casement is hell-bent on discovering 'the truth' as it pertains to the torture that has been reported to him. Like Ahern, Casement believes 'the issue is not one of interpretation, but of fact', as he writes in his diary: 'We are dealing here with first principles of right and wrong, and all the argument in favour of this damnable thing is, originally, inspired by greed, and only maintainable by concealment of fact.'[11] Yet these facts prove elusive as Casement discovers 'while the immensity of the cruelty is beyond question, most of the evidence comes through stories'.[12] Casement encounters an impasse precisely where the fact of torture cannot be logically extracted from the objective evidence he collects. He finds instead that he must read the desire of those around him, and in the process he becomes less a scientist, economist, or journalist, and more a close reader of narratives – a literary critic.

Casement found himself in the Putumayo because of an anonymously authored article published in the magazine *Truth*. Titled, 'A British-Owned Congo', the article detailed atrocities reported in service to the Peruvian Amazon Company, a British-owned rubber supplier. The title, added by 'The magazine's leading investigative journalist',[13] Sidney Patternoster, would have both seriously offended British pride while simultaneously all but guaranteeing Casement would become involved in any Putumayan investigation. In 1903, Casement had investigated reports of abuses against Congolese natives by the representatives of King Leopold managing a Belgian rubber plantation. The report he published in 1904, called 'The Casement Report', resulted in the formation of British and American Congo Reform Associations. The latter counted among its members Mark Twain, who wrote the satirical *King Leopold's Soliloquy* after reading Casement's report.[14] The title of the *Truth* article therefore specifically references Casement and the related British efforts to control and reform Belgian rubber plantations in Africa.

Additionally, Casement's Congo report bases many of its observations on the certainty that British national character can serve as an international check on human rights violations carried out by the racially inferior. Speaking in relation to a group of natives who describe being assaulted and mutilated as they collect rubber, Casement asserts, 'these people were entitled to expect that a civilized administration should be represented among them by other agents than the savages euphemistically termed "forest guards."'[15] He goes on to note that the Congolese 'forest guards', who are representatives of the Belgian La Lulanga rubber company, are supposed to be under the command of 'twenty stations directed by one or more European agents' who are responsible for controlling the forest guards' access to firearms and ammunition.[16] Yet the 'European agents' have allowed the unlicensed guards to amass an illegal amount of weaponry with which they torture the natives who are collecting rubber for the company. Although Casement's report is ostensibly an objective account of the situation in the Congo, the signs of his faith in British moral superiority to Belgian administrative perfidy leak through, especially where Casement suggests the Belgian authorities have produced a situation where innocent natives are in danger. After recounting an interview with 'six natives … wounded by gun-fire' Casement concludes, 'the guns in question could only have come into the hands of their assailants through the permission or the neglect of the authorities'.[17] It is particularly in Casement's ironic use of the terms 'civilizing', 'authority' and 'agency' that the full sense of his rebuke of Belgian rule is apparent: 'In … one case [an] act of mutilation had been committed within a few miles of the head-quarters of a European civilizing agency, and the guilty man was still in their midst, armed with the gun with which he had first shot his victim.'[18] The same voice that can objectively refer to the law as the 'enactments of civilized administrations'[19] can question the civility of the authority that enacts it.

In the Putumayo, however, Casement encounters very similar abuses carried out under the supervision of a British organization: the Peruvian Amazon Company. Casement reports in his diary that on 24 September 1910, in a sweltering room in the government offices in La Chorerra, Peru, he listened to an employee of a British company as he 'own[ed] up to five murders of Indians by his own hands, two he shot, two he beat to death by "smashing their testicles" with a stick'.[20] As he mulls over the situation later in the night, again the words 'civilization' and 'agency' reappear in his vocabulary of terror. But this time they refer to the British authority that formed the ground on which he had so harshly judged the Belgian government. He concludes that the employee's testimony was 'convincing enough for any fair man I should think, that what he had been employed on could not rightly be termed "commerce" or "trade" in any civilized or accepted sense of the term'.[21] This leads him at last to determine 'the Company was a civilized institution, it had inherited the claims of the founders of this method and it *must* sweep away this system and establish a lawful and civilized and humane method of dealing'.[22] While the rug had been pulled out from under the assumed superiority of the British civilizing organizations, Casement believed it was still within their power to re-establish those grounds by excising the grotesque and evil portions of their business in order to purify their otherwise irreproachable institution. This conclusion is clear when he notes, 'The London shareholders and Board are merely the cloak of respectability, and the guarantee for cash. [Local authority Julio César] Arana and his gang in Iquitos are the real Peruvian-Amazon Company'.[23] Casement holds fast to the belief that the system of trade established by the British company is just, and that it is through a malfeasant application of the system that evil is produced.

This assurance wears away over time. In a crucial and often cited entry in his diary, Casement reaches the conclusion that the system of trade in the Putumayo is inherently dependent on the forms of slavery reported to him.[24] Prior to this moment, when Casement says the British corporation must 'sweep away this system', he suggests that civilization and industry are allies in the fight against the inhuman violence he finds in the Putumayo. However, the 'present system' here indicates *capitalism*. The ability to turn a profit on the rubber trade is largely (or entirely, in Casement's opinion) balanced upon the forced servitude of the native people. Rather than trusting the system to sweep away injustice, Casement finds that the system itself must be done in.

Michael Taussig lights upon this argument in Casement's diaries to suggest that he was misguided in his diagnosis of the cause of the horrible practices of the rubber trade. He writes, 'We can say that the culture of terror was functional to the needs of the labour system, but that tells us little about the most significant contradictions to emerge from Casement's report, namely, that the slaughter of this precious labour was on a scale vast beyond belief.'[25] Taussig's ultimate point is to suggest that narrative and storytelling – two factors in Putumayan life that Casement is leery of – contribute in significant ways to the violence produced. For just as 'it is in the coils of rumour, gossip, story and chit-chat where ideology and ideas become emotionally powerful', he argues that 'the colonists and rubber company employees not only feared but also themselves created through narration fearful and confusing images of savagery'.[26] Yet as counterintuitive as it is to suggest that the destruction of labour power can serve a capitalist purpose, it seems clear in the Putumayo that this is precisely the case. When Casement asks whether the rubber or natives will be extinguished first, he does not mean only to emphasize the scarcity of labour, but to draw attention to the all-consuming violence that goes hand-in-hand with market practices. What Taussig seems to miss is that the market itself is a narrative, a story about money where it can become something more than what it is – capital. This fiction contributes in material ways to the stories that are produced in its practice; for without the ur-narrative of the market, there would be no cause for colonists and rubber company employees to produce narratives of native savagery. What Casement saw was not that the violence he was witnessing was all dependent on the cold and calculating logic of the market, but rather that the supposedly impassive logic behind market practices was itself a violent fantasy.

Casement's response is evident from his obsession with charts and figures in the days he spends on his way back to England from Peru. The primary means of enslaving the Huitoto people was by manufacturing debt and then never allowing them to pay it off. By offering a few goods, such as guns and blankets, the rubber company produced a contract that made them legally indebted to the company. While in Venezuela, Casement meticulously collects the variable prices of these products in order to try to prove that their value has been inflated in these contracts that produce the conditions of slavery. When he finally gets a copy of the workers' contracts his excitement is palpable: 'This is a precious document!' he writes, before adding, 'most of the men, it will be seen, are deeply in the Company's debt […] most of this "debt," it is true, is for things that are grossly, nay extraordinarily over priced, and many of them, things that, by the men's contracts (such as medicine, food etc.,) they are entitled to free.'[27] He concludes that very little in the contract connects to an objective reality.[28] Yet for all his excitement Casement demonstrates in his analysis of price inflation only that facts are themselves illusory. Their illusory quality, however, does not in any way diminish their real material effects in the lives of the natives.

Additionally, Casement becomes invested in attempting to match the amount of rubber to the payment of the natives for their work. In a handwritten note, he reminds himself to 'ask to be shown the exact quantities of goods paid' to the natives for the rubber they produce, noting, he saw '8 tons of rubber carried by some 250 human beings, and it would be an object lesson to see exactly what goods go back in return and their value in the books here'.[29] This, too, proves a fruitless task, as the goods the natives receive – clothing, shelter, food – are subject to valuation by a market that is invested in infinitely maintaining debt. Casement is forced to realize that fiction, in this case, bears on reality more intensely than does objective fact. The numbers produced by the rubber trade are less representative of objects than they are of the desire of the subjects who produce them.

Casement transitions so quickly from the position evident in the Congo report – a steadfast belief in the upright character of British manhood – to his role in the attempt to rid Ireland of English rule because he discovers the fantasy situated at the heart of colonial practice. This realization absolutely happens in Peru, where the hard figures of market logic reveal the passionate violence within. Early in his journey, Casement writes in his diary, 'an Englishman educated at an English University should be able to *smell* right and wrong in a case of this kind'.[30] At the end of his trip, in a letter to a friend, his approximation of the English character is quite different:

> I knew the foreign office would not understand the thing, for I realized that I was looking at this tragedy with the eyes of another race of people once hunted themselves, whose hearts were based on affection as the root principle of contact with their fellow men, and whose estimate of life was not something eternally to be appraised at the market price.'[31]

These words express the absolute failure of a system based in fiction to ever express itself through numeric reason – inevitably the desire underneath becomes apparent, and the gesture toward objectivity little more than a convenient lie.

Giovanni Costigan, in his appraisal of Casement's revolutionary motives, dismisses rather quickly the opinion of Sir Arthur Conan Doyle and other English supporters of Casement who suggested in a clemency petition to the Prime Minister that 'his mind might have become affected by his long residence and arduous labors in the tropics'.[32] Rather, Costigan believes that a series of letters between Casement and humanitarian Edmund Dene Morel 'impelled him on the course which was to lead to self-destruction'.[33] While I cannot agree with Doyle's group that Casement had gone mad, I do have respect for their observation that his experience in the Peruvian jungle caused a sudden and profound change in Casement. The decision to invest in revolutionary action is not one usually taken lightly, and Casement's convictions undoubtedly altered while in the Putumayo; it is only there that his faith in the panacean qualities of British character and the market are revealed as destructive fictions. Without the external, objective notion of an impassive economic force, Casement was faced with the difficulty of finding other grounds on which to manifest his authority as a speaking subject.

Fifteen years before Casement became disillusioned with the general economy of capitalist market practice, Sigmund Freud had set out to discover the economy of the human psyche. In an 1895 letter to Wilhelm Fliess, Freud explains, 'I am vexed by two intentions: to discover what form the theory of psychical functioning will take if a quantitative line of approach, a kind of economics of nervous force, is introduced into it, and, secondly, to extract from psychopathology a yield for normal psychology.'[34]

Like Casement, Freud also comes to the conclusion that an economic approach is faulty in its inherent assumptions, and just six months later he reported to Fliess, 'I can no longer understand the state of mind in which I hatched out the "Psychology"; I cannot make out how I came to inflict it on you.'[35] The document Freud produced in this time is his 'Project for a Scientific Psychology', an attempt to propose – as Freud outlines above – the logical economy of emotional energy and a diagram of how that economy functions in normal conditions. In it, Freud produces mathematic variables for the forces he considers necessary to the functioning of the conscious and unconscious, and the pages of the document that result are visually similar to the charts and graphs that Casement collects in his Putumayo journal. Freud assigns Q and $Q\eta$ as representatives for external and internal quantities of excitation, respectively. He uses the Greek symbol φ to indicate the neurons capable of communication, and ψ for the neurons used for memory storage and therefore incapable of communication. Yet even in these early identificatory actions Freud runs into problems. His initial 'inertia theory', that the psyche attempts always to discharge energy, must be immediately revised due to the fact that internal impulses are impossible to release. He notes that endogenous stimuli 'only cease subject to particular conditions, which must be realized in the external world [...] In order to accomplish such an action (which deserves to be named "specific"), an effort is required which is independent of endogenous $Q\eta$ and in general greater, since the individual is being subjected to conditions which may be described as *the exigencies of life*'.[36] Therefore, the internal economy of conscious and unconscious processes is always initiated by a surplus – an internal energy that must be connected to something in the external world. Any inner-subjective economy is always already intra-subjective.

Because the internal psychic processes are beholden to a world beyond the subject, fantasy becomes necessary. The subject is capable of intervening in the world only through the self-asserting and aggressive act of proposing an imagined position for him/herself in a world s/he produces from interpretations of the outside world. Therefore, the passage from internal stimulus to external object necessary includes a process of ideation. Throughout the 'Project' Freud struggles to connect internal processes with what he frequently refers to as 'reality'. He finally settles upon the motor process of speech as the missing link between fantasy and the real world, noting that 'the *indications of speech-discharge* [...] put thought-processes on a level with perceptual processes, lend them reality and *make memory of them possible*'.[37] This finally leads him to conclude that speech is a form of reality, although 'thought-reality not [...] external reality'.[38] In turn, an objective account of reality becomes impossible, for the role of language

– and speech in particular – makes of the objective world a field of potential pleasure and unpleasure as fixed in an economy of fantasy. Jacques Lacan therefore insists, in his essay 'The Function and Field of Speech and Language in Psychoanalysis', that any attempt at segmentation and quantification neglects the foundational gesture of psychoanalysis – its insistence that even the bodily manifestation of symptoms can be treated exclusively through representation. He explains, explicitly addressing Freud's dismissal of a psychic equilibrium theory, 'I do not wish to preach to you the doctrine of the b factor, designating the first, nor of the c factor, designating the second. All I have tried to do is remind you of the neglected a, b, c structure of language, and to teach you to spell once again the forgotten ABC's of speech.'[39] In a capitalist market, figures refer less to the physical quantities or properties of good than they do to the expression of internal desires through external means. Rubber trees, native labourers, bullets, guns, and even dollars and cents become little more than representative functions. The lesson of psychoanalysis is that reducing these things to their functions in speech absolutely does not diminish their potency, but rather amplifies it exponentially. Adding up the profits from the rubber trade is only as impassive as adding up the number of strokes to the testicles it takes to kill a man.

Abandoning objective figures as a basis for reality is in no way a hopeless act; because a link between ideation and reality exists the world that we inhabit is more open to potential change than would be the case were figures to be true expressions of the external world. In his attempt to produce an 'estimate of life' that could avoid an equivalence to numeric valuation, Casement engages in speculation that can manifest in reality. After giving up on the prospect of the British company using market forces to correct the situation in Peru, Casement articulates an alternative plan for addressing the evils he has witnessed. In a small and often overlooked passage in his diary, he suggests art as a potential medium through which to seek justice. After describing the bodies of some of the natives, Casement settles upon one in particular, 'this youth is a bigger boy … a married man of 19, probably or 20 and would make a fine type for Herbert Ward in the group I have in my mind for South America. This has been for some time in my thoughts, to enlist Ward […] on the side of these poor Indians and to do it through their artistic sense.'[40] Here Casement imagines aesthetics circumventing the gridlock he perceives in Putumayo. If the market and system of government is not only contributing to the issue, but is the issue in its entirety, artistic practice opens up a possible space of resistance by appealing to the ethical and aesthetic values of its audience.

There is another important role aesthetics plays in Casement's diary – it provides a method of relief from the horror of the gruesome stories of abuse Casement and his men document all day long. Throughout his diary, Casement details his butterfly chases, and the many different examples he is able to procure: 'to relieve our feelings we began an elaborate butterfly chase there and then on the sandy bank of the river. They were certainly magnificent specimens, and the soil was aflame with glowing wings, black and yellow of extraordinary size, the glorious blue and white, and swarms of reddish orange, yellow ochre, gamboge and sulphur.'[41] Yet the attraction to the beauty of the butterflies bears an ambiguous relation to aesthetics and justice. First, there is a necessarily violent component to the butterfly chase when the attractive animals are killed and turned into specimens for permanent display. Second, butterfly hunting can itself be turned into a convenient fiction, precisely the kind that frustrates Casement – he explicitly compares it in his journal to the lies he is told by the Peruvian Amazon Company.[42] Hence, fiction is both an issue that contributes to the horrors of slavery, and a potential release from those horrors. Casement's aesthetic practice relieves the pressure of dealing with the liars he hopes to expose, but it also makes him of a kind with the liars.

This likeness manifests in other ways as well. It is not only aesthetic practice that Casement believes could make a difference in the Putumayo; throughout his journal he entertains the fantasy of leading the natives in a successful rebellion against the representatives of the company. In a late entry, after going out into the plantation and attempting to haul rubber with the Huitoto people, Casement reflects on his desire to lead them in armed rebellion:

> I would dearly love to arm them, to train them, and drill them to defend themselves against these ruffians. I said to [colleague Juan] Tizon last night that I only wished this were British territory for a year and with 100 men what pleasure I should take in scouring it clean. [...] we both agreed that we should have great pleasure in hanging, if needed with our own hands, many of the Company's staff.[43]

The personal pleasure at stake in violent acts is exposed here – it's not just that Casement wants justice to be served for the native people he finds wronged, he wishes to administer that justice with his own hands, murdering the murderers. Art, and the experience of the beautiful, is therefore not the only pleasurable act that occupies a fantasy space in Casement's relation to the horror he finds in the Putumayo.

Revolution, violence, literature – the terms that initiated this chapter's exploration into modernist Ireland reappear here as modalities of approaching the social scene. Casement finds himself confronted by the same conundrum Freud faced at the failure of his 'Project' to produce an objective account of human mental life: how, if fantasy is the form reality takes for the subject, is it possible to produce something of value at a social level? After being sentenced to hang for treason, Casement delivers a speech emphasizing armed revolution as a form of address whereby a private fantasy can become a social value. He opens the speech by proclaiming his desire that his words be heard by many, saying 'I wish my words to reach a much wider audience than I see before me here.' His emphasis over the remaining lines alights again and again on the word love: 'If true religion rests on love, it is equally true that loyalty rests on love', 'loyalty is a sentiment, not a law. It rests on love, not on restraint', and 'our offence is that we love Ireland more than we value our lives', among other references. Casement here shares much in common with a future revolutionary who writes,

> At the risk of seeming ridiculous, let me say that the true revolutionary is guided by great feelings of love [...] revolutionaries must make an ideal of this love of the people, of the most sacred causes, and make it one and indivisible. They cannot descend, with small doses of daily affection, to the level where ordinary people put their love into practice.[44]

Love, for Casement and Ernesto [Che] Guevara, is a form of social address that can be self-annihilating, that aims directly at the social not only as its end, but the means through which it is expressed. Yet this aim is in itself also of a necessity violent, for it seeks the social from the perspective of the individual in the hope of permanently destroying its current state in order to reimagine it. Therefore, this particular concept of love serves as a locus for the relation of revolution, violence and literature – a mode of address that traverses the private fantasy and enters the social scene.

Ernie O'Malley and Sublimation

> *I would not admit the right of foreign troops to deprive me of a habit.*
> —Ernie O'Malley

In psychoanalysis, this process, wherein a private fantasy is transformed into an object of social relevance, is referred to as sublimation – the sequence of events and reactions which, as Freud puts it in 'Three Essays on the Theory of Sexuality', 'enable excessively strong excitations arising from particular sources of sexuality to find an outlet and use in other fields'.[45] That these 'other fields' are wide and varied is obvious from the fact that Freud calls sublimation and related phenomena 'the origins of artistic activity' (in 'Three Essays'), and in '"Civilized" Sexual Morality and Modern Nervous Illness' identifies them as 'forces that can be employed for cultural activities'.[46] Finally, in his encyclopaedia article on sublimation, Freud identifies the concept as the ability for what was originally a private, internal urge to achieve 'satisfaction in some achievement which is no longer sexual but has a higher social or ethical valuation'.[47] For psychoanalysis, revolution and literature are inherently tied through the process of sublimation – both acts require the transformation of internal impulses into social forces capable of producing monumental change.

This is not to say that the coincidence of revolution and literature should be mistaken for a permanent positive valuation of the concept of revolution – or of literature, for that matter. Freud is clear in his 'New Introductory Lectures on Psychoanalysis' that revolutionary attitudes in general should come under scrutiny. There he writes, 'psychoanalytic education will be taking an uninvited responsibility on itself if it proposes to mold its pupils into rebels. [...] It is even my opinion that revolutionary children are not desirable from any point of view.'[48] Likewise, when asked about the horrors of Stalinism, Gilles Deleuze responded 'revolutions always end badly. Who are they kidding when new philosophers discover that revolutions always end badly? Everyone knows revolutions end badly. [...] all revolutions fail. The whole world knows it, but they pretend to rediscover it now.'[49] For Deleuze, interest in revolutions is misguided when it proposes to solve problems historically, meaning that it is not fruitful to ask of a past revolution why it failed or how a future revolution could be successful. Rather, the focus needs to be on the process of becoming – a concept that centres on the kind of radical change represented in Easter 1916 without the expectation of a progressive bettering of humanity usually associated with revolution.[50] Revolution therefore persists as a concept worthy of study not because it is invested with the hope to save mankind from the tyrannous governments and radical inequalities that define contemporary life, but rather because it relates to human potential without becoming teleological. Focusing on the moment of revolutionary decision offers a chance to analyse the past from the perspective of potential rather than with a backwards-facing ethical judgement.

Hope persists in Deleuze's thought as a crucial element of revolutionary action, particularly where artistic practice is concerned. In *Difference and Repetition*, he explicitly designates art as a revolutionary process through which the habitual repetition of oppressive practices can be broken up from the position of everyday life. He writes:

> the more our daily life appears [...] subject to an accelerated reproduction of objects of consumption, the more art must be injected into it in order to extract from it that little difference which plays simultaneously between other levels of repetition, and even in order to make [...] the habitual series of consumption [resonate with] the instinctual series of destruction and death.[51]

While initially these comments seem counter to those Deleuze makes above in *L'abecedaire*, certain similarities mark them. In *Difference and Repetition*, it is possible to observe the tension between the progressive model of past and future against the possibility of becoming: art is the force that can interrupt or reorient the 'accelerated reproduction' of consumer objects. Like revolution, the artistic moment does not seek answers to why things are bad in the past, but rather attempts to bring something of social value into existence in the present. Violence inevitably plays a crucial role in the process as well, for it is only violently that the potential for revolutionary becoming is able to enter social life, as a form of disruption that gestures towards the death that repetition and progress seeks to conceal.[52]

In an effort to take seriously the concepts of literature, violence and revolution as they relate to the possibility of something called freedom, this section will follow Deleuze's recommendation that the moment of revolutionary decision be taken seriously. Ernie O'Malley provides perhaps the most fitting Irish example for this discussion as the rare figure who is remembered both for his skill as a revolutionary in Ireland's fight for freedom and his skill as a literary figure in committing his memories of revolution to the pages of two memoirs: *On Another Man's Wound* and *The Singing Flame*. Approaching the moment of revolutionary becoming in O'Malley's work therefore means exploring sublimation from two simultaneous angles. O'Malley's decision to oppose the British rule of Ireland will be considered with the decisions he makes in articulating the revolutionary moment in prose.

In both *On Another Man's Wound* and *The Singing Flame*, O'Malley does not make it clear why he chooses to join the Irish Revolution. While from today's perspective it seems silly to ask why O'Malley fights to free Ireland from British rule, in *On Another Man's Wound* in particular, O'Malley maintains a sense of historical contingency. Just as in the moment of the Easter 1916 uprising there is no guarantee that Ireland will ever be an independent country of any shape or character, O'Malley's text demonstrates there is nothing inherent to the moment itself that guarantees his participation in the revolution that follows. In addition to opposing a ruling government, O'Malley's work demonstrates that true revolutionary acts require that one oppose the confirmation bias of popular histories. In this way, O'Malley's works immediately recall Deleuze's thoughts on revolution – neither author is interested in justifying or supporting historical arguments of progress or failure. Due to this focus on revolutionary contingency, O'Malley's acquisition of a sense of Irish national character does not progress through the assumption of well-trodden signifiers of Irishness, but through a process of subtracting and sloughing off popular understandings of what it means to be Irish.

He must, in other words, break through the repetition and habit of the everyday to discover underneath the minimal difference that provides sublimation its force. In coming face-to-face with history as radical intractability – what Deleuze refers to as the 'ultimate repetitions of death' – O'Malley makes the decision to put his life on the line in isolation from the signifiers that popularly characterize Irish history.

Critics who write on O'Malley's memoirs curiously treat his conversion to the revolutionary cause as an afterthought or an indisputable fact. In '"We Knew Where Our Sympathies Were:" Social and Economic Views in *On Another Man's Wound*', Timothy M. O'Neil suggests that witnessing the 1913 Dublin Lockout and Bloody Sunday contributed to O'Malley's political formation. O'Neil's subsequent treatment of O'Malley's conversion to the Republican cause amounts to a sentence fragment: 'After his conversion to Republicanism during the 1916 rising, O'Malley recalls that he read everything he could that the executed leaders had written.'[53] Mary Cosgrove, in her article, 'Ernie O'Malley: Art and Modernism in Ireland', summarizes O'Malley's conversion by describing him as 'A nationalist since the 1916 Easter Rising.'[54] Moreover, Martin Williams argues that O'Malley knew 'nothing of historic mythology' and therefore only after reading about Ireland's mythical past could he 'understand … what he was doing and why he was fighting'.[55] In contrast to these reductive and misleading summaries, O'Malley's words betray a much more complex and obscure genesis of his political convictions.

At the beginning of the memoir, the young O'Malley is not only without political investments, he is also contemptuous of politics in general. He says, 'I had [no politics] to discuss, save to laugh at other people's opinions.'[56] The first decision he makes in response to the excitement of the Easter uprising is to help some Trinity students defend their university. In response to the promise, 'We'll give you a rifle,' O'Malley says, 'I'm going home now, but will be back to see you later.'[57] This does not make O'Malley unique; another IRA memoirist, Tom Barry, is fighting with British troops in Turkey when he hears of the Easter uprising and asks himself, 'What was this republic of which I now heard for the first time?'[58] Barry waits two years before returning to Ireland and reading about 'John Mitchel, Wolfe Tone, Robert Emmet, and the other Irish patriots who strove to end the British conquest'.[59] Barry therefore learns of Ireland's struggle for independence before coming to revolutionary sympathies by reading through the details of Ireland's history. O'Malley, on the other hand, is openly dismissive of revolutionary sympathies, and only comes to a revolutionary decision through the subtraction of his lived relation (i.e. a system of habits and repetitions) to a concept of national historical importance.

The process of subtraction begins on his way home from his meeting with the Trinity students, when he encounters 'a student at the School of Art'. O'Malley is not embarrassed to inform him that he is 'going back to Trinity in the evening' and that he has been 'offered a rifle'.[60] To the young O'Malley, the difference of opinion between himself and the art student is not worth caring about. He writes, 'Was it not pleasant to have a rifle and to feel that there was going to be excitement? This was a lark.'[61] Yet the student responds to O'Malley at length, cautioning him against his plan of action: 'But it's not your university. Remember you'll have to shoot down Irishmen, your own countrymen. You bear them no hatred. If you go in there you cannot leave; and, mark my words, you'll be sorry ever afterward. Think it over.'[62] It is true that this speech is not the end of O'Malley's conversion to the Republican cause; two pages later in the memoir he reports, 'I had no feeling for or against, save irritation at those fellows doing the unexpected, seizing the post office and other buildings.'[63] Yet this encounter with the student at the School of Art marks the beginning of O'Malley's conversion precisely because he makes his first political choice in relation to the Easter uprising: not to join the students in protecting Trinity. In a real sense, this means going against his word – acting in such a way that his promise to return to Trinity becomes a lie. Whether or not he admits it, this amounts to political commitment.[64]

So what makes O'Malley commit to this act? The art student's speech has three primary claims: (1) That Trinity is not his university, (2) that joining the students at Trinity will force O'Malley to 'shoot down Irishmen', and (3) that if O'Malley goes to Trinity he 'cannot leave'. The first claim seems fairly weak. Certainly O'Malley does not attend Trinity, but he also clearly has friends that do attend the school. These acquaintances and the desire to take part in the excitement surrounding their defence of their school no doubt gives him a reason to join them. The second claim at first glance appears more valid: that O'Malley will be forced to shoot Irishmen if he joins his friends at Trinity. Yet one must ask in what sense this advice would be received. Certainly the highly political vocabulary of organizations like the Irish Volunteers and the Gaelic League would insist on a strict differentiation of 'Irishmen' from 'Unionists', but that definition of the term would have been foreign and meaningless to O'Malley. As a young man with, at best, a politically ambivalent family, he undoubtedly would have considered himself and his Trinity friends men who are Irish, so joining either side in the struggle would inevitably mean being forced to shoot Irishmen. Neither of the first two claims can be said effectively to persuade O'Malley.

By process of elimination, the art student's third claim becomes particularly interesting: the student tells O'Malley that he will not be allowed to leave if he joins the

Trinity students. This observation alerts O'Malley to a potentially inextricable political situation he will make himself a part of if he continues with his plan of action. 'Being able to leave' is in fact a fitting metaphor for the young O'Malley's take on politics: his conviction to do nothing other than laugh at those with opinions. This amorphous and plastic satire allows O'Malley to avoid any and all steady signification, to treat every political situation as if it were 'a lark'. Being trapped in Trinity, that is, having his potential exit from a situation subtracted, brings O'Malley uncomfortably close to politics and history as inherent features of Irish life. Like Deleuze suggests above, the casual repetitions of the everyday have been brought into question through their relation to another potential set of repetitions. The art student says to O'Malley, there exists a situation consisting of its own habits from which there is no escape, either through satire or otherwise. O'Malley responds by expressly avoiding that situation, trying to maintain the freedom to engage in political disinterestedness and avoid any permanent political act.

To wit, O'Malley's activities after the encounter with the art student betray an effort to recapture a sacrificed ambivalence. He explains: 'kept a diary of events, entering everything I had heard. When I tried to sum up the day the account was conflicting – rumour, counter-rumour. I had no feeling about it. I might have been a foreign news correspondent who had just landed, knowing nothing about the country, the people or the cause of the present uprising.'[65]

His impulse is to observe as impassively as possible. Yet, in deciding not to join with the armed Trinity students this attempt is already doomed to fail, as it does in a matter of days. O'Malley reports a conversation with one of the rebels, who tells him that the British are being held up in their attempts to reach Dublin. When O'Malley asks what will happen when they get through, the soldier replies, 'Oh, well, when they do it will be hot here.'[66] In the passage that follows, O'Malley attempts to identify this as the moment that his feelings definitively change: 'I went back home in the early morning and got into bed, unnoticed saved by my brothers. I felt faint stirrings of sympathy as I wrote in my diary. I did not feel indifferent now to the men holding Dublin.'[67] Yet it is impossible that O'Malley's sympathy begins here, for as we have seen he has already decided in favour of the rebels at the moment he determines not to give aid in the defence of Trinity. A decision I have argued is related to the threat that should O'Malley aid the Trinity students, he will not be allowed to leave.

This threat is present at the moment when O'Malley claims he 'did not feel indifferent' to the men holding Dublin. In the paragraph immediately following this pronouncement, he notes, 'Civilians fell wounded here and there, the presence of death was close,' before he notes 'I tried to get down to the centre of the city, but I could not get through the cordons.'[68] When it is no longer possible for O'Malley to continue role-playing as a foreign correspondent, or to laugh at those with political opinions, new landscapes of identification must be traversed. The historical circumstances informing his subject position are no longer abstract and distant from him, they are present in the means through which the British prevent him from joining the rebels in the heart of Dublin. Only in being unable to move freely does O'Malley come face to face with the question of what it means to be Irish. As promised above, the subtraction of signifiers of Irishness is not a mental process carried out in isolation from the concrete realities of the everyday, but is instead intimately material to the actual captivity O'Malley experiences. The situation of becoming revolutionary develops from the emergence of a terrifying potential: the need to construct a new identity when yours has been stripped away.

While my argument here bears a resemblance to a kind of neo-liberal 'they didn't come for me so I did not protest' T-shirt slogan; it gets to the heart of the question of what it means to take one's life in one's hands and participate in a revolution. As Deleuze insists, the moment of decision in this process is frequently overlooked, and in the case of *On Another Man's Wound* seems to have been completely elided. While O'Malley often avoids clichés in his memoir, he does occasionally contribute to the obscurity of the question of his conversion by speaking in platitudes. For example, O'Malley bemoans, once the British begin bombarding Dublin, 'It was terrible to watch. Why had I not known about the fight earlier? I thought of all the chances I had had of joining the Irish Volunteers; instead I had laughed and scoffed. Now when I wanted to help I could not.'[69] This is an impossible sentiment because the problem is not that O'Malley does not care about the rebels until it is too late, it is that he cannot care until it is too late. Only the subtraction of the material practices of his daily life, such as his ability to move freely about Dublin, can break through his conservative instincts enough to make the decision to become a revolutionary apparent. Without that material threat the attraction of the rebel cause is not just hard to see, it is impossible to read.

For many of the Irish people O'Malley meets the rebel cause is illegible because they have experienced no threat to their daily lives. O'Malley describes this inertia as a relatively general condition of Ireland at the time of the revolution: 'The people were conservative; they had a hatred of change. They had been driven in on themselves too long, suspicious of changes that had been forced on them by the conquerors. What was good enough for their fathers would be good enough for them.'[70] Freud interprets this colonial impasse in *Civilization and its Discontents*, where he argues that 'the difficulty of cultural development [is] a general difficulty of development', which can be ascribed to 'the inertia of the libido'.[71] One of the hardest things to do, Freud claims, is convince the ego to give up something that pleases it, even if that thing is harmful or crazy. Elsewhere, in 'Creative Writers and Daydreaming', Freud goes so far as to say it is impossible for humans to give up an established pleasure. He writes, 'whoever understands the human mind knows that hardly anything is harder for a man than to give up a pleasure which he had once experienced. Actually, we can never give anything up; we only exchange one thing for another.'[72] O'Malley's description of the 'hatred of change' in the Irish identifies the conservative impulse of Freud's death drive. It is important that, contrary to its depiction in popular media where it has been referred to as a 'subconscious death wish',[73] the death drive is not the desire to hasten one's death. In fact, Freud's description of the death drive is almost the complete opposite: the desire never to have been born. This means, using Freud's words in *Beyond the Pleasure Principle*, energy that results from the production of a change always 'endeavor[s] to cancel itself out'.[74]

Therefore, death is the end of the game for the death drive. As long as the organism stays alive, the death drive is free to preserve a certain satisfaction in its repeated attempts to return to a previous state. Ideas produced by humans, as a result, become ossified whether or not they are beneficial to the individual or society. Breaking through this ossification means nothing less than putting one's life on the line. To commit to revolutionary action one must abandon the pleasures of the ego that consist in being subject to the death drive (i.e. passively allowing the death drive its sway) in order to become a subject of the death drive. Here again, Guevara, who like O'Malley was a former medical student and a child with an upper-class Irish genealogy, can be helpful. Guevara said in 1960 that the process of revolution demands the complete destruction and reassembly of a common vocabulary: 'we realize how mistaken we were in concepts we knew so well; they had become part of us and, automatically, of our consciousness. Every so often we ought to change all our concepts, not just general, social, or philosophical concepts.'[75] Repetition does not just consist in the consumer objects we desire, but in the patterns of speech and clichés that develop alongside them. In other words, as well as instituting a new state, any true revolution seeks also to institute a new language. O'Malley senses among his fellow revolutionaries those not willing to commit themselves to the radical annihilation of their egos, and tellingly describes them like speakers of a foreign tongue: 'They saw the land ahead too much; they questioned themselves at every new departure; they were inclined to count the cost. Talking to some made me feel how inadequate speech could be; you said things that meant nothing unless a man was attuned, and in the conversation there would be two languages.'[76] While the divide between those willing to sacrifice themselves to the cause and those who are unwilling results in two languages, among the former group no language seems to be needed at all: 'Talk was not necessary; an understanding has been firmly set.'[77] Yet, rather than being beyond language, as one might think, these revolutionaries find themselves in the midst of a language that is being rewritten, of signifiers that have given up the ghost of their expected signifieds. This destabilization of the symbolic is accomplished through the radical revolutionary act of becoming a subject of the death drive: of risking death and the subsequent eradication of the death drive's ceaseless play. When death becomes a part of the repetition of daily life, as Deleuze offers above, the former habits of living become impossible.

The decision O'Malley makes to put his life on the line is only possible through the refusal of the objects of ego satisfaction; this refusal begins with a forced subtraction when he is unable to move freely around Dublin. The assault of the British troops on the Irish capital is a violent erasure of signifiers like buildings, landmarks and citizens. O'Malley – like all Dubliners – has structured his experience of the city around the repeated enjoyment of these signifiers, which have been effectively wiped from the world. As a result, O'Malley encounters a certain intractable truth that permits him to make his decision and convert to the rebel's cause. The process of erasure is the modernist act *tout court*, a process that, according to Joan Copjec, 'is intended to foreground historical contingency, to demonstrate … that the cumulate deposits of ego identifications are the result of historical circumstances that could have been otherwise'.[78] Modernist authors therefore seek to reveal that below all the accidentally meaningful signifiers of history exists an 'empty page or blank slate' that symbolizes 'the notion of a universal humanity'.[79] Yet Copjec asks, how do we know this blank slate is not itself another signifier of historical contingency? By eradicating the blank slate as the exception to erasure, we find that 'history is without limit', and what remains when even universal humanity is erased is the inescapability of history.[80] O'Malley revels in a certain universal humanity before the revolution begins; he does not need political or national convictions because he leans on the support of a vague humanism. He is a subject of this modernist 'blank slate'. Once this is stripped away, however, he is faced with an inescapable truth: he is Irish, with or without the signifiers that define that Irishness. The British soldiers who isolate him from his countrymen fighting throughout Dublin make that clear.

O'Malley does have certain sentimental notions about Irish history that he inevitably must shed for the revolutionary cause. In a paradoxical way, the stripping away of common historical Irish signifiers becomes proof of the recalcitrance of Irishness, as in one moment of national nostalgia where O'Malley almost meets his end due to his fondness for Irish myth.

In search of the historical remnants of Irish mythological inheritance embodied in the *Táin*, O'Malley finds it is literally gone – the land of Ireland itself as well as the history related to the national mythology has been removed, erased, made completely anonymous.[81] On the trip to the missing grave, though, O'Malley receives a palpable, material reminder of the war he is caught up in, as his altercation with the police forcibly inscribes him in the struggle to give birth to a nation whose symbols are being systematically destroyed. The words of *Ubu Roi* are therefore proven false; even literally without the earth that makes up Ireland, there would still be Irish. Even without the mythical violence of the *gae bolga*, there still persists the combat at the ford.

Copjec places emphasis on the agency of erasure, of the ability of the author to produce this erasure willingly in order to discover what it is that history means on an individual basis. O'Malley's work gives us insight to the process of erasure that is largely external, and that, rather than being produced through existential thought experiments, takes the form of stream deepenings, bombings, executions, deforestation, and the burning of creameries. This is the inherent double existence of sublimation – the process through which the private enters materially the world of the social. The Ireland of O'Malley's memoir is constantly threatened with elimination, and no cultural practice is safe from restriction, censure, or destruction. Yet rather than producing the conditions under which Ireland becomes less Irish, these practices can do nothing but reveal the Irish as a persistent possibility lurking beneath the habits of the everyday.

It is impossible to end without reflecting back on Deleuze's certainty that all revolutions are failures; Kiberd's words that opened this investigation are a direct reflection of the failure of the Irish war for independence, which produced an 'island of silos and silicon'.[82] O'Malley was himself constantly of the opinion that the promise of independence has been deeply dishonoured in the conditions that it produced, as he reports throughout *The Singing Flame*.[83] Bemoaning that a military chart reduces men's deaths to 'small dots on a map', O'Malley echoes Deleuze's pronouncement that all revolutions are failures in two ways. First, O'Malley implicitly states the similarity between his revolution and the ones that came before it, noting, 'other generations had done this'. It is a telling moment as it puts his actions in relation to a past he had been eager to dismiss in *On Another Man's Wound*.[84] Second, there is a sense of hopelessness that sets in at the end of O'Malley's writing that connects inevitable failure with a kind of fate. The only reason it seems there is no use in 'brooding over it' is that the outcome is foretold.

Yet I wonder if it is too crazy to suggest that both Deleuze and O'Malley admit of a certain hope amid the futility and inevitable failure. O'Malley notes the 'small dots on the map' that make up the stories of men's deaths, of the fights that had been waged. All maps are like this: signifiers of struggles that produced meaning, that mark past acts of violence carried out in space that takes on social value. I find in the small dots on the map not only the remnants of a past that must be justified against all odds, but the legible marks of a struggle for becoming that persist into the present. The small dots – like the Irish tales Yeats claims as the font of his imagination above – provide the possible grounds on which future social bodies can coalesce, can challenge the repetitions of the consumerist marketplace that produce such an unsupportable quantity of meaning in the present. If these dots mark for O'Malley the literal end of life for so many, they also can never be made to stop representing the revolutionary potential of sublimation.

AFTERWORD

CHAPTER ELEVEN

REVOLUTIONARY DISILLUSIONMENT

Roy Foster

Ernie opened the first draft of *On Another Man's Wound* by asking how it might be possible to reconstruct a spiritual state of mind. By the early 1930s, the transfigured moment of commitment and comradeship which he and others had found in the Irish Revolution was an increasingly distant memory; one reason why his extraordinary memoir is so haunting is precisely because it encodes and reflects that sense of loss. The sensation of disillusionment was not his alone: it is reflected in a wide range of contemporary Irish writers, and percolates down to modern fictions too, notably that of John McGahern, who deeply admired O'Malley's writing. Particularly in McGahern's 1990 novel *Amongst Women*, the memory of violence is never far absent, and nor is the negotiation of disillusionment. In a long, intense scene near the beginning, McGahern delineates the annual meeting between two old comrades from the campaign for independence:

> From year to year they used the same handrails to go down into the past: lifting the cartwheel at the crossroads, the drilling sessions by the river, the first ambush, marching at night between the safe houses, the different characters in the houses, the food, the girls … The interrogation of William Taylor the spy and his execution by the light of a paraffin lantern among his own cattle in the byre. The Tans had swarmed over the countryside looking for them after the execution. They had lived for a while

in holes cut in the turf banks. The place was watched night and day. Once the British soldiers came on Mary Duignan when she was bringing them tea and sandwiches. The Duignans were so naturally pale-faced that Mary showed no sign that anything was other than normal and she continued to bring tea and sandwiches to men working on a further turf bank. Seeing the British soldiers, the startled men sat and ate though they had just risen from a complete meal[1]

The vivid compression of this passage, inaugurating a scene which leads on into other memories and ends in barely spoken resentments, suggests the vitality and excitement of life lived at a high pitch of engagement. 'Things were never so simple and clear again.' And the outcome of independence is also queried. 'What did we get for it? A country, if you'd believe them. Some of our own johnnies in the top jobs instead of a few Englishmen. More than half of my own family work in England. What was it all for? The whole thing was a cod'.[2] McGahern's work traces and reflects wider processes of memory and forgetting, amongst the generation who – like his own father – had once lived with an intensity that they would never regain, and who saw the Ireland of their day as a poor reflection of the future they had once hoped and fought for. The gaps and silences which he so consummately indicates also remind us that memory and commemoration are as likely to be divisive as reconciliatory.[3]

The old soldiers, now farmers or cattle dealers, driving up boreens to meet each other and talk about the past, resemble the expeditions of Ernie O'Malley around Ireland in the last years of his life, engaged in compiling the notebooks now being published as *The Men Will Talk To Me*. O'Malley's experience in the revolution and its aftermath is more directly transmuted into fictions such as Roddy Doyle's trilogy *The Last Round-Up* or Ken Loach's film *The Wind that Shakes the Barley*. Doyle's protagonist Henry Smart borrows many of O'Malley's experiences (including hearing ballads composed about his exploits, when attending dances incognito), and O'Malley himself looks in and out of the narrative; while the medical-student hero of Loach's film similarly nods to O'Malley's radicalization (and, perhaps, to his severance from old comrades). This is a testament to the power of his autobiographical writing, but it also suggests that O'Malley's restlessness and disillusionment, vividly conveyed in the letters published in *Broken Landscapes*, reflects a wider sense of disappointment shared by many of the revolutionary generation.[4]

On Another Man's Wound, for all its unique quality, can be seen as reflecting a wider mentality in the Ireland of the 1920s and 1930s; its author's intellectual project also suggests a wider enterprise, engaged upon at various levels, official and unofficial. In the decades of conservatism and restabilization that followed the Treaty, we can trace a very self-conscious process of memorialization on the part of those who had helped bring about the new state. This happened through official channels, such as the Bureau of Military History, explored in Eve Morrison's essay in this volume – a huge though not unproblematic source, only recently opened to historians. To its riches have been added the sources available in the Military Service Pensions records, though these raise sensitive questions, also explored by McGahern in *Amongst Women*: his protagonist's reluctance to claim a pension may be partly because to apply for one necessitated a certain amount of self-presentation and possibly a degree of inflation. Cornelius Kearney's refusal to provide a reminiscence, quoted by Morrison, strikes a McGahern note: 'I look on the events of the period referred to as a very silly and stupid adventure; I remember those times with a feeling of aversion and self-disgust as the years go by.'[5] The 'community of memory', as Morrison's chapter demonstrates, could be competitive and antagonistic as well as consoling.

For this and other reasons, the rich record of autobiographical exegesis in such sources were early on seen as raising matters of extreme sensitivity. The comments of the Chairman of the Advisory Committee, himself a believer in opening the files to bona fide historical researchers, parodied the much more restrictive 'official attitude': 'If every Sean and Seamus from Ballythis and Ballythat who took major or minor or no part at all in the national movement from 1916 to 1921 has free access to the material it may result in local civil warfare in every second town and village in the country.'[6] The impulse behind the enterprise of collecting the materials of memory, as with O'Malley's project, or Richard Mulcahy's efforts to interview and tape-record his contemporaries, has much to do with politics: the traumatic split and Civil War that followed the Treaty in 1921 entailed upon survivors the necessity of gathering material to prove their side was the right one, and their actions consistent with the principles of the revolution. An undercurrent of anxiety persisted, expressed early on in Eimar O'Duffy's 1919 novel *The Wasted Island*, where several prominent revolutionary contemporaries are ruthlessly parodied and mocked. O'Duffy adopted atheism and socialism, and joined the Volunteers (in which he played a decisive and notably militaristic part), fought in the Rising, and became rapidly disillusioned, though continuing to work as a journalist for a number of nationalist publications; like O'Malley, his writing embraced modernist tropes and his life followed a consciously cosmopolitan track, with sojourns in Paris and London. More Hibernocentric, P.S. O'Hegarty's *The Victory of Sinn Féin* (1923) mounted a violent attack on the corruption and degeneration of the nationalist ideal which O'Hegarty saw as inculcated by the Anglo-Irish War and the Civil War, capturing a moment of anger and revulsion that clearly chimed with several other ex-revolutionaries, and with those who had miscalled the 1916 moment, so to speak, and paid for it afterwards. A notable example is Bulmer Hobson, who was condemned by IRB comrades when he agreed to Redmond's takeover of the Volunteers in 1914, and was subsequently excluded from the plans for the Rising, though he had done more between 1900 and 1914 to radicalize nationalist feeling than almost anyone. In 1924, he wrote to another Northern Fenian, Patrick McCartan: 'That period was to me too intense a personal tragedy; I have spent most of the intervening years trying to forget it … I could only continue to live here by assuming an indifference I was far from feeling.'[7]

This did not change. When Richard Mulcahy asked him for his memories thirty years later, Hobson replied: 'I cannot and will not write about the people and times when we were young for reasons that are too long and complicated. Briefly, the phoenix of our youth has fluttered to earth such a miserable old hen I have no heart for it.'[8] Similarly, at the end of Desmond Ryan's autobiographical novel *The Invisible Army* the hero looks on the ruins of Dublin and reflects:

> A thousand similar tragedies had been compressed into five years which history books would never mention or, at best, dismiss in a line: men taken from their beds and shot, struck down on lone hillsides or murdered in fields; women killed by stray or nonchalant bullets; children maddened or smothered in the womb; civilians mangled in the city ambushes; seeds of insanity or consumption sown in the internment camps – epics never to be told, of humble martyrdom already half-forgotten in the lengthening Truce.[9]

There is much more that might be said about the literature of disillusionment in the 1920s and 1930s, brilliantly illuminated in Frances Flanagan's work on Ryan, O'Duffy, George Russell and P.S. O'Hegarty.[10] The roll call of writers who could be further invoked is impressive: these might include Robert Lynd, Brinsley MacNamara, Michael Farrell, Darrell Figgis, Francis Stuart, Stephen McKenna, Seán O'Casey, Peadar O'Donnell, Liam O'Flaherty, Sean O'Faolain and Frank O'Connor. The connection between O'Connor's and O'Faolain's work and O'Malley's writing (often via *The Bell*) is particularly suggestive, especially in O'Connor's short story 'Guests of the Nation'. *On Another Man's Wound* proleptically strikes a note that echoes this literature, rather than the cruder memoirs already appearing from O'Malley's ex-colleagues. Other autobiographical writers (or non-writers) like Tom Barry and Dan Breen had produced naïve, highly coloured morality tales, written in an idiom derived from the nineteenth-century nationalist tracts excoriated by Yeats. By contrast, O'Malley tells his story in cadences influenced by the early Joyce, D.H. Lawrence and American writer friends like Hart Crane, but with a dry assurance all his own. The heroics come through all the more powerfully in his highly polished but economical style.

The supreme example can be found in the closing paragraph of the book. It is July 1921; the freedom fighters, bivouacked out on the hills, suddenly and disbelievingly hear of the Truce, which will soon lead to the Treaty. The conclusion is masterly, not least for the children's jingle which O'Malley adds as a kind of epiphany at the end – recalling the way his Mayo nurse used to end her songs and stories, and hinting caustically at future disappointments for the revolutionary generation.

> Con typed my orders to the five brigades. We sat down to talk about the news in wonder. What did it mean? And why had senior officers no other information than a bald message? Would the Truce last a week, or perhaps two weeks? We were willing to keep up the pressure which had been increasing steadily; soon, in a month or more, the division would begin operations in the towns and use columns by sections. Bewildered, we waited for Mickey Fitz, the Quartermaster, to discuss the speeding up of 'cheddar' and 'war flour'. And so ended for us what we called the scrap, the people later on, the trouble; and others, fond of labels, the Revolution.
>
> Put on the kettle and make the tay, and if they weren't happy, that you may.

The fact that the outcome of the revolution was so disillusioning for so many was a truth which was hard to bear, or to articulate. 'We lived in dreams always,' wrote the old revolutionary Denis McCullough to his comrade-in-arms and brother-in-law General Mulcahy many years later; 'we never enjoyed them. I dreamed of an Ireland that never existed and never could exist. I dreamt of the people of Ireland as a heroic people, a Gaelic people; I dreamt of Ireland as different from what I see now – not that I think I was wrong in this …'[11] The generation of the Irish Revolution lived on in a frame of mind markedly similar to what Robert Wohl has defined as 'the generation of 1914':

> What allowed European intellectuals born between 1880 and 1900 to view themselves as a distinct generation was that their youth coincided with the opening of the twentieth century and their lives were then bifurcated by the Great War. Those who survived into the decade of the 1920s perceived their lives as being divided into a before, a during, and an after, categories most of them equated with the stages of life known as youth, young manhood, and maturity. What bound the generation of 1914 together was not just their experiences during the war, as many of them came later to believe, but the fact that they grew up and formulated their first ideas in the world from which the war issued, a world framed by two dates, 1900 and 1914. This world was the 'vital horizon' within which they began conscious historical life.[12]

The memories of the Irish revolutionary generation, structured by a similar upheaval, were layered by another level of trauma: the fact that the revolution had been followed by internecine strife. The Treaty and Civil War lie behind the contested memory of the revolution, and the response to this traumatic memory often takes the form of evasion or over-compensation. For some, the post-revolutionary dispensation was a chance to repress or eradicate all those foreign and decadent impulses associated with British influence. This is what depressed writers like Eimar O'Duffy. O'Malley's strikingly cosmopolitan approach, his attempt to learn Continental languages (rather than Irish), his far-flung travels, perhaps above all his identification with Mexican artistic culture (vividly conveyed by Róisín Kennedy and Orla Fitzpatrick in these pages) suggest a similar reaction.

This also raises the question of his relation to modernist culture and his adoption as an Irish modernist or proto-modernist. In terms of literary style, the elliptical, challenging tone of *On Another Man's Wound* and *The Singing Flame*, the style well described by Nicholas Allen as 'clipped lyric', along with a certain existentialist swagger, makes a strong case; as does his stated intention behind the book: 'I have endeavoured to explain action as I then saw it, and, as far as was possible, to avoid all retrospective realization of the implications of events. As the survey is seen through my eyes I had to show my own progression in development.'[13] O'Malley's intellectual odyssey into modernism reinforced his powerful affinity with radical forms of contemporary art, particularly that of Jack B. Yeats. O'Malley's insight into Yeats's art locates it sharply in terms of the Ireland which Yeats observed around him, rather than as a fantastical or romantic version of reality.

> Visionary worlds of Tir na nÓg, California, palaces, are opened to us with persuasive paint, and all action is subordinated to thought. Aspects of Dublin workers are searched for inherent character or nobility. Anna Liffey gets its due tribute from one who has the Dubliner's realization of its significance: reflective mood floods people and furniture in light-splashed rooms; or light itself is the subtly dramatic force. He had always a strong sense of man in relation to the impersonality of the Irish scene; isolated figures never dominate the landscape, but they are now more related to it in symbolical significance which increases their stature to bulk in the mind. One departure of his was completely new in Irish painting, the depiction of national events. The memory of the dead makes for a tragic understanding in Ireland. It evokes a feeling of dead generations who served or have died for a common cause, their struggle echoed in each generation.[14]

This is far more insightful and nuanced than the convoluted efforts of Thomas MacGreevy to claim Yeats as a nationalist history painter ('the painter who in his work was the consummate expression of the spirit of his own nation at one of the supreme points of its evolution'[15]). O'Malley stands out from many of his contemporaries for his questioning intelligence and his readiness to deconstruct the predetermined or pious interpretations of Irish experience: his affinities with James Joyce, carefully explicated by Luke Gibbons, and shared with several of the writers listed above, is striking. Like Joyce, the path O'Malley chose was not a straightforward one, and he was not an easy personality. This comes clearly through Richard English's incisive and pioneering 1998 biography, *Ernie O'Malley: IRA Intellectual*, which presented its subject as 'one of modern Ireland's most exciting, distinctive and talented intellectuals'.[16] English's treatment delineated O'Malley's awkward, questioning, contrarian stance and also the disillusionment with simplistic nationalist pieties which characterized his later life. Though the biography uncompromisingly emphasized the intellectual side of his subject, and presented him with considerable empathy, it has attracted some testy sniping from critics determined to enlist O'Malley for a brand of Irish modernism conceived of as a kind of strict correlative to political Republicanism, straitjacketed structuralism and old-style Marxism. (This is an enterprise which sometimes stretches to odd claims on behalf of Samuel Beckett, surprisingly co-opted to the same causes.) Seamus O'Malley's chapter in this volume on his namesake's view of 'the people' is more probing and suggestive – noting that when 'the people' are discussed in *On Another Man's Wound* and *The Singing Flame* the tone becomes vague, cursory, even dutiful. A spiky individuality, and a dislike of 'isms', would characterize O'Malley to the end, and infuse his memory of the revolution – which was also, as he made clear, the story of his own personal development.

The word 'broken' occurs often in O'Malley's writings on Jack Yeats, and there is a sense of unfulfilment and sadness, especially in his later letters. But in the manner of Shakespearean tragedy, the fractures and discontinuities of O'Malley's life reflect a life that could have developed in no other way, given his creative, interrogative, restless personality: he was unafraid to come, as the other Yeats put it, 'into the desolation of reality'. In a thoughtful essay on the twenty-fifth anniversary of the Easter Rising, published in *The Bell* in 1941, Sean O'Faolain remarked: 'here [in Ireland], we know better than most how much a man's emotional bloodstream is made up of memories'.[17] The Irish Revolution, like O'Malley's own history, bristles with ironies, reversals and unanswered questions. In this, he was not alone. Karl Mannheim's influential definition of a political generation suggested that a generation became 'an actuality only where a concrete bond is created between members of a generation by their being exposed to the social and intellectual symptoms of a process of dynamic destabilization';[18] and we can see this happening in O'Malley's life, as it happened in his country. We can also see that the revolutionaries' imagined Utopia was always going to bring disillusionment in its wake. Irish experience between 1890 and 1916 indeed epitomized dynamic destabilization and a revolutionary response, but the revolution took a conservative course and the new state preserved much that British government had created in Ireland over the previous decades. People like O'Malley believed that British government had imposed on Ireland a limiting, grubby, materialistic, collaborationist, Anglicized identity, epitomized by the culture of the old Irish Parliamentary Party, and 'shoneen' admiration of what were perceived as Anglo-Irish values. They would try to substitute a new consciousness, forged in a violent guerrilla campaign which continued into the Civil War. But much of the ethos of the Free State and Republic suggested that many of these values would endure, with a thick top-dressing of authoritarian Catholic social control – imposing yet another area of silence on the national memory. As early as 1928 O'Malley was writing, with ill-concealed impatience, to Sighle Humphreys, who had tried to enlist him as a publicist for the dissident Republican cause:

> What I would write would not suit you for I have the bad and disagreeable habit of writing the truth as I see it, and not as other people (including yourself) realize it, in which we are a race of spiritualised idealists with a world idea of freedom, having nothing to learn for we have made no mistakes and whose mission in life is to broaden the outlook of folks who do not quite see that point of view … I think that often more harm is done by the extremists (not using the term in the generally accepted sense) in organizations than we realize. The spiritualistic interpretation of nationality is the only thing that matters and that no one save the '16 group ever seriously considered. Present organizations ignore it. Result eventual disintegration for their aims are not based on it.[19]

His admission to Paul Strand a few years later is similarly caustic: 'You must have learned a great deal in Mexico. I learned about betrayal, how a people is sold by spurious politicians and the futility of super names like, "revolution" and "republic".'[20]

This is one reason why O'Malley's writing and life resonates so strongly with writers concerned to contest this version of Irish experience – from O'Connor and O'Faolain to McGahern and Doyle. What remains striking about O'Malley's legacy is not only his creation of one of the most remarkable memoirs in Irish literary history, but also the story of the journey of a deeply original and powerful intelligence, coping with the fallout of an extraordinary youth and a saddened middle age. A 1956 letter to his daughter Etain, anticipating his own death a year later, puts it memorably: 'I don't want a Celtic Cross. I wish to have a good slab of granite over me, and face me to the East, towards the old British, for you were once buried in Ireland facing your enemies. Indeed they are no longer my enemies. Each man finds his enemies in himself.'[21]

ENDNOTES

On Another Man's Text: Ernie O'Malley, James Joyce and Irish Modernism

1 Ernie O'Malley, 'The Paintings of Jack B.Yeats' in Roger McHugh (ed.), *Jack B. Yeats: A Centenary Gathering* (Dublin: Dolmen Press, 1971), p. 70; reproduced in Cormac O'Malley and Nicholas Allen (eds), *Broken Landscapes: Selected Letters of Ernie O'Malley, 1924–1957* (Dublin: The Lilliput Press, 2011), p. 395.

2 O'Malley's unease with 'General' is clear from an earlier letter to *The Irish World* (New York); 'I notice in a recent issue of your paper that I am referred to as General O'Maille. I wish to stress the fact that I do not now hold any military title.' Ernie O'Malley to Editor of *The Irish World*, 10 November 1928, in O'Malley and Allen, *Broken Landscapes*, p. 54.

3 [Alice Corbin Henderson], 'Larkin–O'Malley Offerings Win Praise from El Zaguan Audience', *Santa Fe New Mexican*, 20 August 1930, p. 8. Box 21, Folder 32, Ernie O'Malley Papers, Archives of Irish America 060 [hereafter EOM AIA 060], New York University Library. Francis Ledwidge did not participate in the 1916 rebellion but lost his life in the First World War at Ypres, July, 1917; his sympathy for one of the leaders of the Rising, however, was memorialized in one of his finest poems, 'Lament for Thomas MacDonagh'.

4 'O'Malley to Read Joyce on Tuesday', *Santa Fe New Mexican*, undated clipping, November 1930, Box 21, Folder 32, EOM AIA 060.

5 'O'Malley to Make Last Talk Tuesday Evening', *Santa Fe New Mexican*, undated clipping, late November 1930, O'Malley Papers, Box 21, Folder 32, EOM AIA 060.

6 Richard Miller, 'Ernest O'Malley Concludes Talks on Irish Literature', *Santa Fe New Mexican*, undated clipping, late November 1930, Box 21, Folder 32, EOM AIA 060.

7 Box 21, Folder 32, EOM AIA 060.

8 Ibid.

9 Letter Ernie O'Malley to Dorothy Brett, 11 March 1930, O'Malley and Allen, *Broken Landscapes*, p. 69. Writing about 'the Irish understanding of actuality', O'Malley noted: 'Living is so fantastic and strange and un-understandable that they accept the supernatural

or that which cannot be explained as the actual, and with the actual they reverse the effect. The dead are almost closer to us at home than the living, and things called "miracles" seem to fit into life like toast and cream.' Letter Ernie O'Malley to Helen Hooker, 8 May 1935, O'Malley and Allen, *Broken Landscapes*, p. 117.

10 Letter Ernie O'Malley to Edward Weston, 15 February 1931, O'Malley and Allen, *Broken Landscapes*, p. 83.

11 Letter Ernie O'Malley to Paul Strand, 13 July 1932, reporting conversation with Sykes and Clurman, 10 January, 1932, O'Malley and Allen, *Broken Landscapes*, p. 88.

12 Letter Ernie O'Malley to Harriet Monroe, 22 October 1935, O'Malley and Allen, *Broken Landscapes*, p. 109.

13 Writing to Kelleher, O'Malley listed among the studies of Joyce in his possession: '– a book on *Finnegans Wake* by two Americans whose name I forget [Joseph Campbell and Henry Morton Robinson, *A Skeleton Key to Finnegans Wake* (New York, NY: Harcourt Brace & Co., 1944)] – a recently published book here by Faber but not a good book [perhaps T.S. Eliot, *Introducing James Joyce: A Selection of Joyce's Prose* (London: Faber and Faber, 1942, 1945)] – Frank Budgen: *James Joyce*, 1934 – Harry Levine [Harry Levin, *James Joyce: A Critical Introduction* (London: Faber and Faber, 1944] – Louis Goeding: *James Joyce*, 1933 [Louis Golding, *James Joyce* (London: Thornton Butterworth, 1933)] – Charles Duff: *James Joyce and the Plain Reader* (London: D. Harmsworth, 1932) – S. Foster Damon, *The Odyssey in Dublin* (Portland, ME: Hound & Horn, 1929) [paperback reprint of article published in *Hound and Horn* magazine] – Bernard Bandler II: 'Joyce's Exiles', Hound and Horn, Jan. 1933. Letter Ernie O'Malley to John V. Kelleher, 22 October 1947, O'Malley and Allen, *Broken Landscapes*, p. 257.

14 O'Malley moved in advanced Republican circles familiar with Joyce in the early 1920s that included figures such as C.S. Andrews, Sean Dowling, Michael Carolan and Roisín Walsh, but Joyce does not appear in his early reading lists. By the late 1940s, he was sufficiently familiar with the magazine *Klaxon* (1924) to know that the author of 'The *Ulysses* of James Joyce', one of the first extended discussions of *Ulysses* in an Irish periodical, was A.J. ('Con') Leventhal, writing under the pen name 'Lawrence K. Emery'. Box 14, Folder 5, EOM AIA 060.

15 O'Malley visited the newly opened Gotham Book Mart on his first day in New York, and noted 'a dollar edition of [D.H.] Lawrence' on sale, Diary, 12–16 October 1928, O'Malley and Allen, *Broken Landscapes*, p. 49. Nos 8, 13, 15, 19–20, 24, 25, 26 and 27 of *transition* were in his possession, but his notebooks contain passages from many more issues. In 1939, he thanked James Johnson Sweeney for sending issues from New York: Letter Ernie O'Malley to James J. Sweeney, 14 December 1939, O'Malley and Allen, *Broken Landscapes*, p. 179.

16 Box 9, Folder 20, EOM AIA 060.

17 Ernie O'Malley, diary, Coolidge, New Mexico, 4 December 1929, Box 42, Folder 34, 34–9, EOM AIA 060.

18 Richard English, *Ernie O'Malley, IRA Intellectual* (Oxford: Clarendon Press, 1998), p. 73. O'Malley may have delivered some talks from notes rather than completed scripts – as he wrote of a lecture given at Harvard in 1935: 'As usual I worked so much on it that

I nearly wrote a book of notes on Sunday and Monday and had enough material for 8 lectures. I really should write out lectures fully for then I would have a series of small booklets.' Letter Ernie O'Malley to Helen Hooker, 23 April 1934, O'Malley and Allen, *Broken Landscapes*, p. 114.

19 Walter Benjamin, in Rolf Tiedeman (ed.), *The Arcades Project*, trans. Howard Eiland and Kevin McLaughlin (Cambridge, MA: Belknap Press, 1999); Peter Buse, et al., *Benjamin's Arcades: An Unguided Tour* (Manchester: Manchester University Press, 2005).

20 Two notebooks devoted primarily to his initial reading of Joyce date from 1930 to 1935, Box 11, Folders 19 and 20, EOM AIA 060. Three notebooks dealing with his rereading of Joyce and Joycean criticism date from 1947 to 1948, Box 14, Folder 5, EOM AIA 060; Box 14, Folder 6, EOM AIA 060; and Box 14, Folder 7, EOM AIA 060.

21 Hannah Arendt, introduction to Walter Benjamin, *Illuminations*, trans. Harry Zohn (London: Fontana, 1973), p. 47.

22 Many of the original sources consulted by O'Malley are reprinted in Robert H. Deming (ed.), *James Joyce: The Critical Heritage, Volume One 1907–1927* (London: Routledge and Kegan Paul, 1970); *James Joyce: The Critical Heritage, Volume Two 1928–1941* (London: Routledge and Kegan Paul, 1970). I supplement from the original publications where appropriate.

23 James Fitzharris, 'Skin the Goat', was imprisoned for driving the decoy cab that helped the 'Invincibles' escape from the Phoenix Park following the assassination of Lord Frederick Cavendish and Thomas Henry Burke, 6 May 1882.

24 Notes on Stuart Gilbert, 'The "Aeolus" Episode in *Ulysses*', *transition* 18 (November 1929): 129, in Box 14, Folder 4, EOM AIA 060. Quotations in text are O'Malley's transcriptions from original essays or books (sometimes with minor amendments, or in a condensed form): these excerpts constitute the bulk of the notebooks. Original sources will be referenced, where possible, in the footnotes. O'Malley's own glosses or observations will be identified as such, and other passages from the sources will be cited separately in footnotes. It is the highly selective, and at times personal, reading of the secondary literature that is primarily of interest here, as a guide to O'Malley's own responses to Joyce.

25 Gilbert, 'The "Aeolus" Episode in *Ulysses*', p. 132.

26 Ibid., p. 138.

27 Ibid.

28 Ernie O'Malley, *The Singing Flame* (Dublin: Anvil Books, 1978), p. 42.

29 As O'Malley wrote in the course of the fund-raising campaign: 'There is little need to stress the necessity for the paper: anyone who is at all familiar with the present day Irish press can see that it does not represent the country, that it does not interpret our national aspirations, that it has not a dignified national outlook … As a nation, we are not a reading people, not a nation of serious readers, hence newspapers influence our outlook more so than they do that of most other countries' in English, *Ernie O'Malley*, pp. 31–2.

30 Gilbert, 'The "Aeolus" Episode in *Ulysses*', p. 138.

31 Ibid., p. 137. The monosyllable 'AUM' was held to be an occult word containing the secret of creation.

32 John O'Donovan (ed.), *The Topographical Poems of John O'Dubhagain and Giolla na Naomh O'Huidhrin* (Dublin: Irish Archaeological and Celtic Society, 1862), p. xlii.

33 Letter Ernie O'Malley to Paul Strand, 6 August 1953: 'Burrishoole has in ways been associated with our name since the 10th century, and I was anxious to bring the children up related to land and sea until they grew up.' O'Malley and Allen, *Broken Landscapes*, p. 311.

34 O'Malley notes the association of Clew Bay with the fabled Children of Lir in local memory: 'On Inisglora the bewitched Children of Lir took human shape; here they were buried. Within living memory sails were dipped when boats passed Inisglora as was the custom off Caher.' Ernie O'Malley, 'County of Mayo', *Holiday* (28 October 1946), reproduced in O'Malley and Allen, *Broken Landscapes*, p. 403.

35 Notes on Ernst R. Curtius's 'Technique and Thematic Development in Joyce', *transition*, 16–17 (June, 1929), Box 14, Folder 6, EOM AIA 060.

36 For Beckett on Curtius, see 'MacGreevy on Yeats' in *Jack B. Yeats*, p. 71.

37 Curtius, 'Technique', p. 312.

38 Sean O'Faolain, 'Review of *On Another Man's Wound*', *Ireland Today* 1, no. 5 (October 1936), p. 67. See also J.J. Lee, introduction in Cormac O'Malley and Anne Dolan (eds), *No Surrender Here!: The Civil War Papers of Ernie O'Malley 1922–24* (Dublin: The Lilliput Press, 2007), pp. xlviii–xlix.

39 Earnán O'Malley, 'Ireland', *Architectural Digest* 17, no. 7 (July, 1947), reproduced in O'Malley and Allen, *Broken Landscapes*, p. 422. He adds, in a gloss on revolutionary 'extremism': 'The sense of expediency or of compromise, which are commonplace in English politics, are not easy to apply to such fundamental issues.' Tennyson's 'Theirs not to reason why/ Theirs but to do and die' may apply to armies with official backing, given the state's monopoly on the legitimacy of violence, but rebels fighting for a 'provisional' government against the official state have no such assurance. It is as if the verdict of history provides the only vindication in the long run but even at that, Joyce's 'agenbite of inwit' suggests psychological wounds remain when one is in the right. Contrary to the image of 'fanatic hearts', Desmond Ryan recounts how in the GPO during the Rising, Patrick Pearse asked 'if it were the right thing to do' – 'the very last question that I ever expected to hear from him'. Desmond Ryan, *The Man Called Pearse* (Dublin: Maunsel and Company, 1919), p. 58.

40 Donald L. Carveth, *The Still Small Voice: Psychoanalytic Reflections on Guilt and Conscience* (London: Karnac Books, 2013), p. 91.

41 Carveth, *The Still Small Voice*, pp. 103–4.

42 Ernie O'Malley, *On Another Man's Wound* (Dublin: Anvil Books, 2002), p. 373. If conscience weighed heavily, it was also for abject failures, such as the inability to hold the Four Courts at the outset of the Civil War. He wrote of the gun battle that led to his capture in November 1922: 'I would not surrender as I thought I should wipe out the disgraceful surrender of the Four Courts'. 'Details of Military Service, 1916–1924 and List of Wounds' in O'Malley and Dolan, *'No Surrender Here!'* p. lvi.

43 Gilbert, 'An Irish *Ulysses*: "Hades" Episode', *Fortnightly Review* 132 (July 1929): p. 48.

44 Letter Ernie O'Malley to Paul Strand, 28 December 1934, O'Malley and Allen, *Broken Landscapes,* p. 107.

45 Notes on Maurice Murphy, 'James Joyce and Ireland', *The Nation* 129 (16 October 1929), 426 in Box 14, Folder 6, EOM AIA 060.

46 O'Malley, 'Ireland', *Broken Landscapes*, p. 423. There are clear echoes here of Joyce's comparison of the Irish readers and audiences to the 'rage of Caliban' (*U* 1.143) seeing himself in the mirror for the first time.

47 As O'Malley wrote to his future wife Helen Hooker before they left the United States for Ireland in 1935: 'The problem of reality in my country has yet to be faced. It is a bitter country and one without pity ... I mention this because I don't want any romantic idea of the country to obscure its reality.' English, *Ernie O'Malley*, p. 185.

48 Notes on Cyril Connolly, 'The Position of Joyce', *Life and Letters* 2, no. 11 (April 1929): 273–90 in Box 14, Folder 6, EOM AIA 060.

49 Ibid.

50 O'Malley, *On Another Man's Wound*, p. 52; James Joyce, A *Portrait of the Artist as a Young Man* (Harmonsworth: Penguin, 1992), p. 280.

51 O'Malley, *On Another Man's Wound*, p. 143.

52 Ibid.

53 English, *Ernie O'Malley*, p. 151.

54 For the classic liberal position, see John Locke's assertion that no free agent can validly consent to a state of slavery: 'No man, can, by agreement pass over to another that which he hath not in himself, a power over his own life.' John Locke, in Peter Laslett (ed.), *Two Treatises of Government*, Vol. 2 (Cambridge: Cambridge University Press, 1988), p. 285. In keeping with the tenets of a constitutional monarchy, Locke argued consent could be given to a monarchy; modern Republicanism from the American and French Revolutions challenged this as consenting to subjection, particularly in the case of an imposed monarchy.

55 O'Malley, *The Singing Flame*, p. 286.

56 Letter Ernie O'Malley to Sighle Humphries, 25 December 1923, O'Malley and Dolan, '*No Surrender Here!*', p. 473.

57 Peter Burger, *Theory of the Avant–Garde*, trans. Michel Shaw (Minneapolis, MN: University of Minnesota Press, 1984), Chapter 2. See also Andreas Huyssen, *After the Great Divide: Modernism, Mass Culture and Postmodernism* (London: Macmillan, 1986), pp. vii–ix, Chapters 1–2.

58 O'Malley, *The Singing Flame*, p. 181. O'Malley is recalling Joseph Dunn's archaic translation of the *Táin* which, according to his friend John V. Kelleher, was also the version most likely to have been used by Joyce. 'Identifying the Irish Printed Sources for *Finnegans Wake*' in Charles Fanning (ed.), *Selected Writings of John V. Kelleher on Ireland and Irish-America* (Carbondale, IL: Southern Illinois Press, 2002), p. 69.

59 O'Malley, *The Singing Flame*, p. 181.

60 Ibid., pp. 274–5.

61 Ibid., p. 278.

62 *On Another Man's Wound*, p. 51.
63 *The Singing Flame*, p. 276.

'Flamboyant, Gothic, Romanesque': Art and Revolution in the Mind of Ernie O'Malley

1 Ernie O'Malley, *On Another Man's Wound* (Dublin: Anvil Books, 2002), p. 37.
2 John Turpin, *A School of Art in Dublin since 18th century: A History of the National College of Art and Design* (Dublin: Gill and Macmillan, 1995), pp. 192–4.
3 George Noble Plunkett (1851–1948) studied Renaissance and medieval art at Trinity College Dublin. In 1900 he published a biography of *Sandro Botticelli* and in 1911 a revised edition of Margaret Stokes's *Early Christian Art in Ireland*. He was director of the National Museum of Ireland 1907–16, and Minister for Fine Arts in the first Dáil, 1921–22.
4 Eileen McGrane MacCarvill was an important collector of modern Irish art and edited the talks and essays of Mainie Jellett for *An Artist's Vision* (Dundalk: Dundalgan Press, 1958).
5 O'Malley, *On Another Man's Wound*, pp. 238–9.
6 Ernie O'Malley, *The Singing Flame* (Cork: Mercier Press, 2012), pp. 137–8.
7 Ibid.
8 Ibid., p. 244.
9 Nicholas Allen, *Modernism, Ireland and Civil War* (Cambridge: Cambridge University Press, 2009), p. 29. See also M. Cosgrove, 'Ernie O'Malley: Art and Modernism in Ireland', *Éire-Ireland* 40, nos 3–4 (2005), pp. 85–103, for overview of O'Malley's interest in Irish art.
10 Samuel Beckett, in E. O'Brien and E. Fournier (eds), *Dream of Fair to Middling Women* (Dublin: Black Cat Press, 1992), p. 77.
11 O'Malley, *The Singing Flame*, p. 244.
12 Letter Ernie O'Malley to Mary Childers, 26 November 1923, in Richard English and Cormac O'Malley (eds), *Prisoners: The Civil War letters of Ernie O'Malley* (Dublin: Poolbeg, 1991), p. 88; also in Cormac O'Malley and Anne Dolan (eds), *'No Surrender Here!' The Civil War Papers of Ernie O'Malley, 1922–24* (Dublin: The Lilliput Press, 2007), p. 434.
13 Thomas MacGreevy, 'Writers on Art', *Father Mathew Record* (February 1944), p. 4.
14 Nicholas Allen, *Modernism, Ireland and Civil War* (Cambridge: Cambridge University Press), p. 48.
15 Letter Ernie O'Malley to Molly Childers, 5–7 December 1923, in English and O'Malley, *Prisoners*, 110; also in O'Malley and Dolan, *No Surrender Here*, p. 457.
16 Letter Ernie O'Malley to Sighle Humphreys, 5 January 1928 in Cormac O'Malley and Nicholas Allen (eds), *Broken Landscapes: Selected Letters of Ernie O'Malley, 1924–1957* (Dublin: The Lilliput Press, 2011), p. 42.
17 Ernie O'Malley, Introduction to the catalogue for the Jack B. Yeats National Loan Exhibition, National College of Art, Dublin, 1945, in O'Malley and Allen, *Broken Landscapes*, p. 395.
18 John Ruskin, *The Elements of Drawing*, quoted in B. Smith, *The Formalesque: A Guide to Modern Art and Its History* (Melbourne: Macmillan Art Publishing, 2007), p. 107.

19 See R. Hewison, *John Ruskin. The Argument of the Eye* (London: Thames & Hudson, 1976), pp. 132–46.

20 F.S. Connelly, 'The Stones of Venice: John Ruskin's Grotesque History of Art' in F.S. Connelly (ed.), *Modern Art and the Grotesque* (Cambridge: Cambridge University Press, 2003), pp. 156–74, 166.

21 Letter Ernie O'Malley to John V. Kelleher, 7 April 1948, O'Malley and Allen, *Broken Landscapes*, pp. 263–5.

22 While this essay emphasises O'Malley's interest in painting, he had a particular concern with sculpture.

23 Thomas MacGreevy, 'Our National Gallery. A Layman's Ideas, Part II', *Old Ireland* 23 (July 1921), p. 354. The painting is currently catalogued as Filippino Lippi: *Portrait of a Musician,* National Gallery of Ireland, p. 470. For MacGreevy's priorities as an art historian and critic, see R. Kennedy and R. Coulter, '"It is only by learning to fully understand the past that we can most easily come to realize the significance of the present" Thomas MacGreevy, Art Critic and Art Historian' in S. Schrebman (ed.), *The Life and Work of Thomas MacGreevy: A Critical Reappraisal* (London: Bloomsbury Press, 2013), pp. 51–64.

24 See R. Wollheim, 'Giovanni Morelli and the Origins of Scientific Connoisseurship' in R. Wollheim (ed.), *On Art and the Mind* (London: Allen Lane, 1973), pp. 177–201.

25 Letter Ernie O'Malley to Kay Brady, 4 March–26 April 1926, O'Malley and Allen, *Broken Landscapes*, pp. 30–2.

26 Lorenzo di Credi (*c.*1458–1537), Florentine painter, had one work attributed to him, at the time, in the National Gallery of Ireland, *Virgin and Child with two angels*, cat. 519.

27 Letter Ernie O'Malley to Kay Brady, 4 March–26 April 1926, O'Malley and Allen, *Broken Landscapes*, pp. 30–2.

28 Letters Ernie O'Malley to Kay Brady, 24 January 1926 and 27 January 1926, O'Malley and Allen, *Broken Landscapes*, pp. 23–4.

29 The work is catalogued as Pietro Perugino, *Lamentation over the Dead Christ*, *c.*1495, cat. 942, National Gallery of Ireland.

30 J. Knowlson, *Damned to Fame: The Life of Samuel Beckett* (London: Bloomsbury Press, 1996), p. 131.

31 Letter Samuel Beckett to Thomas MacGreevy, 20 December 1931, Knowlson, *Damned to Fame*, p. 131.

32 O'Malley, *The Singing Flame*, pp. 60–2.

33 Ernie O'Malley, *The State of Painting in Ireland*, Lecture at Limerick City Library, Autumn 1946, in O'Malley and Allen, *Broken Landscapes*, p. 404.

34 Letter Ernie O'Malley to Estella Solomons, December 1923, in O'Malley and Dolan, *'No Surrender Here!'*, pp. 439–40.

35 Letter Ernie O'Malley to Eithne Golden, 7 March 1940, O'Malley and Allen, *Broken Landscapes*, pp. 185–7.

36 See, for example, letter of Ernie O'Malley to Helen Golden, 19 January 1931, O'Malley and Allen, *Broken Landscapes*, p. 80.

37 M.A. Staniszewksi, *The Power of Display. A History of Exhibition Installations at the Museum of Modern Art* (Cambridge, MA: MIT Press, 1998); P. Lorente, *The Museums of Contemporary Art: Notion and Development* (London: Ashgate, 2011).

38 Of Irish-American origin, Sweeney was associate editor of *transition* (1935–38), curated *African Negro Art* at the Museum of Modern Art in New York in 1935, becoming MoMA's director of painting and sculpture (1945–6); director of Solomon R. Guggenheim Museum (1952–9), director of Houston Museum of Art (1961–7); member of the Arts Council of Ireland (1967–73) when instrumental in the organization of *Rosc*, 1967 and 1971. For Sweeney as a curator of modernist art, see M. Brennan, *Curating Consciousness: Mysticism and the Modern Museum* (Cambridge, MA: MIT Press, 2010).

39 James J. Sweeney, *Plastic Redirections in 20th Century Painting* (Chicago, IL: University of Chicago Press, 1934), p. x.

40 Ciaran Benson, 'Towards a Cultural Democracy', *Studies* 81, no. 321 (1992), pp. 23–33; B.P. Kennedy, 'The Failure of the Cultural Republic: Ireland 1922–39', *Studies* 81, no. 321 (1992), pp. 14–22.

41 Letter Ernie O'Malley to James J. Sweeney, 18 January 1946, O'Malley and Allen, *Broken Landscapes*, pp. 233–5.

42 Ibid.

43 FNCI was founded in 1924 to secure a permanent home for Lane's Municipal Gallery and to donate artworks to public galleries and museums. See N. Gordon-Bowe, 'The Friends of the National Collections in Ireland' in B.P. Kennedy (ed.), *Art is My Life – A Tribute to James White* (Dublin: National Gallery of Ireland, 1991), pp. 15–30.

44 Letter Ernie O'Malley to James J. Sweeney, 18 January 1946, O'Malley and Allen, *Broken Landscapes*, pp. 233–5.

45 Richard English, *Ernie O'Malley: IRA Intellectual* (Oxford: Clarendon Press, 1998), p. 160.

46 See letter, Ernie O'Malley to Helen Hooker O'Malley, 30 May 1938, O'Malley and Allen, *Broken Landscapes*, pp. 152–3, and *The O'Malley Collection at Irish Museum of Modern Art* (Dublin: IMMA, 1992).

47 O'Malley, 'The State of Painting in Ireland' in O'Malley and Allen, *Broken Landscapes*, p. 403.

48 S.B. Kennedy, *Irish Art and Modernism 1880–1950* (Belfast: Institute of Irish Studies, 1991).

49 Letter Ernie O'Malley to Thomas MacGreevy, 1 May 1939, O'Malley and Allen, *Broken Landscapes*, p. 165. See discussion of relationship between Yeats and O'Malley in Nicholas Allen, *Modernism, Ireland and Civil War* (Cambridge: Cambridge University Press, 2009); B. Arnold, *Jack Yeats* (New Haven, CT: Yale University Press, 1998), and Cosgrove, 'Ernie O'Malley: Art and Modernism in Ireland', pp. 85–103.

50 In addition to *Death for Only One* (1937, Private Collection), O'Malley also acquired *The Band, Dungarvan* (1925, Private Collection), *Paper Bags for Hats* (1925, Private Collection), *Derrynane* (1927, Ireland's Great Hunger Museum, Quinnipiac University), *Evening in Spring* (1937, Private Collection), *Reverie* (1931, Private Collection), *Homage to Bret Harte* (1943, Private Collection) and *The Fighting Dawn* (1945, Private Collection). He also owned several Yeats sketchbooks. See *Joint Exhibition of Jack B. Yeats Paintings from Collections of*

Ernie O'Malley and the Yeats Museum (Sligo: Sligo County Library, 2–20 Aug. 1963).

51 Jack B. Yeats Account Book (1943–51), Y8, Yeats Archive, National Gallery of Ireland.

52 Terence De Vere White, *A Fretful Midge* (London: Routledge, 1957), pp. 113–14.

53 *Paintings by Jack B. Yeats* (Dublin: Victor Waddington Galleries, March 1945) Ernie O'Malley Papers, Archives of Irish America 060, New York University [hereafter EOM AIA 060]. O'Malley bought *Derrynane* at the exhibition.

54 See R. Kennedy, 'The Capuchin Annual: Visual Art and the Legacy of 1916, One Generation on' in J. Bruck and L. Godson (eds), *Making 1916* (Liverpool: Liverpool University Press, 2015).

55 O'Malley, *The State of Painting in Ireland* (Lecture at Limerick City Library, Autumn 1946).

56 Ernie O'Malley, 'Book review of Thomas MacGreevy's *Appreciation and Interpretation of Jack B. Yeats*', *The Bell* 9, no. 4 (January 1946), in O'Malley and Allen, *Broken Landscapes*, pp. 396–7.

57 Ernie O'Malley, Introduction to the catalogue for the Jack B. Yeats National Loan Exhibition, in O'Malley and Allen, *Broken Landscapes*, pp. 391–7.

58 Ernie O'Malley Notebook of 1945, EOM AIA 060.

59 O'Malley and Allen, *Broken Landscape*, p. 395.

60 David Lloyd, 'Republics of Difference: Yeats, MacGreevy, Beckett' in *Samuel Beckett: A Passion for Paintings* (Dublin: National Gallery of Ireland, 2006), pp. 52–9.

61 As a photographer and as the husband of an artist, O'Malley was aware of the physical and intellectual demands of creating art.

62 O'Malley, Introduction to the catalogue for the Jack B. Yeats National Loan Exhibition, in O'Malley and Allen, *Broken Landscapes*, p. 394.

63 O'Malley, 'Review of Thomas MacGreevy' in O'Malley and Allen, *Broken Landscapes*, pp. 396–7.

64 O'Malley, Introduction to the catalogue for the Jack B. Yeats National Loan Exhibition, in O'Malley and Allen, *Broken Landscapes*, p. 395.

65 Letter Ernie O'Malley to James J. Sweeney, 18 January 1946, O'Malley and Allen, *Broken Landscapes*, p. 234.

66 O'Malley put his homes in Dublin and Mayo at Rothenstein's disposal. See letter Ernie O'Malley to John Rothenstein, 26 October 1945, O'Malley and Allen, *Broken Landscapes*, pp. 229–30.

67 John Rothenstein, in Arnold, *Jack Yeats*, p. 328.

68 See Cosgrove, 'Ernie O'Malley: Art and Modernism in Ireland', pp. 100–1.

69 U. Walker, 'Notes and Queries' in E. O'Connor (ed.), *Irish Women Artists 1800–2010* (Dublin: Four Courts Press, 2010), p. 199.

70 Letter, Ernie O'Malley to Jean McGrail, 16–17 March 1955, reprinted in *Broken Landscapes*, pp. 330–2.

71 See R. Kennedy, 'Made in England. Louis le Brocquy's A Family' in *Third Text* (Ireland Special Issue), No.76, 19, Issue 5 (September, 2005), pp. 475–87.

72 Ernie O'Malley, 'Louis le Brocquy', *Horizon* 14 (July 1946), pp. 32–7, in O'Malley and Allen, *Broken Landscapes*, pp. 397–401.

73 See Myles na gCopaleen, 'Crusikeen Lawn', *Irish Times* (Dublin, Ireland), 20 June 1947, p. 4, which derives much amusement from O'Malley's art criticism in *The Bell*.

74 Brian O'Doherty, *The Irish Imagination 1959–1971* (Dublin: Municipal Gallery of Modern Art, 1971). See F. Cullen, *Sources in Irish Art* (Cork: Cork University Press, 2000), pp. 268–73; R. Kennedy, 'The Irish Imagination 1971 – Romanticism or Pragmatism', *Journal of Art Historiography* 9 (December 2013), http://arthistoriography.wordpress.com.

75 Brian O'Doherty, 'Jack B. Yeats: Promise and Regret' in Roger McHugh (ed.), *Jack B. Yeats. A Centenary Gathering* (1971), pp. 77–91.

76 O'Doherty, *The Irish Imagination*, p. 11.

From Mexico to Mayo: Ernie O'Malley, Paul Strand and Photographic Modernism

1 O'Malley was accompanied on this trip by Frank Aiken. For an account of this period, see Evans Bryce and Stephen Kelly (eds), *Frank Aiken: Nationalist and Internationalist* (Dublin: Irish Academic Press, 2014).

2 Letter to Harriet Monroe, 10 January 1935, in Cormac O'Malley and Nicholas Allen (eds), *Broken Landscapes: Selected Letters of Ernie O'Malley, 1924–1957* (Dublin: The Lilliput Press, 2011), p. 109.

3 See Amy Conger, *Edward Weston in Mexico, 1923–26* (Albuquerque, NM: University of New Mexico Press, 1983); Sarah M. Lowe, *Tina Modotti and Edward Weston: The Mexico Years* (London: Merrel, 2004).

4 Weston's impression of their meeting is recorded in Nancy Newhall (ed.), *The Daybooks of Edward Weston, Vol. 2, California* (New York, NY: Aperture, 1973); 14 May 1929, Newhall, *The Daybooks of Edward Weston*, p. 121; 25 May 1929, Newhall, *The Daybooks of Edward Weston*, p. 124; 6 June 1929, Newhall, *The Daybooks of Edward Weston*, p. 125.

5 Diary, Carmel, California, 21 April 1929, O'Malley and Allen, *Broken Landscapes*, pp. 64–5.

6 Newhall, *The Daybooks of Edward Weston*, p. 125.

7 See Helen Delpar, *The Enormous Vogue of Things Mexican: Cultural Relations Between the United States and Mexico, 1920–1935* (Tuscaloosa, AL: University of Alabama Press, 1992).

8 Rose Murphy, *Ella Young, Irish Mystic and Rebel: From Literary Dublin to the American West* (Dublin: The Liffey Press, 2008).

9 During this trip Stewart was researching her book on traditional Mexican shrines: Dorothy N. Stewart, *Hornacinas: Stories of Niches and Corners of Mexico* (Mexico: Editorial Cultura, 1933).

10 Rick López, *Crafting Mexico: Intellectuals, Artisans, and the State After the Revolution* (Durham, NC: Duke University Press Books, 2010), p. 142.

11 See Box 19, Folder 26, Ernie O'Malley Papers, Archives of Irish America 060, New York University Library [hereafter EOM AIA 060].

12 'Irish Film Society', *The Irish Times* (Dublin, Ireland), 15 January 1940.

13 Cormac O'Malley Personal Papers.

14 Patricia Albers, *Shadows, Fire, Snow: The Life of Tina Modotti* (New York, NY: Clarkson Potter, 1999), p. 151. 'The artistic education of Pablo O'Higgins came from working as Diego's assistant for frescoes at Chapingo, the National Agricultural School occupying a bucolic seventeenth-century hacienda east of the capital ... Dominating the mural program are monumental nudes of Virgin Earth and Liberated Earth, whose models were Tina and Lupe, respectively.'

15 William Spratling (1900–67) was an American–born silver designer and artist, best known for his influence on twentieth-century Mexican silver design; Albers, *Shadows, Fire, Snow*, p. 220: 'Frances Toor, who commissioned dozens of shots of masks for a *Mexican Folkways* essay by Miguel Covarrubias' which appears in volume 5, No. 3, July–September 1929.

16 Anita Brenner, *Idols behind Altars* (New York, NY: Payson & Clarke, 1929). Ernie O'Malley had a copy of this book in his library and interestingly it contains a dedication from Brenner to Frances 'Paca' Toor, as follows: 'For Paca, sincere friend of Mexico, Anita Brenner, NY 1929.'

17 Albers, *Shadows, Fire, Snow*, p. 158.

18 Letter to Harriet Monroe, 10 January 1935, O'Malley and Allen, *Broken Landscapes*, pp. 108–10.

19 Maria Morris Hambourg and Christopher Phillips, *The New Vision: Photography Between the World Wars: Ford Motor Company Collection at the Metropolitan Museum of Art* (New York, NY: Metropolitan Museum of Art, 1989), p. 56.

20 Cormac K.H. O'Malley, 'The Publication History of *On Another Man's Wound*', *New Hibernia Review* 7, no. 3 (Autumn 2003), pp. 136–9.

21 Letter to Paul Strand, 19 August 1932, O'Malley and Allen, *Broken Landscapes*, pp. 91–2.

22 'Ford Plant Photos of Charles Sheeler', *Creative Art* 8, no. 4 (April 1931), p. 265.

23 Charles Sheeler, 'Ford Plant Photos of Charles Sheeler' *Creative Art* 8, no. 4 (April 1931), p. 265, cutting located in Box 20, Folder 3, EOM AIA 060.

24 Letter to Paul Strand, 12 July 1934, O'Malley and Allen, *Broken Landscapes*, p. 102.

25 See the following for an overview of Strand's Mexican photography: James Krippner-Martínez, 'Traces, Images, and Fictions: Paul Strand in Mexico, 1932–34', *The Americas* 63, no. 3 (January 2007), pp. 359–83; Krippner et al., *Paul Strand in Mexico* (New York, NY: Aperture Foundation, 2010).

26 Letter to Merriam Golden, 9 April 1935, O'Malley and Allen, *Broken Landscapes*, p. 114.

27 Letter to Paul Strand, 28 December 1934, O'Malley and Allen, *Broken Landscapes*, p. 107.

28 Paul Strand, *Photographs of Mexico* (New York, NY: Virginia Stevens, 1940). Ernie O'Malley's wife owned a copy of this publication. In a letter to Jean McGrail in June 1955 he refers to Strand's 'books on Mexico which I now cannot find when I search my shelves'. See O'Malley and Allen, *Broken Landscapes*, p. 338.

29 The narrative and sequencing of images in this volume are explored by Krippner-Martínez, 'Traces, Images, and Fictions', pp. 359–83.

30 Ibid., p. 370.

31 *Redes, transition: an international quarterly of creative experiment*, no. 25 (Fall 1936), pp. 146–55.

32 A. Philip McMahon, 'New Books on Art: *Modern Works of Art* by Alfred H. Barr; *African Negro Art* by James Johnson Sweeney', *Parnassus* 7, no. 4 (May 1935), p. 44.

33 In a letter to Sweeney, O'Malley states that he knew of him through two publications: '*Negro Art*, which I liked well, and *Plastic Redirections*, excellent', Letter, 19 January 1946, O'Malley and Allen, *Broken Landscapes*, p. 234.

34 Mary Cosgrove, 'Ernie O'Malley: Art and Modernism in Ireland', *Éire-Ireland* 40, nos 3–4 (2005), pp. 96–7.

35 Elizabeth O'Connor, 'Noel Moffett–Review', *Commentary* 1, no. 2 (December 1941), p. 1.

36 Bruce Arnold, *Mainie Jellett and the Modern Movement in Ireland* (New Haven, CT: Yale University Press, 1991), p. 180.

37 *Architectural Design*, Special Issue: Ireland 17, no. 7 (July 1947), pp. 172–5, in O'Malley and Allen, *Broken Landscapes*, pp. 420–4.

38 *Architectural Design*, 175, in O'Malley and Allen, *Broken Landscapes*, p. 420.

39 Earnán O'Malley, 'Louis LeBrocquy', *Horizon* 14, no. 79 (July 1946), pp. 33–7, in O'Malley and Allen, *Broken Landscapes*, pp. 397–401.

40 *Architectural Design*, p. 175, in O'Malley and Allen, *Broken Landscapes*, p. 420.

41 Ibid.

42 Autobiographical statement quoted in O'Malley and Allen, *Broken Landscapes*, pp. 220–1.

43 Box 6, Folder 30, EOM AIA 060. Receipts also show that camera repairs and other services were obtained from Kodak's Irish headquarters at 'Kodak House' in Rathmines. Unfortunately, these receipts do not mention the types of cameras used.

44 Box 6, Folder 30, EOM AIA 060.

45 Turlough O'Riordan, 'Mason, Thomas Holmes' in James McGuire and James Quinn (eds), *Dictionary of Irish Biography* (Cambridge: Cambridge University Press, 2009), accessed on 30 July 2014, http://dib.cambridge.org.

46 Letter to Helen Hooker O'Malley, 29 January 1940, O'Malley and Allen, *Broken Landscapes*, p. 181.

47 O'Malley and Allen, *Broken Landscapes*, p. 125.

48 Patrick F. Wallace, 'Adolf Mahr and the Making of Seán P. Ó Ríordáin' in Helen Roche (ed.), *From Megaliths to Metal: Essays in Honour of George Eogan* (Oxford: Oxbow Books, 2004), p. 263.

49 Ernie O'Malley, 'Book review of Françoise Henry's *Irish Art in the Early Christian Period*' *The Bell* 1, no. 1 (October 1940), 85–7 in O'Malley and Allen, *Broken Landscapes*, p. 390.

50 Françoise Henry, *Irish Art in the Early Christian Period* (London: Methuen & Co. Ltd, 1940), p. xviii. In her introduction Henry states that 'it must also be remembered that I did not intend to write an archaeological treatise. I have tried to reduce technical and typological discussions to a minimum.'

51 Letter to Jean McGrail, 16–17 March 1955, O'Malley and Allen, *Broken Landscapes*, p. 330.

52 Henry, *Irish Art in the Early Christian Period*, plate 38.

53 See Janet T. Marquardt (ed.), *Françoise Henry in Co. Mayo: The Inishkea Journals*, trans. Huw Duffy (Dublin: Four Courts Press, 2014).

54 Letter to Helen Hooker O'Malley, February 1937, O'Malley and Allen, *Broken Landscapes*, p. 137; Letter to Helen Hooker O'Malley, 7–11 June 1938, O'Malley and Allen, *Broken Landscapes*, p. 155.

55 Arthur Kingsley Porter, *The Crosses and Culture of Ireland* (New Haven, CT: Yale University Press, 1931). This book was based on five lectures delivered at the Metropolitan Museum of Art between February and March, 1930.

56 See the following for an account of Porter's life: Pamela Petro, *The Slow Breath of Stone: A Romanesque Love Story* (London: Fourth Estate, 2005) and Lucy Costigan, *Glenveagh Mystery: The Life, Work and Disappearance of Arthur Kingsley Porter* (Dublin: Merrion, 2013).

57 Carol Neuman de Vegvar, 'In the Shadow of the Sidhe: Arthur Kingsley Porter's Vision of an Exotic Ireland', *Irish Arts Review Yearbook* 17 (2001), pp. 48–60; Letter to Eithne Golden, 4 October 1936, O'Malley and Allen, *Broken Landscapes*, p. 131.

58 Letter to James Johnson Sweeney, 14 December 1939, O'Malley and Allen, *Broken Landscapes*, p. 179.

59 29 May 1937, Fassalve [Fassaroe, County Wicklow, location of an unusual granite cross], Evening Light about 3, but tree might be in the way, earlier for head on', Diary 1937, Box 10, Folder 1, EOM AIA 060.

60 Letter to Professor John V. Kelleher, 7 April 1948, O'Malley and Allen, *Broken Landscapes*, p. 264.

61 Letter to Paul Strand, 7 November 1953, O'Malley and Allen, *Broken Landscapes*, p. 310.

62 Fraser Macdonald, 'Paul Strand and the Atlanticist Cold War', *The Journal of the History of Photography* 28, no. 4 (2004), pp. 356–73.

63 Paul Strand and Basil Davidson, *Tir A Mhurain: Outer Hebrides* (London: MacGibbon & Kee, 1962).

64 Martin Parr and Gerry Badger, 'Tir a Mhurain: Outer Hebrides', *The Photobook: A History, Volume I* (London: Phaidon Press, 2004), p. 217.

65 This refers to the International Exhibition of Pictorial Photography which was arranged by the Photographic Society of Ireland and held in the Mansion House, Dublin, in April 1946. See 'Fine Dublin Exhibition of Pictorial Photography', *The Irish Times* (Dublin, Ireland), 2 April 1946; Letter to James Johnson Sweeney from Helen Hooker O'Malley, 22 July 1946, Box 5, Folder 42, EOM AIA.060.

66 'The Background of the Arts in Mexico', *The Bell* 14, no. 5 (August 1947), pp. 56–9, in O'Malley and Allen, *Broken Landscapes*, p. 430.

The Evolution of Ernie O'Malley's Memoir, *On Another Man's Wound*

1 Ernie O'Malley, *On Another Man's Wound* (Cork: Mercier Press, 2013). For historiography of its publication see Section 5 of this chapter.

2 See list of books in his letter of 26–30 November 1922, and later letters, Cormac O'Malley and Anne Dolan (eds), *'No Surrender Here!' The Civil War Papers of Ernie O'Malley, 1922–1924* (Dublin: The Lilliput Press, 2007), pp. 436–7. See also his notebook listing his

readings for 1923–7, in Box 9, Folder 28, The Ernie O'Malley Papers, Archives of Irish America 060 [hereafter EOM AIA 060], New York University Library.

3 The story is told in O'Malley, *On Another Man's Wound*, pp. 342–57.

4 O'Malley, *On Another Man's Wound*, p. 377.

5 See O'Malley's letters written in prison from 7 April 1923 to 12 February 1924 in O'Malley and Dolan, *'No Surrender Here!'*, pp. 368–480.

6 O'Malley, *On Another Man's Wound*, p. 279.

7 In the academic year 1926–7 the newly formed UCD Dramatic Society or 'DramSoc' had to be organized as a committee of the Literary and Historical Society, but, Dr Denis Coffey, President of UCD, allowed it to become an independent society in autumn of 1927 after it had proven itself. See letter, Donough Coffey to Cormac O'Malley, 3 January 1973, Box 23, Folder 2D, EOM AIA 060.

8 Over the years some of O'Malley's early and later notebooks, including his diaries and military notebooks, have been donated to Irish libraries by various people, and these include the Bureau of Military History, Jackie Clarke Collection, Kilmainham Gaol Museum, National Folklore Commission at UCD, National Library of Ireland, and UCD Archives, and perhaps some of the missing diaries will yet surface. The four New Mexican diaries include the second half of September, late November, December 1929 and January 1930 and the eight Mexican diaries cover January to April 1931 but exclude two weeks of that January. O'Malley's Post-Nationalist Papers are held in EOM AIA 060.

9 For European diaries from 1925 to 1926, see Box 9, Folders 28A–D, 29–33, EOM AIA 060.

10 O'Malley had always collected stamps and noted how he steamed off 'surcharged stamps of the Provisional Government and the Free State' while in his internment camp. Ernie O'Malley, *The Singing Flame* (Cork: Mercier Press, 2012), p. 361.

11 Diary, New Mexico, 28 September 1929, Box 42, Folder 32, C91, EOM AIA 060; Diary, New Mexico, 29 November 1929, Box 42, Folder 34, D4, EOM AIA 060.

12 Diary, New Mexico, 2 December 1929, Box 42, Folder 34, D9, EOM, AIA 060.

13 Diary, New Mexico, 23 September 1929, Box 42, Folder 33, B24, EOM, AIA 060; Diary, New Mexico, 23 September 1929, Box 42, Folder 33, B28, EOM, AIA 060.

14 Diary, New Mexico, 3 December 1929, Box 42, Folder 34, D23, EOM AIA 060.

15 Diary, New Mexico, 28 September 1929, Box 42, Folder 32, C102, EOM AIA 060.

16 Diary, New Mexico, 3 December 1929, Box 42, Folder 33, B25, EOM AIA 060.

17 Gweedore, Co. Donegal, was written Guidore in the original diary. O'Malley actually referred to noises at the long bridge of Gweebarra in O'Malley, *On Another Man's Wound*, p. 123; Diary, New Mexico, 27 September 1929, Box 42, Folder 33, B25–26, EOM AIA 060.

18 Robinson Jeffers and his wife, Una, both of whom O'Malley had met in Carmel in the spring of 1929; O'Malley mistakenly wrote this as 'McDougal colony' in his original diary; Diary, Box 42, Folder 33, B30–31, EOM AIA 060.

The Moore reference could have been to Marianne Moore or Harriet Moore, both poets, but the latter published O'Malley's poems in *Poetry* magazine in January 1935 and March 1936 just before she died.

19 The line below about a response seeming monotonous is similar to his 'I felt that Yes, m' would be an answer to all her questions' dialogue referenced in endnote 16; Diary, New Mexico, 9 December 1929, Box 42, Folder 34, D72–73, EOM AIA 060.

20 For Kilkenny, O'Malley, *On Another Man's Wound*, pp. 281–3, 286–92, 295–6; for Dublin Castle, O'Malley, *On Another Man's Wound*, pp. 303, 313–19, 323–5.

21 O'Malley, *On Another Man's Wound*, p. 134.

22 Richard Hakluyt (1553–1616). One of many things Hakluyt undertook was going on seafaring voyages of discovery and writing up his travels; Sir Thomas Malory's ancient telling of this Arthurian tale was published first by William Claxton (1415–92) in 1485 only nine years after he established the first printing press in England.

23 Probably Hakluyt's *Divers Voyages Touching the Discoverie of America and Ilands Adjacent the Same* ... (London: 1582); Daniel Defoe (1660–1731), English author of *The Life and Adventures of Robinson Crusoe* which when published in 1719 was one of the first novels (creating a new genre).

24 Seamus MacManus (1869–1960), Irish storyteller and author of folktales, whose *Donegal Fairy Tales* was his third book (published in 1900); Draft typed MS of *On Another Man's Wound*, Box 40, Folders 2, EOM AIA 060, p. 7.

25 O'Malley, *On Another Man's Wound*, p. 130.

26 Ibid., p. 15.

27 Ibid., p. 15.

28 Ibid., pp. 231, 137, 12.

29 Diary, New Mexico, 3 December 1929, Box 42, Folder 34, D28, D31–33, EOM AIA 060.

30 Diary, New Mexico, 5 December 1929, Box 42, Folder 34, D42–43, EOM AIA 060.

31 Notes, New Mexico, Box 42, Folder 34, D113, D115, EOM AIA 060.

32 O'Malley, *On Another Man's Wound*, p. 11.

33 Mrs Joseph McKiernan of New York City was one of those typists, and O'Malley stayed with the McKiernan family on occasion while in New York. See Cormac O'Malley and Nicholas Allen (eds), *Broken Landscapes: Selected Letters of Ernie O'Malley, 1924–1957* (Dublin: The Lilliput Press, 2011), p. 89.

34 In 2010 and 2012 the working draft notebooks along with several complete typed drafts of O'Malley's memoir were placed in EOM AIA 060. Some of the earlier typed drafts are missing but nevertheless the surviving drafts show significant continuity.

35 The American publisher, Houghton Mifflin, must have thought that the American reader would not understand this subtle Irish saying and changed the title to *Army Without Banners: Adventures of an Irish Volunteer* when it published the American edition in early 1937.

36 Handwritten MS in notebook, Box 1, Folder 23, EOM AIA 060.

37 O'Malley, *On Another Man's Wound*, p. 15.

38 Early draft typed MS for *On Another Man's Wound*, Box 40, Folders 2, EOM AIA 060, 26.

39 Eithne Golden, daughter of Helen Golden, whose car O'Malley drove to Taos, New Mexico, from Pasadena, California in 1929, recalled O'Malley reading sections to her, her siblings and her mother while he lived and travelled with the Golden family in the

1929–32 period. Paul Strand letter to Ted Stevenson, 20 June 1932, in Rebecca Busselle, *Paul Strand Southwest* (New York, NY: Aperture Foundation, 2002), p. 102.

40 George Milburn to Alfred Harcourt, 17 April 1933, Box 4, Folder 43, EOM AIA 060; Box 4, Folder 97, EOM AIA 060.

41 For example, Ella Young wrote O'Malley in March 1932 saying, 'I think that a big book like your book on Ireland takes time. One must stop now and then and do something else to let the work of the book mature in one's mind.' Box 4, Folder 106, EOM AIA 060.

42 O'Malley, *On Another Man's Wound*, pp. 170–7.

43 Alfred Knopf, 10 May 1934, Box 4, Folder 19, EOM AIA 060; *The Forum*, 16 March 1935, Box 4, Folder 22, EOM AIA 060.; *Harper's Magazine*, 21 November 1932, Box 4, Folder 23, EOM AIA 060; Macmillan, 6 October 1933, Box 4, Folder 39, EOM AIA 060; *Atlantic Monthly Press*, 26 March 1935, Box 4, Folder 101, EOM AIA 060; Viking Press, 4 March 1935, Box 4, Folder 107, EOM AIA 060.

44 Alfred Harcourt to General Ernie O'Malley, 14 November 1929, Box 3, Folder 67, EOM AIA 060.

45 Peader O'Donnell told this story to Cormac O'Malley during an interview in Dublin in 1970.

46 Rich & Cowan publishing contract, Box 4, Folder 75, EOM AIA 060.

47 Ernie O'Malley, *On Another Man's Wound* (London: Rich & Cowan, 1936), p. 246. In the 'First Published' edition it was noted as '* * * * / * * * * [Six pages have been deleted by the publishers.]' But these words were deleted in the 'Reprinted October 1936' edition leaving only the asterisks without explanation. For the missing pages, see O'Malley, *On Another Man's Wound*, pp. 312–20.

48 These articles then became the basis for O'Malley's lectures on Radio Éireann in 1953, which in turn became the basis for his *Sunday Press* series which ran from September 1955 to June 1956. They were subsequently published as *Raids and Rallies* by Anvil Press in 1982 and more recently by Mercier Press in 2011.

49 'The Sack of Mallow', *Ireland To-day* 1, no. 4 (September 1936). p. 30. Seamus or James O'Donovan, formerly director of chemicals for the anti-Treaty Republicans, founded this small literary magazine in part with the financial support of O'Malley and others in 1936, but it only lasted two years. Out of friendship O'Malley allowed chapter 14 from his forthcoming *On Another Man's Wound* to be first published there.

50 For more details on the history of the publication, see Cormac K.H. O'Malley, 'The Publication History of *On Another Man's Wound*', *New Hibernia Review* 7, no. 3 (Autumn 2003), pp. 136–9.

51 Letter, Cherry Kearton, Manager, Rich & Cowan, 17 September 1951, Box 4, Folder 75, EOM AIA 060.

52 See *Time* (1 March 1937), pp. 69–70, *New York Herald Tribune Books*, 7 March 1939 in Box 17, Folder 16, EOM AIA 060.

53 See *The New York Times Book Review*, 28 February 1937, Box 17, Folder 16, EOM AIA 060, along with many other clippings of American reviews.

54 Ernie O'Malley, *Army Without Banners* (Boston: Houghton Mifflin, 1937), pp. 288–95.

55 O'Malley's family name was Malley, not O'Malley, the latter being the name he used when he joined the Irish Volunteers in late 1916, probably then as Earnán Ó Máille rather than Ernie O'Malley.

56 O'Malley, *On Another Man's Wound*, p. 12.

The Importance of Being Ernie O'Malley in
Ken Loach's *The Wind that Shakes the Barley*

1 *On Another Man's Wound: Scéal Ernie O'Malley*, DVD, directed by Jerry O'Callaghan (Black Rock Pictures and TG4, 2010).

2 Ibid. See also Ernie O'Malley, *On Another Man's Wound: A Personal History of Ireland's War of Independence* (Cork: Mercier Press, 2013), p. 11.

3 This is, however, precisely what the narrator claims in *On Another Man's Wound: Scéal Ernie O'Malley*. Roy Foster, on the other hand, writes that O'Malley was Damien's 'proto-type'. See Foster, Roy. 'The Red and the Green', *The Dublin Review* 24 (Autumn 2006), accessed 25 April 2014, http://thedublinreview.com/article/the-red-and-the-green/.

4 For an overview of O'Malley's interests in art, see Mary Cosgrove, 'Ernie O'Malley: Art and Modernism in Ireland', *Éire–Ireland* 40, nos 3–4 (2005), pp. 85–103.

5 See David Archibald, 'Correcting Historical Lies: An Interview with Ken Loach and Paul Laverty', *Cineaste* (Spring 2007), p. 27.

6 Paul Laverty, *The Wind that Shakes the Barley* (Ardfield: Galley Head Press, 2006), p. 1. Loach wanted to represent West Cork in the early 1920s as authentically as possible, but did not want to assume the additional responsibility for getting biographical details right for specific people. This would help him avoid the kind of controversy Neil Jordan inspired with his melodramatic reconstruction of the protagonist's love triangle with Kitty Kiernan and Harry Boland, or his historically inaccurate recreations of events in his 1996 biopic, *Michael Collins*.

7 Laverty, *The Wind that Shakes the Barley*, p. 13.

8 In an earlier version of the screenplay, Sinéad's role in the plot was more substantial. See Jill Nelmes, 'Rewriting Paul Laverty's Screenplay – *The Wind that Shakes the Barley* (2006)', *Journal of Screenwriting* 2, 2 (2011), pp. 263–74. According to Nelmes, these and other changes deleted much of the film's 'historical and factual exposition', and 'some fascinating points about the women's movement in Ireland during the war … In D1 the women were presented as a central force in the film; losing Sinéad in the early part of the story in D2, makes the script male-centred, and the focus on the war becomes a mostly masculine battle with much less input from women' (273).

9 Like James Connolly himself, Damien and Dan are motivated by Socialism at least as much as by Nationalism. In this regard, Damien is closer to the contemporary Republican socialist leader Peadar O'Donnell than to O'Malley. For more on this topic, see Donal

Ó Drisceoil, *Peadar O'Donnell* (Cork: Cork University Press, 2001). Also see the essay by O'Malley biographer Richard English, 'Socialism: Socialist Intellectuals and the Irish Revolution' in Joost Augusteijn (ed.), *The Irish Revolution 1913–1923* (New York: Palgrave, 2002), pp. 203–23.

10 Laverty, *The Wind that Shakes the Barley*, p. 14.

11 Archibald, 'Correcting Historical Lies', p. 27.

12 Dalton went on to found Ardmore Studios at Bray in 1957, where he produced many films. One of the first films to come out of Ardmore was *Shake Hands with the Devil*, discussed later in this essay. See Sean Boyne, *Emmet Dalton: Somme Soldier, Irish General, Film Pioneer* (Dublin: Merrion Press, 2015).

13 For a detailed critique of this argument and overview of the debate following it, see Niall Meehan, 'Examining Peter Hart', *The Field Day Review* 10 (2014), pp. 103–47.

14 Archibald, 'Correcting Historical Lies', p. 28.

15 Ibid., p. 29. When pressed by the interviewer, both Loach and Laverty acknowledged that they were adopting a Republican perspective in the film and were not concerned with how the Black and Tans perceived the situation. Laverty said he would like to do a film about a Tan, but this perspective just would not have fit into the current film.

16 Foster thought that *The Wind that Shakes the Barley* snuck its ideology past the gates of reason through a seductively stylish production, while Howe thought the bad ideology sold itself well enough that it would carry an otherwise lacklustre film at the box office. See Stephen Howe. '*The Wind that Shakes the Barley* and Irish History', *openDemocracy* (16 June 2006), accessed 25 April 2014, http://www.opendemocracy.net/arts–Film/loach_3650.jsp.

17 Tom Barry, *Guerilla Days in Ireland: A Personal Account of the Anglo-Irish War* (Boulder, CO: Roberts Rinehart Publishers, 1995), p. 112.

18 Peter Hart, *The IRA and Its Enemies: Violence and Community in Cork, 1916–1923* (Oxford: Oxford University Press, 1998), p. 314.

19 Peter Hart, *The IRA at War 1916–1923* (Oxford: Oxford University Press, 2003), p. 237.

20 Barry, *Guerilla Days in Ireland*, pp. 112–13.

21 He intended the film to be understood as a historically minded protest against the current British government's participation in the US-led occupation of Afghanistan and Iraq.

22 Loach clearly disagreed with most of the opinions voiced by Sir John in the film, but in the DVD's commentary track he acknowledged that the character (like many of his class) regarded themselves as no less Irish than the nationalists themselves.

23 Barry complained that the British press never acknowledged that the IRA were executing Catholics as well as Protestants. See Barry, *Guerilla Days in Ireland*, p. 113.

24 Laverty, *The Wind that Shakes the Barley*, p. 22.

25 O'Malley, *On Another Man's Wound*, p. 44.

26 My thanks to Professor Joe Lee for suggesting the comparison with *The Wind that Shakes the Barley*.

27 See Ernie O'Malley, *The Singing Flame* (Cork: Mercier Press, 2012), pp. 137–8. See Denis Flannery, 'Ernie O'Malley, William Shakespeare's Sonnets, and the Book as Closet Object',

Irish University Review: A Journal of Irish Studies 43, 1 (2013), pp. 102–18. Flannery notes that 'O'Malley emphasizes the thing-status of nearly everything he reads', Flannery, 'Ernie O'Malley', p. 103.

28 See O'Malley, *The Singing Flame*, pp. 156–7.

29 See William Shakespeare, in Colin Burrow (ed.), *The Complete Sonnets and Poems* (Oxford: Oxford University Press, 2002), p. 561.

30 See Flannery, 'Ernie O'Malley', p. 107.

31 William Blake, *Songs of Innocence and Experience. Vol. 2. The Illuminated Books of William Blake* (Princeton, NJ: Princeton University Press, 1991), p. 191.

32 In 1935, Irish playwright Denis Johnston directed Abbey players Cyril Cusack and Barry Fitzgerald in a 49-minute *Guests of the Nation* film (not immediately released commercially). The Irish Film Institute restored it in 2011.

33 Eleftheria Rania Kosmidou, *European Civil War Films: Memory, Conflict, and Nostalgia* (New York, NY: Routledge, 2013), pp. 66–91.

34 For more on this debate, see D. George Boyce and Alan O'Day (eds), *The Making of Irish History: Revisionism and the Revisionist Controversy* (New York: Routledge, 1996) and Ciaran Brady (ed.), *Interpreting Irish History: The Debate on Historical Revisionism 1938–1994* (Dublin: Irish Academic Press, 1999).

35 Kosmidou, *European Civil War Films*, p. 78.

36 See James Chandler, 'Cinema, History, and the Politics of Style: Michael Collins and *The Wind that Shakes the Barley*', *Field Day Review* 7 (2011), pp. 103–21.

37 See Chandler, 'Cinema, History, and the Politics of Style', for an illuminating comparison between the torture scene in *The Wind that Shakes the Barley*, and the conclusion to Roberto Rossellini's *Rome, Open City* (1945).

38 Michael Collins, *The Path to Freedom* (Boulder, CO: Roberts Rinehart Publishers, 2000), p. 14.

39 Collins, *The Path to Freedom*, p. 17.

40 Ibid., pp. 22–3.

41 Frank O'Connor, *Collected Stories* (New York, NY: Vintage, 1982), p. 12.

42 The plot of *Shake Hands* draws upon O'Connor's 'Guests', because the protagonist falls in love with his hostage, Jennifer Curtis (played by Dana Wynter). The film ends more like *The Crying Game* than 'Guests of the Nation'; however, the humane protagonist kills the cold-hearted Republican villain and saves the hostage/love interest.

43 See Frank O'Connor, *The Lonely Voice* (New York, NY: Harper & Row, 1963), p. 16.

44 See Frank O'Connor, *The Big Fellow: Michael Collins and the Irish Revolution* (New York, NY: Picador, 1998), p. 9.

45 O'Connor, *The Big Fellow*, p. 10.

46 Ibid., p. 213.

47 Frank O'Connor, *An Only Child* (London: Pan Books, 1972), p. 162.

48 Ibid., pp. 190–1.

49 Ibid., p. 192.

50 Ibid., pp. 92–3.

51 Ibid., p. 201.

52 O'Connor, *The Lonely Voice*, p. 19.

53 Laverty, *The Wind that Shakes the Barley*, p. 22.

54 See Foster, 'The Red and the Green'.

55 O'Malley, *On Another Man's Wound*, p. 426.

56 Ibid., p. 428.

57 Ibid., p. 431.

58 Barry, *Guerilla Days in Ireland*, p. 112.

59 See Howe, '*The Wind that Shakes the Barley* and Irish History'.

60 These are the lines as delivered in the film rather than as they appear in the published screenplay.

61 Here Laverty's script implies that, had he survived, Damien would have been disappointed at what became of James Connolly's vision. Loach even affords some validity to Sir John's prediction that Ireland will be a 'priest-infested backwater' after the Republican victory, and he explores this idea further in *Jimmy's Hall* (2014), a biopic about James Gralton, the Irish communist leader who had been an IRA volunteer during the War of Independence but afterwards found himself on the wrong side of the Catholic hierarchy and got himself deported as an alien in 1933.

62 O'Malley, *On Another Man's Wound*, p. 428. This was not an overstatement; O'Malley only avoided execution by the British because he successfully concealed his identity. Later, he only narrowly avoided execution in a Free State prison by accident of the fact that he had been grievously wounded during capture in Dublin.

63 I included here the lines as delivered in the film rather than as they appear in Laverty's screenplay, published in 2006.

64 O'Malley, *On Another Man's Wound*, p. 428.

65 Archibald, 'Correcting Historical Lies', p. 29.

On Republican Reading: Ernie O'Malley, Irish Intellectual

1 Ranajit Guha, 'The Prose of Counter–Insurgency' in Ranajit Guha and Gayatri Chakravorty Spivak (eds), *Selected Subaltern Studies* (Oxford: Oxford University Press, 1988), pp. 45–86.

2 Richard English, *Ernie O'Malley: IRA Intellectual* (Oxford: Clarendon Press, 1988).

3 J.J. Lee, Introduction to Cormac O'Malley and Anne Dolan (eds), *'No Surrender Here!' The Civil War Papers of Ernie O'Malley, 1922–1924* (Dublin: The Lilliput Press, 2007), p. xliii.

4 English, *Ernie O'Malley*, pp. 202–3.

5 Lee, Introduction to *'No Surrender Here!'*, pp. xliii–xliv.

6 Tom Barry, *Guerilla Days in Ireland* (Tralee: Anvil Books, 1971), pp. 25.

7 It should be recalled that O'Malley's older brother Frank, to whom he remained close, had joined the British Army.

8 Frantz Fanon, 'On National Culture', *The Wretched of the Earth*, trans. Constance Far-rington (New York: Grove Press, 1968), 223–24.

9 Ernie O'Malley, *On Another Man's Wound* (Cork: Mercier, 2013), pp. 161–2.

10 Richard Kearney, 'Myth and Terror', *The Crane Bag* 2, nos 1–2 (1977), pp. 125–39.

11 Lee, Introduction to *'No Surrender Here!'*, pp. lii, xlvi.

12 O'Malley and Dolan, *'No Surrender Here!'* (Dublin: The Lilliput Press, 2007), p. l.

13 Lee, Introduction to *'No Surrender Here!'*, p. li.

14 Ibid., p. xlix.

15 O'Malley and Dolan, *'No Surrender Here!'*, p. 422.

16 Ibid., p. 423.

17 Ibid., pp. 381, 435, 413, 613, 285.

18 Ibid., p. 423.

19 Letter No. 41, 11 March 1930, Cormac O'Malley and Nicholas Allen (eds), *Broken Land-scapes: Selected Letters of Ernie O'Malley, 1924–1957* (Dublin: The Lilliput Press, 2011), p. 69.

20 Lee, Introduction to *'No Surrender Here!'*, p. xlix; O'Malley and Dolan, *'No Surrender Here!'*, p. l.

21 Ibid., p. l.

22 Ibid., p. l.

23 Ibid., p. 333.

24 Ibid., p. 339.

25 Ibid., p. 339.

26 Lee, Introduction to *'No Surrender Here!'*, p. xlvi.

27 Ernie O'Malley, *The Singing Flame* (Dublin: Anvil Books, 1992), p. 160.

28 Lee, Introduction to *'No Surrender Here!'*, p. xlvi.

29 Ibid., p. xlvii.

30 Bipan Chandra, 'Colonialism, Stages of Colonialism and the Colonial State', *Journal of Contemporary Asia* 10.3 (1980), pp. 272–85; and Benedict Anderson, *Imagined Communities: Reflections on the Origin and Spread of Nationalism* (London: Verso, 2006).

31 Fanon, 'On National Culture', p. 227.

32 O'Malley and Dolan, *'No Surrender Here!'*, p. 432; J.J. Lee, Introduction to *'No Surrender Here!'*, p. xlvii.

33 O'Malley and Dolan, *'No Surrender Here!'*, p. 355.

34 Ibid., p. 473.

35 J.J. Lee, Introduction to *'No Surrender Here!'*, p. xliii.

36 O'Malley, *On Another Man's Wound*, p. 129.

37 See in particular Reynaldo C. Ileto, *Pasyon and Revolution: Popular Movements in the Philippines* (Manila: Ateneo de Manila Press, 1979).

38 See Partha Chatterjee, 'The Nationalist Resolution of the Woman Question' in Kumkum Sangari and Sudesh Vaid (eds), *Recasting Women: Essays in Colonial History* (New Delhi: Kali for Women, 1989), pp. 232–53. One might also invoke, among many others, Shahid Amin's brilliant work on the popular memory of one peculiarly violent moment in Indian

nationalism and its connection to religious understandings of Gandhi, *Event, Metaphor, Memory: Chauri Chaura, 1922–1992* (Berkeley: University of California Press, 1995). Irish historiography has proven sadly limited in this respect by the mythic paradigm circulated by Kearney and others.

39 English, *Ernie O'Malley*, p. 194.

40 For a helpful introduction to Carl Schmitt and Walter Benjamin's reflections on the state, violence and sovereignty, contemporaneous with the Irish war of decolonization, see Giorgio Agamben, *State of Exception* (Chicago: Chicago University Press, 2005), pp. 52–64.

41 Walter Benjamin, 'Critique of Violence', trans. Harry Zohn, in Marcus Bullock and Michael W. Jennings (eds), *Selected Writings: Volume 1: 1913–1926* (Cambridge, MA: Belknap Press, 2003), pp. 239–40.

42 Lee, Introduction to *'No Surrender Here!'*, p. xi.

43 Ibid., p. xi.

44 Ibid., p. xv.

45 Ibid., p. xxii.

46 English, *Ernie O'Malley*, p. 202.

47 Lee, Introduction to *'No Surrender Here!'*, p. xxiii.

48 Ibid., p. xxxi.

49 Ibid., p. xxiv.

50 Ibid., p. xxvi.

51 Carl Schmitt, *Political Theology: Four Chapters on the Concept of Sovereignty*, trans. George Schwab (Chicago, IL: University of Chicago Press, 1985), p. 5.

52 Benjamin, 'Critique of Violence', p. 248.

53 Ibid., p. 242. On O'Higgins's position on this, see John P. McCarthy, *Kevin O'Higgins: Builder of the Irish State* (Dublin: Irish Academic Press, 2006), p. 94.

54 See on this concept of Republicanism, Philip Pettit, *Republicanism: A Theory of Freedom and Government* (Oxford: Oxford University Press, 1997).

55 Thomas MacGreevy, *Jack B. Yeats: An Appreciation and an Interpretation* (Dublin: Victor Waddington Publications, 1945), pp. 25–6, 37–8. Though later critics and biographers, such as Hilary Pyle and Bruce Arnold, tend to sidestep Jack B. Yeats's political affiliations, Thomas MacGreevy, his friend and author of the first lengthy study of his work, discusses a number of political paintings all sympathetic to Republican ideals, which includes this painting, and does so in an explicitly political context.

56 Nicholas Allen, *Modernism, Ireland and Civil War* (Cambridge: Cambridge University Press, 2009).

57 Samuel Beckett, 'MacGreevy on Yeats' in Ruby Cohn (ed.), *Disjecta: Miscellaneous Writings and a Dramatic Fragment* (New York, NY: Grove Press, 1984), pp. 95–7.

58 O'Malley, *On Another Man's Wound*, p. 404.

59 See, for example, Letter to Paul Strand about New York, 6 October 1932, Letter No. 56, O'Malley and Allen, *Broken Landscapes*, p. 92: 'Street corner meetings every night, men talking in clichés. It's stupid, a shirted crowd mostly, waiting eagerly for a few honest, direct

words; instead they get isms. It's brutal and selfish. Why the hell aren't some men trained to talk now, speak out of their hearts?' Elsewhere he laments the lack of 'sturdy independence' among the transients he had been living with: see Letter to Paul Strand from New York City, 12 July 1934, O'Malley and Allen, Letter No. 64, *Broken Landscapes*, p. 103.

60 Letter to Sighle Humphreys, 25 December 1923, O'Malley and Dolan, *'No Surrender Here!'*, pp. 473–4. Bracketed interpolations by the editors. In another letter to Sighle Humphreys, he remarks no less firmly, though less elaborately, that 'The spiritualistic interpretation of nationality is the only thing that matters and that no one save the '16 group ever seriously considered.' Letter to Sighle Humphreys, 5 January 1928, Letter No. 26, O'Malley and Allen, *Broken Landscapes*, p. 42.

61 O'Malley, *The Singing Flame*, p. 286.

62 Ibid., p. 286.

63 Ibid., p. 286.

64 Ibid., p. 286–7.

65 See Sri Aurobindo Ghose, *On Nationalism: First Series* (Pondicherry: Sri Aurobindo, 1965) and W.E.B. Dubois, *The Souls of Black Folk* (Harmondsworth: Penguin Books, 1989), pp. 5–6.

66 On the German tradition of ethnolinguistics and cultural relativity that stemmed from it, see John H. Zammito, *Kant, Herder and the Birth of Anthropology* (Chicago, IL: University of Chicago Press, 2002) and R.L. Brown, *Wilhelm von Humboldt's Conception of Linguistic Relativity* (The Hague: Mouton, 1967).

67 O'Malley and Dolan, *'No Surrender Here!'*, p. 452.

68 Declan Kiberd, *Irish Classics* (Cambridge, MA: Harvard University Press, 2001), p. 632.

69 Letter to Jean McGrail, 20 February 1955, Letter No. 251, O'Malley and Allen, *Broken Landscapes*, p. 327. O'Malley laments to his American friend Jean McGrail about the lack of intellectual support and research funding available to Irish students wishing to research Irish literature.

70 Letter to Jean McGrail, 16–17 March 1955, Letter No. 252, O'Malley and Allen, *Broken Landscapes*, p. 330. Despite having numerous English friends, O'Malley seems to maintain a sardonically amused relation to English culture as he witnessed it, joking about the ignorance of Tories as to their country's relation to Ireland, or commenting ironically on the English feeding pigeons in Trafalgar Square while ignoring the treasures of their National Gallery.

71 O'Malley, *On Another Man's Wound*, p. 171.

72 O'Malley, *The Singing Flame*, p. 289. It is perhaps worth recalling how O'Malley's interest in *Moby Dick* anticipates scholarly interest in the text, given that Carl Van Doren's work on Melville appeared only in 1917, his *The American Novel* not till 1921, while D.H. Lawrence's *Studies in Classic American Literature* only in the early 1920s. F.O. Matthiessen's *American Renaissance* was not to appear till 1941. O'Malley was not alone in finding in *Moby Dick* resources for an alternative political culture or of a radical interpretation of modernity. C.L.R. James's *Mariners, Renegades, and Castaways: The Story of Herman Melville and the*

World We Live In (1953) and Charles Olson's *Call Me Ishmael* (1947) are both very different counter-cultural or 'antithetical' appropriations of Melville.

73 O'Malley, *The Singing Flame*, p. 289.

74 Ibid., p. 105.

75 Kiberd, *Irish Classics*, p. 631.

76 O'Malley, *On Another Man's Wound*, p. 404; On Connolly's sense of Irish history and the specific characteristics of its culture, see David Lloyd, 'Rethinking National Marxism: James Connolly and "Celtic Communism"' in *Irish Times: Temporalities of Modernity* (Dublin: Field Day, 2008), pp. 101–26.

77 Ernie O'Malley, 'Introductory Article', *Architectural Digest* (July 1947) in O'Malley and Allen, *Broken Landscapes*, p. 420. O'Malley's insistence on Ireland's lack of centralization seems to be a fundamental Republican observation, one he shares, for example, with Countess Markievicz. See David Lloyd, 'Nationalism against the State' in *Ireland after History* (Cork: Cork University Press, 1999), pp. 28–9.

78 Letter to Sighle Humphreys from Mexico City, 13 March 1931, Letter No. 49, O'Malley and Allen, *Broken Landscapes*, p. 55.

79 Letter to Eithne Golden from New York, 28 March 1935, Letter No. 70, O'Malley and Allen, *Broken Landscapes*, p. 110.

80 Ernie O'Malley, 'The Background of the Arts in Mexico', *The Bell* 14, no. 5 (August 1947), in O'Malley and Allen, *Broken Landscapes*, pp. 424–30.

81 O'Malley, 'The Background of the Arts in Mexico' in O'Malley and Allen, *Broken Landscapes*, p. 429.

82 Ibid.

83 Ibid., p. 430.

84 O'Malley and Allen, *Broken Landscapes*, p. 390.

85 Ibid.

86 Book review of Francoise Henry, *Irish Art in the Early Christian Period*, in *The Bell* 1, no. 1 (October 1940), in O'Malley and Allen, *Broken Landscapes*, pp. 390–1.

87 Walter Benjamin, 'On the Concept of History', trans. Edmund Jephcott, Howard Eiland and Michael W. Jennings (eds), in *Selected Writings: Volume 4: 1938–1940* (Cambridge, MA: Belknap Press, 2003), pp. 394–5.

88 Ernie O'Malley, Script for BBC Third Programme on 'The Traditions of Mexican Paintings', January 1947, in O'Malley and Allen, *Broken Landscapes*, p. 414.

89 Ibid., pp. 413, 412. See also Letter to Merriam Golden, January 1931, Letter No. 46, O'Malley and Allen, *Broken Landscapes*, pp. 79–81 for comparison of Rivera and Orozco.

90 Ernie O'Malley, Introduction to the catalogue for the Jack B. Yeats National Loan Exhibition, National College of Art, Dublin, 1945, in O'Malley and Allen, *Broken Landscapes*, pp. 391–5.

91 Ernie O'Malley, 'Louis Le Brocquy', *Horizon* 14 no. 79 (July 1946), in O'Malley and Allen, *Broken Landscapes*, pp. 398–9.

92 O'Malley, 'Louis Le Brocquy' in O'Malley and Allen, *Broken Landscapes*, p. 399. His

discussion of le Brocquy's 'Condemned Man', a beautiful cubist-inspired canvas, is both precise and evocative, and understands it as of 'particular interest in a country where gaol was a natural place in which to meet friends or to say goodbye'.

93 Ibid., p. 400.

94 Samuel Beckett, 'The Capital of the Ruins', radio script, 10 June 1946, in *As the Story Was Told: Uncollected and Late Prose* (London: Calder, 1990), pp. 27–8.

95 See Hannah Arendt's discussion of '"The Nation of Minorities" and the Stateless People' in *The Origins of Totalitarianism* (New York, NY: Harcourt Brace, 1976), pp. 269–90 and Giorgio Agamben, 'Beyond Human Rights' in *Means Without Ends: Notes on Politics*, trans. Vincenzo Binetti and Cesare Casarino (Minneapolis, MN: Minnesota University Press, 2000), pp. 15–26.

96 See in particular, Pettit, 'Non-Domination as a Political Ideal', pp. 80–109.

97 It is possible to read the numerous references throughout O'Malley's letters in *Broken Landscapes* to the purchase of tweed for suits, the furnishings of the house at Burrishoole, Co Mayo, the purchase of turf and other local produce, a practical inhabitation of nationalist ideals of self-sufficiency and reliance on local resources, ones which perhaps have regained their force for us in recent decades.

Kindling the Singing Flame: The Destruction of the Public Record Office (30 June 1922), as a Historical Problem

1 An earlier draft of this chapter was given as the plenary lecture at the Old Athlone Society's conference on the Irish Civil War (1922–3), held at Costume Barracks, Athlone, on 23 November 2013. I am grateful to Dr John Keane for extending the invitation to me on behalf of the Old Athlone Society to give the lecture. The Carnegie Trust for Scottish Universities and School of Humanities at the University of Dundee helped fund the research on which the original lecture and this article is based.

2 For a cultural history of the meanings and function given to the destruction of libraries, archives and the printed word in the twentieth century, see Matthew Fishburn, *Burning Books* (Basingstoke: Palgrave Macmillan, 2008).

3 Herbert Woods, 'The Destruction of the Public Records: The Loss to Irish History', *An Irish Quarterly Review* 11, no. 43 (September 1922), pp. 363–78; Herbert Woods, 'The Public Record Office of Ireland Before and After 1922', *Transactions of the Royal Historical Society* 4, no. 13 (1930), pp. 17–49.

4 For a fuller discussion, see John M. Regan 'Irish Public Histories as an Historiographical Problem', *Irish Historical Studies* 37, no. 146 (Nov. 2010), pp. 265–92.

5 Michael Hopkinson, *Green Against Green* (Dublin: Gill & Macmillan, 1988), pp. 115–22.

6 John M. Regan, *The Irish Counter-Revolution 1921–1936: Treatyite Politics and Settlement in Independent Ireland* (Dublin: Gill & Macmillan, 1999), pp. 71–4.

7 Hopkinson, *Green Against Green*, pp. 115–16.

8 Ibid., p. 117.

9 See Donal O'Sullivan, *The Irish Free State and its Senate* (London: Faber and Faber, 1940), p. 63; Dorothy Macardle, *The Irish Republic* (Dublin: Irish Press Ltd, 1951), p. 751; J.C. Beckett, *The Making of Modern Ireland 1603–1923* (London: Faber and Faber, 1966), p. 458; F.S.L. Lyons, *Ireland Since the Famine* (London: Weidenfeld & Nicolson, 1971), p. 459.

10 Ernie O'Malley, *The Singing Flame* (Dublin: Anvil Books, 1978), 115.

11 The original photograph was taken by Dublin-based freelance photographer, Joseph Cashman.

12 Four Courts Garrison – Invitations to Functions, PRES/2005/160/66, National Archives of Ireland [hereafter NAI].

13 See Joseph M. Curran, *The Birth of the Irish Free State 1921–23* (Alabama, AL: Alabama University Press, 1980); Tom Garvin, *1922: The Birth of Irish Democracy* (Dublin: Gill & Macmillan, 1996); David Fitzpatrick, *The Two Irelands 1912–39* (Oxford: Oxford University Press, 1997).

14 John M. Regan, 'Southern Irish Nationalism as a Historiographical Problem', *Historical Journal* 50 (2007), pp. 197–223; John M. Regan, 'Michael Collins, General Commanding-in-Chief, as a Historiographical Problem', *History* 92, no. 307 (July 2007), 318–46; John M. Regan, 'Irish Public Histories'; John M. Regan, 'The 'Bandon Valley Massacre' as a Historical Problem', *History* 72, no. 325 (January 2012), pp. 70–98; John M. Regan, 'The History of the Last Atrocity', *Dublin Review of Books* no. 22 (Summer 2012). These articles and other review essays are republished in John M. Regan, *Myth and the Irish State: Historical Problems and Other Essays* (Dublin: Irish Academic Press, 2013).

15 On sectarianism, see Peter Hart, 'The Protestant Experience of Revolution in Southern Ireland' and 'Ethnic conflict and minority responses' in Peter Hart, *The IRA at War* (Oxford: Oxford University Press, 2003), pp. 223–40, 241–58. Garvin lists 'rape' among the activities engaged in by the anti-Treatyite IRA during the Civil War, but this claim is unburdened by any reference to a source. On the persecution of minorities, see Fitzpatrick, *The Two Irelands*, p. 95. In a discussion of Republican violence Fitzpatrick writes: 'Adulterers, homosexuals, tinkers, beggars, ex-servicemen, Protestants … [were] potentially lethal labels for Ireland's inhabitants in the revolutionary period'; again this statement is made without reference to any sources. Sexual violence and the persecution of minorities was indisputably part of the revolutionary experience, but it is unlikely any such activities were confined to one group or, indeed, left no evidential footprint.

16 Niall Meehan, 'Examining Peter Hart', *Field Day Review* 10 (2014), pp. 103–47.

17 Diarmaid Ferriter, 'Picking a Fight Over the Rights and Wrongs of Our History," *Irish Times* (Dublin, Ireland), 5 April 2014.

18 Regan, *Myth and the Irish State*, pp. 4, 31.

19 Bernard Lewis, *History: Remembered, Recovered, Invented* (Princeton, NJ: Princeton University Press, 1977). The book consists of Lewis' Gottesman lectures, originally delivered at Yeshiva University, New York, in 1974.

20 Ibid., p. 56.

21 George Orwell, *Nineteen Eighty-Four* (Harmonsworth: Penguin, 2013), p. 40.

22 Lewis, *History: Remembered, Recovered, Invented*, p. 69.

23 Ronan Fanning, '"The Great Enchantment": Uses and Abuses of Modern Irish History' in J. Dooge (ed.), *Ireland and the Contemporary World* (Dublin: Gill & Macmillan, 1988), pp. 131–47.

24 See John M. Regan, 'West Cork and the Writing of Irish History', *Dublin Review of Books* (February 2013).

25 For a lengthy but engaging exposition of this technique, see Richard J. Evans, *Telling Lies for Hitler: The Holocaust, History, and the David Irving Trial* (London: Verso 2002).

26 The use of vitriolic personal attacks is an old tactic deployed by vested interests against academic scientists in recent years in the debate over global warming. See Naomi Oreskes and Erik M. Conway, *Merchants of Doubt: How a Handful of Scientists Obscured the Truth on Issues from Tobacco Smoke to Global Warming* (London: Bloomsbury Press, 2010), pp. 216–17. See Eoghan Harris, 'Following IRA's bloody track from the Bandon Valley to South Armagh', *Sunday Independent* (Dublin, Ireland), 26 June 2011; David Fitzpatrick, 'Dr Regan and Mr Snide', *History Ireland* 20, no. 3 (May–June, 2012), pp. 12–13; David Fitzpatrick, 'Ethnic Cleansing, Ethical Smearing, and Irish Historians', *History* 98, no. 329 (Jan. 2012), pp. 135–44.

27 For the experiences of dissenting Israeli 'new historians', see Ilan Pappe, *Out of the Frame: The Struggle for Academic Freedom in Israel* (London: Pluto Press 2010).

28 Ronan Keane, 'A Mass of Crumbling Ruins: The Destruction of the Four Courts in June 1922' in Caroline Costello (ed.), *The Four Courts: 200 Years* (Dublin: Incorporated Council of Law Reporting 1996), p. 167.

29 Garvin, *1922: The Birth of Irish Democracy*, p. 130.

30 Ibid.

31 Ibid. Garvin cites P17b/85, Ernie O'Malley notebooks [hereafter EOM nbks], Ernie O'Malley Papers [hereafter EOM], University College Dublin Archives [hereafter UCDA], and P4/283–84, Hugh Kennedy Papers, UCDA.

32 Garvin, *1922: The Birth of Irish Democracy*, p. 130, citing P17b/85, EOM nbks, EOM, UCDA.

33 P4/283–84, Hugh Kennedy Papers, UCDA.

34 'Destruction of the Four Courts' in P4/284, ff. 210, Hugh Kennedy Papers, UCDA.

35 Fitzpatrick, *The Two Irelands*, p. 170.

36 Regan, *Myth and the Irish State*, pp. 16–17.

37 Michael Laffan, *The Resurrection of Ireland* (Cambridge, MA: Cambridge University Press, 1999), p. 413.

38 O'Malley, *The Singing Flame*, p. 78.

39 Ibid., p. 105.

40 Diarmuid O'Connor and Frank Connolly, *Sleep Soldier Sleep: The Life and Times of Padraig O'Connor* (Dublin: Miseab Publications, 2011), p. 98.

41 O'Connor and Connolly, *Sleep Soldier Sleep*, p. 98. Padraig O'Connor was one of the Free State officers leading the assault on the Public Record Office and oversaw the removal of explosives and incendiaries stored in the building on the night of 29–30 June.

42 Ibid., pp. 98–9.

43 Chief-of-Staff (Richard Mulcahy) to the Dáil Minister of Defence (Michael Collins), 1.30 pm, 5.15pm, 30 June 1922, P7/B/60, Richard Mulcahy Papers, UCDA.

44 O'Malley, *The Singing Flame*, p. 106.

45 See Volunteer Brogan interview, P17b/98, EOM nbks, EOM, UCDA.

46 Simon Donnelly, 'A Brief Account of Attack on the Four Courts Dublin', unpublished handwritten manuscript (June 1923), MS 33,063, National Library of Ireland.

47 O'Connor and Connolly, *Sleep Soldier Sleep*, p. 99.

48 Ibid.

49 Cabinet Minutes Conclusions 4 July 1922, CAB/23/30, United Kingdom National Archives at Kew.

50 O'Connor and Connolly, *Sleep Soldier Sleep*, p. 108.

51 Ibid.

52 See Tim Pat Coogan and George Morrison, *The Irish Civil War* (London: Weildenfeld & Nicolson, 1999), images pp. 226–9.

53 Thomas Johnson to the Secretary of Dáil Éireann, 4 July 1922, D/T S 1581, NAI.

54 Colm Ó Murchadha to Thomas Johnson, 4 July 1922, D/T S 1581, NAI.

55 'The Four Courts 1922', AGO/2002/16/475, NAI.

56 Liz Gillis, *The Fall of Dublin: 28 June to 5 July 1922* (Cork: Mercier Press, 2011), p. 127.

57 Ibid., p. 126.

58 Dermot Keogh, *Twentieth Century Ireland: Nation and State* (Dublin: Gill & Macmillan, 1994), p. 5.

59 Fishburn, *Burning Books*, p. xii.

60 The untranslated wording is: 'Dort, wo man Bücher verbrennt, verbrennt man am Ende auch Menschen'. Heinrich Heine, *Almansor* (Altenmunster: 2012), p. 3.

61 The argument can be traced to the increasingly polemical writings of Conor Cruise O'Brien in the 1970s and 1980s. Conor Cruise O'Brien, 'An Unhealthy Intersection', *New Review* 2, no. 16 (1975), p. 5. For the influence of the fascist interpretation of Republicanism and separatist Republicans in some academic writing, see Regan, *Myth and the Irish State*, pp. 94–112.

62 Conor Cruise O'Brien, 'Blueshirts and Quislings', *Magill* (14 June 1981), p. 25.

63 South Wind Blows Productions received a grant of 350,000 under the Broadcasting Authorities of Ireland's (BAI) Sound and Vision Scheme for the series. BAI to author, 3 February 2015. The three programmes aired on RTÉ 1 television on 1, 8 and 15 June 2010, under the auspices of RTÉ 'Factual'.

64 Programme one of the series, including sections quoted above, can be viewed on YouTube beginning at https://www.youtube.com/watch?v=sV53QsL–oqk.

65 Hopkinson, *Green Against Green*, p. 121.

66 See Elizabeth Yeates to 'Mrs Dickie', 12 July 1922, MS 24,584, National Library of Ireland.

67 A similar fusing of expository history with memories of stories about 1922, is represented in the RTÉ television documentary, *An Tost Fada*, broadcast on 16 April 2012. The documentary alleged experiences of sectarianism in 1922, of a West Cork Church of Ireland

family, the Salters, partly through the testimony of the Reverend Canon George Salter. Identifying factual errors in the programme in a complaint to RTÉ, Tom Cooper contended that there was bias toward a sectarian interpretation of contested events surrounding the so-called, 'Bandon Valley Massacre', of late April 1922. RTÉ conceded factual mistakes were transmitted, and undertook to correct these should the programme be broadcast in the future. RTÉ's response did not address Cooper's assertion that the narration in the programme falsely claimed that a 'sense of fear and series of threats' forced nine members of the Salter family to leave Ireland, and that only one returned. Cooper appealed RTÉ's response to the Compliance Committee of the BAI. Cooper contended the programme was an infringement of current affairs broadcasting, notably in standards relating to 'fairness, objectivity, and impartiality'. On this point the BAI found: 'While the programme focused on a matter of debate and controversy amongst historians ... it did not ... constitute news and current affairs as it was not a matter of current public debate or controversy.' In the *Sunday Independent* on 26 June 2011, Eoghan Harris wrote: 'last Wednesday, neither Morning Ireland, Pat Kenny nor the News at One made a single mention of the report of the [PSNI's] Historical Enquiries team on the Kingsmill Massacre [1976]. This is no time for tribal reporting. By reminding us that sectarianism is not confined to one tradition, RTÉ would have removed some propaganda ammunition from the arsenal of the Recurring IRA.' Harris continued: 'Just as IRA apologists, supported by some academics, created a moral fog around the Bandon Valley murders to protect the myth of a non-sectarian old IRA as a necessary force for Irish self-government, so the same forces conspire to protect the myth of the Provisional IRA as a reaction to sectarian Loyalism and as a necessary prelude to the peace process.' Harris, the narrator and scriptwriter of *An Tost Fada*, does not claim to write as a historian. The *Irish Times* reported 500 people attended public lectures given by the present author and Dr Andy Bielenberg (UCC), in the Imperial Hotel, Cork, on 28 April 2012. Tom Cooper to RTÉ 14 May 2012; Kevin Cummins (RTÉ) to Tom Cooper, 18 June 2012; Chris Morash (BAI) to Tom Cooper 5 October 2012. *Irish Times*, 30 April 2012. *An Tost Fada* claimed to be a response to another RTÉ documentary, *CSÍ: Cork's Bloody Secret*, broadcast 5 October 2009. On that documentary, see Harris's *Sunday Independent* column, 4 October 2009, alongside hundreds of pages of comment on discussion boards on Politics.ie and other websites such as The Cedar Lounge Revolution. I am grateful to the BAI and Tom Cooper for information.

68 For a more balanced interpretation of the destruction of the Public Record Office drawing on much of the primary evidence cited in this article, see *An Léigear*, directed by Andrew Gallimore (1922; Fastnet Films), first broadcast on TG4, 23 October 2013.

69 'Irish Historical Studies school' refers to the historians associated with the journal *Irish Historical Studies*, notably its founding editors in 1938, T.W. Moody and R. Dudley Edwards, who advocated an unbending positivist approach to historical scholarship. J.J. Lee, '"The Canon of Irish History – A Challenge" – Reconsidered' in Toner Quinn (ed.), *Desmond Fennell, His Life and Work* (Dublin: Veritas, 2001), pp. 59–60.

Witnessing the Republic: The Ernie O'Malley Notebook Interviews and the Bureau of Military History Compared

1 Confidential medical examination of Ernest O'Malley by Dr Frank Murray, 19 September 1934 (Military Archives of Ireland [hereafter MAI], Military Service Pensions Collection [hereafter MSPC] /34A6/WDP/760]).

2 Letter, Ernie O'Malley to Helen Golden, August 1933, in Cormac O'Malley and Nicholas Allen (eds), *Broken Landscapes: Selected Letters of Ernie O'Malley, 1924–1957* (Dublin: The Lilliput Press, 2011), p. 95.

3 Ernie O'Malley, Queries from Military Service Registration Board, 30 May and 20 June 1934, 3416/W1RB3572, MSPC, MAI.

4 Letter, Ernie O'Malley to Paul Strand, 12 July 1934, O'Malley and Allen, *Broken Landscapes*, pp. 102–3.

5 Richard English, *Ernie O'Malley: IRA Intellectual* (Oxford: Clarendon Press, 1999), pp. 41–3.

6 Letter, John Kyne to Frank Aiken, 9 August 1934, 34A6/WDP/760, MSPC, MAI.

7 Ernie O'Malley, Wound pension application form, 26 May 1934, 34A6/WIRB3572, MSPC, MAI; Letter, Frank Aiken to Ernie O'Malley, 4 February 1935, Box 3, Folder 20, Ernie O'Malley Papers, Archives of Irish America 060, New York University Library [hereafter EOM AIA 060].

8 Letter, Ernie O'Malley to Paul Strand, 28 December 1934, O'Malley and Allen, *Broken Landscapes*, p. 107. In fact, the 1934 MSP Act covered service only to 30 September 1923.

9 Marie Coleman, 'Military Service Pensions for Veterans of the Irish Revolution, 1916–1923', *War in History*, 20 (2013), p. 205.

10 Dáil Debates, 5 February 1936, vol. 60, cols 25–6 and Seanad Debates, 13 March 1945, vol. 29, cols 1646–9.

11 Patrick Brennan, 'Active Service: Changing Definitions' in Catriona Crowe (ed.), *Guide to the Military Service (1916–1923) Pensions íCollection* (Dublin: Óglaigh na hÉireann , 2012), p. 71.

12 Medical reports on Ernest O'Malley, 14 September 1937 and 28 September 1939, 34A6/WDP/760, MSPC, MAI; English, *Ernie O'Malley*, p. 45.

13 P17b/24–139, Ernie O'Malley notebooks [hereafter EOM nbks], Ernie O'Malley Papers [hereafter EOMP], University College Dublin Archives. The MAI holds one notebook, MAI, Ernie O'Malley notebook, PC 278. Five are held in Box 13, Folders 16a and 16b, EOM AIA 060, Box 14, Folder 2a, AIA 060, and Box 15, Folders 10 and 12, EOM AIA 060.

14 See the biographical note, O'Malley and Allen, *Broken Landscapes*, p. 134; thanks to Dr Róisín Kennedy for drawing my attention to the artist interviews: Box 20, Folder 19, EOM AIA 060.

15 Letter, Ernie O'Malley to John Kelleher, 30 January and 15 February 1950, O'Malley and Allen, *Broken Landscapes*, p. 275.

16 Letter, Ernie O'Malley to Paul Strand, 9 December 1953, O'Malley and Allen, *Broken Landscapes*, p. 313.

17 Letter, Florrie O'Donoghue to Ernie O'Malley, 16 October 1945, P17b/181, EOM nbks, UCDA.

18 Letter, Ernie O'Malley to Liam Manahan, 9 September 1953, O'Malley and Allen, *Broken Landscapes*, p. 308.

19 Interview, Michael Fitzpatrick, P17b/114, p. 11, EOM nbks, UCDA.

20 Eve Morrison, 'The Bureau of Military History as a Source for the Irish Revolution', 2012 MAI website, BMH, Historical essays, pp. 2–3.

21 Sean Moran to Finance, 21 December 1943, S 13081/A, Department of Taoiseach [hereafter TSCH], National Archives of Ireland [hereafter NAI].

22 Ibid.

23 Memo by Maurice Moynihan, 25 June 1946 (NAI, TSCH, S 13081/A). John McCoy, 'Compilation of Evidence for Black and Tan War', 2 June 1949, S 677, Bureau of Military History [hereafter BMH], MAI; Robinson, 'Explanatory Memo', April 1951, S 1151, BMH, MAI.

24 Memo by Maurice Moynihan, 25 June 1946, S 13081/A, TSCH, NAI.

25 http://www.bureauofmilitaryhistory.ie/bmhsearch/search.jsp and http://www.militaryarchives.ie/collections/online-collections/military-service-pensions-collection/search-the-collection

26 O'Donoghue was a member of the Bureau itself until May 1948.

27 Evi Gkotzaridis, 'Revisionist Historians and the Modern Irish State: The Conflict Between the Advisory Committee and the Bureau of Military History', *IHS* 35, no. 137 (May 2006): pp. 99–116; *Trials of Irish History: Genesis and Evolution of a Reappraisal 1938–2000* (London: Routledge, 2006), pp. 81–101. See also Michael Laffan, 'Easter Week and the Historians' in Mary Daly and Margaret O'Callaghan (eds), *1916 in 1966: Commemorating the Easter Rising* (Dublin: Royal Irish Academy, 2007), pp. 323–4. The best account of the Bureau's administration to date is in Gerard O'Brien's *Irish Governments and the Guardianship of Historical Records, 1922–72* (Dublin: Four Courts Press, 2004), pp. 130–53.

28 John McCoy to Director, 2 October 1948, WSO 25, BMH, MAI; McCoy to Ernie O'Malley, 13 November 1951, P17b/196, EOM nbks, UCDA.

29 Note by Paddy Brennan, 28 February 1949; John McCoy to Director, 2 October 1948, WSO 25, BMH, MAI; Interviews with Paddy Brennan, P17b/96, EOM nbks, UCDA; John McCoy, P17b/89, 90, 94, 116, EOM nbks, UCDA; Florrie O'Donoghue, P17b/95, 96, EOM nbks, UCDA; Seamus Robinson, P17b/95, 99, 101, EOM nbks, UCDA; Seamus Conway, P17b/121, 131, EOM nbks, UCDA.

30 Florrie O'Donoghue, P17b/96, pp. 5–6, EOM nbks, UCDA. The most recent analysis of this incident, though still drawing heavily on Peter Hart's original research, is to be found in Andy Bielenberg, John Borgonovo and James S. Donnelly Jr, '"Something of the Nature of a Massacre:" The Bandon Valley Killings Revisited', *Éire–Ireland* 49, no. 3 (2014), pp. 7–59.

31 Minutes, Dept. of Taoiseach, 12 November 1946, S 13081/A, TSCH, NAI; McDunphy, General note, 4 January 1938, S 1, BMH, MAI.

32 O'Brien, *Irish Governments*, pp. 39–40; Marie Coleman, 'McDunphy, Michael' in *Dictionary of Irish Biography*, ed. James McGuire and James Quinn (Cambridge, MA: Cambridge University Press, 2009), http://dib.cambridge.org.elib.tcd.ie/quicksearch.do;jsessionid-B9655CF9124847DAA1BD278D465A3245.

33 *The Irish Press* (Dublin, Ireland), 26 May 1976.

34 Letter, Ernie O'Malley to Liam Deasy, 3 November 1950, MS 43, 556/1–3, Liam Deasy Papers [hereafter LD], National Library of Ireland [hereafter NLI]; Connie Neenan to Cormac O'Malley, 15 June 1972, Box 26, Folder 6, EOM AIA 060.

35 Bureau conference minutes, 1 April 1955 and 30 September 1955, S 1430, BMH, MAI; John McCoy to Charles Holmes, 21 February 1951, S 1644, BMH, MAI; Note by William Ivory, 31 March 1953, S 2136, BMH, MAI.

36 Brian Hanley, 'The Rhetoric of Republican Legitimacy' in Fearghal McGarry, *Republicanism in Modern Ireland* (Dublin: UCD Press, 2003), pp. 167–77, 171.

37 Piaras Béaslaí to Comdt. Ryan, 30 April 1952, S 77, BMH, MAI; Mulcahy to Diarmuid Lynch, 24 April 1948, MS 31, 356, Florence O'Donoghue papers [hereafter FOD], NLI.

38 Cornelius Kearney to John McCarthy, 2 May 1952, S 1971, BMH, MAI.

39 Investigator's notes for WS 1460 Cornelius Kearney, uncatalogued, BMH, MAI.

40 Memo by McDunphy, 25 Nov. 1949, S 851, BMH, MAI.

41 Jack Harty, 7 September 1951, P17b/119, p. 8, EOM nbks, UCDA; Tipperary I Brigade, addresses of men with claims to service on ASU from Oct. 1920 onwards, RO 192A, MSPC, MAI, p. 3; Company Captains, Toomevara (B) Company, 2nd Battalion, Tipperary No. I Brigade and nominal roll for same, 2nd critical date, RO 185, 41, 63, MSPC, MAI.

42 Diarmaid Ferriter, 'In such deadly earnest', *The Dublin Review* 12 (2003), pp. 36–64, 39.

43 Bureau Conference Minutes, 2 October 1951, S 1430, BMH, MAI.

44 On the subject of 'intersubjectivity' as a feature of oral history interviews, see Lynn Abrams, *Oral History Theory* (London: Routledge, 2010), pp. 54–77.

45 Guy Beiner, *Remembering the Year of the French: Irish Folk History and Social Memory* (Madison, WI: University of Wisconsin Press, 2007), p. 23.

46 For a discussion of this, see Paul Thompson, *The Voice of the Past: Oral History* (Oxford: Oxford University Press 2000), p. 133.

47 See Catherine Rooney, Witness Statement [hereafter WS] 648, p. 3, BMH, MAI; Appeal, Catherine Rooney, 25 November 1940, MSP34/3935, MSPC, MAI; Denis F. Madden, WS 1103, p. 14, MAI, BMH.

48 Sean MacEntee to Taoiseach, 29 January 1945, S 13602/A, TSCH, NAI. Presumably MacEntee was referring to former anti-Treaty IRA men who remained active in Sinn Féin after the Civil War. His remarks were made in relation to a 1945 case in which the Supreme Court ruled in favour of the unhappy claimants and against the pensions Referee. For a brief overview of this case, see Caoimhe nic Dháibhéid, *Sean MacBride: A Republican Life, 1904–1946* (Liverpool: Liverpool University Press, 2011), pp. 187–8.

49 Terence A.M. Dooley, *The Land for the People: The Land Question in Independent Ireland* (Dublin: UCD Press, 2004), pp. 84–9.

50 Moss Twomey, quoted in Brian Hanley, *The IRA, 1926–1936* (Dublin: Four Courts Press, 2002), p. 111.

51 Charles Townshend, 'The Irish War of Independence, Context and Meaning' in Catriona Crowe (ed.), *Guide to the Military Service (1916–1923) Pensions Collection* (Dublin: Óglaigh na hÉireann, 2012), p. 110.

52 *Dáil Debates*, 14 February 1945, vol. 96, col. 64, accessed 5 July 2010, www.oireachtas–debates.gov.ie.

53 Memorandum on the procedure, examination of, certification and assessment of claims under the Military Service Pension Act, 1934, undated, *c.*1942, S 9243, TSCH, NAI.

54 Bureau journal II, 1 August 1947, MS 31, 355/1, FOD, NLI.

55 Liam Daly to Diarmuid Lynch, 31 March 1936, MS 11,131, Diarmuid Lynch papers, NLI; N. Laffan and J.F. Shouldice (Four Courts Garrison Committee) to Thos. J. McCann, 28 October 1936, 20/2/A, Contemporary Documents [hereafter CD], BMH, MAI.

56 John Hanratty to Editor, *Irish Times*, 18 December 1944, S 13081/A, TSCH, NAI.

57 Paddy Brennan, confidential note to the Director, 18 October 1949, S 1300, BMH, MAI. The Bureau left the statement as it was, but thereafter the name of the investigator and Bureau insignia were removed from copies of statements issued to witnesses.

58 Nicholas Allen, *Modernism, Ireland and Civil War* (Cambridge: Cambridge University Press, 2009), p. 199.

59 Mrs Sean Beaumont, née Maureen McGavock, WS 385, pp. 7–8, BMH, MAI.

60 Thomas Treacy, WS 1093, 75, BMH, MAI; *The Irish Press* (Dublin, Ireland), 15 December 1936.

61 Richard English, *Ernie O'Malley*, pp. 49–50.

62 Tom Barry, *Guerilla Days in Ireland* (Dublin: Mercier Press, 1989), pp. 158–9.

63 Eve Morrison, 'Kilmichael Revisited: Tom Barry and the "False Surrender"' in David Fitzpatrick (ed.), *Terror in Ireland: 1916–1923* (Dublin: The Lilliput Press, 2012).

64 *Irish Times* (Dublin, Ireland), 26 August 1939.

65 Dan Bryan quoted in Charles Townshend, *The Republic: The Fight for Irish Independence, 1918–1923* (Harmonsworth: Penguin, 2014), p. 207.

66 Ernie O'Malley, *On Another Man's Wound* (Cork: Mercier Press, 2013), p. 269.

67 Interviews with Andy Cooney, P17b/107, p. 16, EOM nbks, UCDA; Joe O'Byrne, P17b/122, p. 47, EOM nbks, UCDA.

68 Joe O'Byrne, P17b/122, pp. 47–8, EOM nbks, UCDA.

69 Sworn statement made by Joseph Byrne, 3 July 1936 and J.V. Joyce to Sec, MSP Board, 17 April 1936, MSP34REF18108, MSPC, MAI.

70 Patrick J. Mullen, WS 621, 10, BMH, MAI; Sworn statement made by Patrick Mullen, 22 February 1935, MSP34REF1103, MSPC, MAI.

71 Tommy Doyle, P17b/115, p. 51, EOM nbks, UCDA; Statement of Thomas J. Doyle, 4 January 1935, MSP34/97, MSPC, MAI.

72 Statement of Patrick Lamb, 1 January 1935, MSP34/102, MSPC, MAI.

73 John Vincent Joyce, W24SP690, MSPC, MAI.

74 *Irish Times* (Dublin, Ireland), 6 March 1958.

75 ASUs, Dublin Brigade, RO 9, MSPC, MAI; see also memo by P.J. Brennan, Liam Tobin, October 1949, S 90, BMH, MAI.

76 Andy Cooney, P17b/107, EOM, UCDA; Sworn statements of Andy Cooney, 4 December 1936 and 8 April 1937, WMSP34REF/20320, MSPC, MAI; Albert Rutherford, P17b/107, EOMP, UCDA;

Sworn statement of Albert Rutherford, 18 December 1936, MSP34REF/22365, MSPC, MAI.

77 Florrie O'Donoghue, 'Memorandum of Procedure on the Taking of Evidence' 9 July 1947, Ms 31,360/2, FOD, NLI and S 851, BMH, MAI.

78 Taking of Evidence. Instructions to Representatives of the Bureau, 10 May 1948, S 851, BMH, MAI.

79 Director's 9th Progress Report, 12 May 1948, no ref. number supplied, BMH, MAI.

80 Bureau conference minutes, 4 January 1956 and 3 April 1956, S 1430, BMH, MAI; Patrick J. Deasy, Maurice Fitzgerald, John J. Lucy and Mark Wickham, uncatalogued, BMH, MAI; Tom Barry to McDunphy, 4 July 1948, WSO 26, BMH, MAI; Barry to P.J. Brennan, 21 October 1958, S 894, BMH, MAI.

81 See Jack Lane's introduction to Seán Moylan, *In his Own Words: His Memoir of the Irish War of Independence*, with a selection of speeches and poems (Millstreet, Co. Cork, Aubane Historical Society, 2004), pp. 5–6; Peter Hart, *The IRA at War 1916–1923* (Oxford: Oxford University Press, 2003), p. 82; David Fitzpatrick 'History in a Hurry', review of Gerard Murphy, *The Year of Disappearances: Political Killings in Cork, 1921–1922* (Dublin, 2010) (http://www.drb.ie/essays/history-in-a-hurry).

82 Anne Dolan, 'Killing and Bloody Sunday, November 1920', *The Historical Journal*, 49 (2006), pp. 789–810.

83 Josephine Clarke, WS 699, p. 16, BMH, MAI.

84 Lynn Abrams, *Oral History Theory*, p. 80.

85 Quoted in Alessandro Portelli, *The Death of Luigi Trastulli and other Stories: Form and Meaning in Oral History* (Albany, NY: State University of New York Press, 1991), p. 1.

'The People' of *On Another Man's Wound*

1 Ernesto LaClau, *On Populist Reason* (New York, NY: Verso, 2005).

2 Ibid., p. 77.

3 Ibid.

4 R.F. Foster, *Modern Ireland: 1600–1972* (London: Allen Lane, 1989), p. 257.

5 Ernie O'Malley, *On Another Man's Wound* (Cork: Mercier, 2013).

6 LaClau, *On Populist Reason*, p. 81.

7 Ibid. De Valera's 1937 Constitution is the ultimate product of this dynamic, both temporally and conceptually: it encodes in law the limits and horizons of Irish Republican populism, and marks the moment when the term ceases to operate oppositionally. As if on cue, Flann O'Brien begins his career-long sarcastic usage of the phrase, alongside the equally ironic 'plain people of Ireland' and 'good people of Ireland'.

8 LaClau, *On Populist Reason*, p. 81.

9 Ibid.

10 Nevertheless, his book began a high-profile spat between himself and Slavoj Žižek in *Critical Inquiry*. Later reprinted in *In Defense of Lost Causes* (London: Verso, 2008), Žižek

writes that populism is 'by definition, a negative phenomenon' (268), and that 'in populism, the "big Other", although (potentially) suspended in the guise of procedural *formalism*, returns in the guise of the People as the *substantial* agent legitimizing power' (265). As a result the enemy is 'never the system as such, but the intruder who corrupted it ... not a fatal flaw inscribed into the structure as such, but an element that does not play its part within the structure properly' (279). This clearly applies to the case of Irish nationalism, for whom the British presence is the corrupting agent in the discourse of Irish populism, and the resultant revolution was, as Kevin O'Higgins famously remarked, led by 'the most conservative-minded revolutionaries', who removed the foreign agent but left the system unaltered. Laclau defended himself in a 2006 *Critical Inquiry* article, 'Why Constructing a People is the Main Task of Radical Politics': 'In a heterogeneous world, there is no possibility of meaningful political action except if sectorial identity is conceived as a nucleus and starting point in the constitution of a wider popular will' (*Critical Inquiry* 32, no. 4 (2006), pp. 646–80, 674). Despite the acrimonious nature of the exchange, both theorists seem to agree on the structural workings of populism, and differ only in their estimation of its potential for positive political change.

11 In *The Absolute Bourgeois: Artists and Politics in France 1848–1851* (Berkeley, CA: University of California Press, 1999 [1973]), T.J. Clark writes of Eugene Delacroix's painting: 'The very terms of the myth – the story the bourgeois told of himself – suggested its own dissolution. If you took it seriously and gave it form, the bourgeois disappeared. If the new revolution really was heroic and universal, if it went to make a new definition of man, if people and bourgeoisie were true allies, then the People must be *represented* – and the bourgeois was going to find himself in their midst, one against four, or one against a hundred, a colonial planter surrounded by slaves' (19).

12 T.J. Clark, *Farewell to an Idea: Episodes from a History of Modernism* (New Haven, CT: Yale University Press, 1999), p. 47.

13 Ibid.

14 Ibid., p. 28.

15 Ibid., p. 27.

16 Ibid., p. 38.

17 Ibid.

18 Ibid., p. 43.

19 Ibid., p. 18.

20 LaClau, *On Populist Reason*, p. 96.

21 Clark, *Farewell to an Idea*, p. 43.

22 Ibid., p. 35.

23 Ibid., p. 22.

24 Ibid., p. 48.

25 Although see W.J. McCormack's *Dublin 1916: The French Connection* (Dublin: Gill & Macmillan, 2012), where he argues that the French influence on Irish nationalism was of a Catholic, conservative, late-nineteenth-century variety instead of the earlier secular Republicanisms.

26 Michael Hopkinson, *The Irish War of Independence* (Montreal: McGill-Queen's University Press, 2004), p. 15.

27 Hopkinson, *The Irish War of Independence*, p. 25.

28 Richard English, *Ernie O'Malley: IRA Intellectual* (Oxford: Clarendon Press, 1998), pp. 76, 84.

29 O'Malley, *On Another Man's Wound*, p. 363.

30 Ibid., p. 139.

31 Ibid., p. 59.

32 Ibid., p. 162.

33 Ibid., p. 12.

34 On vagueness, LaClau writes that 'the language of populist discourse … is always going to be imprecise and fluctuating: not because of any cognitive failure, but because it tries to operate performatively within a social reality which is to a large extent heterogeneous and fluctuating. I see this moment of vagueness and imprecision – which, it should be clear, does not have any pejorative connotation for me – as an essential component of any populist operation.' LaClau, *On Populist Reason*, p. 118.

35 O'Malley, *On Another Man's Wound*, p. 182.

36 This does not necessarily mean that populism always rests upon homogeneity: LaClau argues that the process of equivalence that produces the people '*does not attempt* to eliminate differences. [It is] because a series of particular social demands were frustrated that the equivalence was established in the first place – if the particularity of the demands disappears, there is no ground for the equivalence either. So difference continues to operate within equivalence, both as its ground and in a relation of tension with it.' Laclau, *On Populist Reason*, p. 79.

37 O'Malley, *On Another Man's Wound*, p. 410.

38 Ibid., p. 29.

39 Ibid., p. 64.

40 Ibid., p. 248.

41 Ibid., p. 335.

42 Ibid., p. 166.

43 We have to wonder if underlying this attention to region is the spectre of Partition, the near future of the action of the memoir, and an increasingly settled fact by the 1930s. O'Malley may be charting the regional tensions in the areas in which he is organizing, but the Free State ultimately incorporated them, and while O'Malley fought against the government in 1922–3, by 1936 he, like the majority of Republicans, had a less antagonistic relationship to the state. This is not to downplay the tensions that remained well into the mid-century between the hardline Republicans and the Irish political establishment, but the reality of partition and Ulster throws such animosity into relief. As the nation unified throughout the mid-century, the north was increasingly isolated until the 1960s.

44 David Lloyd addresses this in a suggestive footnote to his essay 'The Poetics of Politics: Yeats and the Founding of the State', included in *Anomalous States* (Durham, NC: Duke University Press, 1993). Drawing upon Derrida's work on the American Declaration of

Independence, Lloyd writes that 'representation is said to take place in the sense of a representation which participates in that which it represents, as should the founder in the people in whose name he speaks. In the absence of an external point of origin, can that which originates also represent that which it brings into being?' (85 n. 18).

45 LaClau, *On Populist Reason*, 108.

46 Lady Augusta Gregory, *Poets and Dreamers: Studies and Translations from the Irish* (New York, NY: Haskell House Publishers, 1973), 21.

47 O'Malley, *On Another Man's Wound*, p. 122.

48 Ibid., p. 152.

49 Nicholas Allen, *Modernism, Ireland and Civil War* (Cambridge: Cambridge University Press, 2009), p. 160.

50 O'Malley, *On Another Man's Wound*, pp. 162–3.

51 O'Malley's papers contain several notebooks with notes on Joyce. Ernie O'Malley Papers, Archives of Irish America 060, New York University Library [hereafter EOM AIA 060].

52 O'Malley, *On Another Man's Wound*, p. 162.

53 Ibid.

54 English, *Ernie O'Malley*, p. 151.

55 Mary Cosgrove, 'Ernie O'Malley: Art and Modernism in Ireland', *Éire-Ireland* 40, nos 3–4 (2005), p. 93. Here is a brief excerpt of the content: *Éire-Ireland* 40, nos 3–4 (2005).

56 Cormac O'Malley and Nicholas Allen (eds), *Broken Landscapes: Selected Letters of Ernie O'Malley, 1924–1957* (Dublin: The Lilliput Press, 2011), p. 413.

57 O'Malley and Allen, *Broken Landscapes*, p. 424.

58 English, *Ernie O'Malley*, p. 150.

59 The poem is included in his 'Final' collection of typed poems. Box 1, Folder 39, EOM AIA 060.

60 An earlier version of the poem has the phrase 'quiet sad' instead of 'quien sabe', Box 1, Folder 33, EOM AIA 060.

61 O'Malley, *On Another Man's Wound*, p. 166.

62 Box 2, Folder 58, EOM AIA 060.

63 Ernie O'Malley, *The Singing Flame* (Cork: Mercier Press, 2012).

64 O'Malley and Allen, *Broken Landscapes*, p. 392.

65 Allen, *Modernism, Ireland and Civil War*, p. 148.

66 O'Malley and Allen, *Broken Landscapes*, p. 393.

67 Ibid., p. 394.

68 O'Malley, *On Another Man's Wound*, p. 124.

69 O'Malley and Allen, *Broken Landscapes*, p. 396.

70 Ibid.

71 O'Malley, *On Another Man's Wound*, p. 107.

72 Ibid., p. 122.

73 In his introduction to *Broken Landscapes*, Nicholas Allen writes, 'This landscape is informed by practice and study, O'Malley's correlation of visual art and literature a recurring concern of post-Civil War Irish modernism. In this mode the experiment of modernism

is not registered in the malformation of signs. Its innovation depends on the register of a particular historical deficit imaginable in the reader between the Ireland fought for and the Ireland won', O'Malley and Allen, *Broken Landscapes*, p. xxiii. Allen thus sees not just history in the abstract in O'Malley's landscapes, but a particular set of historical traces that speak to struggles for hegemony still not worked out. David Lloyd, in his essay for *Broken Landscapes*, 'On Republican Reading', argues that 'The aesthetic sense that O'Malley espouses becomes a capacity for grasping the distinctive in Irish (or Mexican) art precisely by the juxtaposition of what is contemporary with what is past, what is foreign with what is local, through comparison and differentiation alike. It is, in effect, a refusal of what Walter Benjamin termed historicism, that insistence on the continuity of history or tradition through "empty homogeneous time", a refusal that is perhaps crucial to a culture whose experience of history has been that of rupture rather than continuity and for whom the artefacts of often jarringly disparate traditions are often violently pressed into alignment' (O'Malley and Allen, *Broken Landscapes*, p. 384). Unlike the teleological vision of history found in both narratives of capitalist expansion and orthodox Marxism, O'Malley, like the Fenians and James Connolly, 'always affirmed other possibilities than the destructive passage through industrialization and modernization for the radical transformation of the colonial order'. O'Malley and Allen, *Broken Landscapes*, p. 386.

74 O'Malley and Allen, *Broken Landscapes*, p. 163.
75 Ibid., p. 399.
76 O'Malley, *On Another Man's Wound*, p. 121.
77 O'Malley and Allen, *Broken Landscapes*, p. 397.
78 Ibid., p. 407.
79 R.F. Foster, *W.B. Yeats: A Life*, Vol. 2 (Oxford: Oxford University Press, 1997), p. 294.
80 Ibid., p. 297.
81 Elizabeth Bowen, *The Last September* (New York, NY: Anchor Books, 2000), p. 117.
82 Foster has noted the 'distinctly Protestant "we"' in Yeats's writings from this time, Foster, *W.B. Yeats: A Life*, Vol. 2, p. 295. When Yeats incorporated some of the language of his speech into 'The Tower', he writes of 'The pride of people that were / Bound neither to Cause nor to State', and of 'The people of Burke and of Grattan', and in *On the Boiler* (1938) he asserts that 'Berkeley, Swift, Burke, Grattan, Parnell, Augusta Gregory, Synge, Kevin O'Higgins, are the true Irish people', *The Collected Works of W.B. Yeats, Volume V: Later Essays* (New York, NY: Scribner, 1994), p. 242.

Literature, Violence, Revolution: Roger Casement and Ernie O'Malley

1 P17b/89, O'Malley Military Notebooks, Ernie O'Malley Papers, University College Dublin Archives [UCDA].
2 Alain Badiou, *Being and Event*, trans. Oliver Feltham (New York, NY: Continuum, 2007), p. 376.

3 Thomas MacDonagh, *Literature in Ireland, Studies Irish and Anglo-Irish* (New York, NY: Frederick A. Stokes, 1916), p. 7.

4 '[The Irish mode] enters literature at a period which seems to us who are of it as a period of disturbance, of change […] it stands as another element of disturbance, of revolution; it is comparatively free from the old authority imposed by the Renaissance […] this it is necessary to note in order to understand the reception given to the Irish Mode. It has come in its due time.' MacDonagh, *Literature in Ireland*, pp. 7–8.

5 '[T]he colonized writer, after having tried to lose himself among the people, with the people, will rouse the people. Instead of letting the people's lethargy prevail, he turns into a galvanizer of the people. Combat literature, revolutionary literature, national literature emerges. During this phase a great many men and women who previously would never have thought of writing, now that they find themselves in exceptional circumstances, in prison, in the resistance or on the eve of their execution, feel the need to proclaim their nation, to portray their people and become the spokesperson of a new reality in action.' Franz Fanon, *The Wretched of the Earth*, trans. Richard Philcox (New York, NY: Grove Press, 2004), p. 159.

6 Declan Kiberd, *Inventing Ireland* (Cambridge, MA: Harvard University Press, 1996), p. 480.

7 Ernie O'Malley, *The Signing Flame* (Dublin: Anvil Books Limited, 1979), p. 286.

8 Nicholas Allen says of a passage in *On Another Man's Wound* that nothing better 'associates the forms of art and the practice of revolution'. Nicholas Allen, *Modernism, Ireland, and Civil War* (Cambridge: Cambridge University Press, 2009), p. 147.

9 'Taoiseach Calls for Casement Enquiry', *History Ireland* 7, no. 3 (Autumn 1999), p. 9.

10 Peter Costello, '"The Amazon Journal of Roger Casement" by Angus Mitchell, Roger Casement's Diaries, 1910; The Black and the White by Roger Sawyer." Review', *Studies: An Irish Quarterly Review* 87, no. 346 (1998), p. 210.

11 Roger Casement, MS1622, p. 77, Roger Casement Papers and Diaries, National Library of Ireland Archives.

12 Michael Taussig, 'Culture of Terror – Space of Death: Roger Casement's Putumayo Report and the Explanation of Torture' in Nancy Scheper-Hughes and Philippe Bourgois (eds), *Violence in War and Peace, An Anthology* (Malden, MA: Blackwell Publishing, 2004), p. 45.

13 Jordan Goodman, *The Devil and Mr Casement: One Man's Battle for Human Rights in South America's Heart of Darkness* (New York, NY: Farrar, Straus and Giroux, 2009), p. 4.

14 Dean Pavlakis, *British Humanitarianism and the Congo Reform Movement, 1896–1913* (London: Ashgate, 2015).

15 Casement, MS1622, p. 58.

16 Ibid., p. 58

17 Ibid., p. 58

18 Ibid., p. 58

19 Ibid., p. 42.

20 Ibid., p. 8.

21 Ibid., p. 8.

22 Ibid., p. 9.

23 Ibid., p. 19.

24 Ibid., p. 60. 'Immediately [that] anything resembling civilised dealing with the Indians is instituted, no 10% of the actual rubber produced will be brought in. That is to say, 90% of it "at least" in [colleague Louis] Barnes' view comes from vile oppression and slavery. I put it at 100% I think and largely agree with the statement [...] that under the present system, the question is, which will be exhausted first, the Indians or the rubber trees.'

25 Taussig, 'Culture of Terror', p. 44.

26 Ibid., p. 50.

27 Casement, MS1622, p. 232.

28 Ibid., p. 236. 'The contract ... has been violated again and again. The medicines, for instance, the not being left destitute, and many others of the clauses. Also that referring to work to begin "the day after arrival at the above mentioned place." Here a double fraud was committed. There is no such place as Putumayo, nor as Igara Parana. The former is a huge river, fully 1000 miles long, the latter a tributary river about 400 miles long.'

29 Ibid.

30 Ibid., p. 70.

31 Brian Inglis, *Roger Casement* (New York, NY: Penguin, 2002), p. 131.

32 Giovanni Costigan, 'The Treason of Sir Roger Casement', *The American Historical Review* 60, no. 2 (1955), p. 284.

33 Costigan, 'The Treason of Sir Roger Casement', p. 285.

34 Roger Casement, Letter 25, Roger Casement Papers and Diaries, National Library of Ireland Archives.

35 Roger Casement, Letter 36, Roger Casement Papers and Diaries, National Library of Ireland Archives.

36 Sigmund Freud, 'Project for a Scientific Psychology (1896)', *The Standard Edition of the Complete Psychological Worlds of Sigmund Freud*, Vol. 1, trans. James and Alix Strachey (London: The Hogarth Press and the Institute for Psycho-Analysis, 1953–74), pp. 296–7.

37 Freud, 'Project for a Scientific Psychology', p. 366.

38 Ibid., p. 373.

39 Jacques Lacan, 'The Function and Field of Speech and Language in Psychoanalysis', *Écrits*, trans. Bruce Fink (New York: W.W. Norton and Co., 2006), p. 264.

40 Casement, MS1622, p. 248.

41 Ibid., p. 87.

42 Ibid., p. 55. 'We, in search of the truth, proceed as if we were the liars and wrongdoers, and hold our meetings in secret, and constantly pledge ourselves to be "prudent" and "silent", and to show no one of our local hosts what we think of them or of the things we are hourly looking at. We play a part the whole day, and when investigating (as far as we can) a most appalling crime like that told this morning, pretend to be butterfly catching!'

43 Ibid., p. 218.

44 Ernesto Che Guevara, in David Deutschmann (ed.), *Che Guevara Reader* (New York, NY: Ocean Press, 1997), p. 211.

45 Sigmund Freud, 'Three Essays on the Theory of Sexuality', *The Standard Edition of the Complete Psychological Worlds of Sigmund Freud*, Vol. 7, trans. James and Alix Strachey (London: The Hogarth Press and the Institute for Psycho-Analysis, 1953–74), p. 209.

46 Sigmund Freud, '"Civilized" Sexual Morality and Modern Nervous Illness', *The Standard Edition of the Complete Psychological Worlds of Sigmund Freud*, Vol. 9, trans. James and Alix Strachey (London: The Hogarth Press and the Institute for Psycho-Analysis, 1953–74), p. 178.

47 Sigmund Freud, 'Two Encyclopaedia Articles', *The Standard Edition of the Complete Psychological Worlds of Sigmund Freud*, Vol. 18, trans. James and Alix Strachey (London: The Hogarth Press and the Institute for Psycho-Analysis, 1953–74), p. 243.

48 Sigmund Freud, 'New Introductory Lectures on Psychoanalysis', *The Standard Edition of the Complete Psychological Worlds of Sigmund Freud*, Vol. 22, trans. James and Alix Strachey (London: The Hogarth Press and the Institute for Psycho-Analysis, 1953–74), p. 90.

49 Gilles Deleuze, *L'abécédaire de Gilles Deleuze*, directed by Pierre-André Boutang and Michel Pamart (Sodaperaga Productions. Film, 1996), television production. All translation is original.

50 Ibid. 'Historians mix two absolutely different things by confusing history with situations in which the only way to be human consists in "revolutionary becoming." [...] Theorists speak of "the future of revolutions," but this is not an accurate way to approach the issue. They want to trace it back far enough to demonstrate that, if the future was bad, this is because everything was bad to begin with.. But the concrete problem is how and why people become revolutionary.'

51 Gilles Deleuze, *Difference and Repetition*, trans. Paul Patton (New York: Columbia University Press, 1994), p. 367.

52 Ibid. 'Art [...] discovers underneath consumption a schizophrenic clattering of the jaws, and underneath the most ignoble destructions of war, still more processes of consumption. It aesthetically reproduces the illusions and mystifications which make up the real essence of this civilization, in order that Difference may at last be expressed with a force of anger which is itself repetitive ... in other words, a freedom for the end of a world. Each art has ... the critical and revolutionary power [that] may attain the highest degree and lead us from the sad repetitions of habit to the profound repetitions of memory, and then to the ultimate repetitions of death in which our freedom is played out.'

53 Timothy M. O'Neil, '"We Knew Where Our Sympathies Were": Social and Economic Views in *On Another Man's Wound*', *New Hibernia Review* 7, no. 3 (2003), p. 141.

54 Mary Cosgrove, 'Ernie O'Malley: Art and Modernism in Ireland', *Éire-Ireland* 40, nos 3–4 (2005), p. 85.

55 Martin Williams, 'Mythology and Revolutionary Ideology in Ireland 1878–1916', *The Historical Journal* 26, no. 2 (1983), p. 326. To make this claim, Williams ignores both *On Another Man's Wound*'s opening line, 'Our nurse, Nannie, told my eldest brother and me stories and legends,' and O'Malley's decision to shoot at British soldiers *before* he begins reading through Irish history.

56 Ernie O'Malley, *On Another Man's Wound* (Boulder, CO: Roberts Rinehart Publishers, 1999), p. 33.

57 Ibid.

58 Tom Barry, *Guerilla Days in Ireland* (Dublin: Anvil Books, 1955), p. 2.

59 Barry, *Guerilla Days in Ireland*, p. 2.

60 O'Malley, *On Another Man's Wound*, p. 33.

61 Ibid., p. 33.

62 Ibid.

63 Ibid., p. 35. Emphasis mine.

64 Richard English tries to argue that a sense of belonging is what attracts O'Malley to revolutionary work. He writes, 'The attractions of being part of a meaningful, distinctive, and purposeful group; the excitement of action; the ignition of imaginative patriotism – one can begin here to trace the development of the youthful Revolutionary,' Richard English, *Ernie O'Malley: IRA Intellectual* (Oxford: Clarendon Press, 1991), 7. Yet in the context of the memoirs, this cannot be the case. O'Malley's first political investment is to turn away from such belonging by avoiding the students at Trinity.

65 O'Malley, *On Another Man's Wound*, p. 38.

66 Ibid., p. 39.

67 Ibid.

68 Ibid. Emphasis mine.

69 Ibid., p. 41.

70 Ibid., p. 137.

71 Sigmund Freud, 'Civilization and its Discontents', *The Standard Edition of the Complete Psychological Worlds of Sigmund Freud*, Vol. 21, trans. James and Alix Strachey (London: The Hogarth Press and the Institute for Psycho-Analysis, 1953–74), p. 71.

72 Sigmund Freud, 'Creative Writers and Day-Dreaming', *The Standard Edition of the Complete Psychological Worlds of Sigmund Freud*, Vol. 9, trans. James and Alix Strachey (London: The Hogarth Press and the Institute for Psycho-Analysis, 1953–74), p. 149.

73 Matthew Weiner, 'Smoke Gets in Your Eyes', *Mad Men*, directed by Alan Taylor (19 Jul 2007), television production.

74 Sigmund Freud, 'Beyond the Pleasure Principle', *The Standard Edition of the Complete Psychological Worlds of Sigmund Freud*, Vol. 18, trans. James and Alix Strachey (London: The Hogarth Press and the Institute for Psycho-Analysis, 1953–74), p. 32.

75 Guevara, *Che Guevara Reader*, p. 115.

76 O'Malley, *On Another Man's Wound*, p. 144. Emphasis mine. Compare here the insistence on Casement's revolutionary practices including the valuation of humanity by something other than market forces, and O'Malley's observation that unwilling revolutionaries had the habit of 'count[ing] the cost'.

77 Ibid.

78 Joan Copjec, *Imagine There's No Woman: Ethics and Sublimation* (Cambridge, MA: MIT Press, 2002), p. 92.

79 Copjec, *Imagine There's No Woman*, p. 92.

80 It is important to note here that Copjec's history is not Deleuze's history. Copjec defines history not as a narrative of progress that situates the present in relation to meaning, but rather (borrowing Lacan's terms) a 'teeming void' from which meaning is derived.

81 O'Malley, *On Another Man's Wound*, p. 126. 'The Táin almost brought me to trouble near Ardee. The name meant the Ford of Ferdia; here he had been buried, after death at the weapons of his friend and enemy, Cuchulain. I cycled to look at the burial mound close to the stream in the town, but I ran into police who tried to halt me in the street. I back-kicked one in the face with the studded strength of a heavy boot, then drawing my gun on his partner, who was trying to open a holster flap, I cycled out of sight. Later I found that the grave had been cut away during a deepening of the stream.'

82 Kiberd, *Inventing Ireland*, p. 480.

83 O'Malley, *The Signing Flame*, p. 42. 'We had given ourselves to this land with death or imprisonment as a reward. Other generations had done this. The dead, what did they think? Small dots on the map showed where men had died. […] Here Martin Conway, the fearless, had fallen in action against police and soldiers, and lower down on the map the wounded Tobin had dragged himself to die, there, outside his mother's house. Here we had been chased, there we had stood and fought. What was the use of brooding over it?'

84 O'Malley, *On Another Man's Wound*, p. 220. Upon meeting an elderly man who had marched with the Fenians, O'Malley asserts: 'But the Fenians did not do much … Why didn't they fight?'

Revolutionary Disillusionment

1 John McGahern, *Amongst Women* (London: Faber and Faber, 1990), p. 15.
2 Ibid., p. 5.
3 Diarmaid Ferriter, 'Commemorating the Rising, 1922–65: A Figurative Scramble for the Bones of the Patriot Dead?' in Mary E. Daly and Margaret O'Callaghan (eds), *1916 in 1966: Commemorating the Easter Rising* (Dublin: Royal Irish Academy, 2007), pp. 199–219.
4 For an extended treatment, see Chapter 9 of my *Vivid Faces: The Revolutionary Generation in Ireland, 1890–1923* (London: Allen Lane, 2014).
5 Ibid.
6 Diarmaid Ferriter, 'In Such Deadly Earnest', *The Dublin Review* 12 (2003), p. 45.
7 Letter from Bulmer Hobson to Patrick McCartan, 13 February 1924, Box 6, Maloney Papers, New York Public Library.
8 30 April 1956; P120/17, Denis McCullough Papers, University College Dublin Archives.
9 Desmond Ryan, *The Invisible Army: A Story of Michael Collins* (London: A. Barker Ltd., 1932), p. 182.
10 Frances Flanagan, *Remembering the Irish Revolution: Dissent, Culture and Nationalism in the Irish Free State* (Oxford: Oxford University Press, 2015).

11 Quoted in Tom Garvin, *Nationalist Revolutionaries in Ireland, 1858–1928* (Oxford: Oxford University Press, 1987), p. xi.

12 Robert Wohl, *The Generation of 1914* (London, 1980), p. 210.

13 Ernie O'Malley, *On Another Man's Wound* (Dublin: Anvil Press, 1979), p. 12.

14 'The Ernie O'Malley Introduction, 1945', originally in the catalogue of *Jack B. Yeats 1871–1957*, accompanying the exhibition of Yeats paintings from the Ernie O'Malley Collection, the Yeats Museum and private owners in Sligo County Library, 2–20 August 1963, 8–9; reprinted in Cormac O'Malley and Nicholas Allen (eds), *Broken Landscapes, Selected Letters of Ernie O'Malley, 1924–1957* (Dublin: The Lilliput Press, 2011), pp. 391–95.

15 Thomas MacGreevy, *Jack B. Yeats: An Appreciation and an Interpretation* (Dublin: Victor Waddington Publications, 1945), pp. 3–4.

16 Richard English, *Ernie O'Malley: IRA Intellectual* (Oxford: Clarendon Press, 1998), p. vii.

17 Ferriter, 'Commemorating the Rising, pp. 199–219.

18 Karl Mannheim, 'The Problem of Generations' in Paul Kecskemeti (ed.), *Essays on the Sociology of Knowledge* (Oxford: Oxford University Press, 1952), p. 303.

19 O'Malley and Allen, *Broken Landscapes*, p. 42.

20 Ibid., p. 107.

21 Ibid., p. 363.

BIBLIOGRAPHY FOR ERNIE O'MALLEY (1897–1957)

by Cormac K.H. O'Malley

PUBLICATIONS by Ernie O'Malley

Books

On Another Man's Wound (England/Ireland: London/Dublin: Rich & Cowan, 1936; London: Four Square Books, 1961; Dublin: Anvil Books, 1979, revised edition 2002; Cork: Mercier Press, 2013, revised edition with footnotes and photographs).

Germany: *Rebellen In Irland* (Berlin: Alfred Metzner, 1937, and again in 1942 and 1943).

United States of America: *Army Without Banners* (Boston, MA: Houghton Mifflin, 1937); *On Another Man's Wound* (Boulder, CO: Roberts Rinehart, 1999, revised edition).

The Singing Flame (Dublin: Anvil Books, 1978; Cork: Mercier Press, 2012, revised edition).

Raids and Rallies (Dublin: Anvil Books, 1982; Cork: Mercier Press, 2011, revised edition).

Rising Out: Sean Connolly of Longford: 1890–1921 (Dublin: UCD Press, 2007), edited by Cormac O'Malley.

Books based on Ernie O'Malley's military notebooks

The Men Will Talk to Me: Kerry Interviews by Ernie O'Malley (Cork: Mercier Press, 2012), edited by Cormac O'Malley and Tim Horgan.

The Men Will Talk to Me: Galway Interviews by Ernie O'Malley (Cork: Mercier Press, 2013), edited by Cormac O'Malley and Cormac Ó Comhrai.

The Men Will Talk to Me: Mayo Interviews by Ernie O'Malley (Cork: Mercier Press, 2014), edited by Cormac O'Malley and Vincent Keane.

The Men Will Talk to Me: West Cork Interviews by Ernie O'Malley (Cork: Mercier Press, 2015), edited by Andy Bielenberg, John Borgonovo and Pádraig Óg Ó Ruairc.

The Men Will Talk to Me: Clare Interviews by Ernie O'Malley (Cork: Mercier Press, 2016), edited by Pádraig Óg Ó Ruairc.

Articles by Ernie O'Malley in journals, magazines, newspapers

'Introduction' to the daily serial publication of *On Another Man's Wound*, in *The Irish Press*, starting October 1936.

Book Review of Françoise Henri's *Irish Art in the early Christian Period*, *The Bell* I, no. 1 (Dublin: October 1940), reprinted in *Broken Landscapes*.

Book Review of Thomas MacGreevy's *Appreciation of Jack B Yeats*, *The Bell* XI, no. 4 (Dublin: January 1946), pp. 914–16, reprinted in *Broken Landscapes*.

'County of Mayo', *Holiday*[Magazine] (London, 28 October 1946).

'Renaissance' [in French on Irish neutrality], *La France Libre* XIII, no. 74 (London, December 1946 / January 1947), pp. 139–42, reprinted in *Broken Landscapes*.

'Ireland', *Architectural Design*, XVII: 7 (London, July 1947), pp. 172–4, reprinted in *Broken Landscapes*.

Newspaper series

The Irish Press, a daily serial of *On Another Man's Wound*, October 1936–7.

The Sunday Press, a weekly serial of *Raids and Rallies*, September 1955–June 1956.

Published correspondence

Cathair na Mart, Journal of the Westport Historical Society 9, no. 1, 1989, pp. 1–20, letter from Kilmainham Gaol to Molly Childers, 21–4 November 1923.

Prisoners: The Civil War Letters of Ernie O'Malley, edited by Richard English and Cormac K.H. O'Malley (Dublin: Poolbeg Press, 1991).

No Surrender Here: The Civil War Papers of Ernie O'Malley, 1922–1924, edited by Cormac K.H. O'Malley and Anne Dolan, with introduction by J.J. Lee (Dublin: The Lilliput Press, 2007).

Broken Landscapes: Selected Letters of Ernie O'Malley, 1924–1957, edited by Cormac K.H. O'Malley and Nicholas Allen (Dublin: The Lilliput Press, 2011).

Published art criticism

'Introduction' to the catalogue for the Jack B. Yeats National Loan Exhibition, National College of Arts and Design (Dublin, June–July 1945), reprinted in *Broken Landscapes*.

'Louis le Brocquy', *Horizon Magazine* XIV:79 (London, July 1946), reprinted in *Broken Landscapes*.

'Traditions of Mexican Art', *The Listener* (London, BBC, 23 January 1947), pp. 146–7, reprinted in *Broken Landscapes*.

'Painting: The School of London', *The Bell* XIV, no. 3 (Dublin, July 1947), reprinted in *Broken Landscapes*.

'The Background of the Arts in Mexico', *The Bell* XIV, no. 5 (Dublin, August 1947), reprinted in *Broken Landscapes*.

Poetry

Poetry [Magazine], Chicago, January 1935, pp. 192–4 and March 1936 pp. 304–5.
Dublin Magazine, Dublin, October 1937.

Radio programmes

BBC Home Service, Third Programme, 'Traditions of Mexican Painting', 2 January 1947, reprinted in *Broken Landscapes*.
Radio Éireann, Music Programme: 'From Japan to Tunis', 1947.
BBC Home Service, Third Programme, Compere, Country Magazine, 7 September 1947.
Radio Éireann, 'Raids and Rallies', series of talks of War of Independence encounters, 1953.

Excerpts of Ernie O'Malley' writings republished

More Escapers in War and Peace, edited by Eric Williams (London: Collins, 1968) reproduced segment on escape from Kilmainham Gaol from *On Another Man's Wound*.
Field Day Anthology of Irish Literature (Derry: Field Day Publication, 1991) with excerpts from *On Another Man's Wound*.
Sources in Irish Art: A Reader, edited by Fintan Cullen (Cork: Cork University Press, 2000), pp. 133–40 (reproduced 1945 Introduction to the catalogue for the Jack B. Yeats National Loan Exhibition.
Louis Le Brocquy, edited by Dorothy Walker (Dublin: Ward River Press, 1981) reproduced 1946 article on Louis le Brocquy from *Horizon Magazine*.

PUBLICATIONS about Ernie O'Malley

Biographies

The Ernie O'Malley Story by Padraic O'Farrell (Cork: Mercier Press, 1983).
Ernie O'Malley: IRA Intellectual by Richard English (Oxford: Clarendon Press, 1998).

Articles about Ernie O'Malley

New Hibernian Review 7, no. 3, Autumn 2003 (St. Paul, MN), pp. 136–48: 'Radharc ar gGul: A Backward Glance with three articles': Timothy M. O'Neil, 'We Knew Where Our Sympathies Were: Social and Economic Views in *On Another Man's Wound*'; Cormac O'Malley, 'The Publication History of *On Another Man's Wound*'; and Mary Cosgrove, 'Ernie O'Malley's Art References in *On Another Man's Wound*'.
Éire-Ireland 40, nos 3–4 (2005) (Morristown, NJ: Irish American Cultural Institute), pp. 85–103, with illustrations, 'Ernie O'Malley: Art and Modernism in Ireland' by Mary Cosgrove.
Times Literary Supplement, 17 June 2005 (London), 'A Sinn Féin Classic' by John McGahern.

Films, videos, etc., referencing Ernie O'Malley

Hidden Ireland, RTÉ, 23 November 2003 concentrating on Sighle Humphreys and Ernie
   O'Malley (52 min).

The Irish Press and de Valera, RTÉ documentary, 2004 focusing on role in fundraising for *The
   Irish Press* in the United States in 1928–9 (52 minutes).

'*On Another Man's Wound:* Sceal Ernie O'Malley', TG4 documentary, 2008, directed by Jerry
   O'Callaghan (now on DVD).

Publications/films using Ernie O'Malley as a reference or basis for a character

Frank Gallagher, *The Challenge of the Sentry* (1930), with two short stories, 'Shadows in the
   Prison Yard' and 'The Starting Sheep' modelled loosely on Ernie O'Malley.

Thomas Flanagan, *The End of the Hunt* (1995), the principal character was Dublin medical
   student modelled loosely on Ernie O'Malley.

Roddy Doyle, *A Star Called Henry* (1999) and *The Dead Republic* (2010) with characters
   modelled loosely on Ernie O'Malley.

Ken Loach (director) and Paul Laverty (scriptwriter), feature film *The Wind that Shakes
   the Barley* (2006), with medical student who went anti-Treaty modelled loosely on Ernie
   O'Malley.

ARCHIVAL HOLDINGS with Ernie O'Malley Papers

Ernie O'Malley [Nationalist] Papers, University College Dublin Archives

P17a has general military papers for War of Independence, Civil War and other matters.

P17b has interviews with 450 survivors of the independence struggle in First and Second
   Series Military Notebooks.

P17c has military papers from Civil War period, which will be catalogued in 2017.

Ernie O'Malley [Post-Nationalist] Personal Papers, Archives of Irish America, Collection #060, New York University Library (50,000 pages)

Correspondence, manuscripts for published works, working notebooks, poetry, art research,
   personal papers, including unpublished works such as articles; book and film reviews;
   journals/diaries *Climbing the Pyrenees*, memoir of 1924–6 life in the Pyrenees; diaries: 1925
   France, 1925–6 travels in Europe, 1926 Pyrenees, 1928 New York and Boston, 1929 San
   Francisco, Carmel; 1929–30 New Mexico, 1931 Mexico, 1937, 1939, 1941 (Aran), 1944,
   1948, 1949, 1951 Ireland, 1955–6 (Aran); lectures: history of modern art, autumn 1947
   at Limerick City Library and Gallery; poetry: about New Mexico and Ireland, written
   in 1928–35 period; short stories: five, written in 1928–35 period; research work done in

preparation for book on Spanish Armada and sixteenth-century Ireland (1939); notes on lives of thirty-five Irish artists (1945–7) and other miscellaneous works.

Other institutional holdings

Irish College, Rome, correspondence to and from Monsignor John Hagan, Rector.

Jackie Clark Collection, Mayo County Library, Ballina: collection of various editions of EOM's published books and many other brochures and pamphlets owned at one time.

Military Archives, Cathal Brugha Barracks, Dublin with four collections including the Bureau of Military History, Captured Documents and others.

National Archives of Ireland, Dublin, including papers from the Office of the Taoiseach, December 1922–January 1923 [NAI D/T S1369/17].

National Library of Ireland, Dublin, including #10973, a deposit of Ernie O'Malley papers made by Cormac O'Malley in 1961, as well as correspondence in other files including letters from or to or about Ernie O'Malley in the collections of Joseph McGarrity, Sean O'Faolain, Fiona Plunkett and others.

National Museum of Ireland, Collins Barrack, Dublin: boltcutter handles used in 1921 escape from Kilmainham Gaol and pistol.

Trinity College Library Archives, Dublin, including letters from Ernie O'Malley in the collections of Erskine Childers, Frank Gallagher, Seamus O'Sullivan and Estella Solomons.

University College Dublin Archives, including military and personal letters from or to Ernie O'Malley in the collections of Frank Aiken, Desmond Fitzgerald, Sighle Humphreys, Richard Mulcahy, Ernie O'Malley, Moss Twomey and others.

University of Arizona, Center for Creative Photography, Paul Strand Archives and Edward Weston Archives.

Others: Raidió Telefís Éireann Archives; Tate Gallery Archives, London (John Rothenstein); University of Chicago Library (*Poetry* [Magazine]); University of Indiana at Bloomington, Indiana (John Ford); Yaddo Foundation.

CONTRIBUTORS

Nicholas Allen is Franklin Professor of English and Director of the Willson Center for Humanities and Arts at the University of Georgia. His current project is a cultural history called *1916: Empire, War and Rebellion*. His books and edited collections include *Broken Landscapes: Selected Letters of Ernie O'Malley, 1924–1957*; *Modernism, Ireland and Civil War*; *That Other Island*; *The Proper Word*; *George Russell and the New Ireland* and *The Cities of Belfast*. Allen's work is located at the intersection between literature, history and visual culture. His interests include the study of modernism, empire and, increasingly, writing about ocean and archipelago. Dr Allen has taught previously at the University of North Carolina at Chapel Hill and the National University of Ireland, Galway, where he was Moore Institute Professor.

Orla Fitzpatrick is a librarian and photographic historian. She has held the post of Head Librarian at the National Museum of Ireland since 2003. Orla has contributed articles on Irish photographic history and material culture to journals such as *Éire-Ireland* and *Irish Architectural and Decorative Studies*. She is a regular contributor to *Source* photographic review. Her essay on the Easter Rising and photography appears in Lisa Godson and Joanna Brück (eds.), *Making 1916: Material and Visual Cultures of the Easter Rising* (2015). In 2016, Fitzpatrick completed her doctorate at Ulster University on the subject of Irish photographic publications and modernity.

Roy Foster is Carroll Professor of Irish History at the University of Oxford and the author of many books on modern Irish history and culture, including *Modern Ireland 1600–1972* (1989), *Paddy and Mr Punch* (1993), *The Irish Story: Telling Tales and Making It Up in Ireland* (2001), *Luck and the Irish: A Brief History of Change, 1970–2000* (2007); the prizewinning two-volume biography of W.B. Yeats, *The Apprentice Mage, 1865–1914* (1997) and *The Arch Poet, 1915–1939* (2003); *Words Alone: Yeats and his Inheritances*. (2011), based on his 2009 Clark Lectures at Cambridge, dealing with a number of Irish writers of the nineteenth century. He has also written biographies of Charles Stewart Parnell (1977) and Lord Randolph Churchill (1981). His most recent book is *Vivid Faces: The Revolutionary Generation in Ireland, c. 1890–1923*

(2014). He is also a well-known cultural commentator, broadcaster and critic. He has received honorary doctorates from the University of Aberdeen, Queen's University Belfast, Trinity College Dublin, the National University of Ireland, Queen's University, Kingston, Ontario and the University of Edinburgh; he is also a Fellow of the Royal Historical Society, a Fellow of the Royal Society of Literature, an honorary Fellow of Birkbeck College University of London, an honorary Member of the Royal Irish Academy, and a Fellow of the British Academy.

Luke Gibbons is Professor of Irish Literary and Cultural Studies at Maynooth University. He was formerly Keough Family Professor of Irish Studies at the University of Notre Dame, Indiana, Lecturer, Dublin City University, and Visiting Professor at New York University. His recent publications include *Joyce's Ghosts: Ireland, Modernism, and Memory* (University of Chicago Press, 2015); Co-editor (with Kieran O'Conor), *Charles O'Conor and Eighteenth-Century Ireland* (Four Courts Press, 2015); 'Introduction' to Dorothy Macardle, *The Uninvited* (Tramp Press, 2015); *Limits of the Visible: Representing the Irish Great Hunger* (Quinnipiac: Great Hunger Museum, 2014). Among his other publications are *Gaelic Gothic: Race, Colonialism and Irish Culture* (Arlen House, 2004); *Edmund Burke and Ireland: Aesthetics, Politics and the Colonial Sublime* (Cambridge University Press, 2003); *The Quiet Man* (Cork University Press, 2002); *Transformations in Irish Culture* (University of Notre Dame Press, 1996), and *Cinema and Ireland* (Routledge, 1988), with Kevin Rockett and John Hill. He was a contributing editor to Seamus Deane, ed., *The Field Day Anthology of Irish Writing* (1991), co-editor, *Re-Inventing Ireland: Culture, Society and the Global Economy* (with Peadar Kirby and Michael Cronin, 2002), and co-editor (with Dudley Andrew), of 'The Theatre of Irish Cinema', a special issue of *The Yale Journal of Criticism* (2002).

Róisín Kennedy is an art historian and curator. She teaches in the School of Art History and Cultural Policy in University College Dublin. She is former curator of the State Collection at Dublin Castle (1998–9) and author of *Dublin Castle Art* (1999). She was Yeats Curator at the National Gallery of Ireland (2006–8), where she curated *The Fantastic in Irish Art* and *Masquerade and Spectacle: The Travelling Fair in the Work of Jack B. Yeats* in 2007. Her research focuses on censorship and art, the role and function of art writing post 1880, on the position of women as artists and subjects in modernist art, and on the critical reception of modernist art in Ireland. She has contributed to *Circa*, *Third Text*, the *Journal of Art Historiography* and numerous edited collections of essays including *Making 1916: Material and Visual Culture of the Easter Rising* (Liverpool University Press, 2015), *Creating History. Stories of Ireland in Art* (Irish Academic Press, 2016) and *Atlas of the Irish Revolution* (Cork University Press, forthcoming, 2017).

David Lloyd, Distinguished Professor of English at the University of California, Riverside, works primarily on Irish culture and on postcolonial and cultural theory. He is the author of *Nationalism and Minor Literature* (1987); *Anomalous States* (1993); *Ireland After History* (1999) and *Irish Times: Temporalities of Irish Modernity* (2008). His most recent book is *Irish Culture and Colonial Modernity: The Transformation of Oral Space* (Cambridge University Press, 2011). He has recently completed a study of Samuel Beckett's visual aesthetics, forthcoming in 2014, and is beginning a series of essays on poetry and violence. His *Arc & Sill: Poems 1979–2009* was published by Shearsman Books in the UK and New Writers' Press, Dublin, 2012. He has co-published several other books, including *The Nature and Context of Minority Discourse* (1991), with Abdul JanMohamed; *Culture and the State*, co-authored with Paul Thomas (1997); *The Politics of Culture in the Shadow of Capital* (1997), with Lisa Lowe; and *The Black and Green Atlantic: Cross-Currents of the African and Irish Diasporas* (2008), edited with Peter D. O'Neill.

Eve Morrison studied history at Trinity College Dublin, receiving her BA in 2003. She continued her studies in modern Irish History as an Irish Research Council of the Humanities and Social Sciences (now IRC) postgraduate scholar at TCD, researching the Bureau of Military History. She was awarded her PhD in 2011, and was an IRC postdoctoral fellow at University College Dublin from 2013 to 2015. She is currently teaching in UCD, working on a critical guide to the Ernie O'Malley military notebook interviews, and writing a book based on her doctoral work, for Liverpool University Press.

Cormac K.H. O'Malley studied history at Harvard but only returned to historical research after his retirement from an international legal career in 1999. Since then he has pursued various aspects of the life and heritage of his father, Ernie O'Malley, including co-editor with Anne Dolan, *'No Surrender Here:' The Civil War Papers of Ernie O'Malley, 1922–1924* (The Lillitput Press, 2007), editor *Rising Out: Sean Connolly of Longford, 1890–1921* by Ernie O'Malley (UCD Press, 2007), co-editor with Nicholas Allen, *Broken Landscapes, Selected Letters of Ernie O'Malley, 1924–1957* (The Lilliput Press, 2011), a series of co-edited books with Mercier Press, *The Men Will Talk to Me: Interviews by Ernie O'Malley: Kerry* (2012), *Galway* (2013), *Mayo* (2014); as well as revised editions with Mercier Press of Ernie O'Malley's works: *Raids and Rallies* (2011), *The Singing Flame* (2012) and *On Another Man's Wound* (2013); and co-editor with Juliet Christy Brown, *Western Ways: Remembering Mayo through the Eyes of Helen Hooker and Ernie O'Malley* (Mercier Press, 2015). He is a Visiting Scholar at New York University and a Research Associate at Trinity College Dublin.

Seamus O'Malley is an Assistant Professor of English at Stern College for Women, Yeshiva University. His book *Making History New: Modernism and Historical Narrative* was published by Oxford University Press in 2015. He has also published on W.B. Yeats, Ford Madox Ford, Rebecca West, Robert Louis Stevenson, Frank McGuinness, Edmund Wilson, D.H. Lawrence and Alan Moore, and co-edited the volume *Ford Madox Ford and America* (Rodopi, 2012). He is currently co-editing a research companion to Ford for Routledge, and writing a book on populism in Irish literature.

John M. Regan lectures in British, Irish and public histories at the University of Dundee. After completing his doctorate at Queen's University Belfast in 1994, Dr Regan became the Irish Government's Senior Scholar at Hertford College, Oxford. He was later elected to a Research Fellowship at Wolfson College, Oxford, and was awarded a British Academy Postdoctoral Fellowship. In 1999, he published *The Irish Counter-Revolution 1921–36: Treatyite Politics and Settlement in Independent Ireland* (Gill & Macmillan), and in 2013 *Myth and the Irish State: Historical Problems and Other Essays* (Irish Academic Press). He has published articles and review essays in *Historical Journal*, *Irish Historical Studies*, *History*, *Reviews in History*, *Dublin Review of Books*, and *The Journal of British Studies*.

Macy Todd is a lecturer at Buffalo State College. He is co-editor, with Chris Sylvester, of the 2013 issue of *Umbr(a)*, *A Journal of the Unconscious* titled 'The Object'. His research interests include psychoanalysis, revolution, Irish studies, and the relation between numbers and literature.

Nathan Wallace is an Associate Professor of English at the Ohio State University in Marion where he teaches courses in British, Irish and Comics Studies. He is the author of *Hellenism and Reconciliation in Ireland from W.B. Yeats to Field* Day (Cork University Press, 2015), and his essays on Edmund Burke, Matthew Arnold, James Joyce and William Shakespeare have appeared in *Prose Studies* and *ELH*. His second book project is a study of James Joyce and early cinema, entitled *Ulysses at the Movies*.

INDEX

1916 Rising, *see* Easter Rising
Aiken, Frank, 9, 61, 125, 130
Allen, Nicholas, 18, 19, 34, 93, 151, 154, 190
Anderson, Michael, 62
Anglo–Irish, 5, 71, 98, 101, 142, 157–8, 192
Anglo–Irish Treaty, xi–xii, 57, 64–6, 71,
    74–5, 108, 131, 186–90
Anglo–Irish Truce, *see* Anglo-Irish Treaty
Anglo–Irish War, *see* War of Independence
Aran Islands, 48
Architectural Design [magazine], 35
Artists,
    American: Calder, Alexander, 34, 52;
        Charlot, Jean, 31
    English: Constable, John, 155
    French: Daumier, Honoré 155; David,
        Jacques–Louis, 143–5, 147, 150,
        158; Delacroix, Eugeèe, 143–4, 147,
        150, 156, 158, 188; Lurcat, Jean, 22;
        Rouault, Georges, 22; Vlaminck,
        Maurice, 22
    German: Dürer, Albrecht, 18; Klee,
        Paul, 34
    Irish: Hanlon, Jack, 126; Hone, Evie,
        22–3, 26, 94, 126; le Brocquy, Louis, 26,
        36, 94, 103–4, 126, 156; Jellett, Mainie,
        xv, 23, 35, 94; McGuinness, Norah, 23,
        126; Reid, Nano, 23, 94, 126; Tuohy,

Patrick, 17; Yeats, Jack B. Yeats, *see*
    Yeats, Jack B.
    Italian: Botticelli, 20; Crivelli, Carlo,
        20; del Sarto, Andrea, 100; della
        Francesco, Pierro, 18, 100; di Credi,
        Lorenzo, 20; Lippi, Filippino, 20;
        Lotto, Lorenzo, 20; Perugino, Pietro,
        20; Raphael, Sanzio da Urbino 20;
        Vecchio, Palma, 20; Veronese, Pablo,
        20; del Verrocchio, Andrea, 20;
        Vivarini, 20
    Mexican: Orozco, José Clemente, 21,
        30–1, 103, 152–3, 157; Rivera, Diego,
        21, 30–1, 103, 152; Siqueiros, David,
        103
authoritarianism, 112, 119

Barry, Tom, xvi–xvii, 57–60, 63, 72, 82, 136,
    138, 174, 188
Béaslaí, Piaras, 130
Beckett, Samuel, xv, 10, 18, 20, 23, 80, 94,
    104, 191
Benjamin, Walter, 7, 90–1, 103, 140, 230
Black and Tans, 56, 59, 185
Blake, William, 18, 43, 63, 99
blood sacrifice, 84, 96
Bloody Sunday, 1920, 136–7, 139, 174
Brady, Kay, 20

Breen, Dan, xvii, 188
Brennan, Paddy, 129
Brennan, Seán, 129
Bryan, Dan, 134, 136
Buchan, John, 83–4
Bureau of Military History [BMH], xiii, 127–139, 187
Burke, Edmund, 86, 157–8
Byrne, Joe, 136–7

Casement, Roger, xiii, 160–71
Chandler, James, 64–5
Childers, Erskine, 43, 85, 87
Childers, Mary (Molly) Alden, 18, 85–6, 88
Civil War, see Irish Civil War
Clark, T.J., 143–6, 158
Clarke, Josephine, 136, 139
Collins, Michael, 57–8, 62, 64–8, 74, 96, 108, 118
Copjec, Joan, 179–80
Cosgrove, Mary, 35, 152, 174
Cumann na mBan, xvii, 57, 125, 131, 134
Curran, Constantine (Con) P., 22–3

de Valera, Éamon, xiv, 9, 28, 37, 53, 64–5, 94, 129, 141, 145, 149
decolonization, 79–81, 88–9, 94–8, 105
Deleuze, Gilles, 172–4, 176–7, 179–81
Devlin, Denis, 6, 44, 94
Dolan, Anne, 81, 83–89, 139
Donnelly, Simon, 117
Doyle, Roddy, 186, 192
Doyle, Thomas J., 137

Easter Rising, xi–xii, xvii, 14, 16, 32, 60–1, 108–9, 125, 128, 131, 145, 160–2, 172–5, 187–8, 191
Edwards, Robert Dudley, 128–9
Emergency [the], xv, 22, 25, 27, 104, 133, 157, 172–5
Emmet, Robert, 12, 157–8, 174

English, Richard, 14, 81, 85, 88–9, 91, 99, 146, 151, 191
Evans, Walker, 31–2, 34

Fanon, Frantz, 82–3, 87–8, 153, 160–1
fascism, 95, 97, 119
Ferriter, Diarmuid, 111–12, 120–2
Fianna Éireann, 125, 131, 134,
Fianna Fáil, 22–3, 109, 125, 127, 129–30, 133–5, 162
Fitzgerald, Desmond, 87
Fitzgerald, Mabel, 97
Fitzgibbon, John, 142
Fitzpatrick, David, 115–16, 122, 138
folk art, 29–30, 103
folk tradition, 152
folklore, 30, 43, 45, 48–50, 54, 102, 126, 154
    folk tales: Bricriú's Feast, 48;
        Conchubar, 48; Fionn, 48, 51;
        Hakuylt's sea tales, 48; Story of Burnt
        Njal, 48; Táin Bó Cúailnge, 15, 180;
        Till Eulenspiegel, 48
Four Courts, xi, 9, 18, 62, 100, 107–10, 115–22
Fox, R.M., 135
France, 44, 99
Free State, see Irish Free State
French, Feirn, 53
Freud, Sigmund, 167–72, 177–8
Friends of the National Collection of Ireland, 22

Gallagher, Frank, 146
Garvin, Tom, 115–16, 122
General Post Office [GPO], 17
Gilbert, Stuart, 6, 9–10, 12
Grattan, Henry, 157–8
Gregory, Lady Augusta, 43, 142, 150, 153
Grennan, Elizabeth, 130
Griffith, Arthur, 108, 149
guerrilla warfare, xii, xvi, 55–6, 82–4, 99, 105, 192

Guevara, Che, 82, 171, 178

Hales, Sean, 57–8, 63, 73, 74
Hales, Tom, 57–8, 73, 74
Hart, Peter, 56, 58–9, 63, 72, 138
Harty, Jack, 131
Hayes, Liam, 131
Heaney, Meahey, 37
Henry, Françoise, 38, 102
Herbert, Robert, 36–8
Hibernian Rifles, 125, 131
historical research, 107–9, 112–14, 127
historiography, xvii, 64, 89–90, 141
Hobson, Bulmer, xvii, 188
Holland, Robert, 135
Hooker [O'Malley], Helen, xv, 10, 22–3,
    36–7, 40
Hopkinson, Michael, 146
Horizon [magazine], 26, 36
Humphreys, Síghle, 19, 86, 95, 192

invented history, 111–16, 123
IRA, *see* Irish Republican Army
Ireland:
    Co. Clare: 19, 37, 48; Burren, 39; Ennis
        Abbey, 37; Kinvara, 19
    Co. Galway: Galway, 19, 39; Tuam, 19
    Co. Kildare: Curragh, 16, 96, 99; Kilteel
        Church, 37
    Co. Kilkenny: 43, 47, 136, 139
    Co. Mayo: Burrishoole, 10, 126;
        Castlebar, 10; Clew Bay, 36
Ireland Today [magazine], 53
Irish art, 19, 22–3, 26–7, 35, 38, 101–3, 147
Irish Citizen Army, 61, 125, 131, 134–5
    Old Irish Citizen Army Comrades
        Association, 135
Irish Civil War, xi–xii, xiv, xv, 6, 9, 13–16,
    18, 31, 33, 38, 43, 49, 52–3, 55–8, 62,
    64–9, 73–5, 80, 82, 86–8, 92–4, 105, 107,
    109–11, 115, 119, 122, 124–6, 128–36,

139, 146–7, 153, 187, 190, 192
Irish Exhibition of Living Art, 23, 126
Irish Film Society, 30
Irish Free State, xvii, 15–16, 52–3, 56–8,
    62–4, 67–8, 70, 73, 75, 80, 84, 87, 89, 91–4,
    100, 108–10, 116–19, 120, 136, 139, 192
Irish Republican Army [IRA], 43, 45, 47–8,
    53, 56–4, 66–7, 69–70, 72, 75, 82, 84, 108–
    11, 115–22, 124–6, 128, 130–5, 146, 148–9
    Old IRA, 133–5
    Provisional IRA, 69, 111–12, 119, 122
Irish Revolution, 74, 81, 89–90, 95, 169, 173
    185, 189, 191
Irish Volunteers, xiii, xvii, 63, 70, 82–3, 88,
    108, 125, 131, 135, 175, 177, 187–8
Italy, 44, 99, 119

Johnson, Thomas, 118
Jooss Ballet, 35, 40
Jordan, Neil, 64–6, 72–3
    Crying Game [film], 66, 73
    Michael Collins [film], 64, 72
Joyce, James, xii, xviii, 3–11, 13–16, 43, 145,
    151, 188, 191
    Ulysses [novel], 4–12, 14
    Work in Progress [novel section], 6
Joyce, John V., 136–7

Keane, Ronan, 115–16, 118
Kearney, Cornelius, 131, 187
Kearney, Richard, 84
Kelleher, John V., 5, 126
Kiberd, Declan, 98–100, 161, 180
Kieley, Jerry, 149
Kilmainham Gaol, 15, 18, 43, 97, 99, 149

La France Libre [magazine], 157
Laclau, Ernesto, 141–44, 150
Laffan, Michael, 115–16, 122
Lamb, Patrick, 137
Laverty, Paul, xvi, 56–61, 63–5, 67, 71, 74–5

INDEX

Lawrence, D.H., 5, 85, 188
Lee, J.J., 79, 90–1, 123
Lewis, Bernard, 111–14, 116
Lloyd George, David, 91, 95
Loach, Ken, xvi, 55–6, 58–60, 62–3, 65, 70–2, 74–5, 186
 The Wind that Shakes the Barley [film], xvi–xvii, 55, 57–8, 60–6, 69, 71–4, 186
Lynch, Liam, 88, 127
MacNeill, Eoin, 120–22
MacCarvill, Eileen (McGrane), 23
MacEntee, Seán, 133
MacGreevy, Thomas, xv, 17–20, 22, 25, 80, 94, 104, 155, 190
MacLir, Mananaan, 8, 10
Maguire, Tom, 130
Mahr, Adolf, 37–8
Malley, Frank, 85–6
Malley, Charles, *see* O'Malley
Malley, Marion [O'], 86–7
Marat, Jean-Paul, 144–6, 150
Mayhew, Patrick, 98–9
McCartan, Patrick, 188
McCoy, John, 127, 129, 134
McCullough, Denis, 189
McDunphy, Michael, 128–9, 138
McGahern, John, xvii–xviii, 185–7, 192
McGavock, Maureen, 136
Melville, Herman, 43, 99
memory, 107, 110, 119, 123, 135, 185–7, 190–2
 akasic memory, 9
 collective memory, 112, 119
 improvement of memory approach, 112–14
 social memory, 132, 154
Mexican art, 21, 31, 34, 94, 102, 146, 152
Mexican Folkways [magazine], 29–30
Mexico, xiv, xv, 28–33, 39, 41, 43–4, 95, 99, 101, 105, 152–3, 192
Military Service Pensions [MSP]: 125–28; 132–5, 137, 140, 187

Modern
 Irish modernism/modern art, 21–3, 27, 191
 modernism/modernist, ix, xii, xiv, 4, 13–15, 17, 19, 21–4, 26–7, 31, 34, 92, 100, 103–4, 144–6, 151, 179, 187, 190
 modernization, 32, 100, 105–6
 photography, 28, 31
Mooney, Jimmy, 84–5
Mountjoy Gaol, 118
Mulcahy, Richard, 96, 130, 187–89
Mullen, Patrick, 137
Murphy, Des, 49
Murray, Frank, 124
Museum of Modern Art [MoMA], 34, 40
National Gallery of Ireland, 19–21
National Library of Ireland, 37
National Museum of Ireland, 37
nationalism, 19, 32, 69, 72, 80, 89, 93, 94, 96–8, 100, 141, 142, 149–51, 154
Native American: Shalako, 45–6, 49; Zuni, 49
Nolan, Dan, 53–4
Northern Ireland, 89–90, 92, 98, 122
O'Brien, Conor Cruise, 119
O'Connor, Frank, 56, 58, 64, 66–73, 80, 188, 192
O'Connor, Nuala, 120
O'Connor, Padraig, 117
O'Connor, Rory, 62–3, 110, 115, 120–2
O'Doherty, Brian, 26–7
O'Donnell, Peadar, xv, 35, 52–3, 66, 80, 130, 188
O'Donoghue, Florence, 126, 128–9, 134, 138
O'Donovan, Jim, 53
O'Duffy, Eimar, xvii, 187–8, 190, 192
O'Faolain, Sean/O'Faoláin, Seán, 11, 66, 81, 188, 191–2
O'Flaherty, Liam, 6, 66, 80, 86, 94, 188
O'Hegarty, Diarmuid, 130
O'Hegarty, P.S., 187–8
O'Higgins, Kevin, 92–3

O'Kane, Louis, 127, 132
O'Malley, Charles, 84, 86
O'Malley, Cormac, xvi
O'Malley, Ernie
　　diaries, xiii, 36–8, 42–50, 54, 126
　　Director of Organization, IRA, 124
　　Dramatic Society, UCD, founder, 44
　　folklore collector, 45, 126
　　friends:
　　　　Mexico: Aleksandrov, Grigori, 30;
　　　　　　Beals, Carleton, 31; Crane, Hart,
　　　　　　31, 43, 94, 153, 189; Eisenstein,
　　　　　　Sergei, 30; Goddard, Theodora,
　　　　　　29; Stewart, Dorothy, 29; Toor,
　　　　　　Frances, 29–30;
　　　　New Mexico: Brett, Dorothy, 5,
　　　　　　46, 85, 101; Golden, Eithne, 21;
　　　　　　Golden, Helen Merriam, 33;
　　　　　　Luhan, Mabel Dodge, xiv, 29,
　　　　　　46, 52; Lujan, Toni, 46; Otis,
　　　　　　Raymond, 4; Staples, Berton, 48;
　　　　　　Young, Ella, 29, 45–6
　　　　New York: Clurman, Harold, 5;
　　　　　　Group Theatre, 5, 94–5; Milburn,
　　　　　　George, 52; Odets, Clifford, 94;
　　　　　　O'Keefe, Georgia, 21, 32, 94, 153;
　　　　　　Stieglitz, Alfred, 21, 32; Strasberg,
　　　　　　Lee, 94; Sweeney, James Johnson,
　　　　　　xv, 21–2, 25, 34, 39–40; Sykes,
　　　　　　Gerald, 5; Todd, Betty, 52; Vorse,
　　　　　　Mary Heaton, 52
　　health: neurasthenia, 124, 126
　　hunger strike, 15, 18, 69, 95, 125, 128
　　in Mexico/New Mexico, xiv, 6, 21, 28–32,
　　　　43–4, 48, 85, 94–5, 101, 146, 151–3
　　in Pyrenees, 44, 46
　　Irish Press fundraising trip, 6, 9, 28, 44
　　medical student, 56, 60, 62, 136, 149, 151
　　medieval sculpture, 19, 35–6; 38–40
　　notebooks, xiii–xiv, 6–8, 49–50, 94, 126,
　　　　138, 159, 186
　　on art, xiv–xv, 21, 26, 102–4, 190
　　on Jack B. Yeats, xiv, 190
　　oral history pioneer, 126
　　pension, disability, 124–5
　　poetry, 'Time of Day Cordova', 152
　　publications:
　　　　Army Without Banners [memoir,
　　　　　　Boston], 53
　　　　articles:
　　　　　　La France Libre [magazine], 157
　　　　　　Horizon [magazine, on Louis le
　　　　　　　　Brocquy], 26, 36
　　　　　　The Bell [magazine], 102, 152,
　　　　　　　　155, 157, 188
　　　　On Another Man's Wound [memoir,
　　　　　　Dublin, London], xii–xiv, xvi, xviii
　　　　　　16, 32, 42, 47, 54–5, 61–3, 71, 73–4,
　　　　　　81, 83, 88, 125, 129, 135–6, 142, 145,
　　　　　　147, 151–5, 162, 173–4, 177, 180,
　　　　　　185–6, 188, 190, 191
　　　　Rebellen in Irland [memoir, Berlin],
　　　　　　53
　　　　The Singing Flame [memoir, Dublin],
　　　　　　6, 9, 15–16, 18, 54–5, 62, 81, 87,
　　　　　　99–100, 109, 117, 147, 153, 173,
　　　　　　180, 190–1
O'Neil, Timothy M., 174
O'Sullivan, Gearóid, 130
oral history, 126, 132, 138
oral testimony, 122, 132, 140

Paris, France, 8, 11, 22–3, 34, 47, 187
Parnell, Charles Stewart, 12, 61, 157–8
Pearse, Padraig, 3, 19, 86, 96, 160
pension, 124, 125, 127–8, 130–5, 137, 187
people, the, 14–15, 33, 48, 50, 83, 89, 141–71,
　　188–9, 191
Peruvian Amazon Company, 163–5, 170
photographers:
　　American: Blossfeldt, Karl, 34; Brehme,
　　　　Hugo, 30; Lotar, Eli, 34; Nagy,

Moholy, 34; Man Ray, 34; Sheeler, Charles, 32; Stieglitz, Alfred, 21, 32; Strand, Paul, *see* Strand, Paul Weston, Edward, *see* Weston, Edward

Irish: Moffett, Noel, xv, 35–6

Mexican: Modotti, Tina, 29–31

Plunkett, Joseph Mary, 3, 17, 160

populism, 141–5, 150

Porter, Arthur Kingsley, 38, 39

propaganda, 60, 64, 84, 96, 113–14, 116–19, 122–3

public history, 108, 110, 122

Public Record Office, 107, 109–10, 115–23

Putumayo, Peru, 162–5, 167–70

Republic of Ireland, Department of Defence, 125, 127, 133–4

Republican, 9, 13–4, 35, 55–60, 62–72, 79–81, 84, 86–9, 91–7, 99–102, 104, 109, 114, 119, 129–30, 136, 145, 147, 153, 174–5

anti–Treaty, 14, 56, 62, 64–7, 75, 84, 93, 108–10, 115–22, 124–5, 130–1, 134, 137, 139

pro-Treaty, 108, 110, 120, 125, 129, 131

Republicanism, 6, 13, 57, 64, 66–7, 69, 79–81, 84, 89, 91–2, 95–6, 99, 104–5, 110, 112, 115, 119, 122, 146, 191

Revisionism/Revisionist, 58–9, 64, 79, 81, 87, 91, 92, 94, 138

Robinson, Lennox, 17

Robinson, Seamus, 128–9, 134

romanticism, 26, 58, 60, 64–6, 68, 71–2, 97

Rothenstein, John, xv, 25–6

Royal Hiberian Academy, 23

Royal Society of Antiquaries of Ireland, 37–8

Ruskin, John, xv, 18, 19, 21, 26

Russell, George (Æ), xii, xviii, 4, 11, 96, 188

Ruttledge, P.J., 130

Ryan, Desmond, xvii, 188

Schmitt, Carl, 90–1

Shake Hands with the Devil [film], *see* Loach, Ken

Shakespeare, William, 9, 11, 43, 62–3, 98–100, 191

Sinn Féin, 97, 108, 130, 133, 142, 149

sovereignty, 14, 89–91, 95

Spain, 44, 95, 99

Stephens, James, 3, 43

Stuart, Francis, 80, 188

Strand, Paul, xv, 13, 21, 28, 31–6, 39–40, 94, 125–6, 153, 192

Synge, John M., 4, 13, 18, 100

Taussig, Michael, 165–6

The Bell [magazine], 35, 102, 152, 155, 157, 188, 191

The Irish Press [newspaper], 6, 9, 28, 44, 53, 94

The Irish Times [newspaper], 30, 111

The Limits of Liberty [documentary], 120, 122

Tobin, Liam (Billy), 139

transition [magazine], 6, 9, 10, 34

Traynor, Oscar, 110, 116–17, 137

Twain, Mark, 43, 163

Twomey, Moss, 130, 134

United States

California: xv, 29; Carmel, 28, 46, 62, 64; Pasadena, 44; San Francisco, 44, 49

New Mexico: 6, 29, 44, 48, 85, 94–5, 99, 101, 146, 151–53; Santa Fe, xii, 3–4, 8, 49; Taos, 29, 32, 44–6, 52, 85, 94, 101

New York: 5–6, 21–2, 31–2, 44, 49–50, 94, 146

University College Dublin, 26, 42, 60, 126

Vasari, Giorgio, xv, 18–19, 26, 100

Villon, François, 99

Vize, Joseph, 130

Waddington, Victor, 23

War of Independence, xi, xvi, 11, 17, 31, 49,
52, 55–8, 69, 74, 82, 124–5, 128, 161, 187
West Cork Flying Column, 57–8, 61, 64, 69
Weston, Edward, xv, 5, 21, 28–30, 32–3,
35, 94
Whelan, Pax, 130
Whitfield, Niamh, 121–2

Yaddo Foundation, 32, 52, 94
Yeats, Jack B., xiv, xviii, 3, 18–19, 23–7, 36,
80, 93–4, 100, 103, 104, 146, 153–7, 190–1
National Loan Exhibition, xiv, 23–4, 154
Yeats, William Butler, xii, 4, 13, 16, 43, 86,
145, 157–9, 160, 181, 188